How to Paint Like the IMPRESSIONISTS

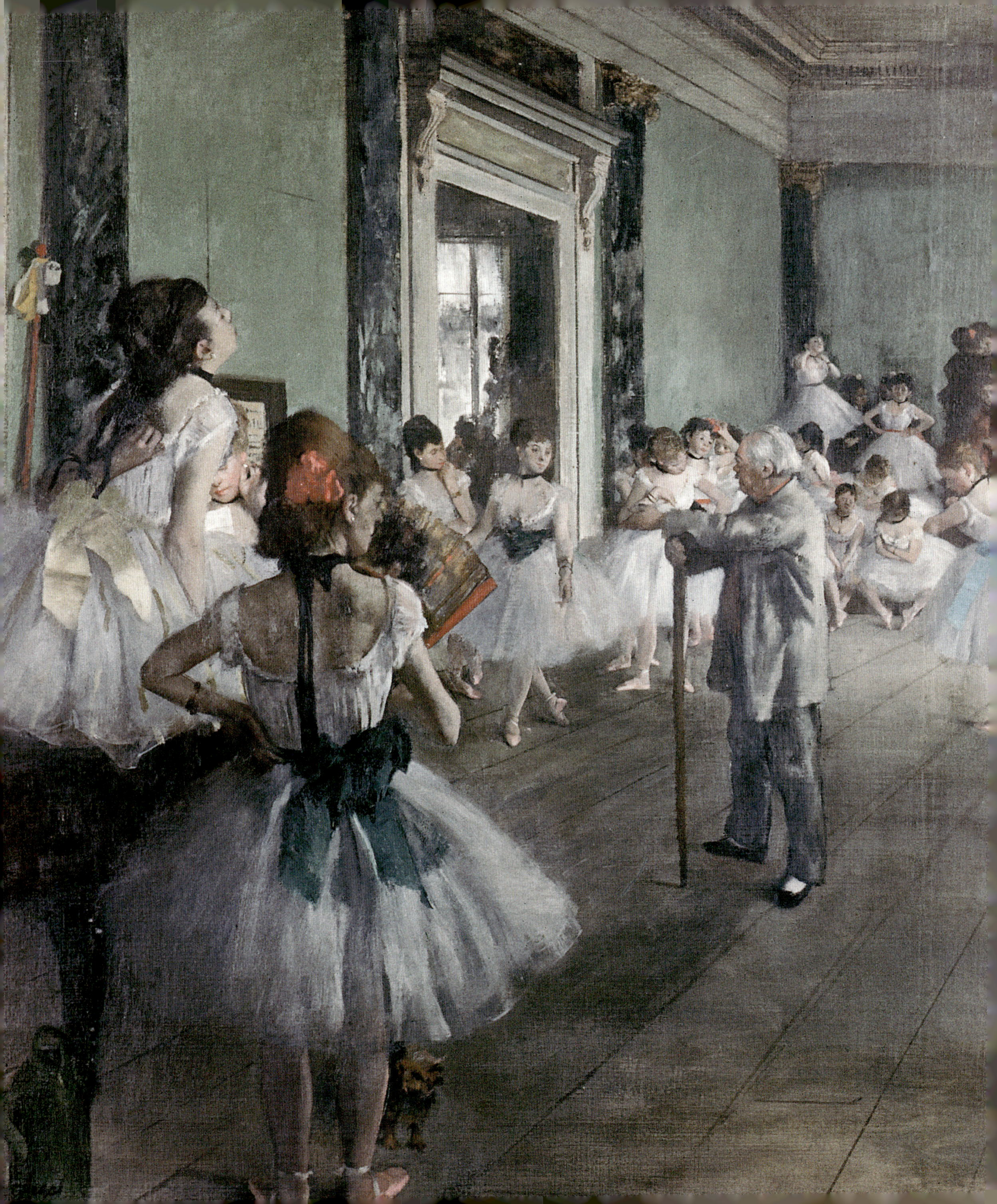

How to Paint Like the IMPRESSIONISTS

A practical guide to re-creating your own Impressionist paintings

Susie Hodge

HARPER DESIGN
An Imprint of HarperCollinsPublishers

First published in 2004 by:
HARPER DESIGN
An Imprint of HarperCollins*Publishers*
10 East 53rd Street
New York, NY 10022
Tel: (212) 207-7000
Fax: (212) 207-7654
harperdesign@harpercollins.com
www.harpercollins.com

Distributed throughout North America:
HarperCollins*Publishers*
10 East 53rd Street
New York, NY 10022
Fax: (212) 207-7654

CREATED BY The Bridgewater Book Company
EDITOR Susie Behar
DESIGNER Kevin Knight
STEP-BY-STEP PAINTINGS Ivan Hissey
PHOTOGRAPHER Ian Parsons

Library of Congress Control Number: 2004101632

ISBN 978-0-06-074791-6
Second Printing, April 2014

Color reproduction by Colourscan, Singapore
Printed and bound in China

Author acknowledgments:
I would like to thank Cathy Gosling and Caroline Churton at HarperCollins. My special thanks go to Jason Hook, Terry Jeavons, Michael Whitehead, Susie Behar, and Sarah Doughty at Bridgewater Books, as well as to Ivan Hissey, Claire Musters, Kevin Knight, and Fiona Biggs. Many thanks in particular to Lynda Marshall. Thanks to everyone for their hard work and commitment!

Picture credits:
Bridgewater Books would like to thank the following for permission to use copyright material: **AKG-London:** p. 20. **Bridgeman Art Library:** p. 6, Courtauld Institute Gallery, London; 25b, Brooklyn Museum of Art, New York; 26t, Musée Marmottan, Paris/Giraudon; 27tr, Ackermann and Johnson Ltd., London; 27b, Musée D'Orsay, Paris/Giraudon; 46, Private Collection; 48, Musée D'Orsay, Paris/Giraudon; 128, J. Paul Getty Museum, Los Angeles; 136, Courtauld Institute Gallery, London. **Corbis Images:** pp: 7, 17t, 21, 23, 30, 31, 34, 40, 44, 60, 66, 90, 117, 129, 130/131, © Archivo Iconografico, SA; 100, 104, 108, © Barnes Foundation, Pennsylvania; 24c, 87, 125, Bettmann; 18t, 52, © Alexander Burkatowski; 32–33, 45, 80, © Burstein Collection; 8, 11, 19, 76, Christie's Images; 10, © Angelo Hornak; 14, 15, 110, © Edimedia; 12, 13, 16, 17b, 18b, 22, 58, 59, 72, 73, 75, 86, 96, 102, 114, 115, 122–123, 138, © Francis G Mayer; 9, 38–39, 54, 68, 88, 94–95, 118, 132, © National Gallery Collection, by kind permission of The Trustees, London; 62, 82, 101, © Philadelphia Museum of Art. **Winsor & Newton:** pp: 24bl, 25t, 26b, 27c, reproduced by kind permission.

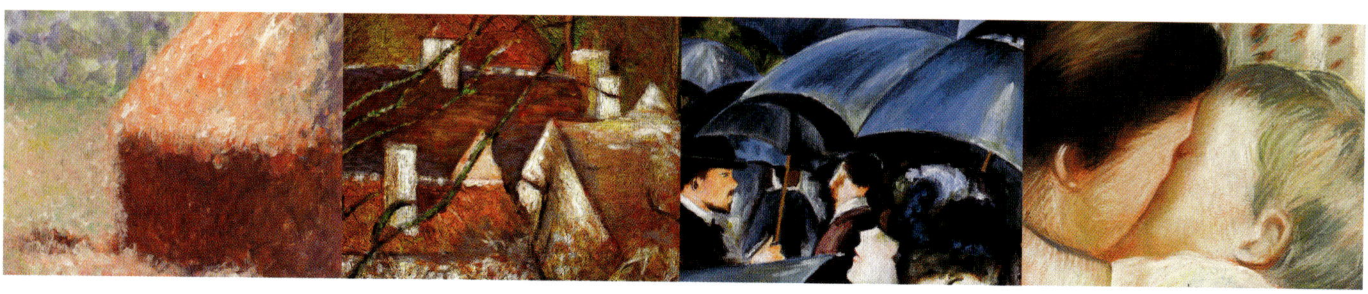

CONTENTS

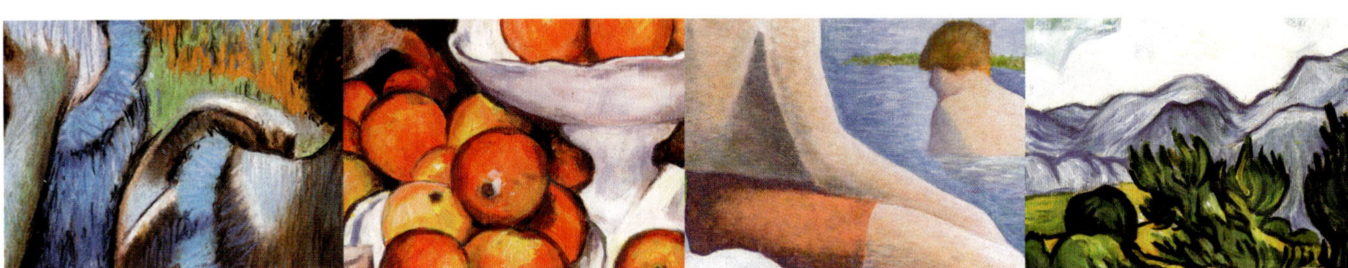

Chapter one

INTRODUCTION

Splashes of white on a sapphire sea, dashes of emerald and turquoise on water, and spatters of vermilion in a verdant field. These are aspects of paintings by a group of artists who were simply trying to capture the fleeting effects of light and atmosphere. Together, these painters created one of the most famous movements in Western art.

BELOW
Alfred Sisley, BOATS ON THE SEINE, c.1877, oil on canvas, 14½ x 17¼ inches (37 x 44 cm).
Sisley, one of the original Impressionists, captured scenes from the world around him and depicted his own vision of sunlight on water.

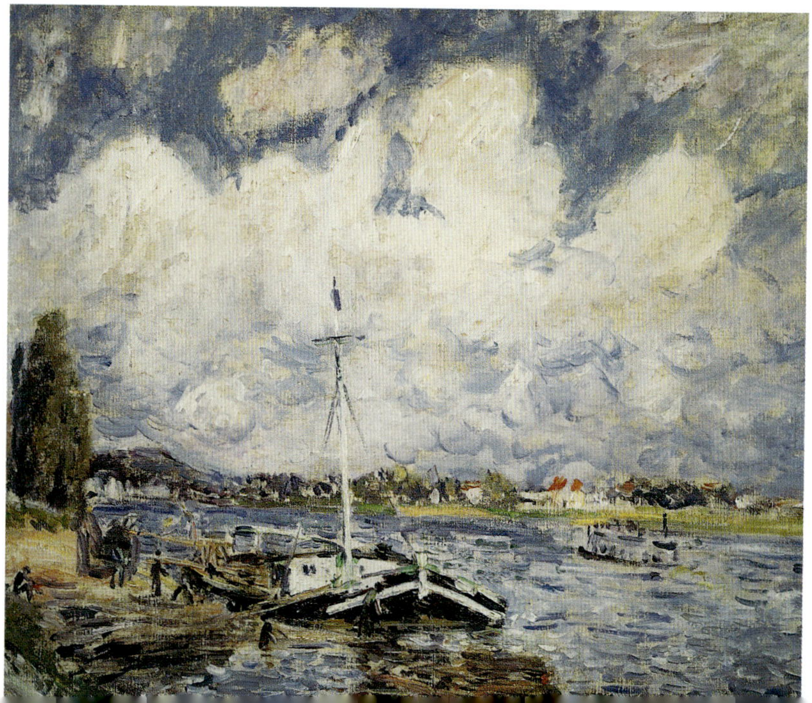

IMPRESSIONISM HAS CAPTURED the imaginations of people all over the world since the artists' first group exhibition was held in a photographer's studio in Paris on April 15, 1874. The name of the group was actually coined by journalist Louis Leroy. It was meant to be derogatory and was taken from Claude Monet's (1840–1926) painting *Impression, Sunrise,* which was on display there. Accustomed to detailed pictures painted in studios, visitors derided what they regarded as unfinished sketches by the exhibitors.

The unknown artists who were exhibiting included Frédéric Bazille (1841–1870), Paul Cézanne (1839–1906), Edgar Degas (1834–1917), Claude Monet, Berthe Morisot (1841–1895), Camille Pissarro (1830–1903), Auguste Renoir (1841–1919), and Alfred Sisley (1839–1899). Originally calling themselves the Société des Anonyme des Artistes—literally, "a group with no name"—they were reacting against academic traditions of art. Between 1874 and 1886, they put on eight independent exhibitions, gradually losing their scandalous reputation and adopting the name Impressionism themselves.

What the public and critics had found slapdash is exactly what subsequent generations value most about the art. The Impressionists were not consciously advocating social change, but they reflected it. They painted what they saw around them, instead of historical subjects, and they were particularly concerned with capturing fleeting moments.

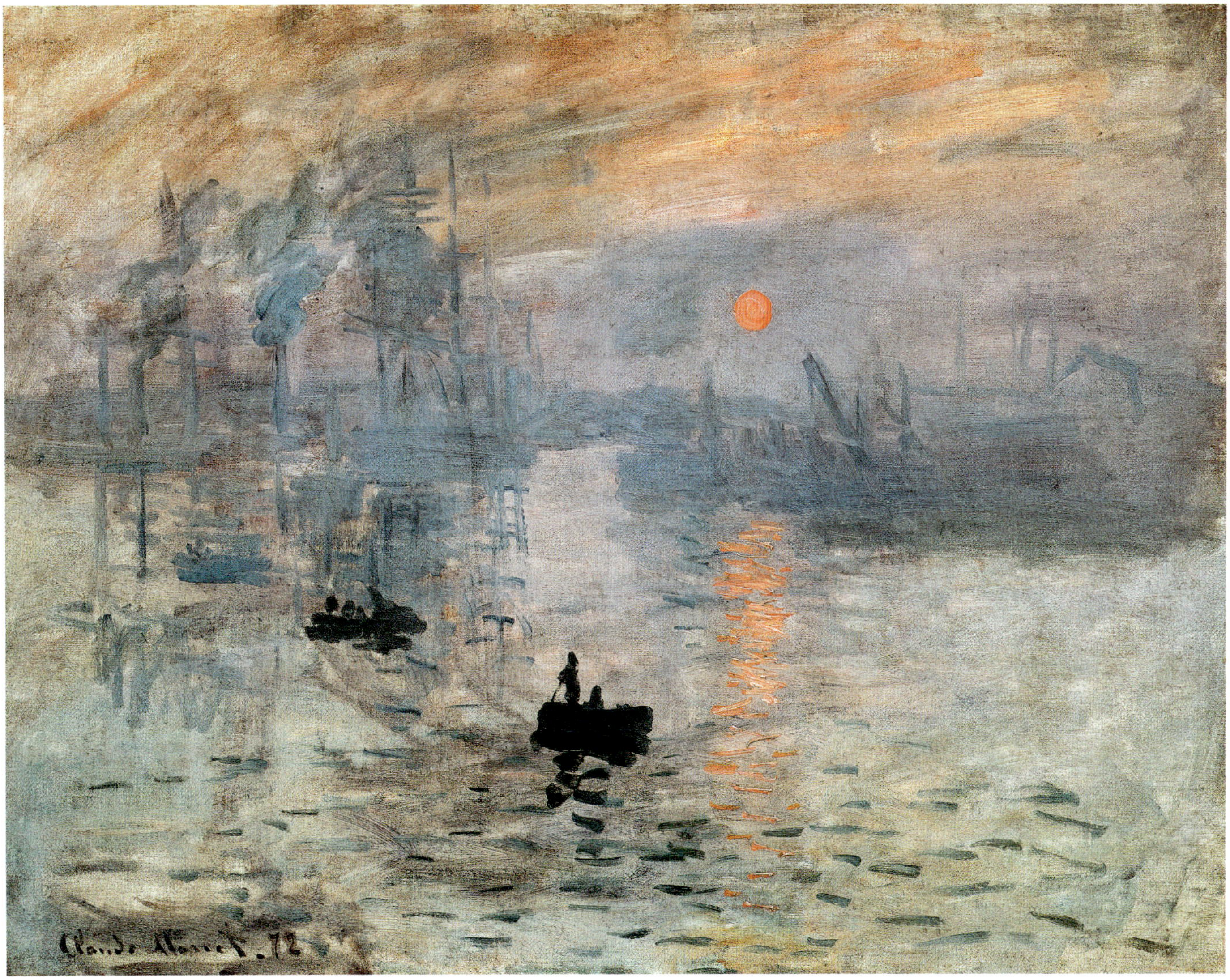

ABOVE
Claude Monet, IMPRESSION, SUNRISE, 1872–73, oil on canvas, 19 x 24¾ inches (48 x 63 cm).
Monet exhibited two harbor scenes in the 1874 exhibition. By calling this one an "impression" he unwittingly provided a name for the group. This painting of the harbor at Le Havre was not an accurately depicted seascape, but a record of impressions formed while looking at it.

How this book works

This book deconstructs and evaluates some of the greatest paintings by the Impressionists, as well as some of their immediate successors' paintings, giving step-by-step, practical demonstrations to enable you to re-create their styles and techniques. There are sections on a variety of techniques, such as pointillism, impasto, two-dimensional brushwork, and palette knife application.

The book discusses what background surfaces were used, how paintings were prepared, how color was used so effectively, and how tones were built up. It then shows how you can emulate the same effects with modern materials.

Step-by-step instructions illustrate how to re-create details from 16 paintings by eight artists. In order to get the most from the instructions, you should have some knowledge and practical experience of basic painting terms and techniques. Then, with just a few brush strokes, you can make sunlight sparkle, water glisten, skin tones glow, and shadows flicker. In other words, you will be able to re-create aspects of some of the most esteemed and appreciated paintings in the world.

INSPIRATION AND INFLUENCES

BELOW
Claude Monet, MONET'S GARDEN AT VÉTHEUIL, 1881, oil on canvas, 59½ x 47½ inches (151.5 x 121 cm).
In this painting, Monet captured a moment in time. The dominant colors of blue, yellow, and green are dappled with white sunlight and deep mauve shadows. A striking contrast between the forces of nature and man is depicted in the tall flowers and small children.

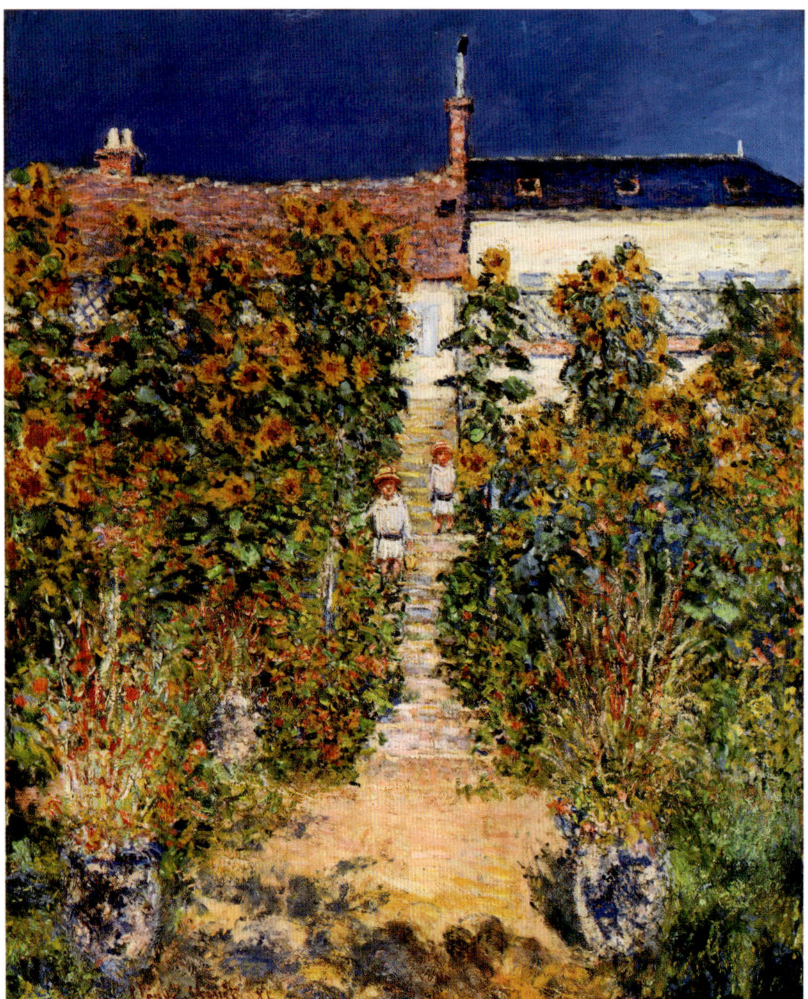

ALTHOUGH IMPRESSIONISM DID NOT have one common theory or practice, the main aim of most of the artists was to paint the effects of light, movement, and color, often on the contemporary environment, breaking away from the highly finished technique of traditional academic art. Landscapes included railway bridges and factory chimneys, while people sat or danced in cafés, attended the races, or worked. The artists were centered around Paris, living and working in the suburbs, and did not restrict themselves to conventional standards.

One of their preferred methods was painting in the open air (known as *en plein air*) to capture the real, observed effects of light outdoors and convey a sense of life and atmosphere. Although they were the first to make light the main subject of their paintings, they were not the first artists to paint in the open air and to capture light on the landscape.

Throughout the nineteenth century, it had been common practice for landscape painters to make rapid oil sketches outside in direct observation of a scene. Most of these sketches were taken back to the studio to be used in creating finished paintings. In Britain, John Constable (1776–1837) and J. M. W. Turner (1775–1851) made sketches in situ to capture atmospheric effects.

The first painters to work as a group outdoors, capturing nature at its source, were French landscapists who became known as the Barbizon School. Charles-François Daubigny (1817–78), one of the leading Barbizon artists, was among the first to use *plein air* paintings as finished pictures.

A looser approach

The Impressionists took this idea of working outdoors to capture atmosphere and pushed it one step further. Disregarding the accepted subjects of the day—history, mythology, and religion—they created images of contemporary life and brief moments in time. Not all of them worked in the open air, but for many this was the essence of their work. Painting outside required a free, almost shorthand technique due to the constant change of light. The traditional smooth and detailed process of academic art would have been too time-consuming to capture this, so the Impressionists worked in a new way.

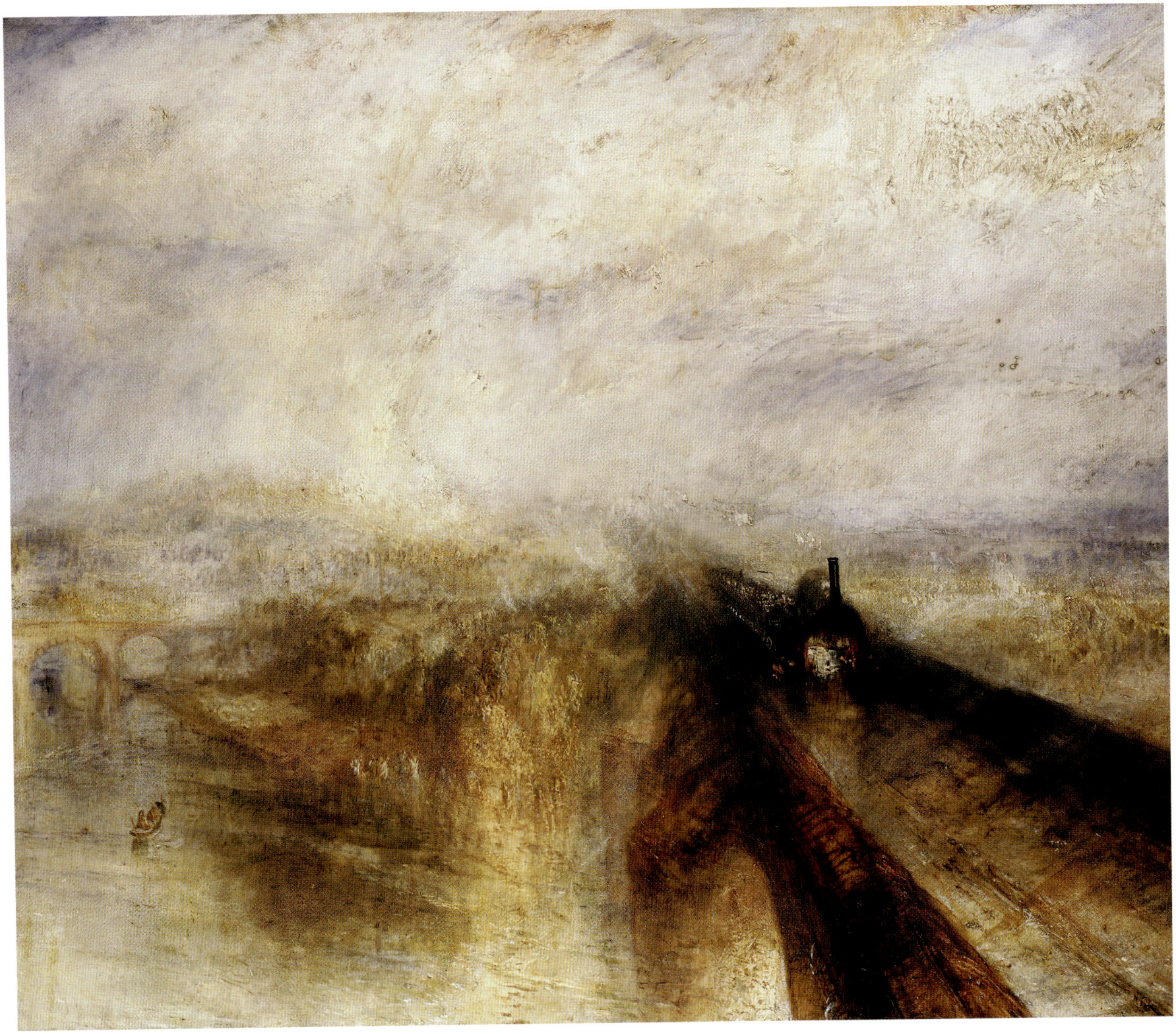

Most Impressionists avoided the harsh brightness of the midday sun, and they frequently painted diffused light effects created by clouds, reflections, or the low light of early mornings and late afternoons. They also studied qualities that change light, such as the softening and dissolving effects of fog and snow.

Each artist had his or her own creative agenda that was usually different from anyone else's, but they often used each other's ideas as starting points for their explorations of the effects of light. Scenes involving rippling and reflective water fascinated some, mottled light on the skin or speckled shadows cast by vegetation intrigued others, and some of them focused on capturing diffused or reflected light through smoke, steam, and glass.

All of these subject matters provided plenty of scope for the exploration and application of the Impressionists' revolutionary approach to painting.

ABOVE
J. M. W. Turner, RAIN, STEAM, AND SPEED, THE GREAT WESTERN RAILWAY, 1844, oil on canvas, 35¾ x 48 inches (91 x 122 cm).
Turner was one of the first painters to include trains and other evidence of modernity in his work. With this painting, Turner created a new artistic concept—painting a transitory moment.

ART AND DESIGN

THE NINETEENTH CENTURY was a period of social, political, and cultural change. It was the Industrial Age, when new inventions and scientific discoveries happened frequently, so it was natural that some artists questioned the rigid boundaries of traditional art. Both artists and designers experimented with different styles and approaches at around the same time.

While the Industrial Revolution brought wealth to some, there was a growing awareness of social discontent and poverty. Art and literature often reflected this or portrayed a desire to escape from the modern age, often into the romanticized past of the Middle Ages. The growth in popularity of landscape art in the United States and Europe was partly a reaction against the newly built towns, cities, and railways and what many saw as the erosion of the countryside.

In the mid-nineteenth century, a group of young British artists, calling themselves the Pre-Raphaelite Brotherhood, rebelled against the academic art of their country. They looked back to the art of the fifteenth century, and were inspired by what they believed was "truth to nature"—serious subjects, intricate brushwork, and clear, bright colors. They painted subjects from poetry, the Bible, myths, and the Middle Ages. Among the first painters to use chemically produced pigments, they painted bright colors directly onto wet, white background surfaces, giving lighter, fresher results than contemporary works, which were usually painted onto dry brown canvases.

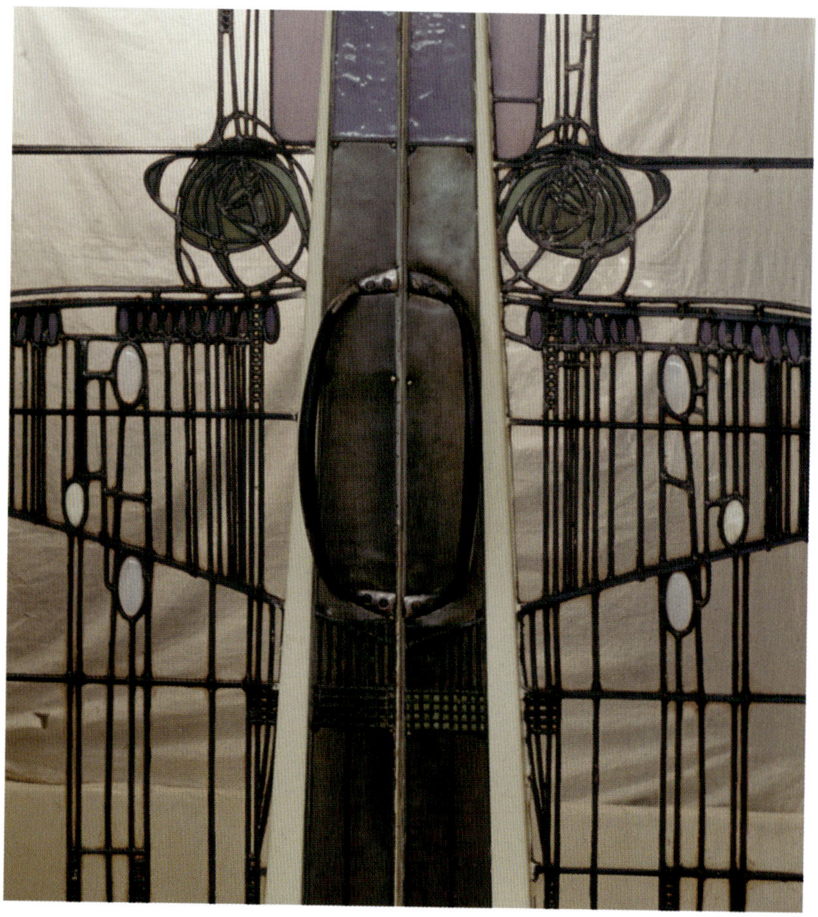

RIGHT
Charles Rennie Mackintosh, DOORS TO THE ROOM DE LUXE, 1898, Willow Tea Rooms (detail).
Charles Rennie Mackintosh (1868–1928) designed buildings, interiors, and elegant furniture, as well as painting delicate watercolors. His approach to Art Nouveau was unique, which can be seen in this original design of stained glass doors for tea rooms in Glasgow. He didn't allow past traditions to impose on his imaginative designs and innovative use of materials.

RIGHT
Dante Gabriel Rossetti, PROSPERINE, 1874, oil on canvas, 49¾ x 24 inches (126.5 x 61 cm).
Almost 30 years after he had first painted as a Pre-Raphaelite, Rossetti (1828–82) continued to use harmonious color contrasts and subdued light to create moods and atmosphere. For this painting, he worked with about 10 colors, including Sap Green, Ivory Black, Raw Umber, Cobalt Blue, Ceruleum Blue, Chrome Yellow, Cadmium Red, Burnt Sienna, Titanium White, and Yellow Ocher.

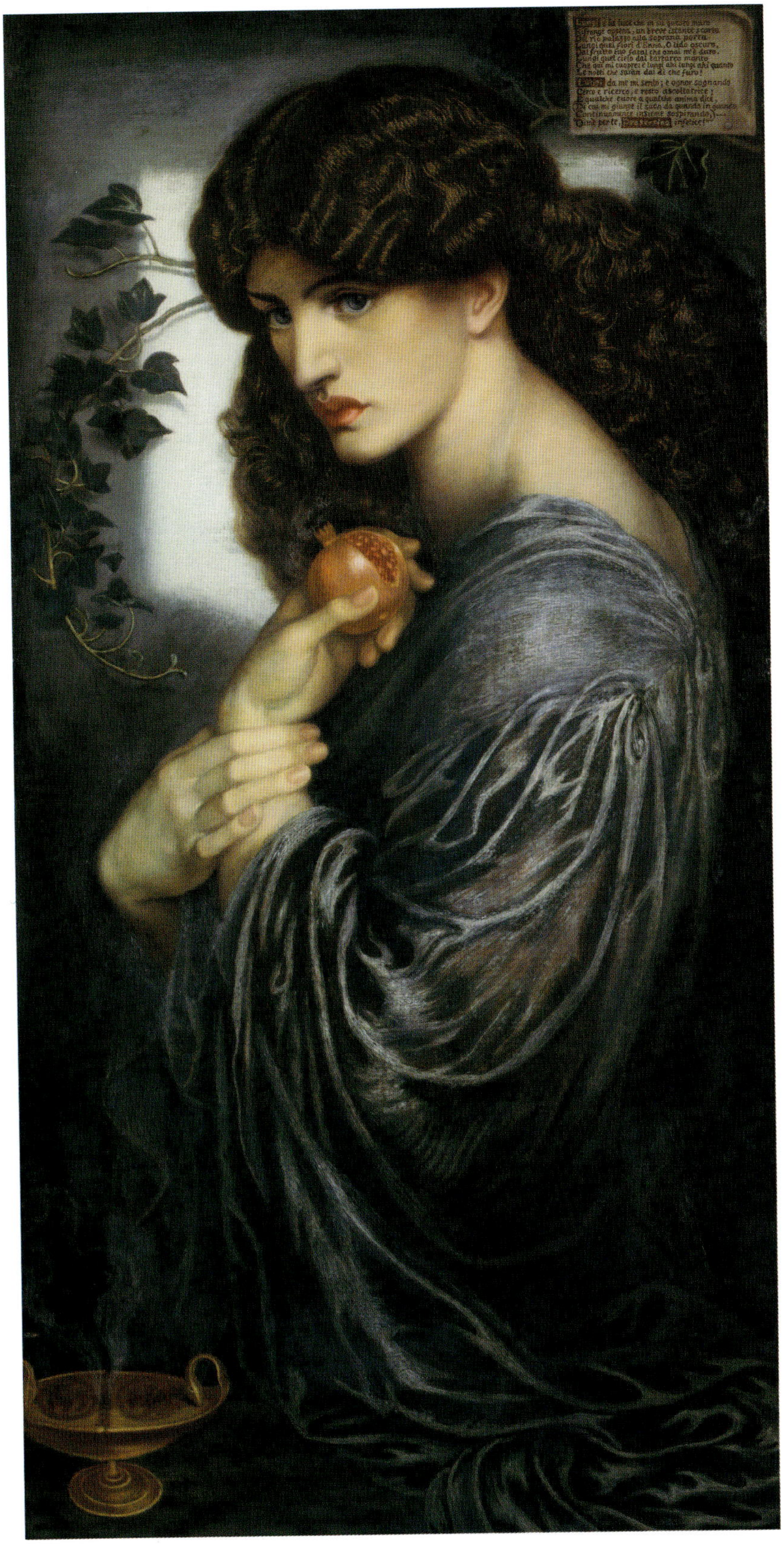

They explored the idea of colored shadows, as the Impressionists were to do, but, unlike the Impressionists, they were not interested in the changing effects of atmosphere and light.

The Realist movement

Social and economic problems also inspired Realism, which began in France at the same time. This was partly a reaction against the style of painting advocated by the academies, which involved the smooth application of paint and almost imperceptible brush strokes. Realists applied paint with broad brushes or palette knives in earthy colors—a technique the Impressionists admired. Realist art was concerned with the present, not the past, and with the tangible, not the spiritual. Realists painted people as they really were: shop assistants, beggars, prostitutes, or waitresses. Although criticized for being vulgar, Realism tried to highlight many social problems and changed the way artists looked at landscape. Edouard Manet (1832–83) and Gustave Courbet (1819–77) were both Realists, learning their techniques from Classical painters, but both portrayed provincial life. They believed that artists should only paint what they could experience. This had a profound and lasting influence on the Impressionists.

By the end of the nineteenth century, when the Impressionists were well established, a new art known as Art Nouveau emerged—it encompassed architecture, interior design, ornament, and fine art. Utilizing "modern" materials, such as iron, glass, silk, and pewter, artists and designers used undulating, sinuous lines based on natural plant forms, stylized flowers and tendrils, and female forms, all in flowing asymmetry. It was an earnest endeavor to achieve a completely new and contemporary style. The idea was not to hark back to the past, but to make something "of the age."

POST-IMPRESSIONISM

THE TERM POST-IMPRESSIONISM was invented after the artists it describes had died. Although inexact, it roughly covers the period from the last Impressionist exhibition in 1886 through to 1910. During the 1880s, some of the artists who had begun by painting with the Impressionists started to experiment with different styles, reacting against the overriding concern with visual appearances and wanting to introduce more complex meanings and emotional content into their art. Although grouped together under the name Post-Impressionists, the artists had extremely diverse styles and talents. Exploring new ways of expressing color and ideas, they often exhibited together, but, unlike the Impressionists—a close and sociable group—each artist mainly painted alone. The following artists are some of the most well-known Post-Impressionists. They socialized with the Impressionists and tried some of their techniques before developing their work in slightly different directions.

Paul Gauguin (1848–1903) learned how to paint under Pissarro. He developed a style that was characterized by flat patterns of brilliant color often outlined in black, like stained glass. His flat, asymmetrical compositions came from his admiration of primitive woodcuts, Japanese and medieval art, and the Symbolists—who admired his expression of moods and emotions. In 1891, he moved to Tahiti and worked in solitude for the remainder of his life.

Paul Cézanne (1839–1906) was inspired in his early years by Delacroix (1798–1863)—a huge influence on the Impressionists—and Courbet and Manet. He later began working with Pissarro and took part in the first Impressionist exhibition of 1874, but he moved to the South of France in 1877 and rarely exhibited again. By then, he had become uncomfortable with capturing the constantly changing effects of light and color on nature. He developed a systematic style based on the underlying geometric structure of all forms.

Vincent van Gogh (1853–90) experienced little success in his short and tragic life. His early paintings were dark until he moved to Paris and met the Impressionists. Intrigued by their ideas, he lightened his palette and also briefly experimented with the ideas of Seurat and Paul Signac. Gradually, his explosive and unpredictable behavior alienated almost everyone but his brother Theo. He moved

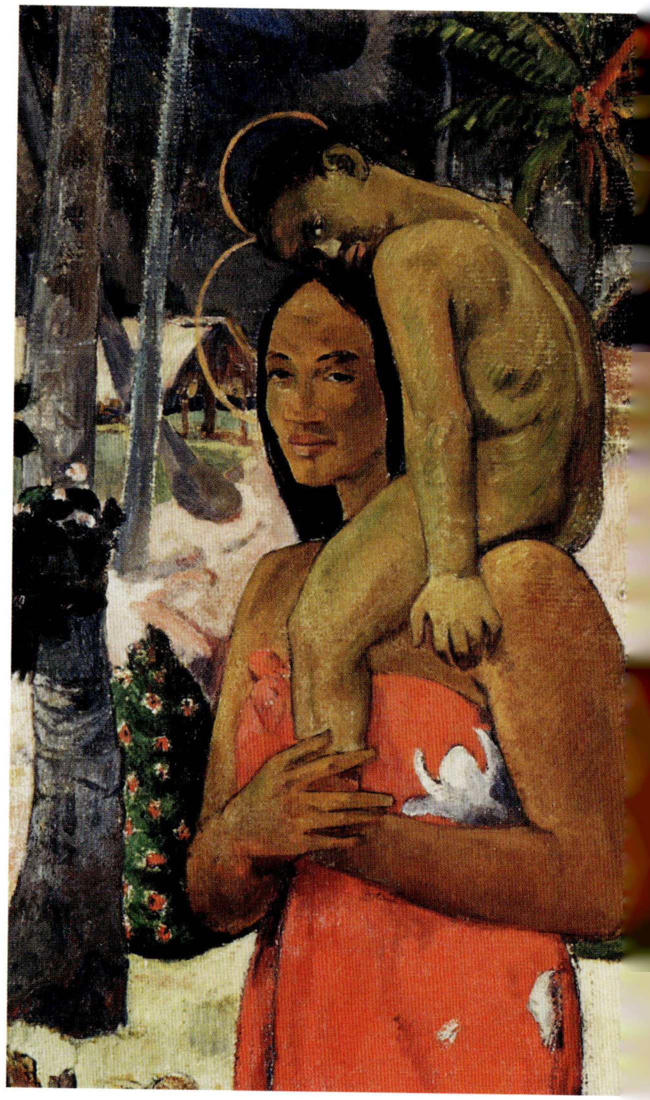

RIGHT
Paul Gauguin, WE GREET THEE, MARY, 1891, oil on canvas, 44 x 35¾ inches (112 x 90 cm).
This painting combines religious emotion with the exotic elements that had drawn Gauguin to Tahiti—beauty, splendor, and mysticism. His painting style involved creating broad, flat areas of color and subtle variations of hue. Because of financial problems, his paint was always thinned, even when he used a palette knife, and he often painted on unprimed burlap or wood.

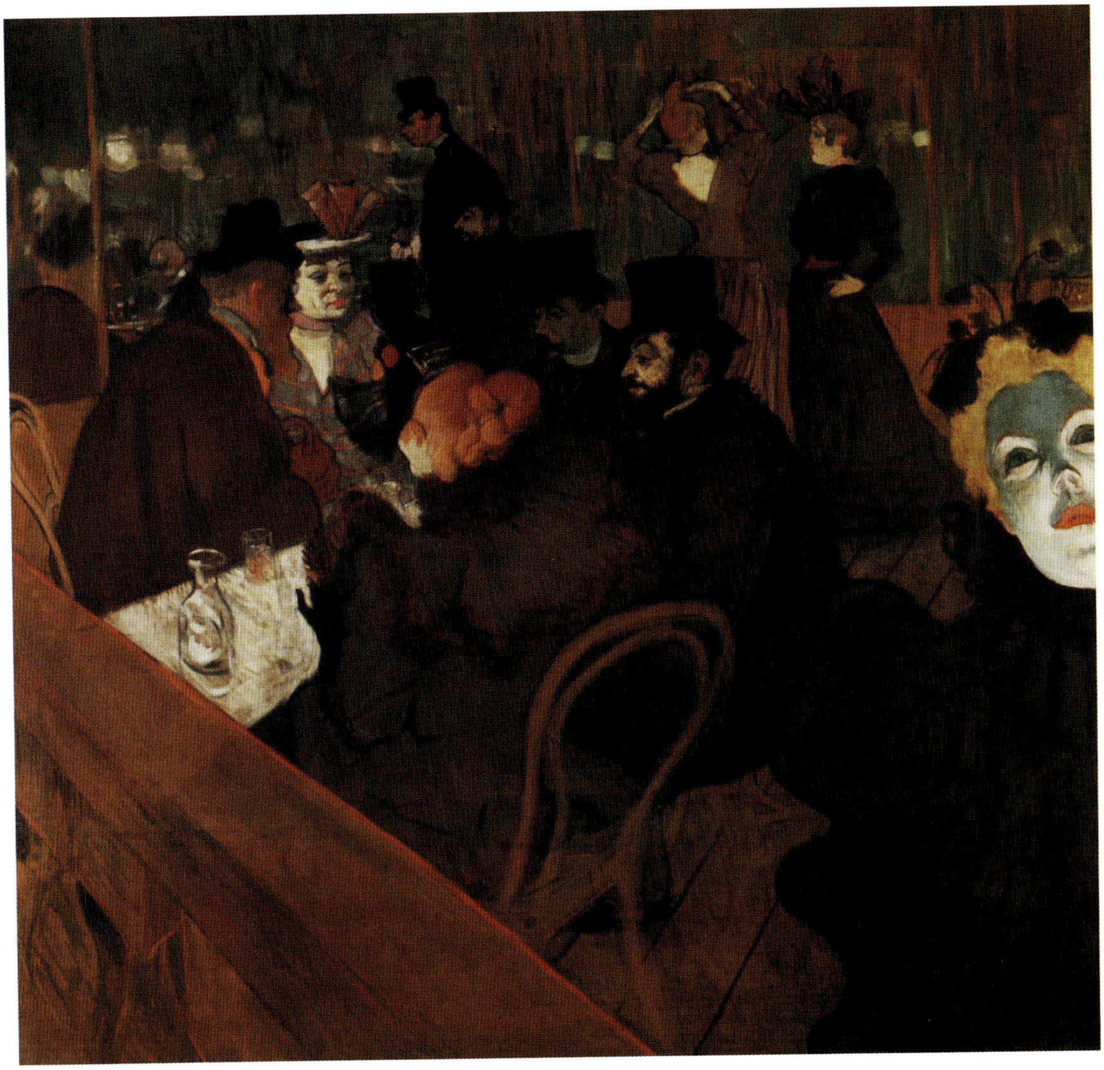

LEFT
Henri de Toulouse-Lautrec, IN THE PROMENOIR OF THE MOULIN ROUGE, c.1894–95, oil on canvas, 48½ x 55½ inches (123.5 x 141 cm).
This was Toulouse-Lautrec's last major work based on the subject of dance halls, which had fascinated him for a decade. As with most of his paintings, he has created an unusual, diagonal composition, the paint is thinly applied, and the eerie atmosphere pervades the entire scene and envelops the figures. The artificial light and shadows reflect Viridian on the faces.

away from Paris, and, using the ideas of colored shadows that the Impressionists had emphasized (see page 23), painted his now distinctive images using varied, emphatic brushwork and radiant colors that were inspired by his emotions.

Georges Seurat (1859–91) produced highly organized and meticulously executed paintings as a response to the Impressionists' handling of light and color, the ideas of Delacroix, classical compositions, and contemporary color theories. He developed a scientific process that combined moods and emotions with line and color. This scientific approach to color was also called Neo-Impressionism.

From an aristocratic family, Henri de Toulouse-Lautrec (1864–1901) was physically deformed and was rejected by many of his class. Yet in spite of the dissipated life he led, he was remarkably productive. He used the Impressionist idea of making ordinary people at their daily tasks the subject of his paintings. He painted and printed the seedy side of Paris nightlife in a vibrant, fluid way that distorted line and color and captured the vitality of city life.

In general, Post-Impressionism led away from the naturalistic approach of Impressionism and toward the two major movements of the early twentieth century: Cubism and Fauvism.

Chapter two

TECHNIQUES

The Impressionists experimented with various techniques in order to produce their colorful fleeting images effectively. Some of their techniques were original to them; others had been used previously by different artists but were adapted by the Impressionists to create the unique style for which they are famous.

BELOW
Claude Monet, REGATTA AT ARGENTEUIL, c.1872, oil on canvas, 19 x 29½ inches (48 x 75 cm).
Monet built up thick, opaque slabs of color in broad, directional, form-following brush strokes. He painted the reflections in horizontal slabs of complementary colors.

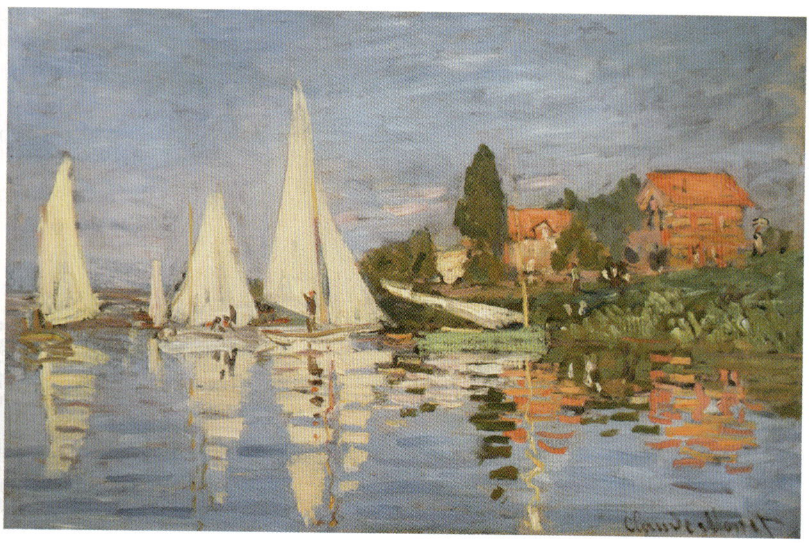

THE IMPRESSIONIST PAINTERS constantly experimented with new techniques. Below are the main methods that they used to create the stunning effects of light and atmosphere that are the hallmarks of their art.

Alla prima

Alla prima or "single sitting" painting literally means "at the first" when translated from the Italian, or "first cut" from the French *au premier coup*. It involves painting an entire picture in one sitting—that is, without putting it aside or reworking it later. It was one of the methods closest to the Impressionists' original ideals of capturing fleeting moments, yet few of their paintings were completely created in this way. They often began alla prima when painting outdoors directly in front of their subject, where speed was of the essence, but most paintings required at least a little tidying up afterward, before they were displayed in front of the critical public.

Monet's painting *Bathers at La Grenouillère* (see pages 38–39) was painted largely alla prima, with final accents applied in the studio afterward, as were his paintings *Grain Stacks* (see pages 34–37) and *La Gare Saint-Lazare* (see pages 32–33). Gustave Caillebotte, Renoir, and Pissarro also began many paintings in this way. A good indicator of whether a work was painted alla prima is the size of the canvas, because portability was vital.

Sisley (1839–99) was one of the few Impressionists who adhered to the alla prima method throughout his life. His painting *Boats on the Seine* (see page 6) is painted completely alla prima using a restricted palette and short brush strokes. The general alla prima method usually entailed little or no initial underpainting, although some artists did begin by making quick sketches in charcoal, pencil, or thinned paint. Next, they applied the paint rapidly, laying down each area of color across the canvas. The paint could be thin or thick, depending on the artists' preferences—most artists who painted in this way used a limited palette and bold, expressive brushwork.

To work alla prima, the artists had to have a clear idea of what their final image would look like, or at least what effect they wanted. Sometimes they worked wet-in-wet (layering wet paint over still wet paint), altering the first colors they laid down or scraping off unsuccessful marks with a palette knife. However, they were careful to keep alterations to a minimum, otherwise the spontaneity and freshness would have been lost. Few alla prima works are elaborate, as there is no time for really detailed work.

Slabs of color

Many of the Impressionists picked up the idea of using pure colors beside each other without premixing them, although they experimented in different ways. The label Neo-Impressionists is often used to refer to the artists who experimented with color to an even greater degree. Some of their works were made up of bright "slabs" of color, with each one being placed next to the color that would enhance it most (see pages 20–23). Many of Paul Signac's (1863–1935) works were produced like this. Similarly, to capture the evanescent effects of light and atmosphere, Monet and Caillebotte often applied contrasting slabs of bright color on their canvases, frequently in a seemingly haphazard yet deliberate fashion.

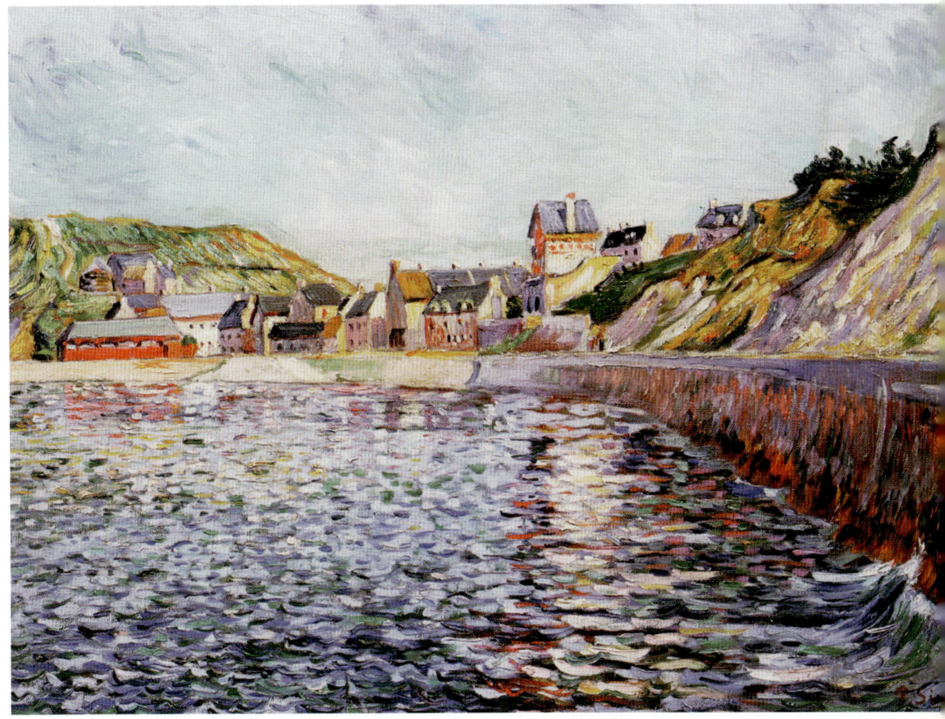

ABOVE
Paul Signac, PORT-EN-BESSIN, 1884, oil on canvas, 19 x 26½ inches (48.5 x 67.5 cm).
This painting, by Neo-Impressionist Paul Signac, shows how far Impressionism led some artists of the time. It had opened up new avenues for experiments with color and style that had not been possible previously. Signac was among a group of artists who had watched Impressionism come to be accepted and aimed to make their own mark on the art world.

Pointillism

Seurat took the Impressionist practice of applying broken colors to suggest shimmering light and movement to the extreme and set out to systemize the broken color of the Impressionists. He painstakingly painted thousands of tiny dots and thin slashes of contrasting color side by side across huge canvases, believing that the colors would merge and appear brighter to viewers than if they'd been mixed on the palette beforehand. This effect was called optical mixing and the painting technique became known as pointillism (although he preferred the term divisionism). Several other artists tried variations of it themselves, particularly Signac, Pissarro, and van Gogh. For further details on Seurat's techniques, including pointillism, see pages 122–127.

BELOW
Vincent van Gogh, ROAD WITH CYPRESS AND STAR, 1890, oil on canvas, 36¾ x 29 inches (92 x 73 cm). ***Retaining his great admiration for Rembrandt's lively, dramatic style, van Gogh applied impasto paint as the seventeenth-century master had done. He worked rapidly on his paintings, desperate to capture the immediacy of his perception and feelings. The composition here is dramatic, the colors are bold and simplified, and the brushwork is rhythmic and thick.***

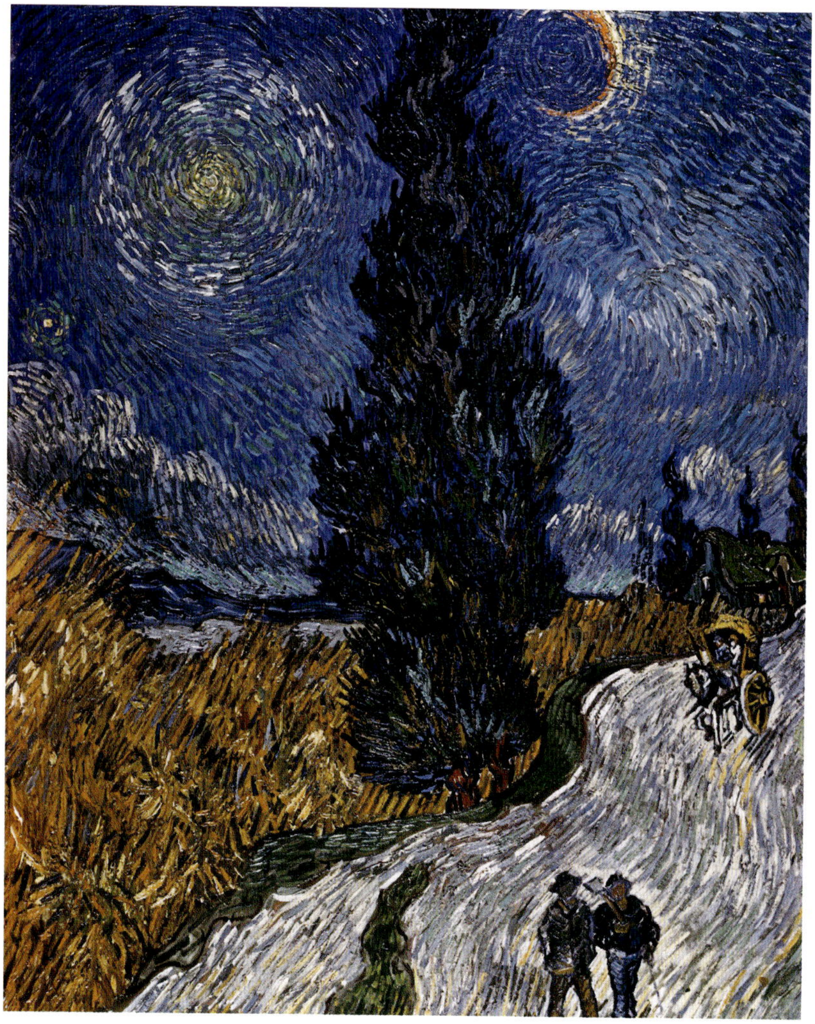

Impasto

The term impasto refers to the technique of applying oil paint thickly and liberally, so that it retains the marks and ridges left by the brush on the picture surface. Van Gogh's characteristic style of thick textured paint and rapid, slashing brush strokes is a good example of this, although the other Impressionists, including Monet, Renoir, Pissarro and Cézanne, often worked with an impasted technique too.

From early on, van Gogh worked in impasto, but later, when he moved to Paris and met many of the Impressionists, he lightened his palette and began using even thicker, more vigorous brush strokes for both expressive and decorative purposes. Using complementary color contrasts enhanced his impasto brushwork even more.

Although he painted for only 11 years, van Gogh completed over 800 paintings. His later works are a mixture of intense unblended colors applied in thick, slashed, or choppy impasto brush strokes. For more details on his impasto application, see pages 130–135.

Palette knife painting

Painting with a palette knife is a versatile and expressive technique in which layers of thick impasto are built up, creating a richly textured paint surface. Palette knives were a standard piece of painter's equipment during the Impressionists' time. Pissarro, van Gogh, and Cézanne, among others, experimented with knife painting, working on some parts of their paintings with the fast, direct, and bold way that knives allow to give these works a great sense of energy. (For an example of how to work with a knife like Cézanne, see pages 102–107). Knife painting is ideal for working alla prima, although it is also successful when painting over several sessions. The Impressionists often used knives as corrective tools, removing and replacing unsuccessful layers of paint while they were still wet. In this way, they could repaint the same area several times and still have something that looked spontaneous.

Textured brushwork

Pissarro tried out various techniques during his career, due partly to his great ability to interpret and adopt others' theories. He was able to select precisely what he wanted from each artist's work and to use it in his own individual way, but throughout his career he remained committed to giving viewers a "fresh sensation." By about 1877, he had tried out a large variety of techniques, including what has been described as

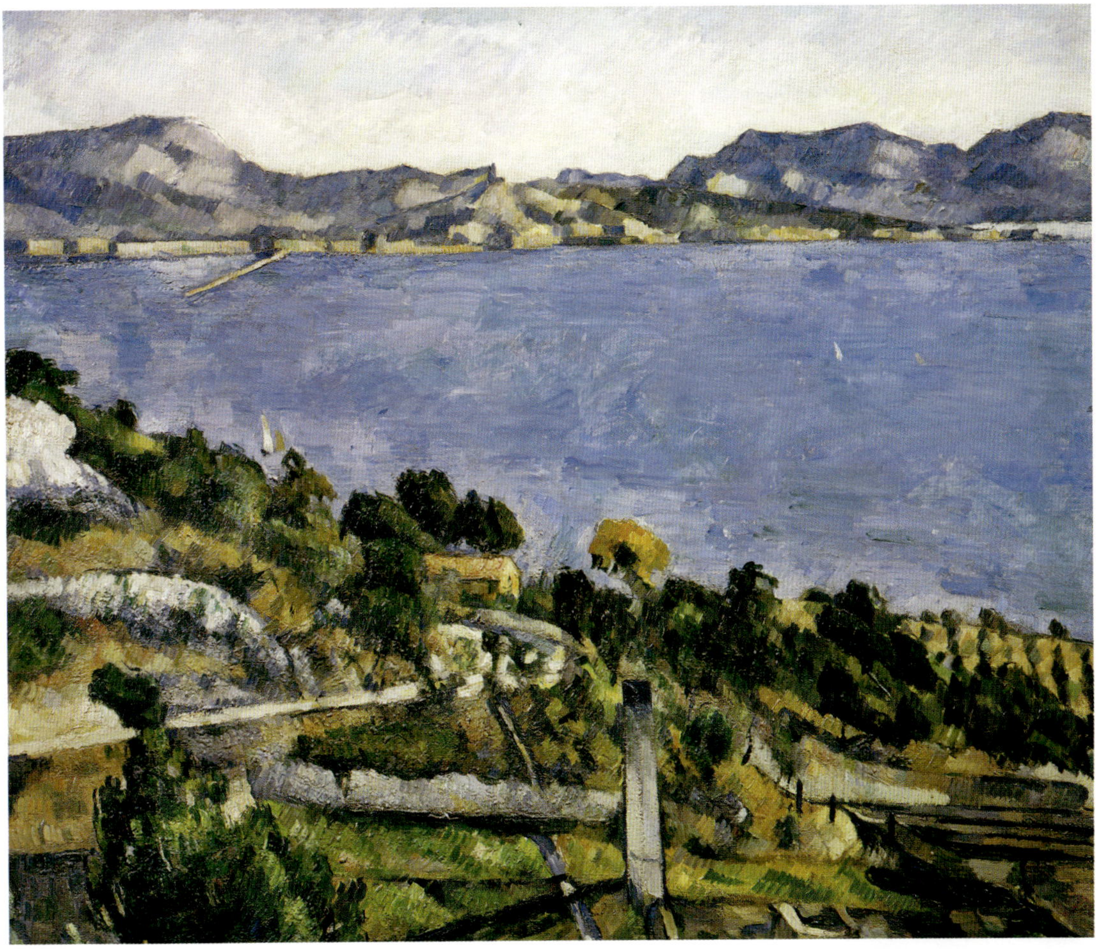

LEFT
Paul Cézanne, GULF OF MARSEILLES, 1882–85, oil on canvas, $22^{3}/_{4}$ x $28^{1}/_{4}$ inches (58 x 72 cm).
Cézanne painted this subject a number of times from different viewpoints and largely with a knife. He was particularly attracted by the middle-distance of the bay itself, a flat area of color in the center of the picture, and he offset it with strong forms in the far distance and foreground.

"woven," or two-dimensional, brush strokes. These are not the thick, raised marks of impasto, but instead multiple, patterned, flatter marks. In some parts of his paintings, small strokes have been layered on top of each other in diagonal dashes or in repeated comma-like brush marks. This is different from the spontaneity of *plein air* painting. By working in this way, Pissarro was able to create a strong tension between the surface pattern and the texture of the painting. For further explanation of how he painted in this way, see pages 46–57.

Similar small, gridlike brush strokes are also evident in some paintings by Sisley and Mary Cassatt (1844–1926). Sisley's are made up of thinner, less precise brush strokes, while Cassatt's include more dragged marks.

RIGHT
Camille Pissarro, CAFÉ AU LAIT, 1881, oil on canvas, 25 x $21^{1}/_{2}$ inches (64 x 54.5 cm).
Pissarro often painted peasants living and working. Here, light enters through the open window, softening the peasant girl's outline. Her arm echoes the "L" shape of the window and the green of the foliage outside is echoed on the handle of the mug she is holding. Pissarro applied the paint in myriads of comma-like brush marks, giving the impression of a tapestry and linking the peasant girl with the background through surface texture.

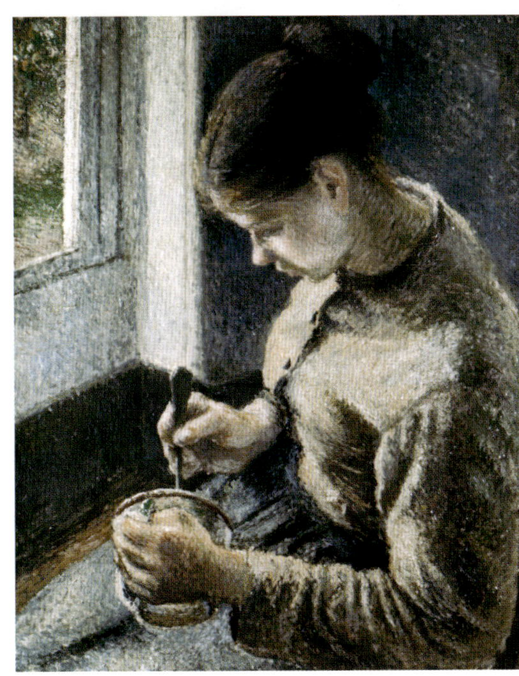

Japanese art

After Japan began trading with the West in 1868, Japanese art and objects became extremely popular in France and had a major impact on the Impressionists.

During the eighteenth century, Japanese artists had become skilled at color printing from woodblocks. These Ukiyo-e, or "images of the Floating World," included unexpected subjects, fresh colors, and new ways of composing pictures, which appealed to the Impressionists because these elements invigorated and reinforced their ideas. They particularly liked the simple line drawings, flat areas of bold color, and the way that the main subject was often off-center. Many prints had no single point of focus, so viewers' eyes were led all around the picture. Busy and calm areas were held together with rhythmic outlines, emphasizing surface patterns instead of trying to create an illusion of depth. Subjects and surrounding spaces created an equal amount of tension—this idea of space taking an active role in a composition had been previously unseen in the West. Japanese artists' disregard for perspective involved unusual viewpoints and figures cut off at the edges of pictures. Instead of this causing disjointed images, it held viewers' interest.

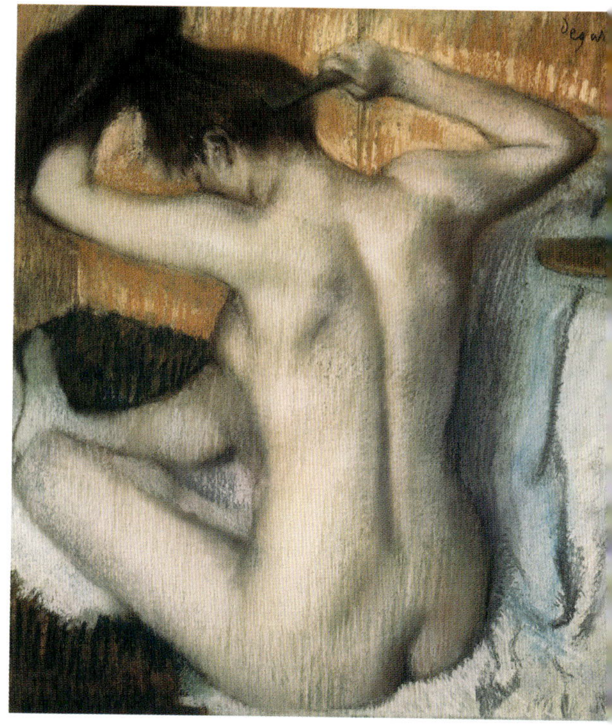

RIGHT
Edgar Degas, WOMAN COMBING HER HAIR, c.1885, pastel on card, 20¾ x 20½ inches (53 x 52 cm).
Degas created many paintings capturing moments that made it seem as if the viewer was simply looking through a keyhole. However, these were well-planned poses, prepared through photographs and other studies. This drawing is the result of many sketches and an understanding of the lighting, composition, and angles that are used in photography.

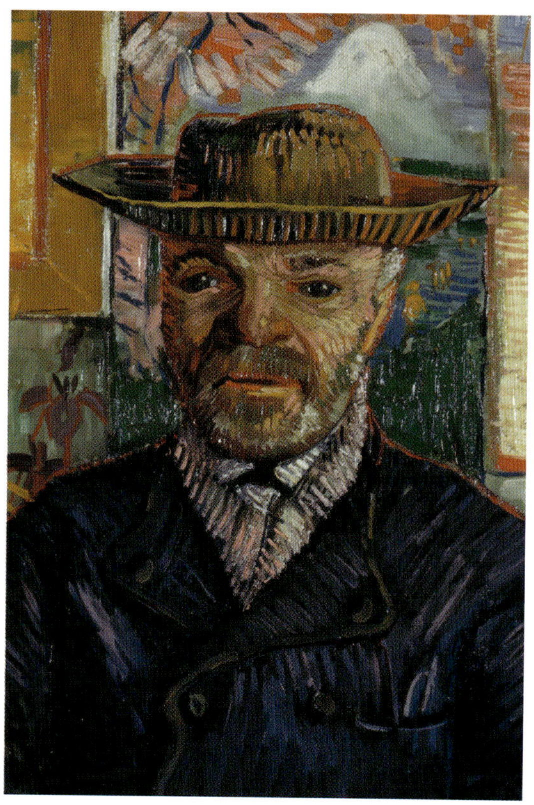

RIGHT
Vincent van Gogh, PÈRE TANGUY, 1887, oil on canvas, 36¾ x 29½ inches (92 x 75 cm).
Van Gogh and many of the Impressionists bought their art supplies from Julien Tanguy's shop in Paris. His shop was also well stocked with Japanese woodcuts and some can be seen behind his head. By including them here, van Gogh was affirming his admiration of them. The colorful vivacity of this painting demonstrates the regard he had for Japanese items.

Many of the Impressionists collected Japanese prints and began using some of the devices in their own work. Van Gogh's experiments with unusual viewpoints and flat areas of color reflect his collection's influence. (For more advice on how to paint using Japanese compositional techniques, such as van Gogh's, see pages 136–141). The artist Hokusai (1760–1849) particularly inspired Degas, and many of his subsequent bathers and dancers are in similar, balanced, asymmetrical formats surrounded by space. Degas passed his love for Japanese prints to his good friend Cassatt. In 1890, she worked on a set of 10 colored aquatints done "as an imitation of Japanese methods." After studying the prints of the eighteenth-century print-maker Utamaro (1753–1808), she experimented with new ways to paint the theme of mother and child.

One of the methods that the Impressionists found especially appealing about Japanese prints was the sharp contrasts of light and shade that were used, not necessarily to give the idea of depth, but often to simply create decorative effects.

Photography

Photographs were invented in 1839, which means that the Impressionists were working at the dawn of the photographic era. Several of them, such as Cassatt, Degas, Morisot, and Renoir, used photographic effects in their paintings and were subsequently criticized for what some traditionalists saw as their lack of imagination. However, photography gave them a means of looking at light with fresh eyes. It inspired new ways of depicting simplified, more direct impressions of the natural world. It also introduced such ideas as cropping figures at the edges of pictures, stark contrasts, smooth application of paint, informally posed models, and painting movements in a blurred way (see pages 94–99). In the late 1880s, the first small box camera was invented, which allowed almost anyone to take snapshots. From then on, the Impressionists' "frozen moments in time" no longer seemed so extreme.

BELOW
Claude Monet, TERRACE AT SAINTE-ADRESSE, 1867, oil on canvas, 38½ x 51¼ inches (98 x 130 cm). ***Stark contrasts of light and shade are used to create a decorative effect instead of to model form and space. Bright colors are concentrated into flat shapes, reminiscent of Japanese prints. The composition is similar to one by Hokusai from a series of his prints, but the complementary colors show the Impressionists' knowledge of modern color theories.***

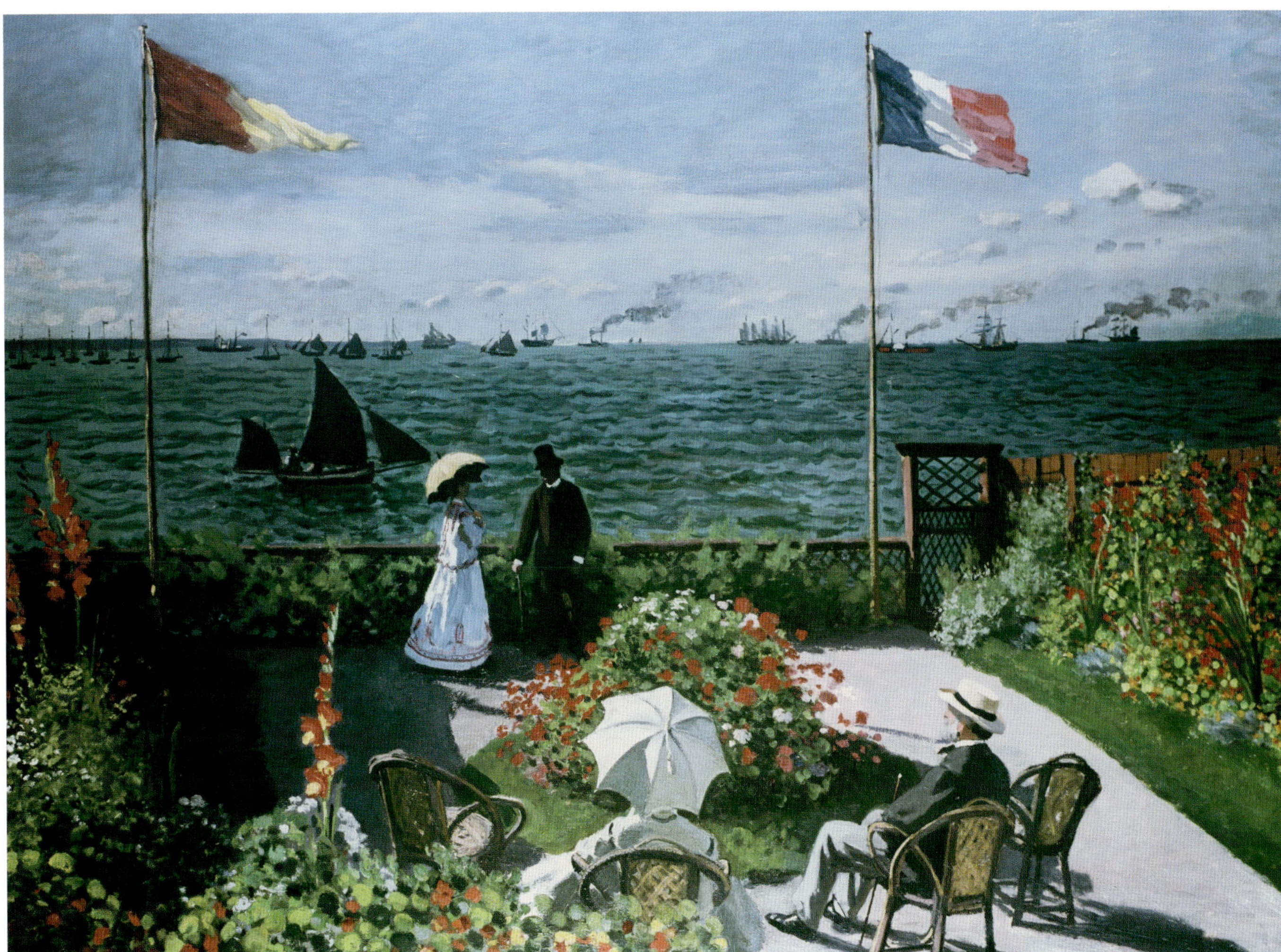

Chapter three

COLOR

The Impressionists made their most expressive break from academic tradition in their use of color. They used color in a radical way and were aware of contemporary scientific color theories, many of which evolved from Sir Isaac Newton's 1666 discoveries of the spectrum and of primary and secondary colors.

BELOW
Chevreul's color circle, 1839.
Chevreul's "law of simultaneous contrast" formed the basis of the Impressionists' use of color. Chevreul constructed this precise color wheel, which is divided into 72 sections, to demonstrate the relationships between colors. Complementaries are opposite to each other, which results in the following three pairings: red and green; orange and blue; and yellow and violet. The colors on the blue side are considered cool and appear to recede, while those on the red side are considered warm and appear to come forward.

IN 1810, THE GERMAN SCIENTIST and poet Johann Wolfgang von Goethe (1749–1832) had published *Farbenlehre* (*Theory of Colors*), which explored how colors relate to perception and the feelings of the observer. In 1805, the enhancing visual effects of placing certain colors beside each other was noted, and, in his 1820 book *Théorie des couleurs*, Gaspard Grégoire

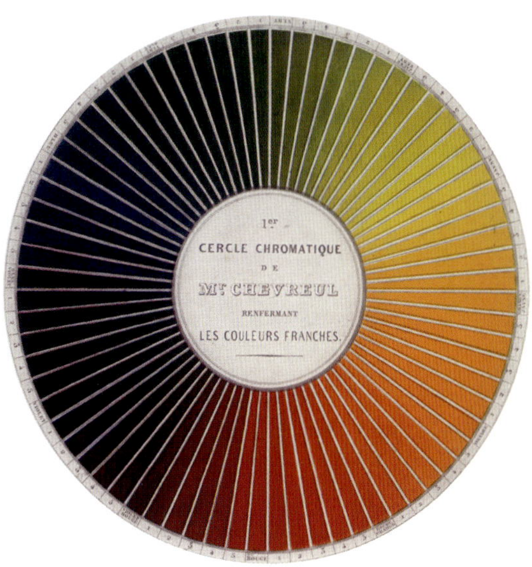

(1751–1846) described how to make black by mixing three primaries—Gamboge, Ultramarine, and Carmine.

Perhaps the most influential of all the color theorists was Michel-Eugène Chevreul (1786–1889), a chemist and the director of dyeing at the Gobelins tapestry works. He had been asked to investigate the dullness of certain colors when they appeared in some tapestries. He discovered that the apparent brightness of a particular color depended more on the colors surrounding it than on the depth of the dye. As a result, he wrote *The Law of Simultaneous Contrast of Colors*, which was published in 1839. This describes the brightening effect when colors opposite each other on the color circle, known as complementary colors, are placed side by side. The Impressionists used these complementary contrasts to enhance their painting effects and also used the idea of juxtaposing warm and cool colors to depict form instead of conventional methods of painting tones.

By the 1860s and 1870s, several handbooks and artists' journals had

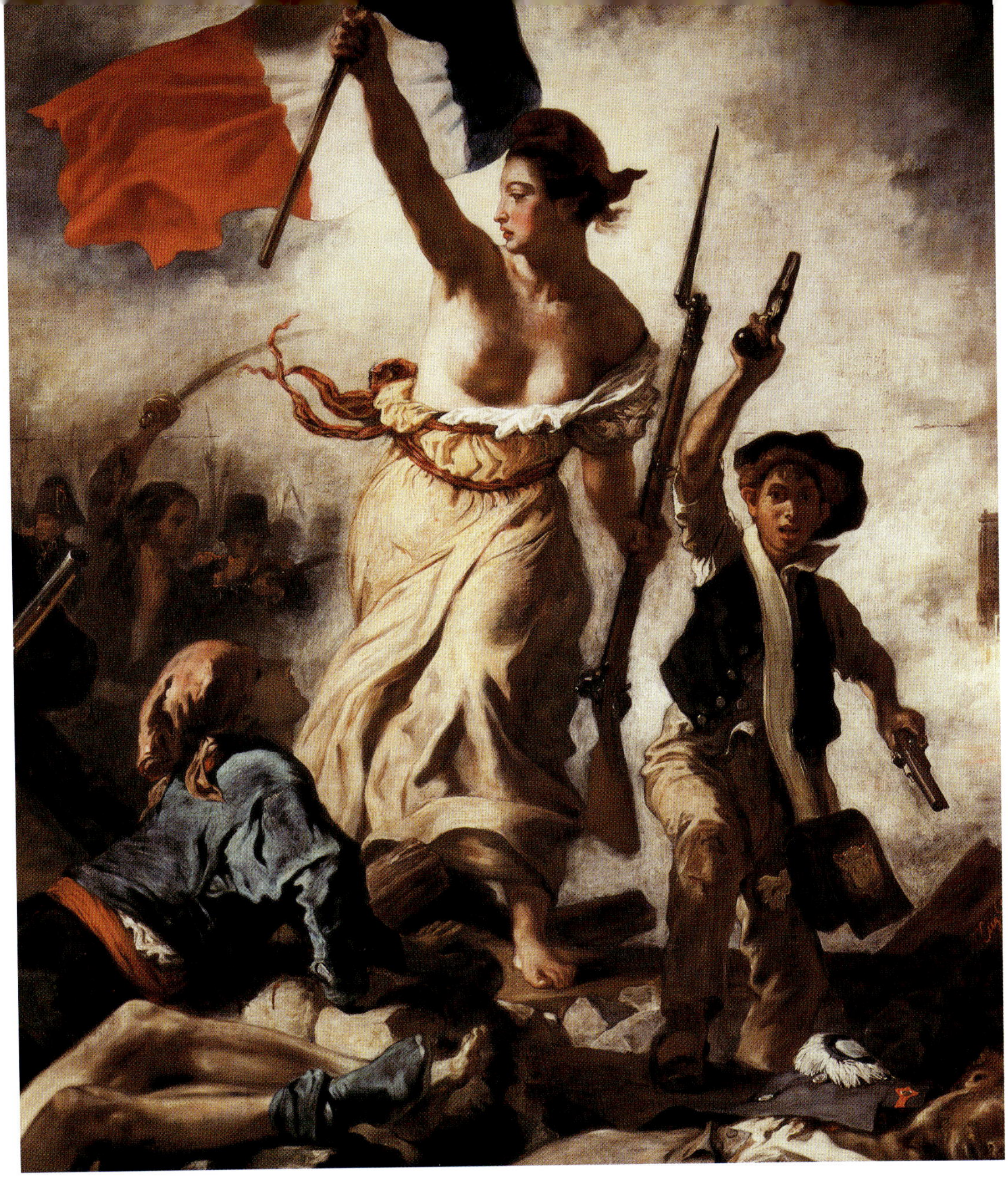

LEFT
Eugène Delacroix, LIBERTY LEADING THE PEOPLE, 1830, oil on canvas, 128 x 102¼ inches (325 x 261 cm).
The Impressionists admired the expressive color that Delacroix had applied in his paintings. He valued the use of bold color above meticulous draftsmanship, and he juxtaposed complementary colors to increase their individual brilliance. He also used color in shadows—discarding the traditional notion that shadows should be gray. Another of his ideas was to mix all his colors with white to brighten the overall effect.

acknowledged the color theories mentioned above. The Impressionists probably also knew about the color mixing studies of Hermann von Helmholtz (1821–94), who had written about contrasting colors in 1852. By the 1850s, these theories had already been investigated by the leader of the French Romantic movement, Eugène Delacroix, whom the Impressionists particularly admired for his use of brilliant color in bold, quick brush strokes. Delacroix wrote about color theories in his journals and explored them in his paintings. He had also become friendly with the famous art critic Charles Blanc (1813–82) in around 1850. In his book *Grammaire des arts du dessin* (1867), Blanc analyzed Chevreul's theories. Seurat, Signac, Pissarro, Gauguin, and van Gogh, among others, read this book avidly.

Further books on color were written and published throughout the century, with varying impact. Ogden Rood (1831–1902), an American physicist, wrote a book especially for painters, including precise charts of the results that would be achieved when certain colors were mixed.

IMPRESSIONIST USE OF COLOR

RIGHT
Georges Seurat, SEATED MODEL (STUDY FOR THE MODELS), 1887, oil on canvas, 9½ x 5½ inches (24 x 14 cm). ***This is a preliminary study for a large painting that Seurat undertook of three nudes. It is a good example of the way in which he placed his dots beside each other to create a merging of colors. Although you might think that the woman's hair and the dark area behind her feet were painted with black, on closer inspection you can see that there is absolutely no black in this painting—the darks have been produced with violet or dark blue. This technique makes it possible to render softness without loss of precision and keeps the painting dynamic, although not formless.***

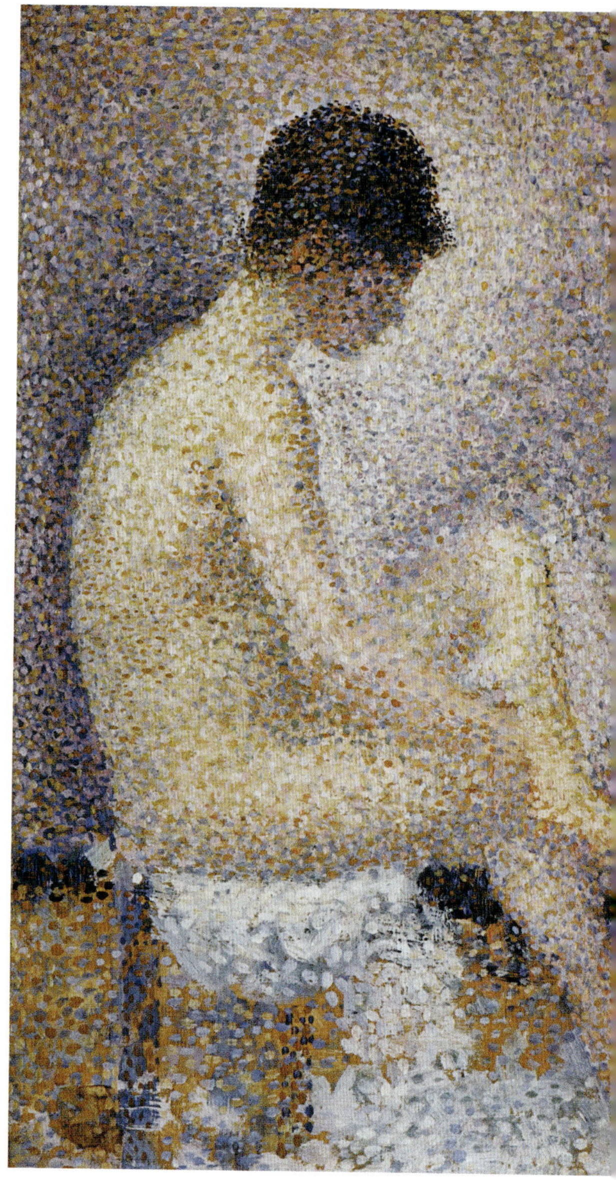

THE BASIS OF ALL Impressionist painting was the representation of color and light. This was more accessible for them than for previous painters, because suddenly, after centuries of innovation, an explosion of new pigments was available. Paint technology was developing rapidly and new chemical pigments were being invented more frequently than ever before. There is no unique Impressionist palette, but the artists used a relatively consistent range of colors that was biased toward the new materials (12 out of the 20 main pigments they used were synthetic). Favorite colors included Emerald Green, artificial Ultramarine, Chrome Yellow, Chrome Orange, Cadmium Yellow, and Viridian. As the complementary to Sunshine Yellow, most of them used Violet extensively, whether mixing it from Cobalt Blue or Ultramarine and Crimson Lake or using the commercially made violet pigments that were being produced by the 1850s and 1860s.

The Impressionists mixed color directly on the canvas or placed hues next to each other, which allowed viewers' eyes to mix them; the technique is known as optical color mixing. They also explored "local" and reflected color. Local color describes the actual color of objects, such as green leaves or red strawberries. The painters observed that every object's local color is altered by reflected colors from nearby objects and by the light. So, once more challenging accepted conventions within the establishment, instead of painting only the local color of objects, they painted what they actually saw. Monet explained, "When you go out to paint, try to forget what objects you have before you, a tree, a house, a field, or whatever. Merely think here is a little square of blue, here an oblong of pink, here a streak of yellow, and paint it just as it looks to you, the exact color and shape, until it gives your own naïve impression of the scene before you."

The color of their canvases was important to the Impressionists, because they usually used the background surface as part of each painting. They often used white or light-colored surfaces and left certain amounts showing through the finished compositions.

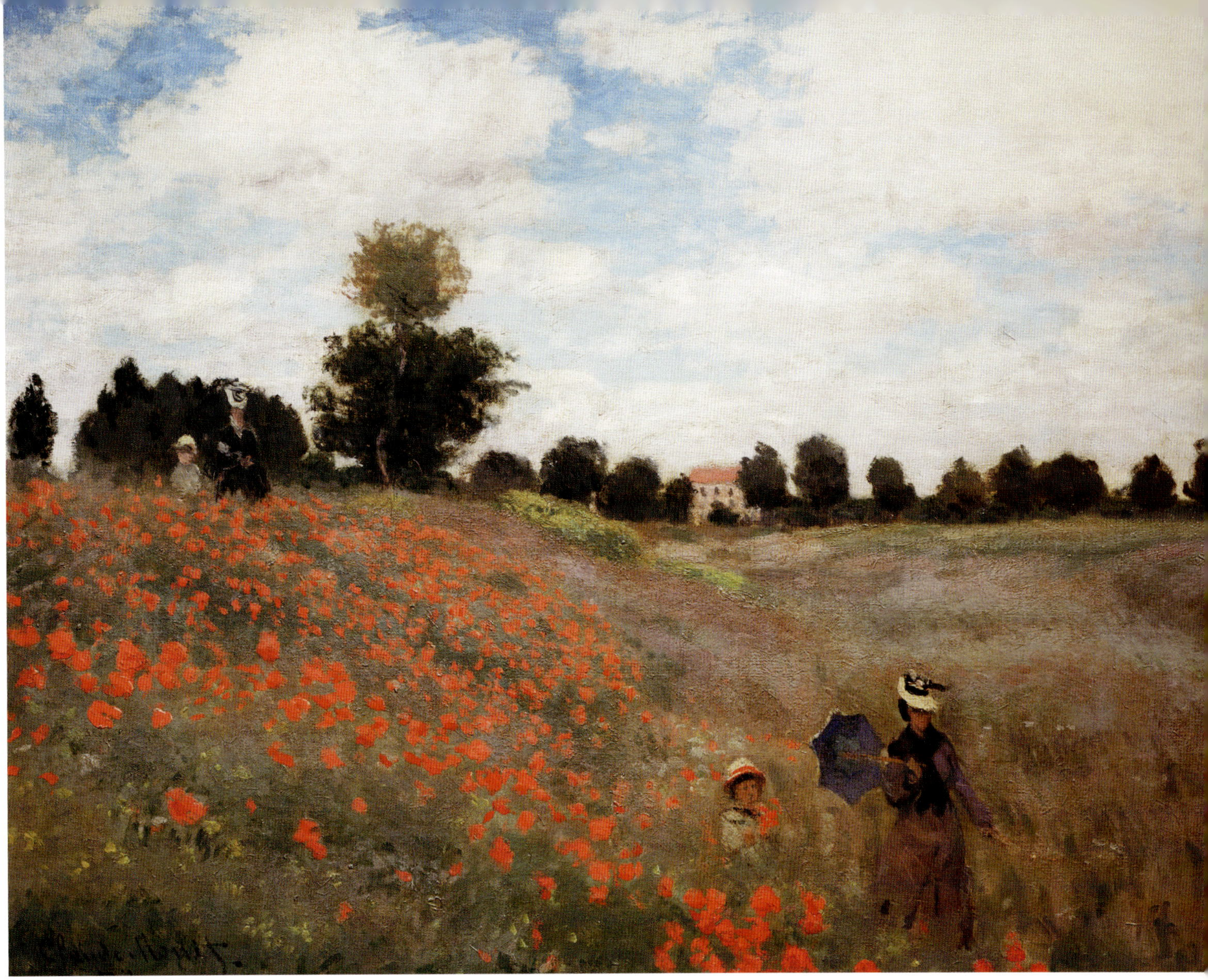

ABOVE
Claude Monet, WILD POPPIES NEAR ARGENTEUIL, 1873, oil on canvas, 20 x 26 inches (51 x 66 cm).
Monet employs the technique of including complementary contrasts, such as the vibrant red poppies scattered on a shimmering green field. The soft tranquillity reflects the warm summer's day and the figures (his wife and son) merge with their surroundings. Painted in an almost abstract style, the splashes of red dominate.

The awareness of color theories led the Impressionists to discard earthy tones and deal almost solely with the seven colors of the solar spectrum (red, orange, yellow, green, blue, indigo, and violet). Their views of black and white were another matter.

Absence of black

They believed that white reflects all colors; so all surfaces that appear to be white must include other colors as well, such as yellow, violet, blue, or green. White—usually Lead White as Delacroix had advocated—was the most-used color on their palettes, and they mixed other colors with it. Conversely, black was considered to be the absence of color. The artists argued that pure black is not found in nature and so they rarely used it. Occasionally, some used it for accents, but never in shadows. "No shadow is black," said Renoir, "it always has a color." Van Gogh agreed: "Absolute black does not really exist." Even in his paintings of sooty stations, such as *La Gare Saint-Lazare* of 1877 (see pages 32–33), Monet avoided black. To make a color close to black, colors (except for white and yellow) were mixed together—the belief being that even the darkest tones are full of color. Shadows rarely included black but were made of blended colors.

Chapter four

MATERIALS

The Impressionists lived in an age of great social change as well, as radical technical innovation. The modernization of the world greatly affected them. The struggle between modernity and tradition was particularly apparent in their paintings, and the way in which they portrayed their wonderment has become for us a cheering reflection of the past.

RIGHT
Collapsible tin tubes. ***These were invented and patented in London by the American artist John Goffe Rand in the early 1840s.***

BELOW
William Winsor's first Patent Tubes, 1840. ***These early Winsor and Newton products reflect the innovations in paint technology and its means of storage.***

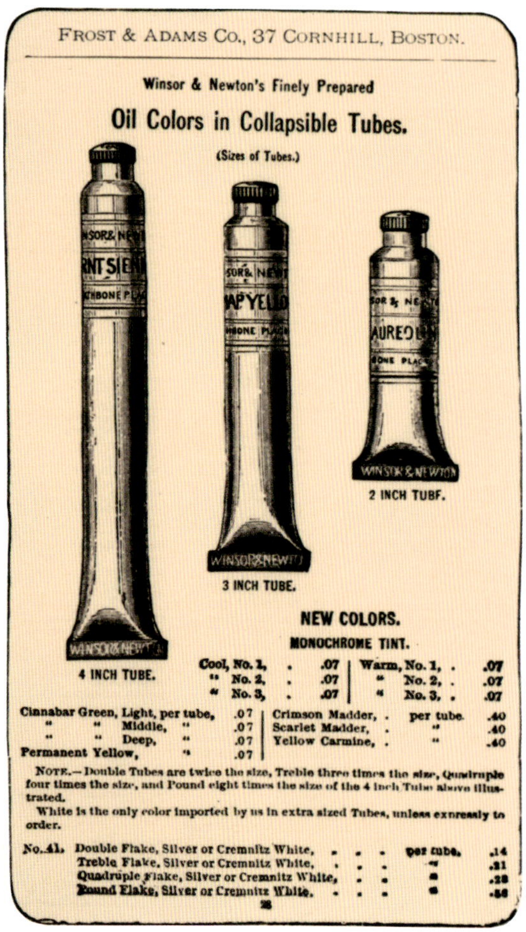

FROST & ADAMS CO., 37 CORNHILL, BOSTON.

Winsor & Newton's Finely Prepared

Oil Colors in Collapsible Tubes.

(Sizes of Tubes.)

4 INCH TUBE.

3 INCH TUBE.

2 INCH TUBF.

NEW COLORS.

MONOCHROME TINT.

Cool, No. 1,	.07	Warm, No. 1,	.07
" No. 2,	.07	" No. 2,	.07
" No. 3,	.07	" No. 3,	.07

Cinnabar Green, Light,	per tube,	.07	Crimson Madder,	per tube.	.40
" " Middle,	"	.07	Scarlet Madder,	"	.40
" " Deep,	"	.07	Yellow Carmine,	"	.40
Permanent Yellow,	"	.07			

NOTE.—Double Tubes are twice the size, Treble three times the size, Quadruple four times the size, and Pound eight times the size of the 4 inch Tube above illustrated.

White is the only color imported by us in extra sized Tubes, unless expressly to order.

No. 41.	Double Flake, Silver or Cremnitz White,	per tube,	.14
	Treble Flake, Silver or Cremnitz White,	"	.21
	Quadruple Flake, Silver or Cremnitz White,	"	.28
	Pound Flake, Silver or Cremnitz White.	"	.56

28

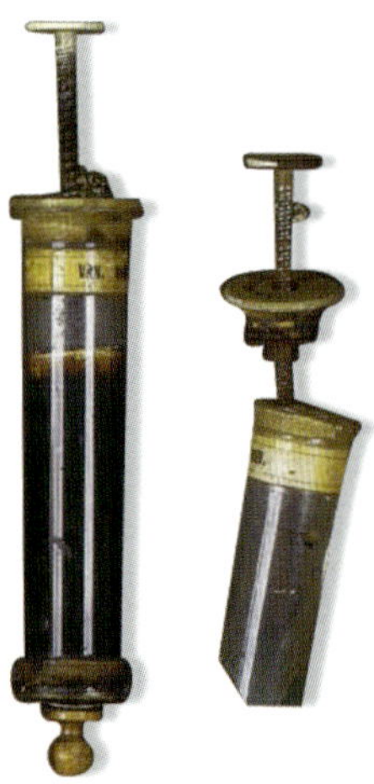

AT THE BEGINNING of the nineteenth century, painters still kept their colors as dry pigments that had to be mixed with oil in order to make paint. The alternative was to buy oil colors already mixed by colormen, who were professional suppliers of art materials and who ground the paints by hand. Linseed oil was originally used to mix up the paints. However, of all the oils used for painting, linseed is the most prone to yellowing, and it also forms a skin when thickly applied. The Impressionists, therefore, favored poppy oil, because it gives paint a smooth, even quality and is slow drying, which is particularly useful when reworking paintings. Once paints were mixed, they were wrapped in pieces of pig's bladder and tied with thread. Painters pierced the skin with an ivory tack, squeezed out the paint, and used the tack as a plug. However, unfortunately, paints in bladders hardened and deteriorated rapidly once they were pierced, so manufacturers experimented with adding waxes, fats, or more oils to the paints, with varying degrees of success.

By the mid-nineteenth century, one of the most significant developments was mechanical pigment grinding, allowing mass production of artists' colors. Soon after, there was a steady increase in chemically prepared colors, which resulted in brilliant pigments that had not been achievable before.

Perhaps the most important technological advance of all was the invention of metal tubes in the 1840s, which allowed for the long-term storage of oil paints and made outdoor painting trips more practicable.

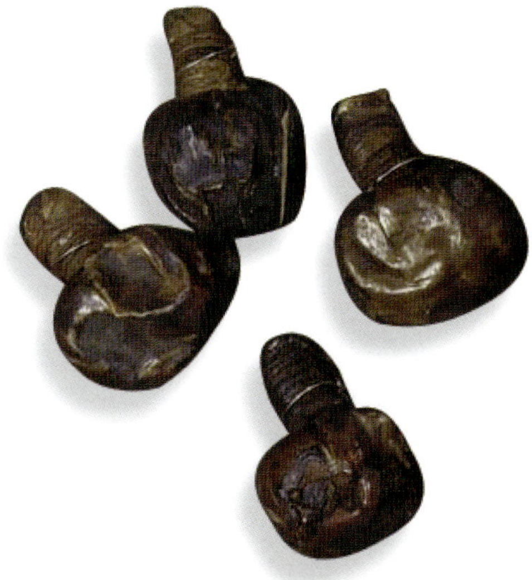

RIGHT
Pigs' bladders.
Used by artists before 1840, they were perforated and closed with ivory tacks.

BELOW
John Singer Sargent, PAUL HELLEU SKETCHING WITH HIS WIFE, 1889, oil on canvas, 26 x 32 inches (66.5 x 81.5 cm).
The freedom that the new portable paints and equipment gave artists is clearly shown in this relaxed and colorful painting.

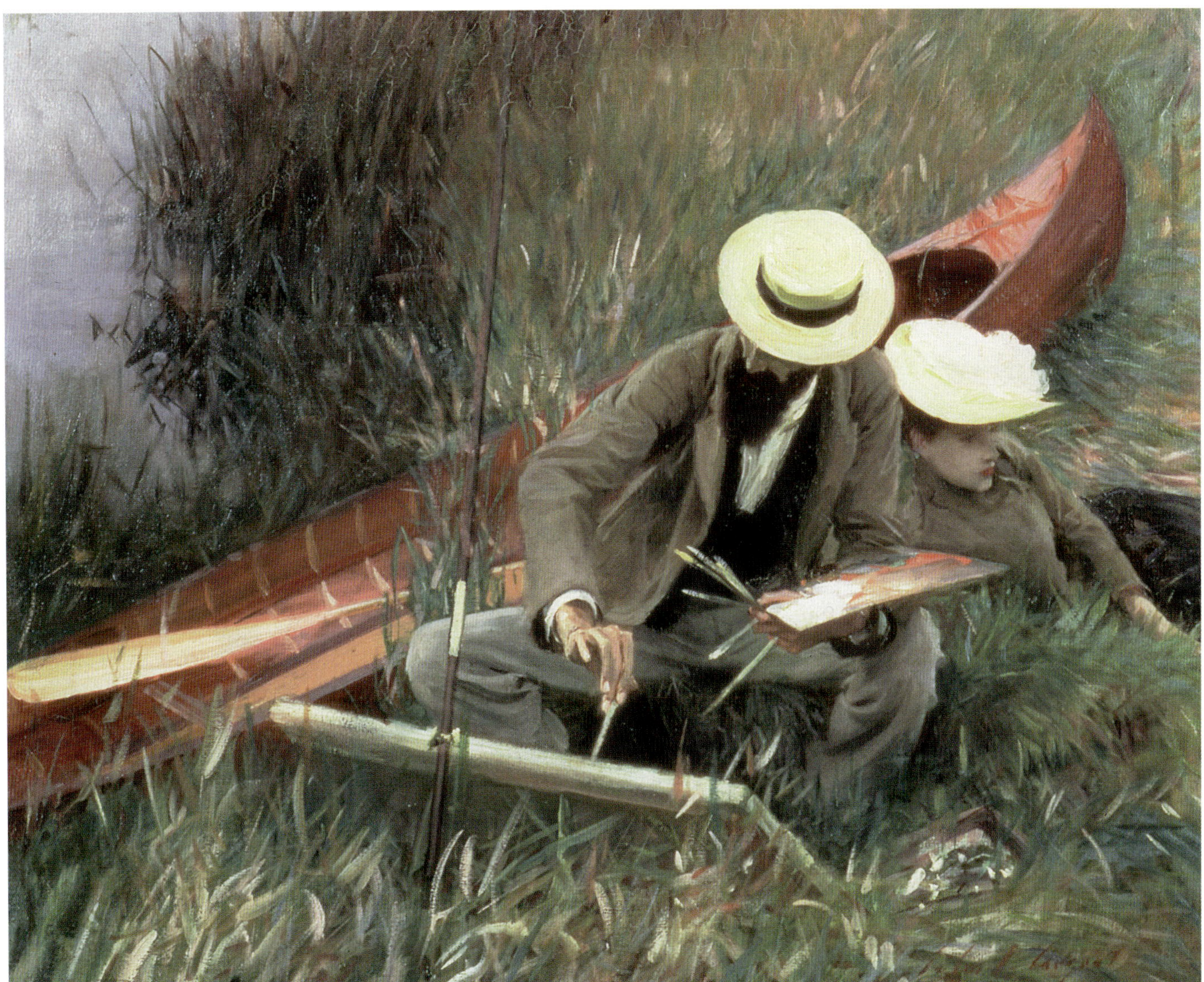

IMPRESSIONISTS' MATERIALS

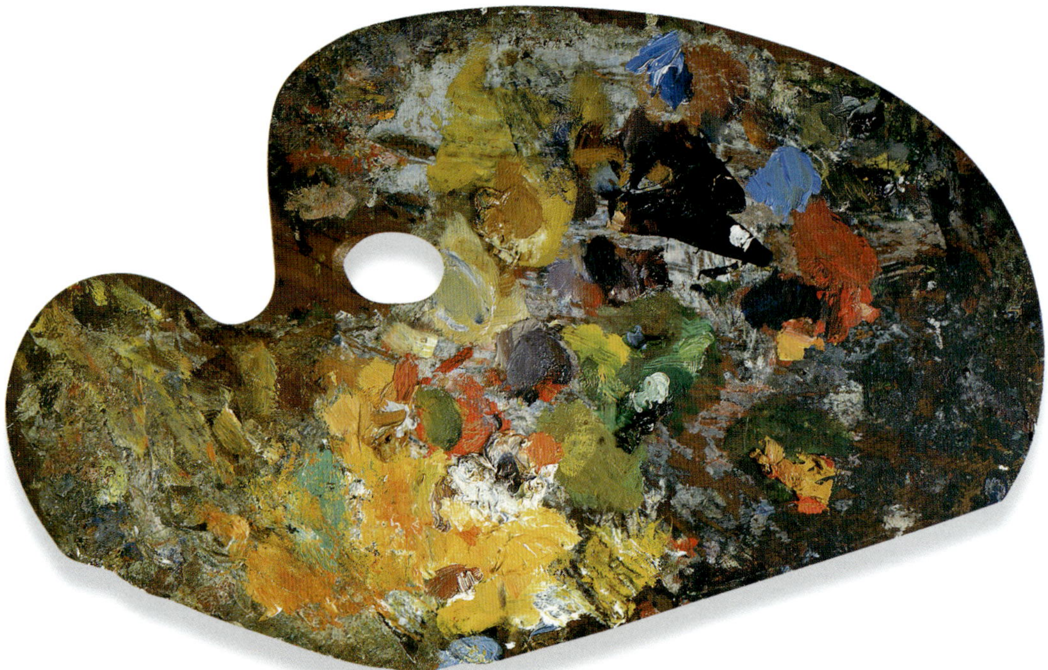

RIGHT
Monet's palette, 13 x 20 inches (32.5 x 51 cm).
Monet used this palette during the 1880s. The colors include Cobalt Blue, Viridian, Vermilion, White, Cadmium Orange, and Cadmium Yellow. The Impressionists either cleaned or changed their brushes when applying different colors.

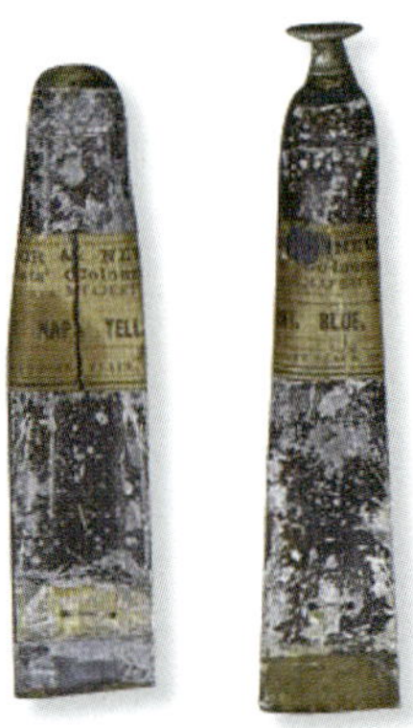

ABOVE
Early makes of metal tubes, about 1841.
The first tubes were made of tin.

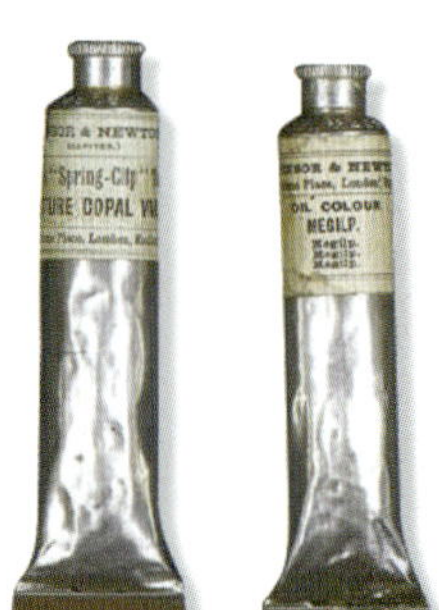

ABOVE
Some later tin tubes.
Tin was soft enough to be malleable and sufficiently inert not to react with and discolor the paint.

BY THE 1870S, many colormen began opening stores or factories. Several Impressionists preferred small suppliers who made up paints to their specific requirements, and they debated the merits of hand grinding as opposed to machine grinding. Some Impressionists and Post-Impressionists including Cézanne, Pissarro, Renoir, and van Gogh preferred the varied consistencies and textures of traditional hand-ground paints to the firm consistency of machine-made paints.

Paints

Although the practical sections of this book includes more details about the actual colors each artist used, here is a selection of the main colors found in the Impressionists' paintbox:

Red At first, Vermilion was the most reliable bright red available. When Cadmium Red was introduced toward the end of the nineteenth century, several artists were reluctant to use it but both Cadmium and Deep Madder eventually became popular. Alizarin, discovered in 1868, became the synthetic replacement of the natural madder. The natural Red Lakes and the synthetic Alizarin were important components of several Impressionists' palettes.

Yellow Cadmium Yellow was introduced slowly as it was more expensive than Chrome Yellow. Cadmium Yellow soon became available as lemon and deep or bright yellow. Most artists continued to use Yellow Ocher.

Green Viridian and Emerald Green were two of the most exciting new colors available to the Impressionists, and most of their palettes contained at least one of them. Viridian was the most popular green, but its recipe was kept secret and, thus, its price was expensive until 1859, when it was patented in France.

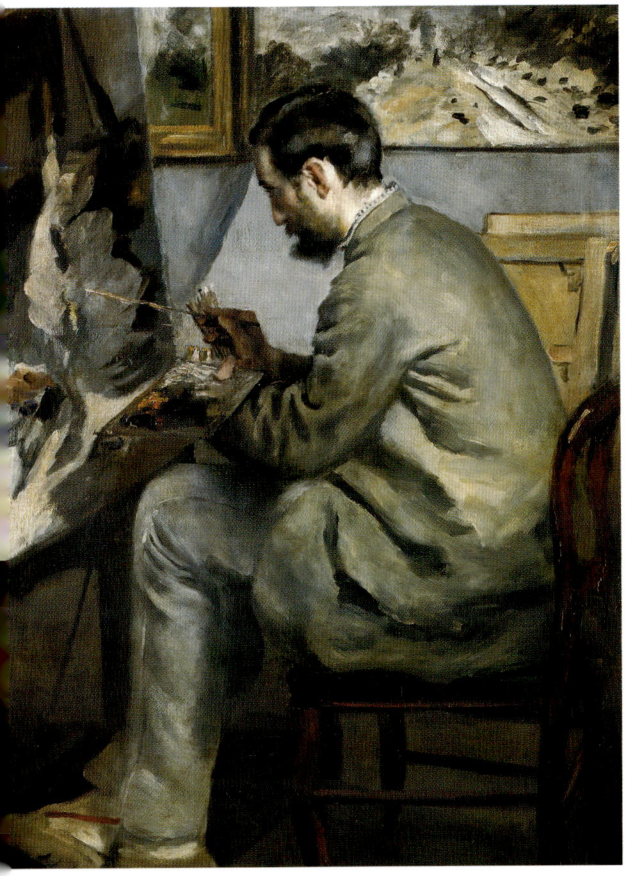

Blue Ultramarine was originally made from the semiprecious stone lapis lazuli. After 1828, when a prize had been offered for the production of a less costly pigment, a synthetic version was produced. By the 1870s, artificial French Ultramarine was the standard blue for painters and it featured prominently in the Impressionists' palettes. Ceruleum Blue is a cool greenish blue that was first produced in 1860 and was extensively used by the Impressionists afterward. Cobalt Blue was also widely used.

White Lead White was the Impressionists' most prevalent color. It had the greatest opacity of any white oil pigment. In a bid to find a less toxic color, some painters occasionally used Zinc or Titanium White, but these were more expensive and didn't have the opacity of Lead White.

Other materials

As well as paints, the materials used by the Impressionists' were not that different from the ones we use today.

Canvases were stretched over wooden frames, which is still done today. The Impressionists usually used commercially prepared canvases, which were primed with white or other pale colors, such as oatmeal, cream, and pinkish or bluish gray. These were supplied in two finishes—*à grain*, which was textured, and *lisse*, which had a smoother finish. Most Impressionists preferred *à grain*.

Brushes were similar to those we use now: short or long and made of bristle or hogs' hair in three basic shapes: round, flat, and "cat's tongue" (filbert). Long, flat brushes were popular with the Impressionists due to their versatility and the variety of marks they produce. Soft or sable-haired brushes were also used, but not as widely as stiffer bristle brushes. The blender or fan-shaped brush was used by artists to smooth the accents of the brush marks.

Easels and palettes were wooden and oval or rectangular. Palette knives were similar to contemporary knives, resembling small trowels. Charcoal and pencils were often used for preliminary sketches. Sketchbooks have hardly changed since the late nineteenth century and several of the Impressionists worked in pastels on textured, colored paper (usually buff or light brown). Pastels have also changed little. The Impressionists used handmade pastels made with varying quantities of chalk, binder, and pigment.

A wide range of portable equipment also became available, including various lightweight sketching easels and the *boîte de campagne*, a complete outdoor painting kit.

LEFT
Auguste Renoir, BAZILLE AT WORK, 1867, oil on canvas, 41¼ x 29 inches (105 x 73.5 cm).
Renoir painted this portrait of his friend Bazille at work in his studio, holding a traditional wooden palette with a thumbhole securely in his left hand and clasping the long brush relatively far back in his right hand. Behind his right hand you can see several other brushes, which would have been used for different colors to avoid making the hues muddy.

BELOW
Nineteenth-century artist's watercolor paintbox.
This box, made from wood and enamel by R. Ackermann in about 1820, is the type that would have been used by the Impressionists when they were out on location. It was convenient for such artists, whose work relied on painting in the open air.

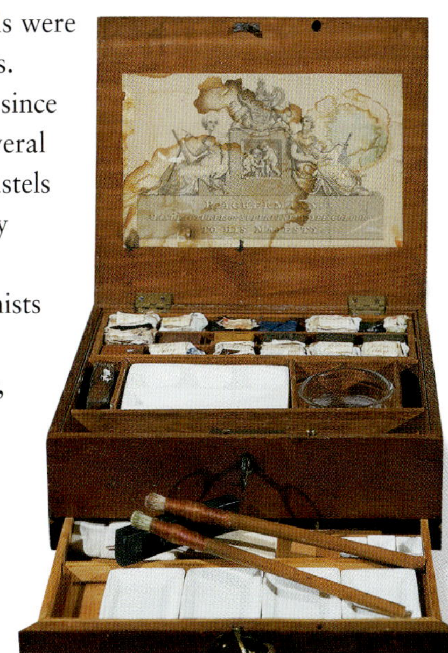

MODERN MATERIALS

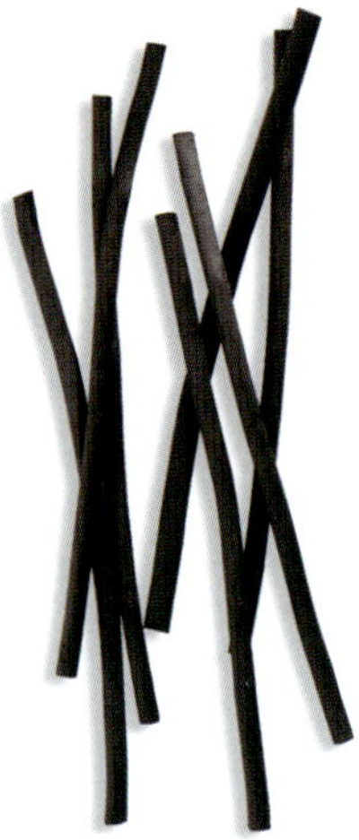

charcoal sticks

MANY OF THE MATERIALS that are available today are similar to those used by the Impressionists. Easels, palettes, pastels, brushes. and sketchbooks, as mentioned, have changed little. Pencils, charcoal, and Conté crayons are also much the same today. (The Impressionists' rejection of academic principles did not mean a rejection of drawing, and many of their paintings were made on top of light drawings.)

Several brands of pastels are still made by hand in the way in which they were produced in the Impressionists' time. It's worth trying different types to see what suits you best, because some are soft and smooth, while others are harder and chalkier. Often a mixture of materials answers all needs, such as using harder pastels for detailed areas and softer pastels for looser, sketchier parts.

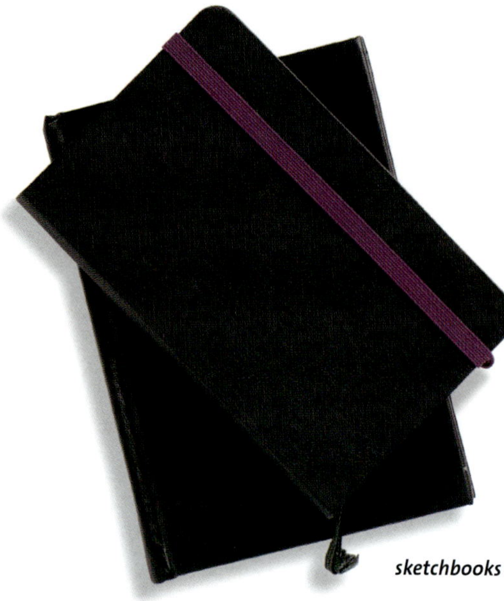

sketchbooks

Brushes, although barely changed from the sizes and styles that the Impressionists used, are available in a wide assortment of animal- and synthetic-haired varieties and also in different price ranges. Many of the newer synthetic varieties are more versatile than the animal-haired brushes, but, as with pastels, experiment to find your personal preference.

Crank-handled palette knives were standard pieces of the Impressionists' equipment and remain extremely useful. These days, most commercially prepared canvases are primed with white acrylic, but to create alternative light tints apply a light wash

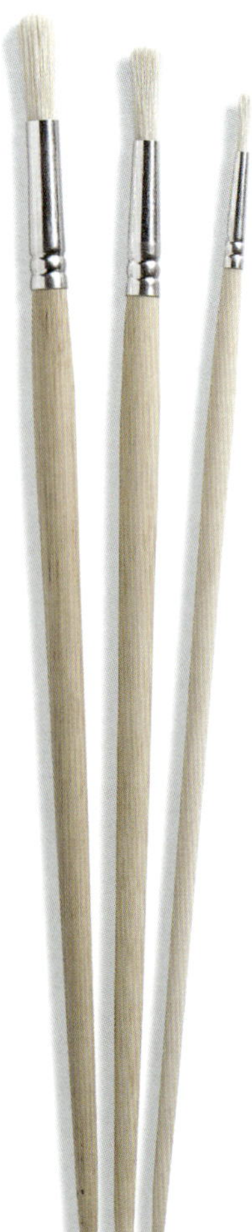

bristle brushes

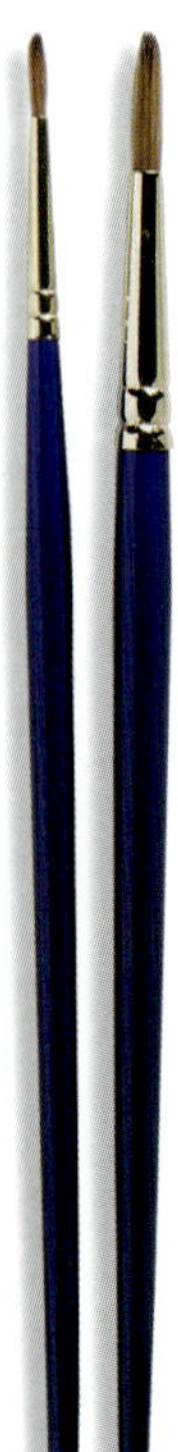

sable/synthetic mix brushes

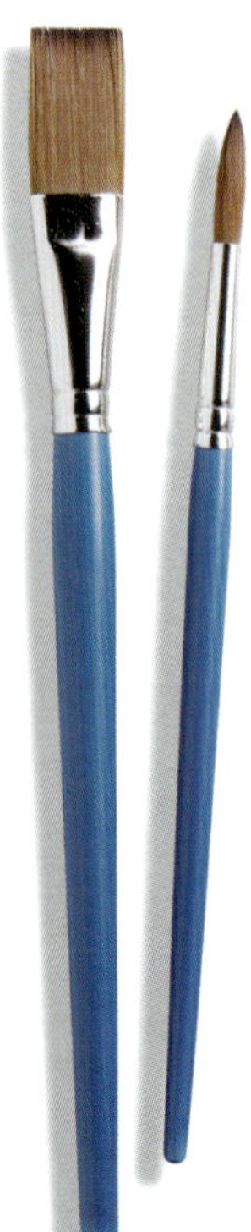

synthetic brushes

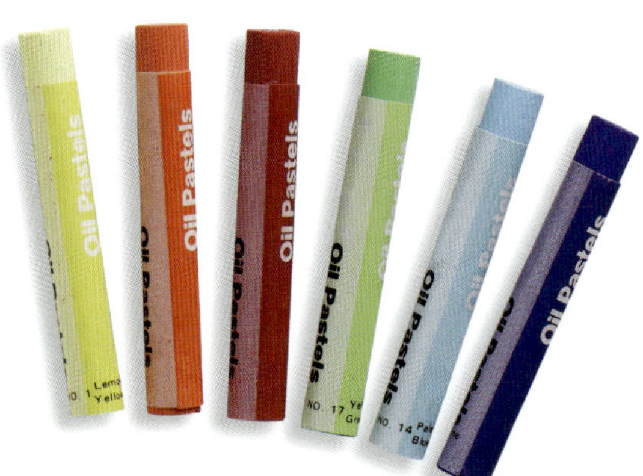

oil pastels

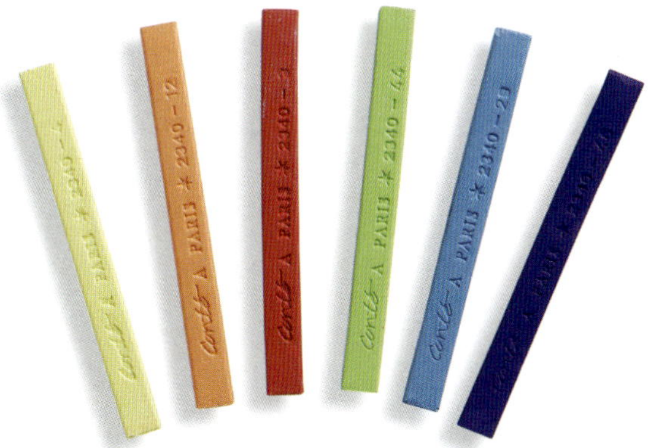

Conté crayons

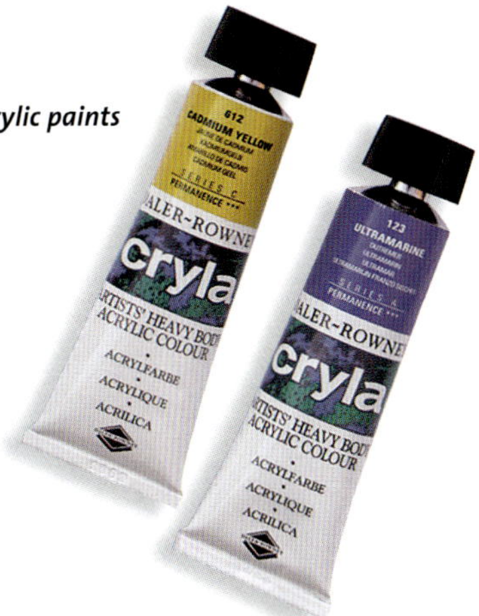

acrylic paints

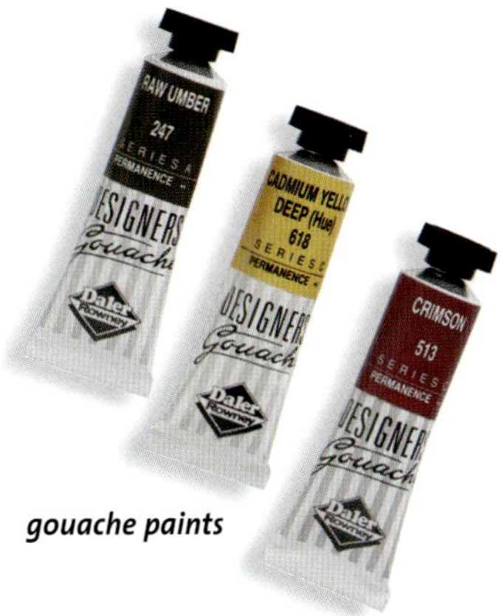

gouache paints

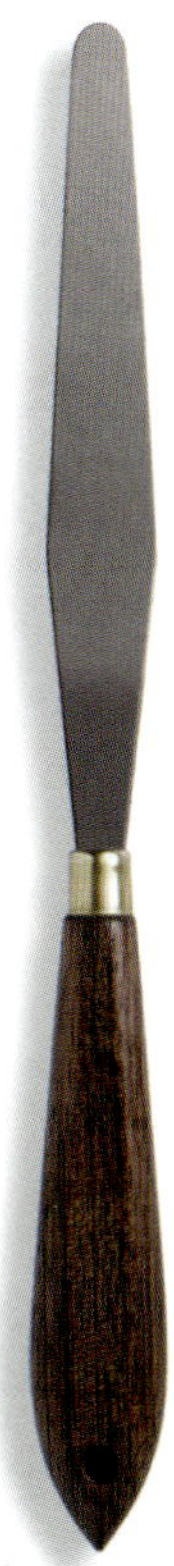

palette knife

of acrylic in the appropriate shade. This can also be done on the canvas-textured boards that are now available.

Types of paint

As far as modern paints are concerned, again, experiment with a few different makes and types to find the consistency and colors you like. Most of the paintings in this book can be created with oil paints, water-mixable oils, or acrylics. Some are more specifically suited to pastels or gouache. Each type of paint has its own merits and most come in colors and textures similar to those of the Impressionists.

Oil paints are available in two different grades: artists' and students'. Artists' colors are of better quality, which is reflected in the price. Water-mixable oil paints respond in a similar way to regular oil paints but, as the name implies, they can be mixed and cleaned with water instead of with mineral spirits.

Gouache is opaque watercolor. Degas, Toulouse-Lautrec, and Pissarro often used gouache, usually on paper instead of on canvas. Many modern gouache paints are made for designers and do not have the permanence necessary for fine art, so check for this when you are buying.

Acrylic paints are mixed with water and can imitate the effects of oils. Quick drying, they can be applied thickly or thinly and are available in most of the same colors as oil paints. When dry, their faint surface sheen gives the impression of oil paints, although there are differences in the final effect.

It is possible to mix acrylic, gouache, and oil paints, but this might alter the finished look of your picture.

primed canvas and canvas board

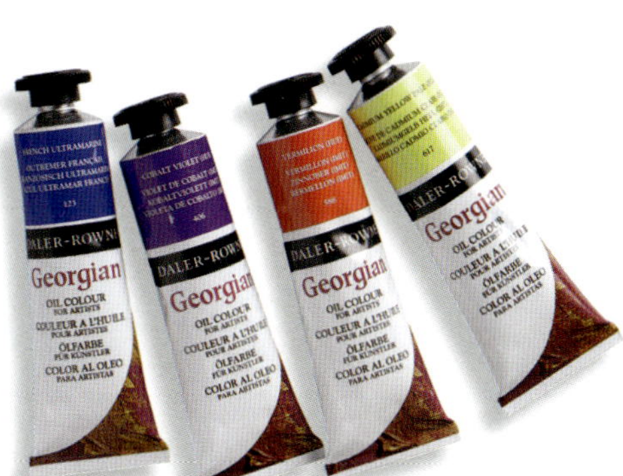

oil paints

Chapter five

MONET

The words Monet and Impressionism are virtually synonymous. After all, his painting Impression, Sunrise *gave the movement its title. Monet lived the longest of all the Impressionists, and he is probably the best-known artist of the movement, dedicated to exploring the effects of light and color.*

RIGHT
RUE MONTORGEUIL: FÊTE NATIONALE DU 30 JUIN, 1878, oil on canvas, 31½ x 20 inches (80 x 50.5 cm).
Monet worked across the canvas, making hundreds of impasto brush strokes to represent fluttering flags, people, and windswept clouds. The flicks of paint indicate bustling crowds, obliterating the lines of the architecture and creating a vivid sense of movement.

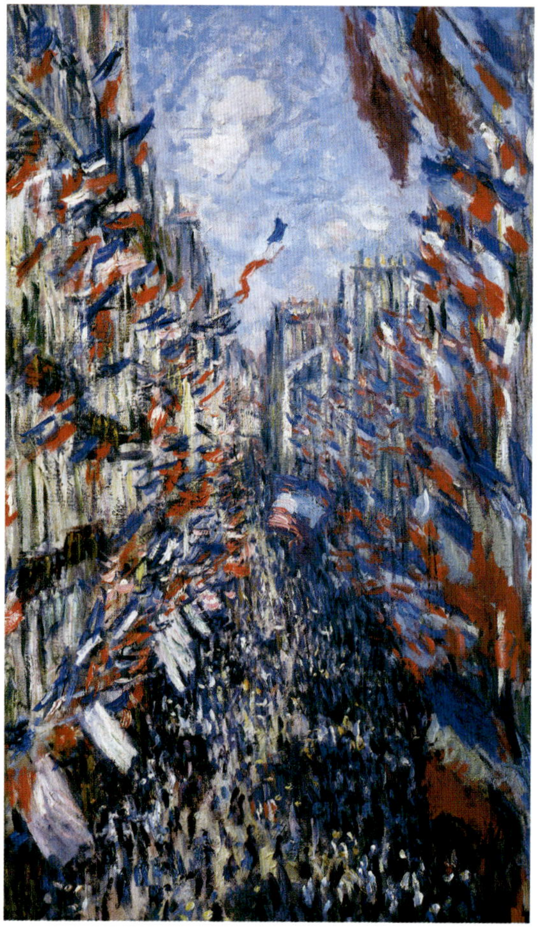

OSCAR-CLAUDE MONET (1840–1926) was gregarious and confident. Born in Paris, he grew up in Le Havre from the age of five. As a teenager, he was encouraged by the painter Eugène Jouis Boudin (1824–98) to stop drawing caricatures and to travel around the coast painting in the open air. From his teenage years, Monet admired the natural realism of such artists as Jean-Baptiste Camille Corot (1796–1875), Gustave Courbet (1819–77), and the Barbizon painters (see page 8). Boudin introduced him to Johan Barthold Jongkind (1819–91), from whom he learned to use bright colors and to paint the same landscapes in different light.

Devotion to nature

In 1859, Monet went to Paris. Instead of following the convention of studying academic painting, he chose to work in an independent studio. There, he met other young artists, including Bazille, Renoir, and Sisley, who shared his dissatisfaction with established academic art. In complete contrast to traditional paintings with idealized social or

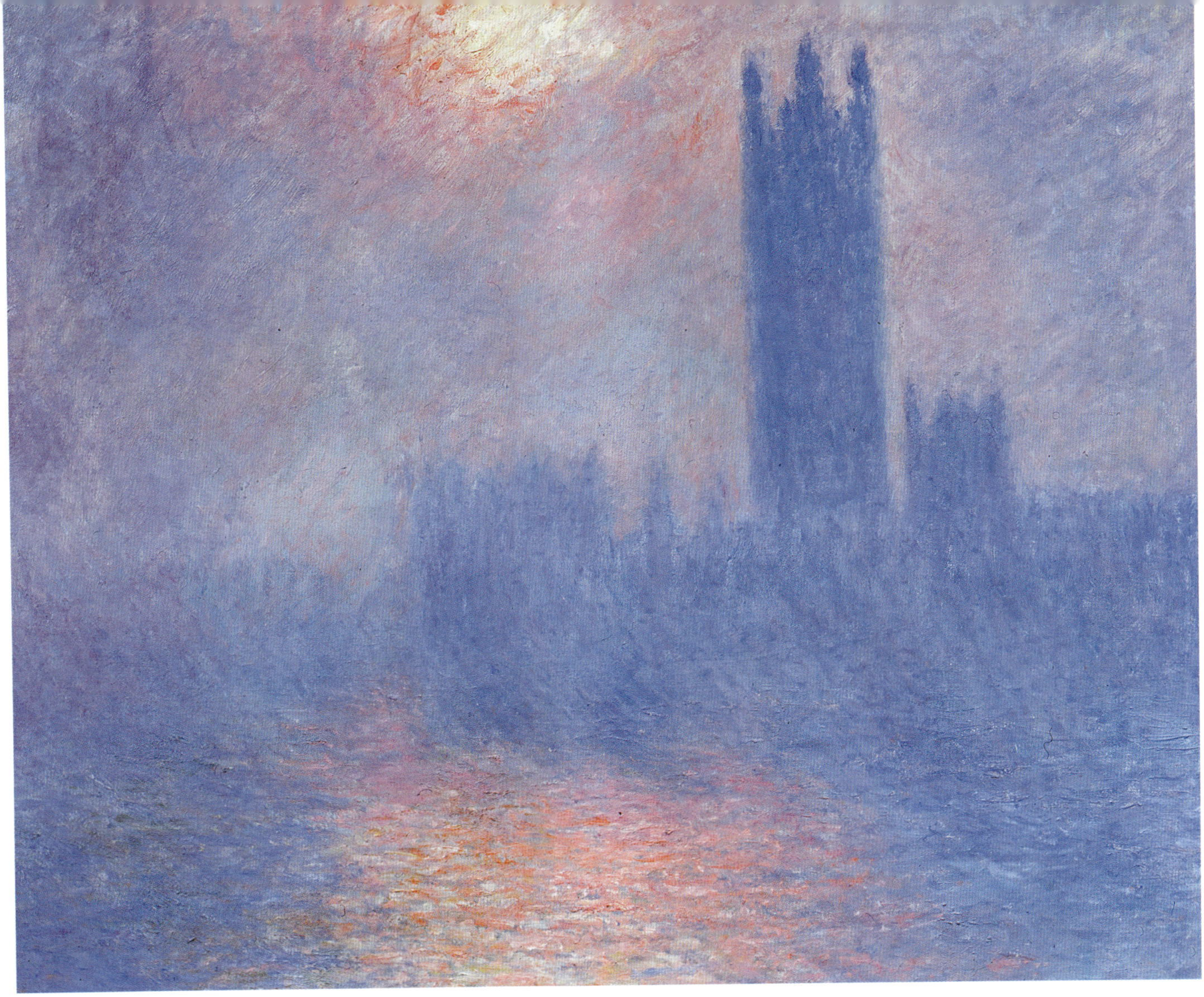

ABOVE
HOUSES OF PARLIAMENT, LONDON, SUN BREAKING THROUGH THE FOG, 1904, oil on canvas, 32 x 36¼ inches (81 x 92 cm). ***Monet painted with thin, translucent washes, then accented highlights with touches of impasto. The technique is similar to the*** sfumato, ***or "smoky," method used by painters of the Italian Renaissance.***

religious messages, he painted objectively what he saw in front of him. He wrote, "I have no other wish than a close fusion with nature."

As well as their devotion to nature, Monet and the other Impressionists were fascinated by the new technology that was transforming the countryside in the form of railways and steel bridges. Modern life became as much a part of Monet's work as timeless landscapes. Painting from direct observation, he used quick brush strokes to record the overall image. This gave the effect of spontaneity, although most of his works were carefully planned and often completed in the studio over several sessions. His ideas of capturing the light and weather effects he saw around him never wavered.

Throughout his life, Monet's brushwork was strongly descriptive, catching the character of different phenomena; at times, it became almost calligraphic with short, horizontal dashes or slabs, abrupt zigzags, and small, diagonal marks or curving strokes. In some of his paintings, the canvas can be seen through thin paint; in others, colors are layered on top of each other. Following the abounding color theories, even his shadows became diffused with color, replacing the traditional dark brown or gray. (The color of his signature is often a clue to the last color that he used on a painting.) Later in life, Monet recorded the changing effects of light and weather in his much-loved "series" paintings, such as his depictions of water lilies.

CAPTURING FLEETING MOMENTS

CENTER
LA GARE SAINT-LAZARE, 1877, oil on canvas, $31^3/_4$ x $38^1/_2$ inches (80.5 x 98 cm). ***This painting captures the moment in which the steam and smoke blend with the hazy sunlight filtering in from the background. The broken color and dense impasto brushwork add to the sense of atmosphere and movement.***

BELOW
LA GARE SAINT-LAZARE, detail. ***The paint varies in thickness, most dense in the clouds and steam that dissolve the details of the structures.***

THROUGHOUT HIS LIFE, Monet was fascinated by light effects and the challenge of capturing their appearance in paint. His method was to look beyond the obvious and to capture a fleeting moment in time. He was not only fascinated with light and color, but also by textures and his brush strokes imitate many of the textures visible in nature. Seen from a distance, his paintings give instant impressions of a complete image. Magnified, you can see the richly textured brush marks and quality of the paint surfaces combining to create energetic and vibrant patterns of color. The spontaneous appearance of Monet's paintings was created by the sketchlike application of paint in broken dabs of color, using brush marks of varying widths and shapes.

Many of Monet's paintings were completed rapidly and largely alla prima, although, increasingly, he finished works in the studio, because he was accomplished enough not to lose the sense of spontaneity. When he worked on his "series" paintings, he often painted up to seven canvases at a time, dashing from one to the other as the light changed. Paint was applied both in successive layers and in carefully placed slabs of color side by side. Monet experimented with

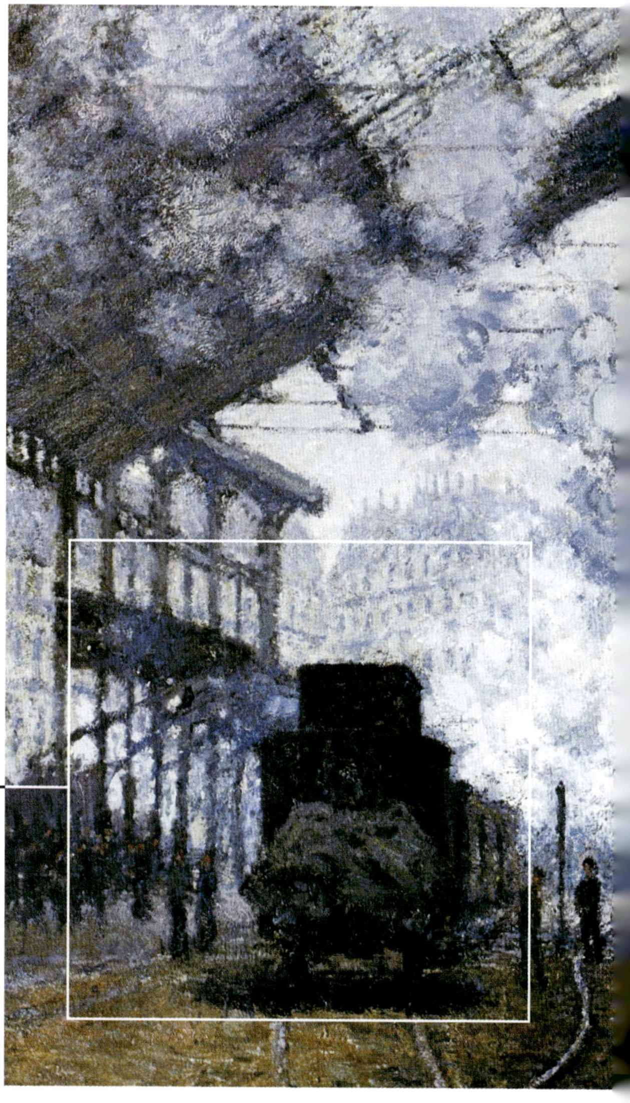

varying degrees of finish throughout his career, but it was not until the 1880s that he exhibited his sketch-like work publicly.

La Gare Saint-Lazare

Part of the fascination with Monet's treatment of fleeting moments is the fact that he painted timeless landscapes and images of modern life with equal vivacity. His sequence of paintings of the Gare Saint-Lazare gives us an insight into his technique at this time. Saint-Lazare station served most of his favorite locations around Paris. Between January and March 1877, Monet produced 12 paintings of the station, which became labeled his "modern life" paintings. They were made largely in situ using a restricted palette of about nine colors. To work speedily, he mixed his paints with turpentine to help the color flow freely.

What little color is used reinforces warm and cold tones, as well as light and shade. For example, the cool Cobalt Blue swirls of steam contrast with the warm Yellow Ocher-tinged background surface. Monet painted in direct, unbroken brush strokes, varying the thickness of the paint; in addition, the breadth and scale of each brush was related to the size of the object being painted. Color and tone are broken everywhere and small strokes of paint have been delicately touched in. The overall effect is atmospheric and captures a sense of movement.

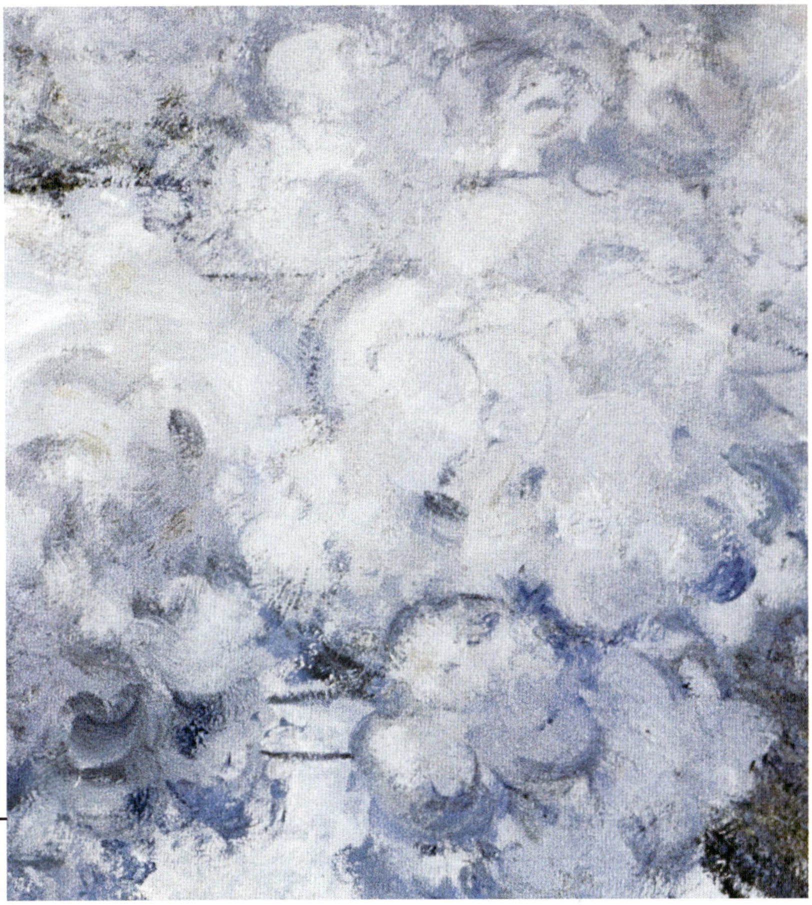

ABOVE
LA GARE SAINT-LAZARE, detail.
Although Monet painted quickly, the paint was applied with great precision. Here, the tumbling clouds of smoke and steam have been held static by Monet's purposeful use of complementary colors.

HOW TO DO IT

YOUR PALETTE

Your palette will be simple and reasonably limited for this painting:

1 Zinc White
2 French Ultramarine
3 Cadmium Yellow
4 Viridian
5 Rowney Emerald
6 Vermilion
7 Crimson Alizarin
8 Cobalt Violet

Monet often used colors straight from the tube, but for this painting most colors were blended with varying amounts of Zinc White to create a pastel-like luminosity.

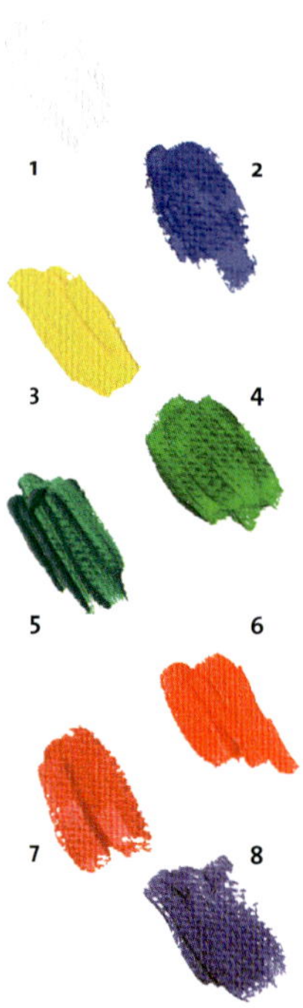

MONET'S PAINTINGS APPEAR to be a haphazard mixture of color and texture. Closer examination, however, reveals the careful planning of his work, which stemmed from his overriding objective to capture transitory moments in time. By carefully following the steps shown here, you can paint a detail that demonstrates how lighting effects can portray fleeting moments.

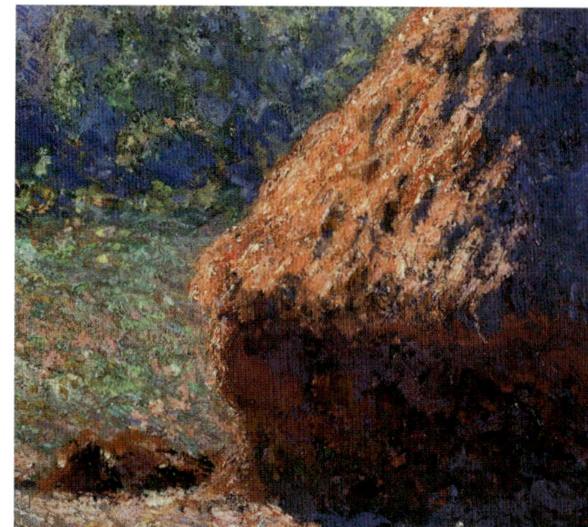

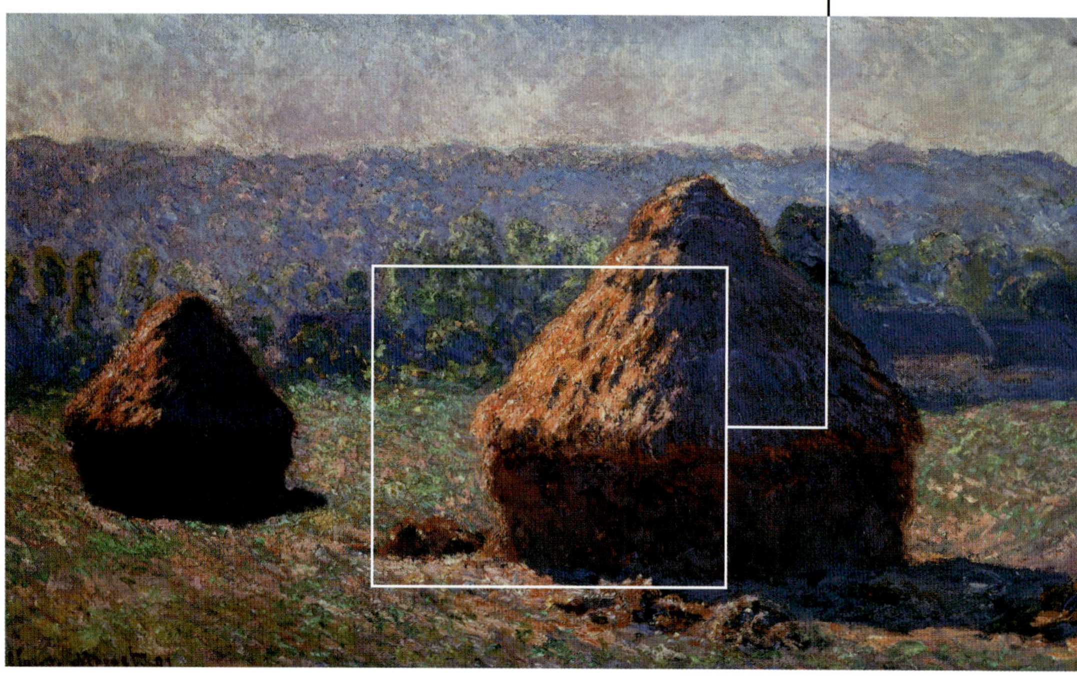

ABOVE

GRAIN STACKS, END OF SUMMER, MORNING, 1891, oil on canvas, 23¾ x 39½ inches (60.5 x 100 cm).

During a walk, Monet saw a distant haystack shimmering in the sun. He rushed home for his paints, only to discover on his return that the light and colors had changed. The result was a series of over 30 paintings that concentrated on recording changing light.

The main techniques

Your palette is based on the palette of Monet's mature work: still dark, but filled with brighter, more colorful harmonies. Monet usually painted on standard-sized canvases with white, warm beige, or light-gray priming. He did little underpainting, but worked all over the canvas at the same time. Monet's natural attraction for brighter, sunlit scenery emerged after the 1860s and, thereafter, his palette continued to lighten as he gained confidence.

You should work vigorously across the canvas, mixing colors with Zinc White to create light, opaque hues and adding pure colors where necessary to re-create Monet's vivid, brilliant accents.

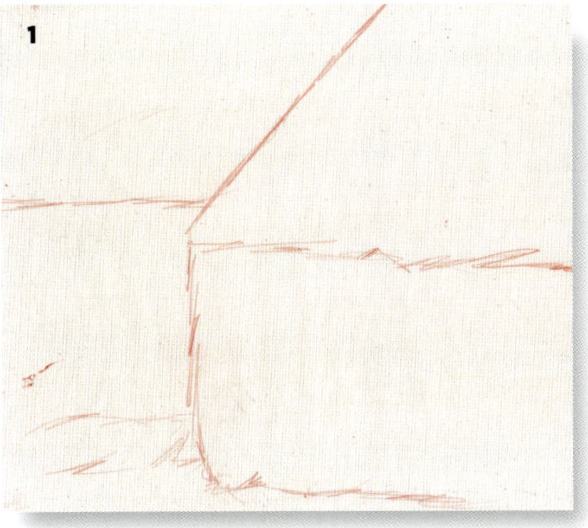

STEP 1 To begin, prepare your canvas with a light oatmeal or putty-colored wash. If you can't find this color commercially prepared, blend Zinc White with a touch of Cadmium Yellow and even smaller amounts of Vermilion and French Ultramarine. Apply this mixture with a large brush in smooth, fluid strokes and allow it to dry. For this picture, Monet painted rapidly, largely in situ, so a lot of wet paint will overlay the lower color. Lightly draw the outline of the haystack in red chalk or charcoal, dividing your canvas into key areas.

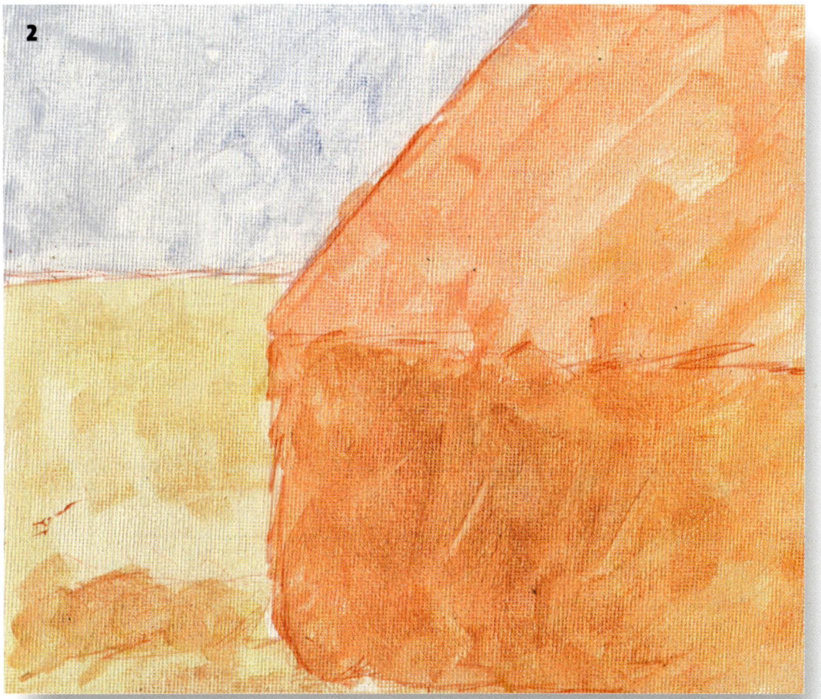

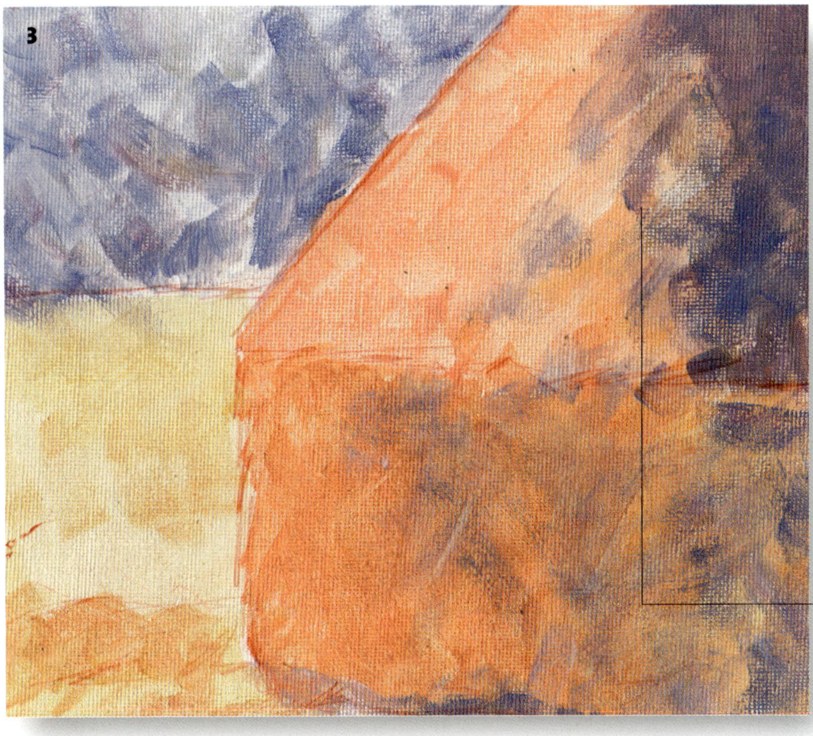

STEP 2 Monet liked to keep his canvas balanced as he worked, so cover the area with some broad scumbles (see page 143) of local color. Use relatively thin paint over the dry background surface, allowing patches of the underlying color to show through (you may need to mix a little turpentine with this). The background sky is made up of French Ultramarine and White and the foreground and haystack are made up of Crimson Alizarin, Cadmium Yellow, and Zinc White (use a touch more of the Crimson in the haystack) applied with a medium flat brush.

STEP 3 Apply a loose scumble of Cobalt Violet plus a little Zinc White to strengthen the shadows in the distance and on the side of the haystack. Begin to introduce a touch of Cadmium Yellow to indicate background foliage. Dab on the paint to break up the surface over the original colors. It is important that you do not try to be too precise.

Remember to work vigorously as you apply a loose scumble of paint to capture the vibrancy of the play of light.

STEP 4 Use light touches of Viridian, French Ultramarine, Cadmium Yellow, and Zinc White to continue creating the background tree foliage, as well as the field. Spread this around vigorously in small dabs and patches to give a vague sense of the scenery as a whole.

As you apply small dabs of French Ultramarine, Cadmium Yellow, and Zinc White, you should begin to get a sense of how these different colors can give the impression of light playing on the foliage in a specific moment.

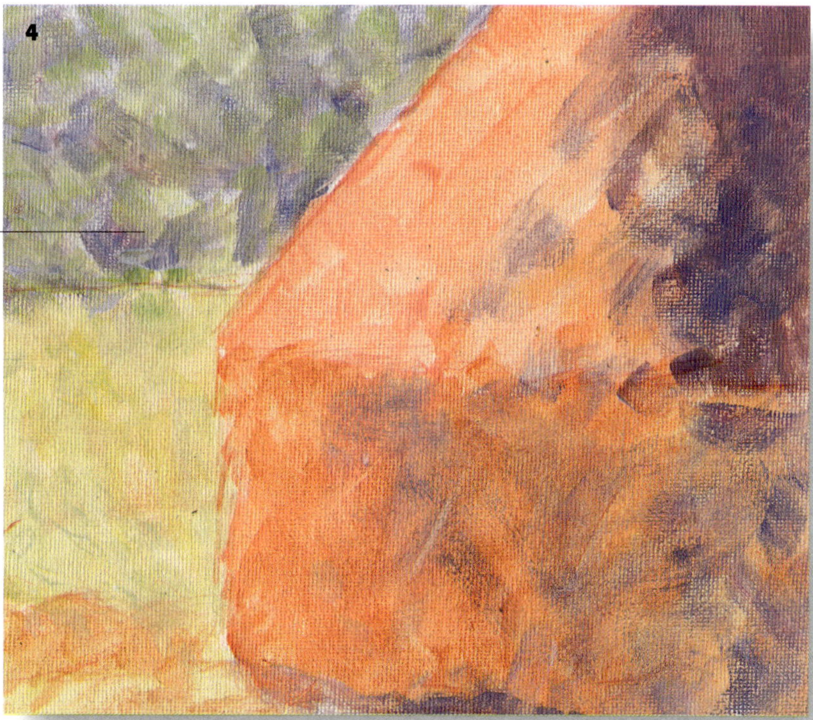

Use a No. 8 flat brush to apply Crimson Alizarin to create the shadow on the side of the haystack.

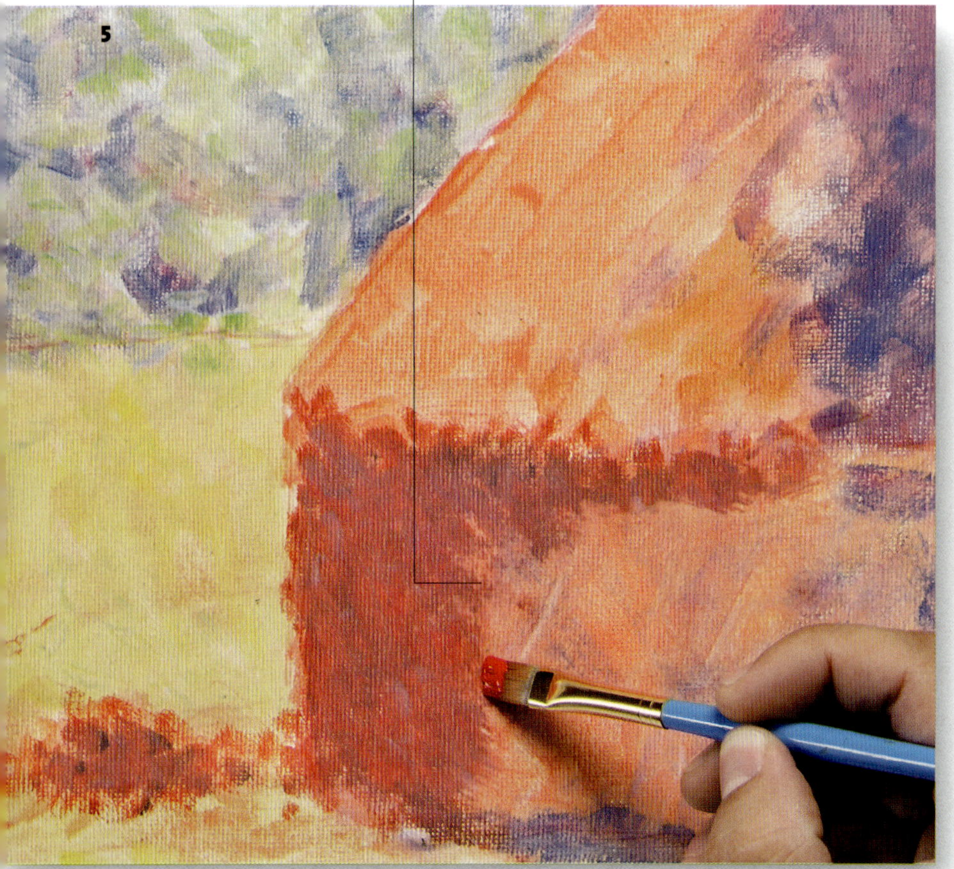

STEP 5 Monet's brush strokes do not imitate physical features as in his earlier works, but are secondary to the effect of light and cast shadow. Darken the base of the haystack with Vermilion, French Ultramarine, and Cadmium Yellow, using a smaller round brush.

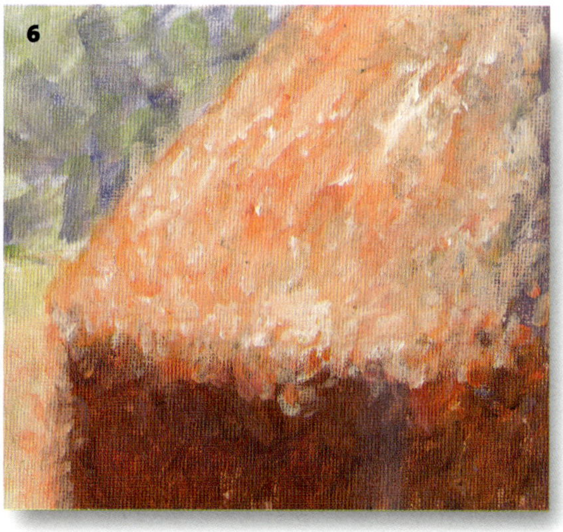

STEP 6 Enhance the values of the haystack by lightening it at the top with White, Cadmium Yellow, and a little Vermilion. The purpose of this is to give the painting vibrancy, so apply the paint in relatively thick dabs.

STEP 7 Working wet-over-dry to develop the impression of the detail and texture of stubble, lighten the field by applying Zinc White, Cadmium Yellow, Emerald Green, and a little Vermilion. Then, with a relatively dry brush, add dabs of Cadmium Yellow blended with Viridian. Establish the shadows of the haystack and the distant foliage with small dabs of Cobalt Violet, Zinc White, French Ultramarine, and Crimson Alizarin.

STEP 8 Begin to darken the distant trees with the application of Ultramarine, Emerald Green, and White. To make the side of the haystack, field, and foliage appear as if they are shimmering in sunlight, paint on irregular dabs of pure white with a small brush to create highlights. Keep your brushwork light and broken, and squint your eyes during the process to ensure that you create enough contrast.

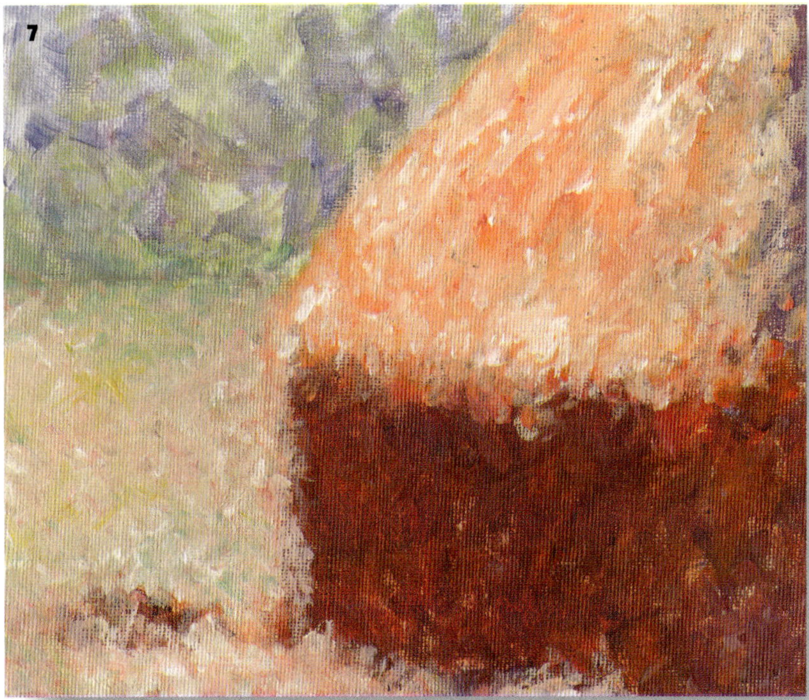

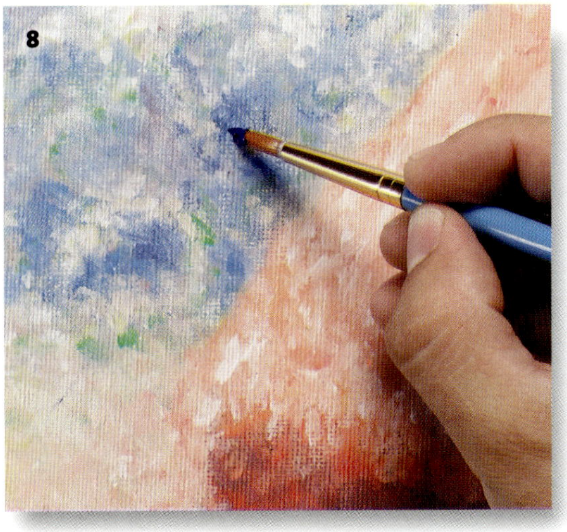

The vital finishing touch, by which you capture the fleeting moment of the shimmering light, is achieved with dabs of pure Zinc White.

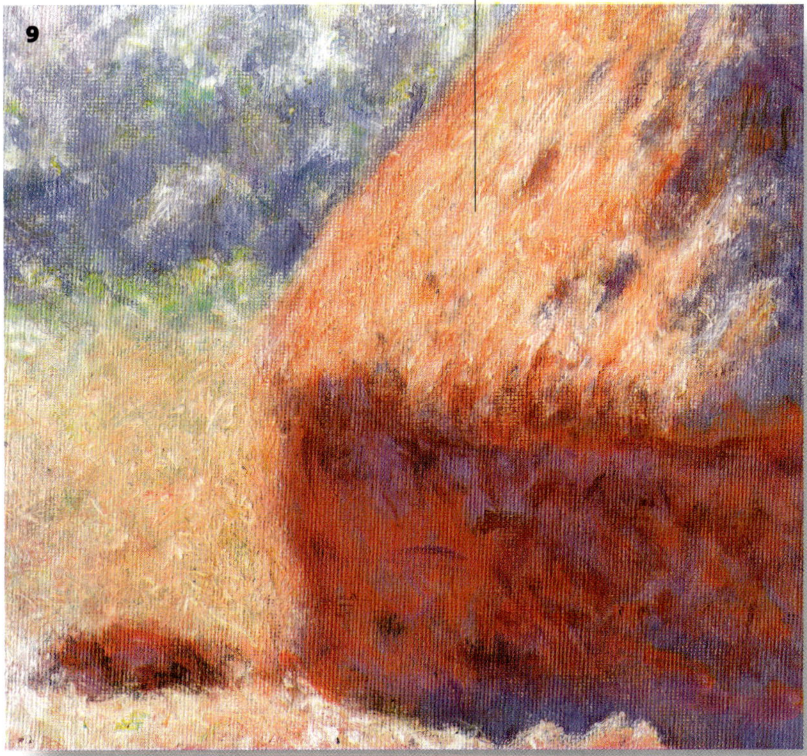

STEP 9 To finish the painting, deepen the shadows on the haystack with French Ultramarine and Vermilion and also enrich its local color with dabs of Cadmium Yellow mixed with Crimson Alizarin and a touch of Zinc White. Add some Cobalt Violet blended with a little Vermilion, Cadmium Yellow, and Ultramarine to the base of the haystack using broken brushwork. Bring out the violet shadows on the side of the haystack and the reflected shadow on the background surface by adding dabs of Cobalt Violet, holding your brush at right angles to the canvas. To complete the painting, use touches of Zinc White, Viridian, Vermilion, and French Ultramarine to strengthen the shapes within the background and haystack. This will brighten any overblended marks and bring out the full effect of the brilliant sunlight.

PAINTING WATER AND SNOW

CENTER
BATHERS AT LA GRENOUILLÈRE, 1868, oil on canvas, $28^{3}/_{4}$ x $36^{1}/_{4}$ inches (73 x 92 cm).
Because it was painted mainly alla prima, this is not a highly finished work but retains a deliberate sketchiness. The brush strokes are bold, broad, often overlapping, and descriptive—for example, short, broad strokes are used for the ripples in the water, while longer, thinner strokes describe the sides of the boats. It is a freely painted blocked-in sketch; boldly divided across the middle by the walkway, the lower half is in shadow, while the upper contains the liveliest and most varied brushwork.

RIGHT
BATHERS AT LA GRENOUILLÈRE, detail.
Short horizontal slabs of colors indicate broken reflections on the surface of the water. The water in the background is paler than in the foreground, giving the impression of distance.

MONET HAD A PASSION for painting water—its colors, nuances, and reflections allowed him to explore techniques and effects. Whether he painted a turbulent indigo sea, rippling azure waves, or smooth, glassy lakes and ponds, he repeatedly explored the effects of water against the elements. With water, he could study the ideas of local and reflected color and the effect of atmospheric conditions. Water also gave him the chance to paint unstructured areas of color, using dribbles, spatters, smears, and thick and thinned paint. Monet mixed his paints into each other as he painted, constantly changing and adapting his technique to match the qualities of the particular water and atmosphere he was observing. Monet said: "I adore the sea, but I know that to do her justice you have to view her every day, at all hours, at the same vantage point, to learn how she lives."

For the last 20 years of his life, Monet painted images of his personally created water scene, his much loved lily pond at Giverny. In these paintings, he interwove colors and shapes to create a myriad dazzling images that retain the effect of tone and structure, no matter how abstract they may appear to the viewer at first.

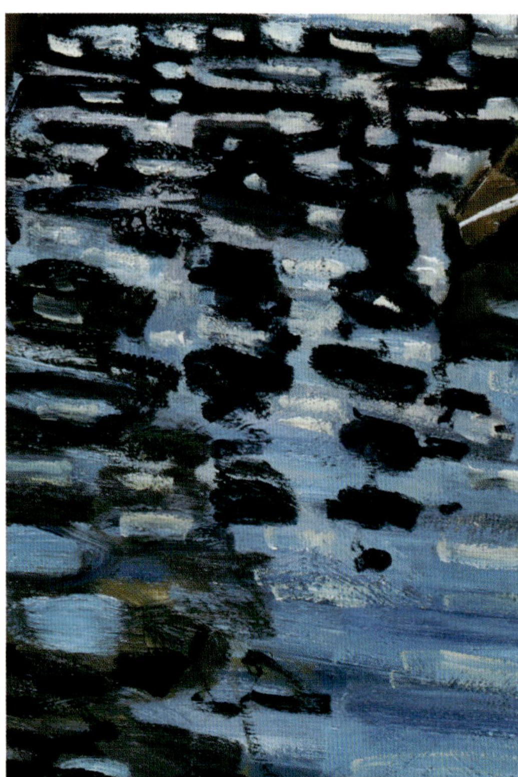

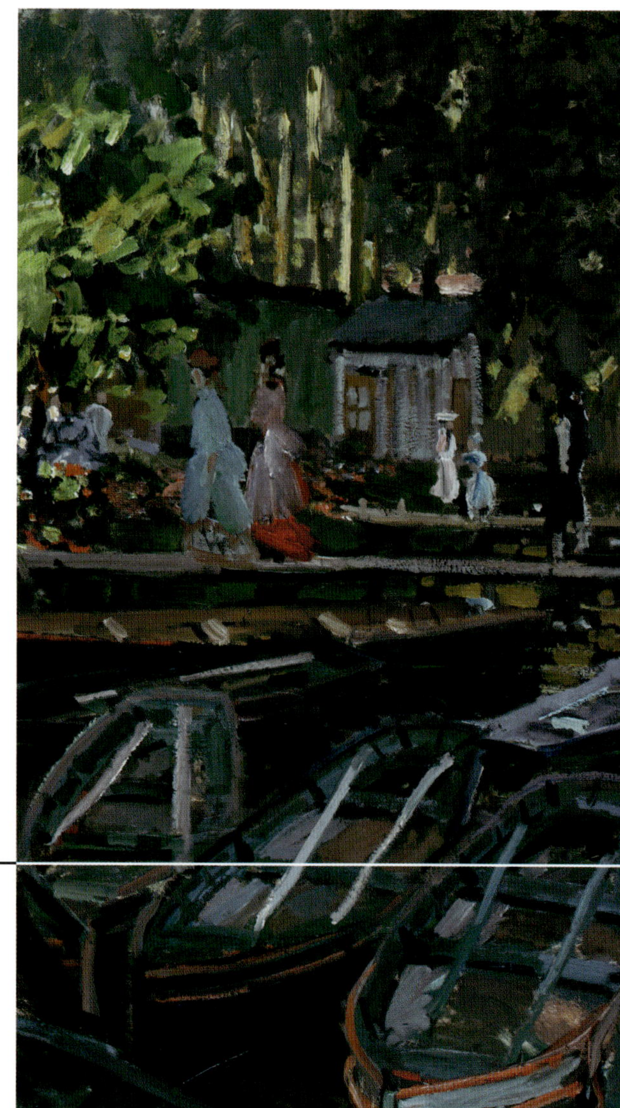

Colored snow

Snow scenes were another vehicle used by Monet to investigate shadows and reflections. He realized early on that snow was rarely completely white, but instead reflected colors from all around it. He also noted that shadows on dazzling snow are multicolored. For a period during the early 1870s, Monet, Sisley, and Pissarro particularly devoted themselves to creating winter landscapes, seeing them as a way to discover the truth of colors in nature. For these snow paintings, Monet layered opaque colors on top of each other, building up glazes of soft colors to create a gleaming effect.

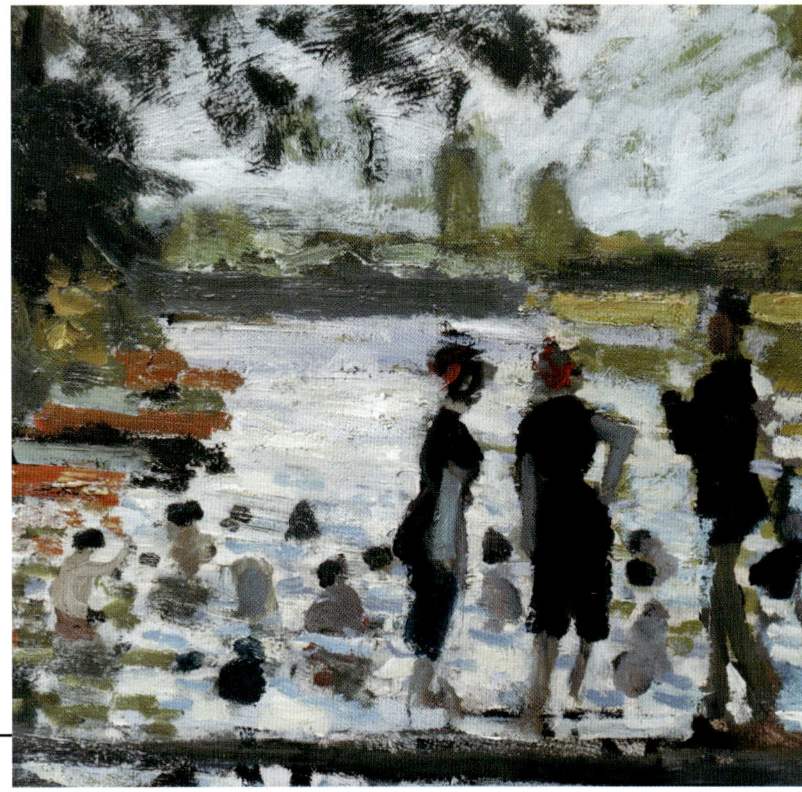

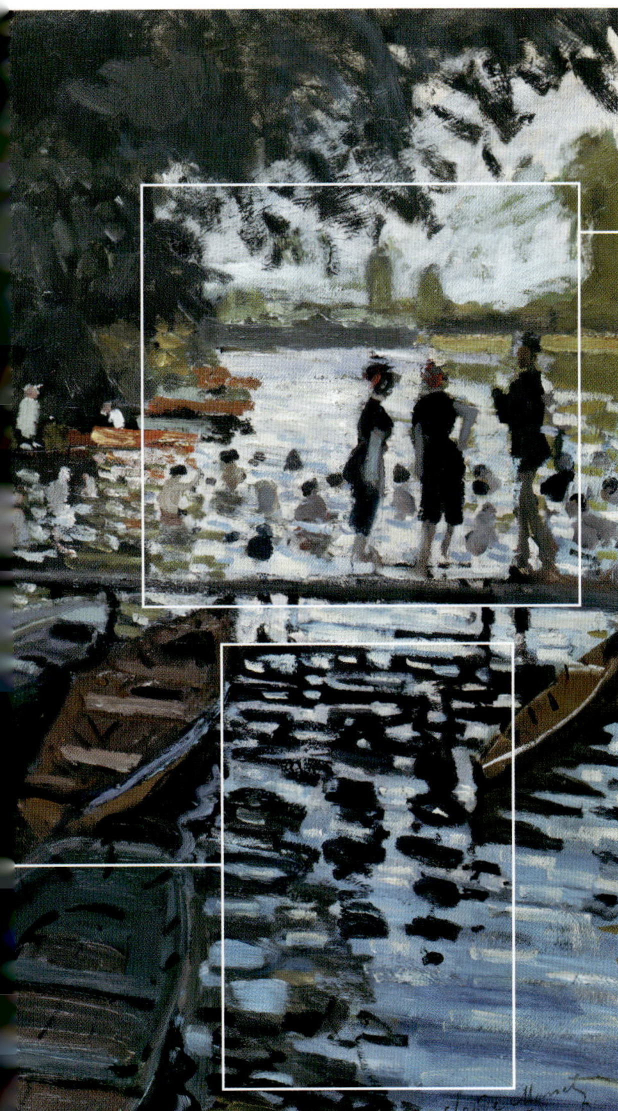

ABOVE
BATHERS AT LA GRENOUILLÈRE, detail.
Figures are indicated with a few quick strokes of paint from a flat brush, with Prussian Blue used straight from the tube for the swimsuits. Vermilion has been blurred and blended wet-in-wet for the figures' hats and Chrome Yellow has been blurred and blended into green for the foliage.

Although Monet probably completed many of his snow scenes in the studio, there is no doubt that he worked outdoors on many of his smaller works—even in severe weather conditions.

Some of Monet's snow scenes were painted from unusual viewpoints, which echo the compositions in Japanese prints, while others are brilliantly colored, and still others are chalky and emphasize warm and cool contrasts in loosely applied strokes. Monet often included "colored grays" in his snow paintings. These are subtle, softly colored grays that he created by combining white with a mixture of either red, yellow, and blue or of combined complementaries, such as red and green or blue and orange. Monet understood that the key to making these colored grays lively is to include both warm and cool colors.

HOW TO DO IT

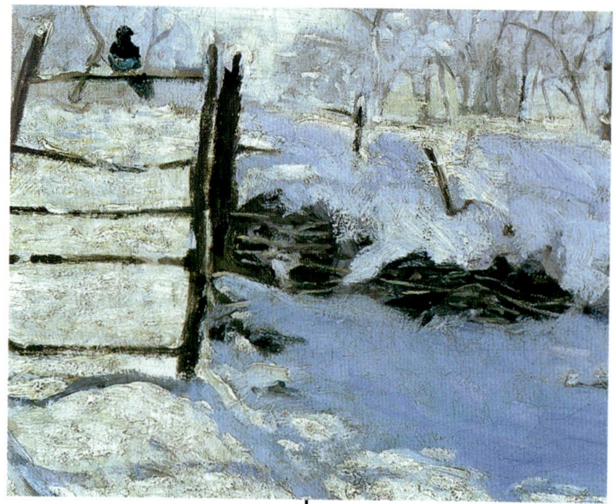

YOUR PALETTE
This picture requires a relatively limited palette, with no black at all. You will need:

1 Zinc White
2 Chrome Yellow
3 French Ultramarine
4 Cobalt Blue
5 Cobalt Violet
6 Vermilion
7 Viridian
8 Lemon Yellow

As with most Impressionist paintings, you should heighten the brilliance of the colors by applying fresh dabs of paint over the dried layers at the end.

A WHITE OR LIGHT-COLORED background surface adds to the radiance of the colors in this picture, especially where the paint is applied in thin layers. To re-create Monet's snow scene, you should work with direct brush strokes, laying colors and tones next to each other. For the initial applications, thin the paint with turpentine, but use it as close to its natural tube consistency as possible afterward.

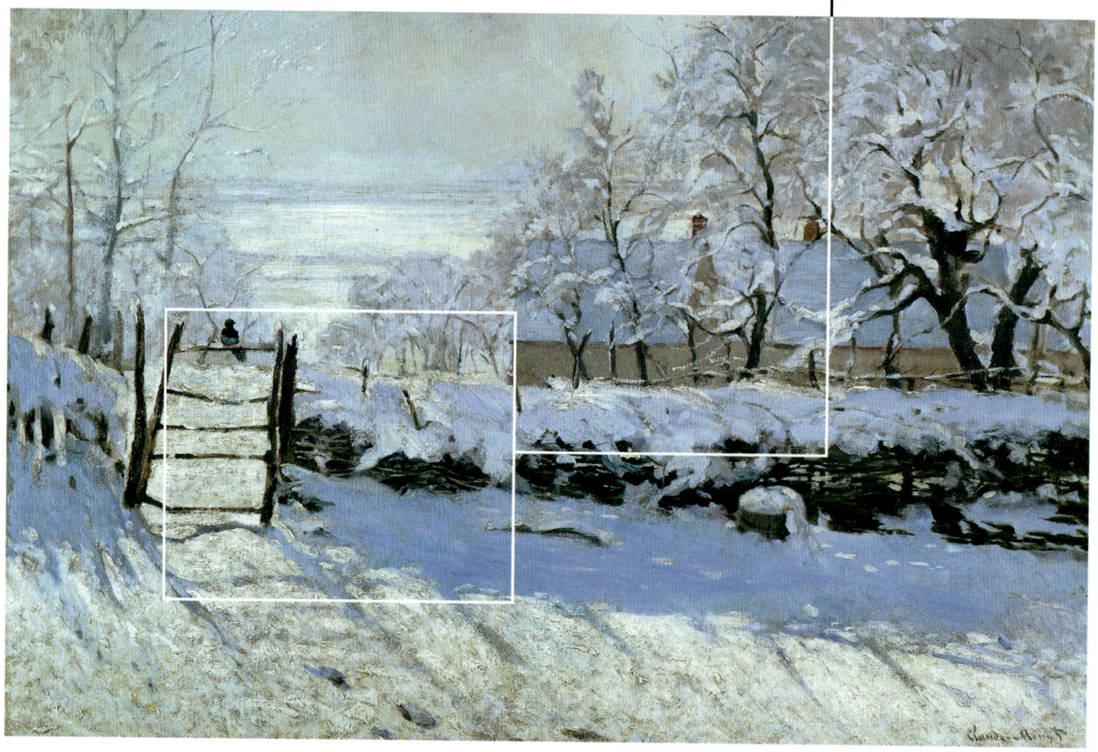

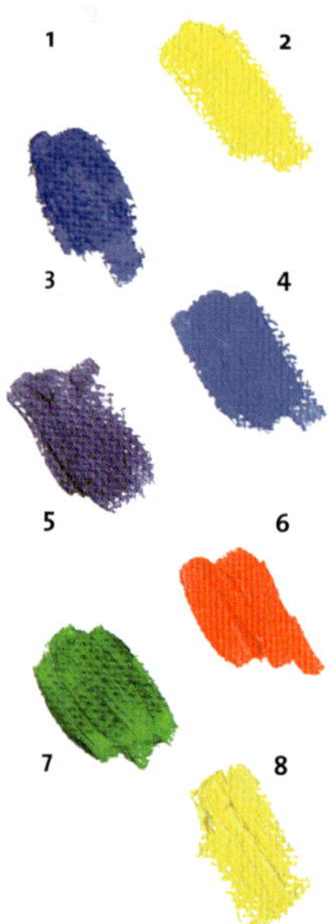

The main techniques

To create the snow, apply the paint in vigorous, broken brush marks in the directions that you are describing. Using impasto, be careful not to muddy the colors as you blend and try to match your brush strokes to the motif with the size and shape of mark. Long and short horizontal strokes describe snowfall well. Use small dabs for highlights. Choose firm bristle brushes that are about ½–¾ inches (1–2 cm) wide—try Nos. 10, 6, and 4.

ABOVE
THE MAGPIE, 1869, oil on canvas, 33 x 51 inches (89 x 130 cm).
Here, Monet has captured the pristine qualities of fresh snow in the prevailing light, adding luminescence with soft complementaries. He painted 140 snow scenes, reducing the objects to subtle colors and shapes. In this painting, he contrasted blues and mauves with peach, lemon yellow, beige, and cream. He divided the gate, roof, trees, and even the clouds into a grid, changing this into diagonals beneath the fence. The magpie is made out of the darkest hues, contrasting with the dazzling colors surrounding it and drawing the viewers' eyes into the scene.

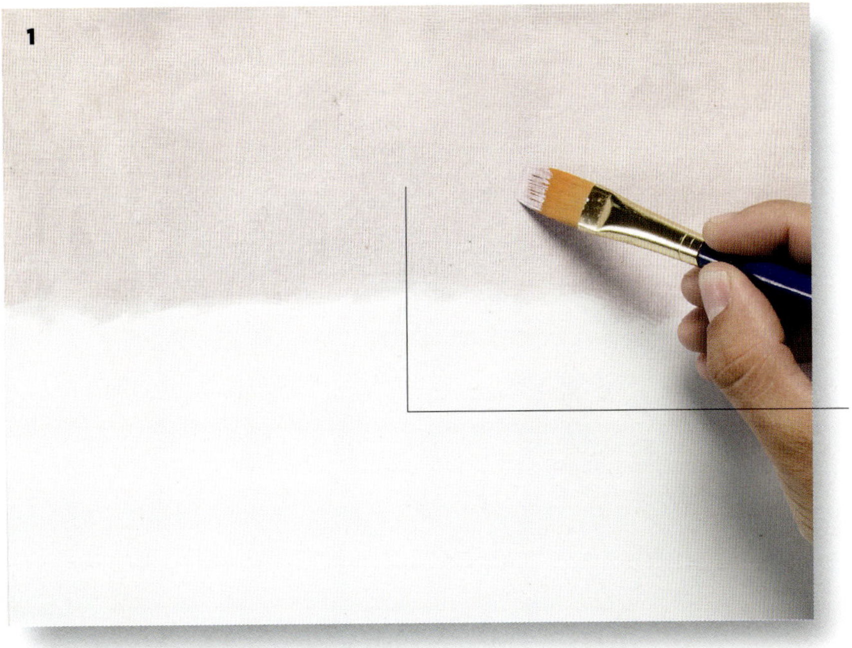

Using a flat brush, drag the colored gray mixture across the top of the canvas and blend it well with Zinc White on the bottom half.

STEP 1 Prepare the canvas with a light wash of gouache, acrylic, or diluted oil paint in Zinc White, French Ultramarine, and small amounts of Vermilion and Chrome Yellow over the top half and Zinc White over the bottom. This will provide the final painting with depth, but it should be a very thin wash, so it does not detract from the surface texture.

STEP 2 Lightly underpaint the essential outlines, using Vermilion and Chrome Yellow for the gate, fence, and magpie and Cobalt Violet for the snow shadows. Paint relatively quickly using a stiff brush.

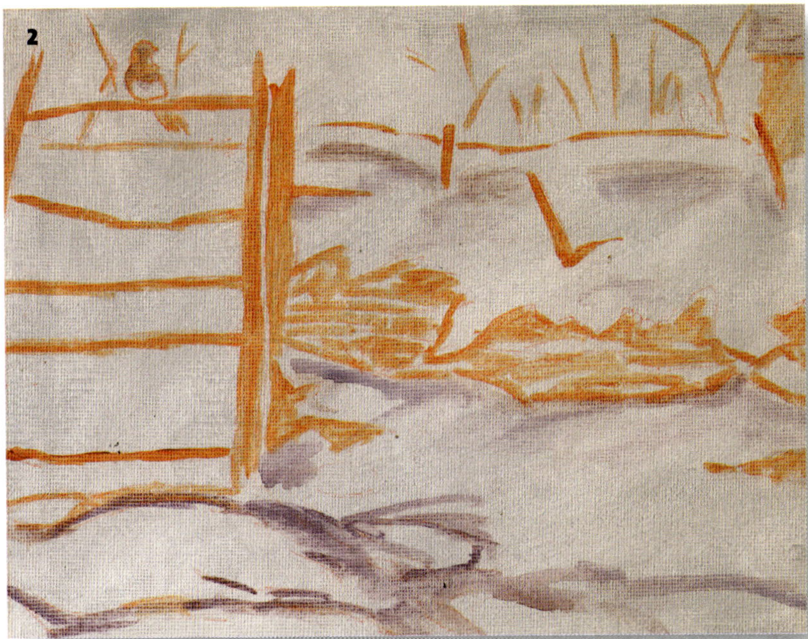

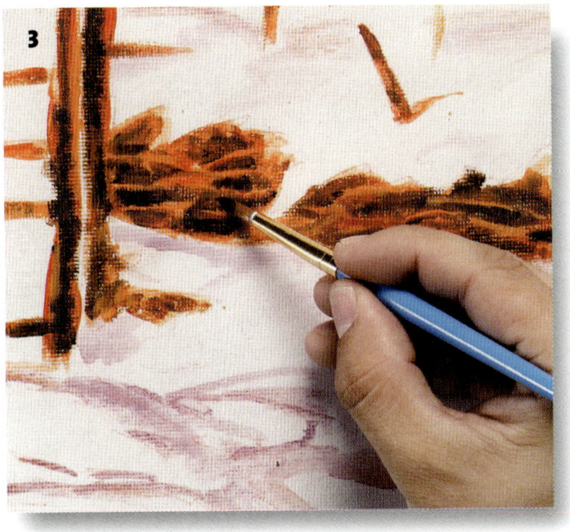

STEP 3 Begin to darken the fence and gate areas (as well as the magpie), using French Ultramarine, Viridian, Vermilion, and Chrome Yellow. You should adjust the ratio of colors to reach the desired darkness as you work. The paint should be applied in a relatively thin consistency and you may need to adjust the shapes later by overlaying wet-on-dry.

STEP 4 Begin to lay Cobalt Blue, Cobalt Violet, a small touch of Chrome Yellow, and Zinc White in horizontal strokes across the foreground. In Monet's painting, this is made up of several shades of blues and mauves, so don't worry if you mix and apply different variations.

The snow is built up out of loosely applied layers of soft hues. You can soften these with layers of Zinc White if they seem too bright, but ensure that you build up the right tones. The snow on the fence is scumbled and stroked on in shapes that indicate the soft formations of snow as it begins to melt and slide.

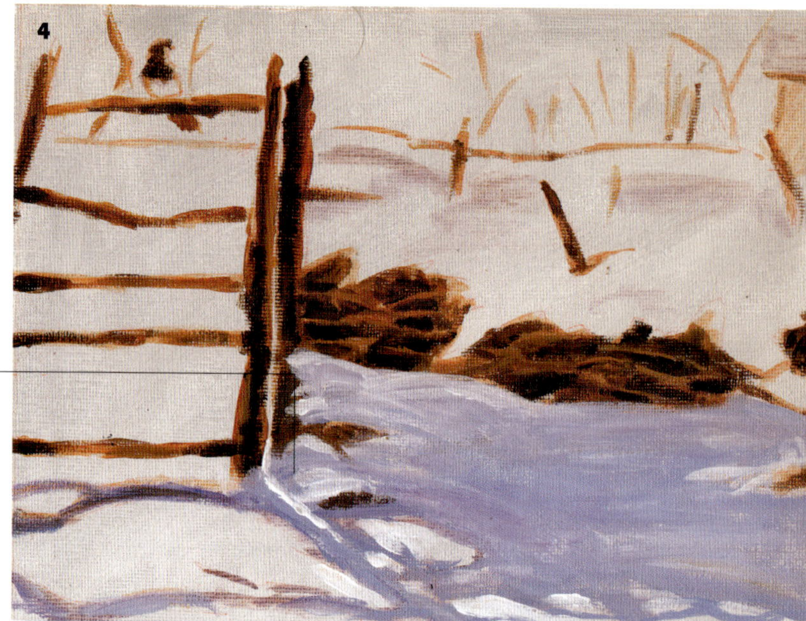

STEP 5 Continue painting the mauve tones and gradually build up the color in the foreground, as well as along the top of the fence. Then add streaks of Zinc White as highlights, applying shorter, broken brush strokes on the fence, with longer, broken brush strokes on the background surface. Using a thin, dry mixture of Cobalt Violet, smooth on some hazy distant trees.

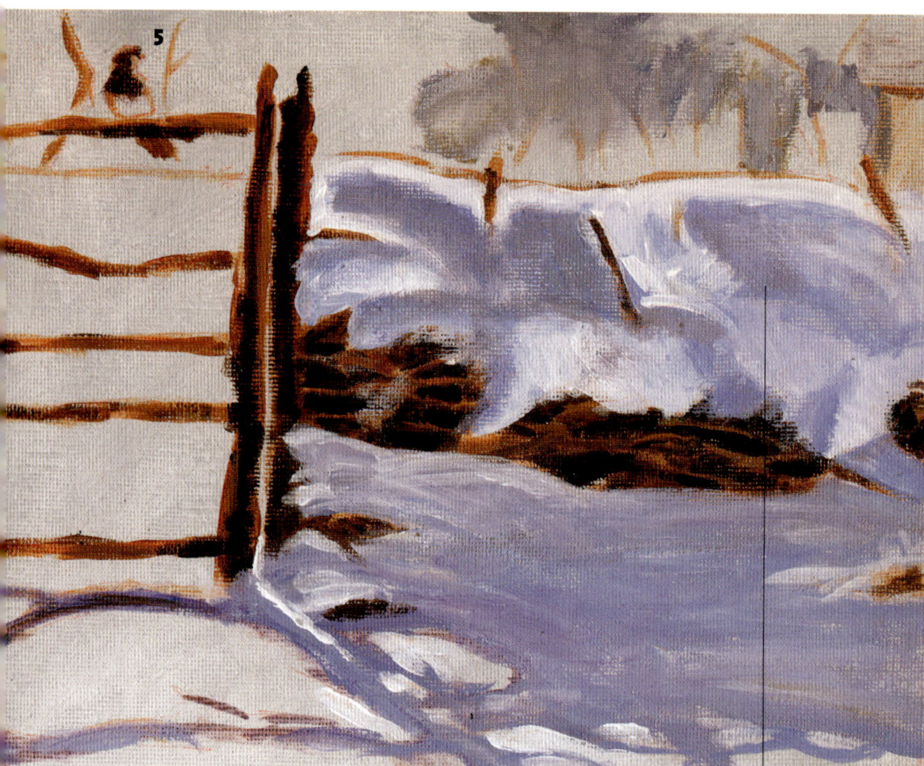

All the colors you add to the snow should be mixed with Zinc White and blended carefully together to create subtle lights and tints.

STEP 6 Refine the trees and distant edge of the building, using Cobalt Blue, Cobalt Violet, and Chrome Yellow on a small, flat brush about ½ inches (1 cm) wide. Try smudging the violet-hued tones, then pick out some fine distant branches with the earlier brown mixture. Angle the brush so that it's flat to the canvas as you do this. Then use a fine brush to pick out small highlight details on the trees and building.

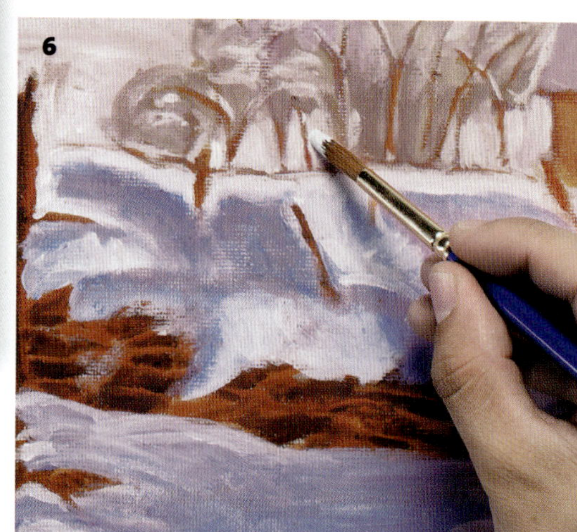

STEP 7 Highlight the snow behind and between the gate and in the foreground with pure Zinc White scumbled over a light wash of Lemon Yellow. You may need to apply this again when the first layer is dry in order to give the image vibrancy. So far, your painting should be predominantly lemon, brown, and mauve with white. These areas of color give the composition solidity and hold the painting together.

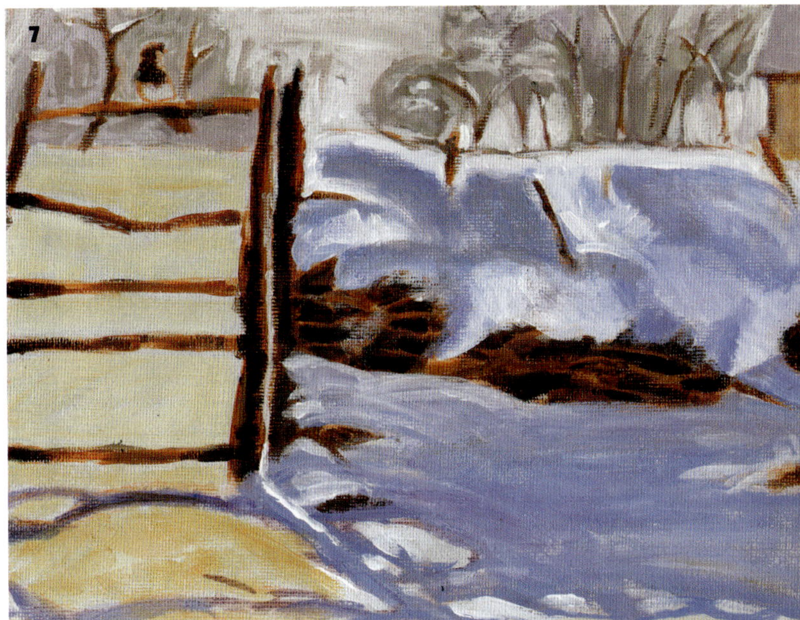

STEP 8 Using a fine brush, create the final details by using broken dabs of Zinc White over the (dry) foreground, the Lemon tints, the top of the gate, and the sky. Finally, add definition to the magpie and fence with a fine brush and a mixture of Viridian, Vermilion, Chrome Yellow, and French Ultramarine.

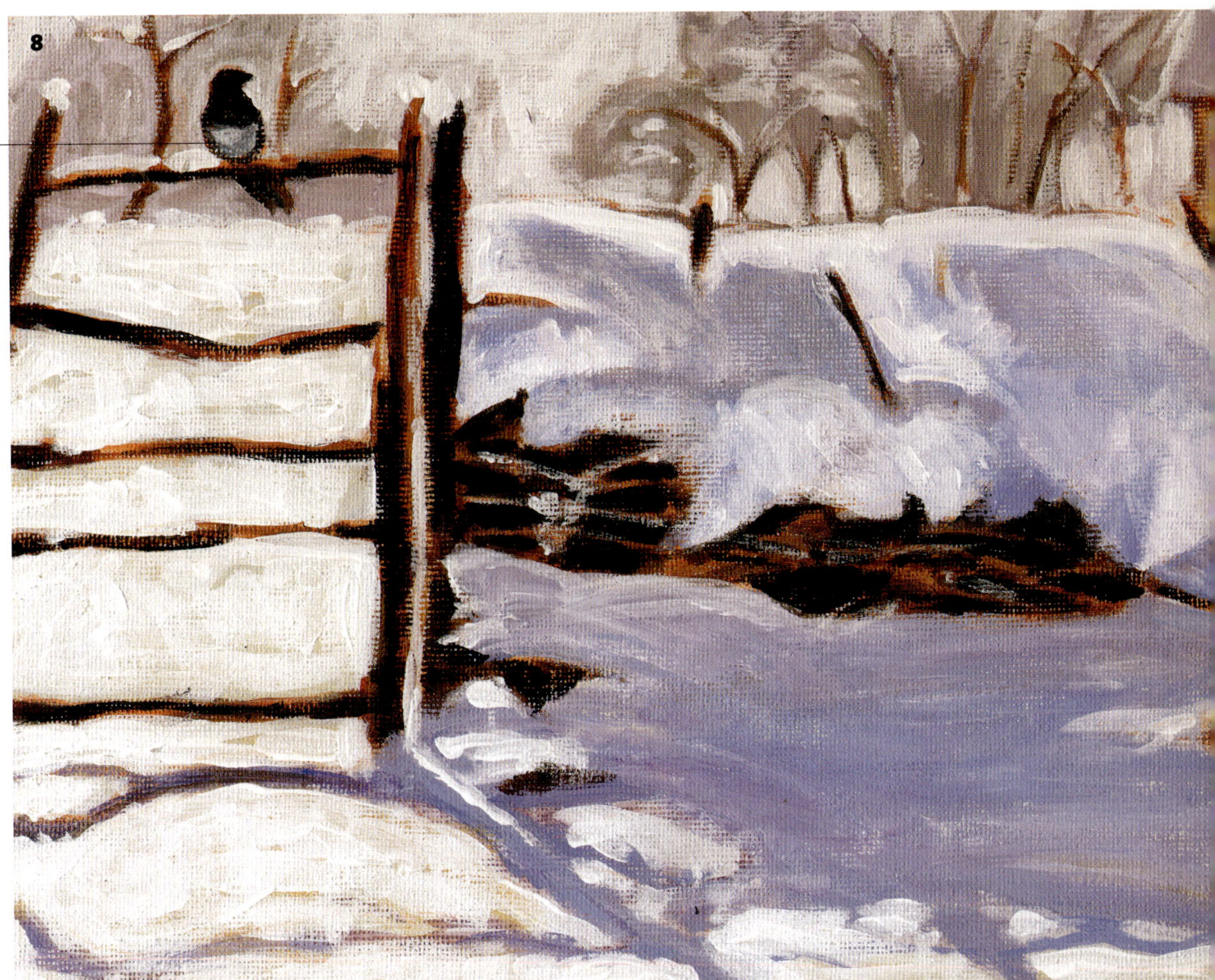

With a fine brush, pick out the small details on the magpie, adding white highlights on the top of its head and blue shadows on the white feathers at the front.

Chapter six

PISSARRO

A major supporter of the Impressionists from the outset, Pissarro was keen to be part of a group who painted and exhibited without any association with French academic conventions. Although stylistically his work changed greatly over the course of his life, he always tried to maintain a sense of energy in his paintings.

BELOW
ENTRANCE TO THE VILLAGE OF VOISINS, 1872, oil on canvas, 18 x 21¾ inches (46 x 55.5 cm).
Pissarro painted thickly and densely, dabbing on short, broken strokes. He built the picture in stages and layered the paint over several sessions.

CAMILLE PISSARRO (1830–1903) was born on the Caribbean island of Saint Thomas but moved to Paris at the age of 12. He studied at the official art school of Paris, the École des Beaux-Arts, and at independent studios, but he also received direction from the great landscape artist Corot. A patient and inspiring teacher himself, Pissarro lacked confidence in his own work but always encouraged other painters when they were rejected or couldn't sell their work. Indeed, fellow Impressionists recognized him as a mentor and guide. "He was like a father to me," Cézanne recalled.

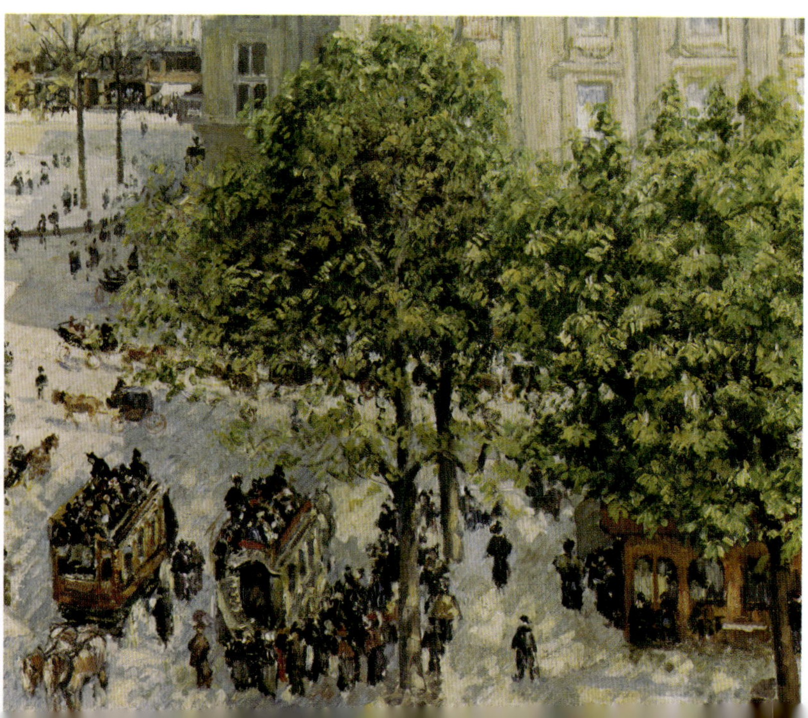

Pissarro was always willing to take inspiration from other artists, whether they were older or younger than he was. For example, in 1870 and 1871 he met Monet in England and viewed the work of Turner and Constable. This had a significant effect on his style, increasing his awareness of color and light. Later, he worked with Seurat and Signac and began experimenting with the pointillist techniques that they were developing.

As a socialist and anarchist, Pissarro was extremely aware of contemporary social problems and chose to dedicate the subjects of many of his paintings to peasants and their hardships. In keeping with his social and political beliefs, he was also one of the first artists to depict factories and the realities of modern life in his paintings.

Despite his frequent stylistic experiments, there are a number of consistent technical

RIGHT
MARKET PLACE AT GISORS, 1885,
gouache and pastel on paper, 32¼ x 32¼ inches (82 x 82 cm).
Pissarro's interest in market scenes began in the 1880s, and, over the following 15 years, he executed numerous drawings and paintings of the subject. Here, using gouache and pastel, Pissarro gives the impression of a passing moment but, of course, he has carefully composed it. The two figures in the foreground lead the eye into the picture and the trees break the image into different heights without blocking any view.

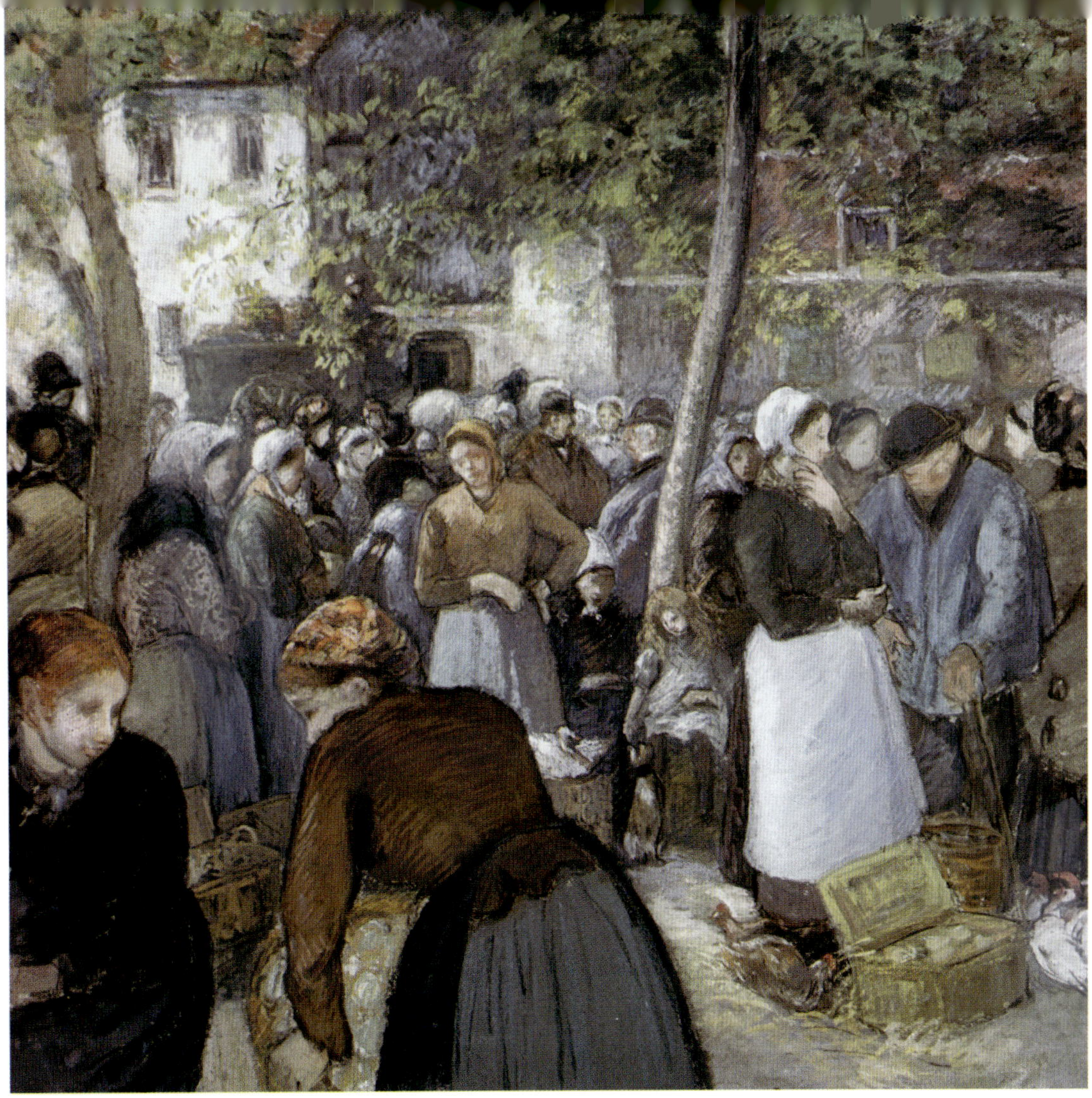

features that run throughout Pissarro's work. He almost always used white canvases and began paintings with light pencil sketches. However, he maintained that precise painting hampered the overall impression of a piece and destroyed its visual energy. He recommended that artists should paint as much as possible initially, covering the canvas in the first session, balancing tones with small brush strokes across the whole image and keeping everything balanced. Once the canvas had been covered in this way, small, angled brush marks were applied on top to build up the picture.

From the 1870s, Pissarro's brushwork became design-led—the short, delicate, and regular strokes that he used often formed hatched patterns on the picture surface. The resulting richness of pattern and color on his canvases almost contradicted the natural qualities he insisted on.

By this time, he was applying and contrasting the light and dark, as well as the cool and warm colors that had become so prominent in his work when he experimented with pointillism. By the late 1880s, his association with Seurat and Signac and his research into scientific color theory and Neo-Impressionism resulted in his brushwork evolving into irregular but neat dots. Most of these dots are not completely round, but are in the shape of small brush marks. Sometimes they are hatched or crosshatched and curve around the forms depicted. By the end of the century, he completely adhered to Chevreul's theory of simultaneous contrast, and placed only complementary colors next to each other.

TWO-DIMENSIONAL BRUSHWORK

While Pissarro's style developed and evolved constantly, he always retained his personal direction. In Cézanne's opinion, of all of the Impressionists, Pissarro came the closest to capturing nature.

Pissarro remained a technical artist throughout his life, but he changed styles, colors, and compositions. He always captured essential shapes before adding details, then applied rich, buttery paint in small brush strokes. From 1865, he stopped using black and terra-cotta paint, as well as bitumen (a form of tar that was traditionally used by artists to create the darkest tones in oil paintings). By about 1872, he also stopped using commercially prepared greens as he had enough blues and yellows in his palette to create a large range of his own greens.

At this time, Pissarro began applying paint to the canvas in diagonal dashes that looked like little chevrons or commas. For a while, he built up speckled surfaces, then he began to layer crusty, impasted paint in long, thin threads of color, dots, or dashes. He usually kept his paint relatively dry, applying it carefully using wrist gestures to flick the marks across the canvas. For a time, he also created variegated marks, which were applied delicately with his brush or a palette knife to leave textured patterns across his canvases.

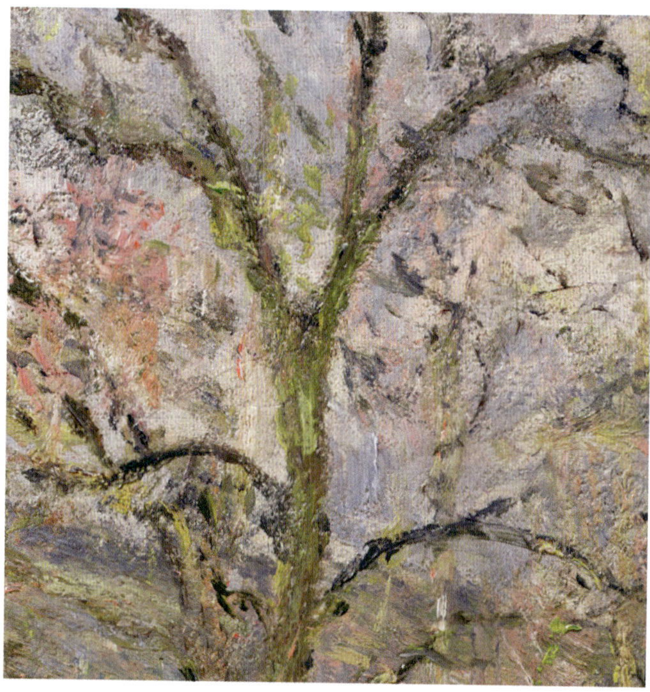

CENTER
ORCHARD AT PONTOISE, 1877, oil on canvas, 25¾ x 31½ inches (65.5 x 80 cm). *This is a clear example of Pissarro's two-dimensional brush stroke technique. Instead of dragging paint across the canvas to create a smooth surface, he quickly applied his loaded brush in dashes or commas of pure pigment. The first touches on the canvas were large strokes in many different directions, which covered the area loosely. Pissarro superimposed smaller strokes later. The buildup of paint caused by this technique is so thick in parts that it stands out in relief from the picture surface.*

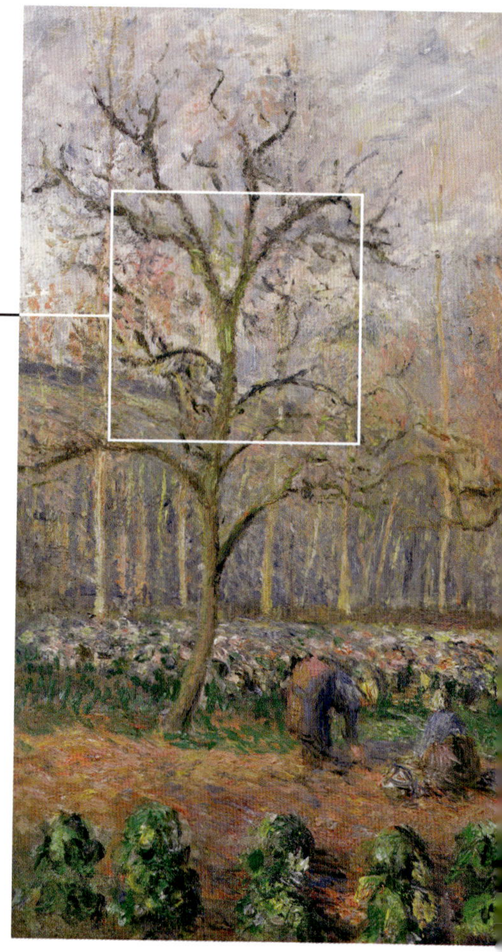

RIGHT
ORCHARD AT PONTOISE, detail. *The trees are built up with short, vertical strokes, with pale pink highlights added to the branches, indicating the fall of sunlight. These soften the contours of the trees, so that they blend into the sky.*

This way of applying paint is often described as two-dimensional, or textured, brushwork, because of the way it angles and criss-crosses across the surface of the canvas. Two-dimensional brushwork became characteristic of Pissarro's work mainly during the 1870s and 1880s, although his style often varies even within the same painting.

Layered surfaces

Pissarro often reworked surfaces in several layers over a period of time, painting wet-over-dry and sometimes wet-in-wet. These layers of little marks—hatchings, commas, and dashes—were used skillfully to establish mass and form, as well as to provide vibrancy within each painting. His varied brushwork created vigorous and descriptive surface patterns, which gave almost a textured-weave appearance to his canvases. He used color to enhance this effect. For example, he purposely added warm colors to enliven areas that were dominated by cool colors, and light and dark complementaries were often placed next to each other. He often reworked canvases with several layers over a period of time, painting wet-over-dry and sometimes wet-in-wet. He applied small strokes in rapid flicks, creating a mosaiclike pattern across the canvas. Colors were not overblended, but were kept "clean" on the picture surface, so, close up his pictures are a multitude of bright colors, with contrasting ranges juxtaposed. He balanced cool and warm colors across the canvas, and used delicate, broken contours to outline.

BELOW

ORCHARD AT PONTOISE, detail.

Among the colors layered on the background surfaces are greens, blues, and violets, with orange-yellow depicting sunlight dappling through the branches.

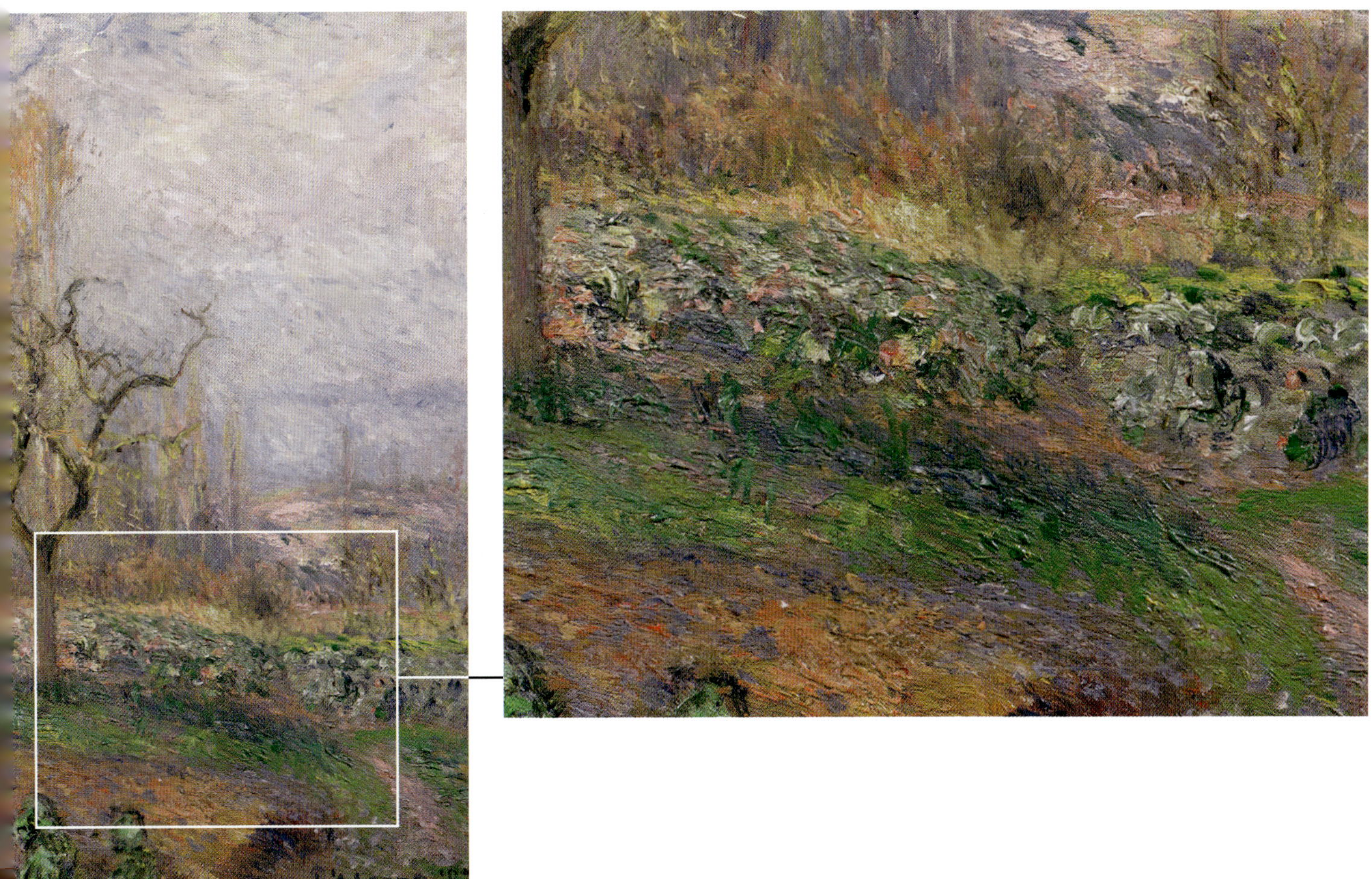

HOW TO DO IT

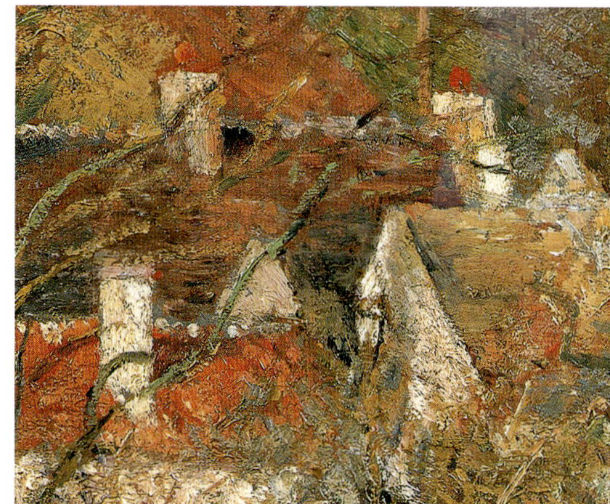

YOUR PALETTE
Your palette should consist of two yellows, two reds, two blues, green, and white:

1 Yellow Ocher
2 Cadmium Yellow
3 Cadmium Red
4 Crimson Alizarin
5 French Ultramarine
6 Ceruleum Blue
7 Viridian
8 Zinc White

While you work, follow the advice that Pissarro himself once gave: "Use small brush strokes and put down your perceptions immediately . . . Work at the same time upon the sky, water, branches, ground . . ."

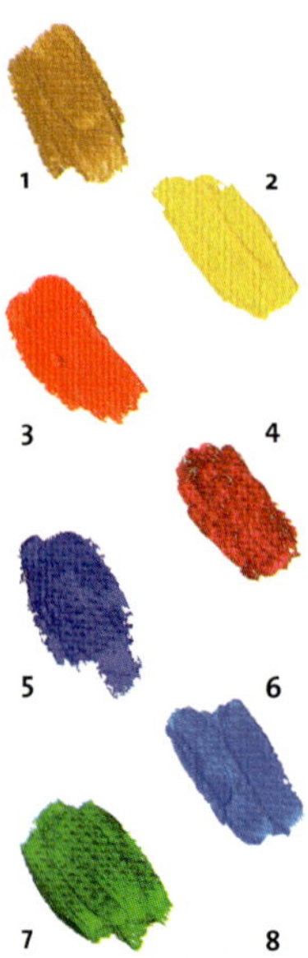

PISSARRO'S SLABLIKE brush strokes allowed him to build up structure and to describe forms. One of his favorite color combinations was red and green, which helped to bring his broken brush marks (known as "taches") to the attention of the viewer. You should work these small brush marks wet-in-wet for the bulk of this painting.

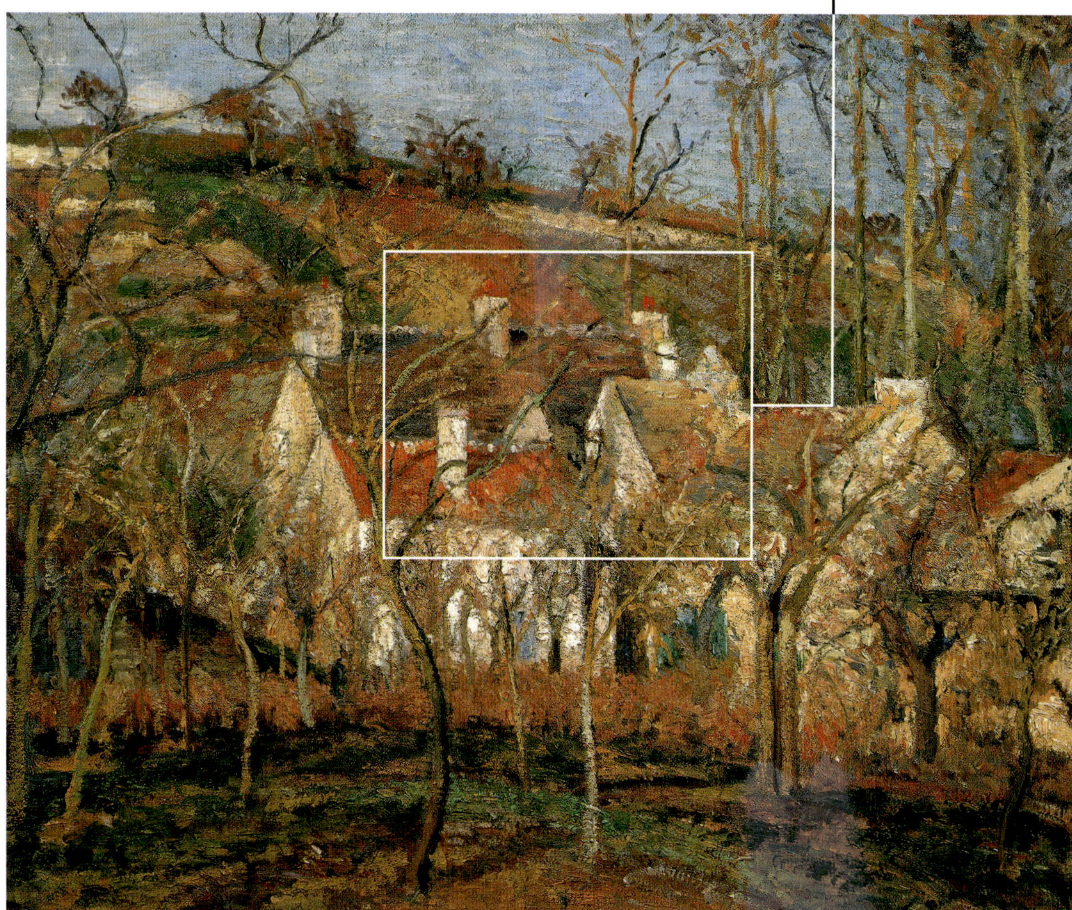

The main techniques

Use a textured canvas for this painting and move progressively across it with layer upon layer of small, well-spaced brush strokes. Aim to keep the colors fresh and separate. If they blend too much, the colors will blur.

ABOVE
RED ROOFS, VIEW OF A VILLAGE IN WINTER, 1877, oil on canvas, 21½ x 25¾ inches (54.5 x 65.5 cm).
Pissarro layered the paint using small, criss-crossed brush marks. Painted over a previous painting, he reworked the scene over an extensive period. He blended the paint, applying it wet-in-wet and wet-over-dry, which resulted in cross-hatchings of color and surface texture.

1

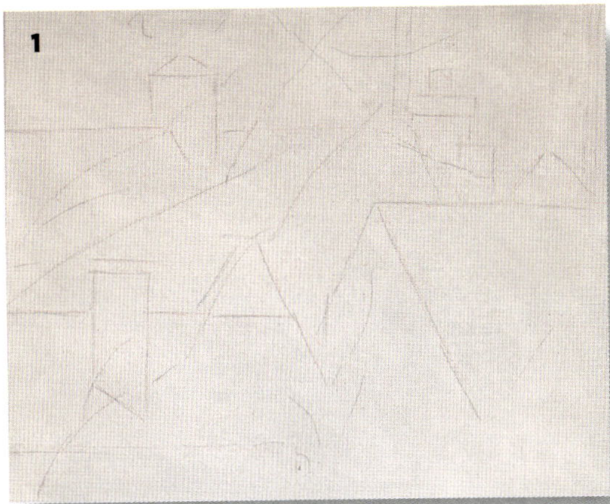

STEP 1 For this painting, Pissarro used a twill canvas. To imitate this, select a background surface with a slight texture. Pissarro painted over a previous painting and probably used a pale warm gray priming over it. He usually drew his pictures lightly in pencil first, so draw a light outline with a soft pencil.

Using a small flat brush, loaded with a blend of the two yellows, paint the roofs in broken brush strokes, imagining where the sun would scatter its rays.

2

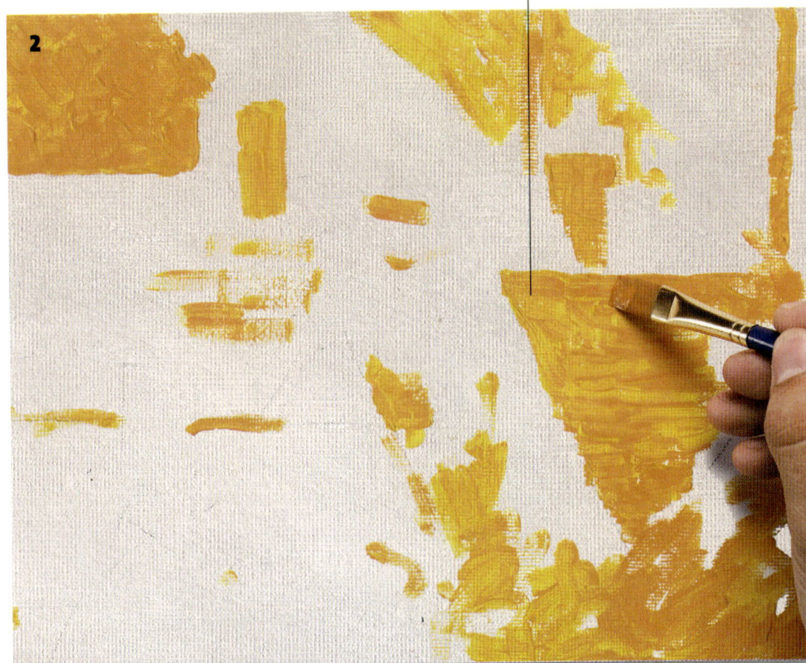

When the underpainting is dry, use small, angled brush marks to build up blocks of color on the central roof.

3

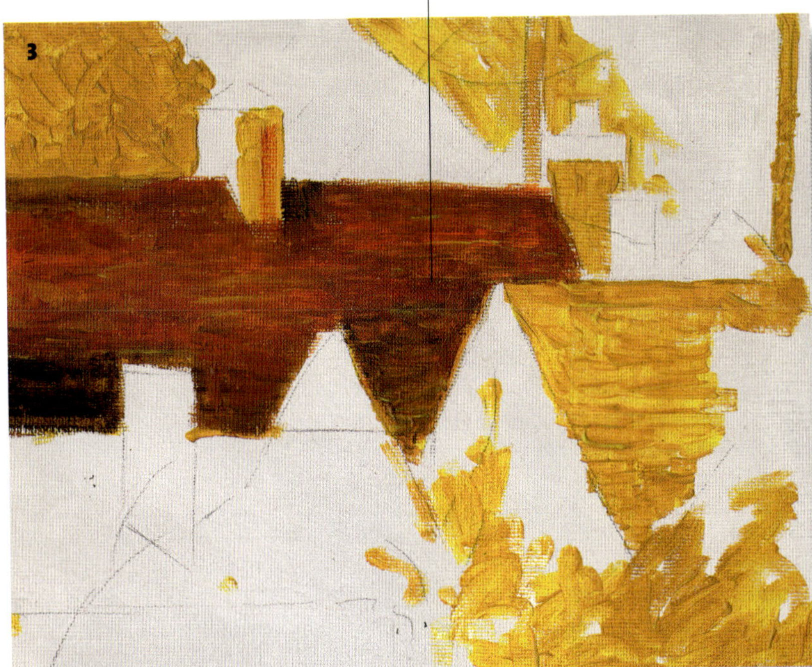

STEP 2 Begin with an underpainting for the fields and roofs. Paint these lightly with thinned paint of Yellow Ocher and a touch of Cadmium Yellow, then start painting behind the roofs, using thick impasto paint and stubby brush marks.

STEP 3 Once the underpainting is dry, build up blocks of color in warm russets, reds, and red-browns on the central roof and darken the ocher tone behind this using small, angled brush marks. Make these tones from various mixtures of Cadmium Red, Crimson Alizarin, and touches of Yellow Ocher and French Ultramarine. Experiment with varying amounts of colors to create a variety of hues.

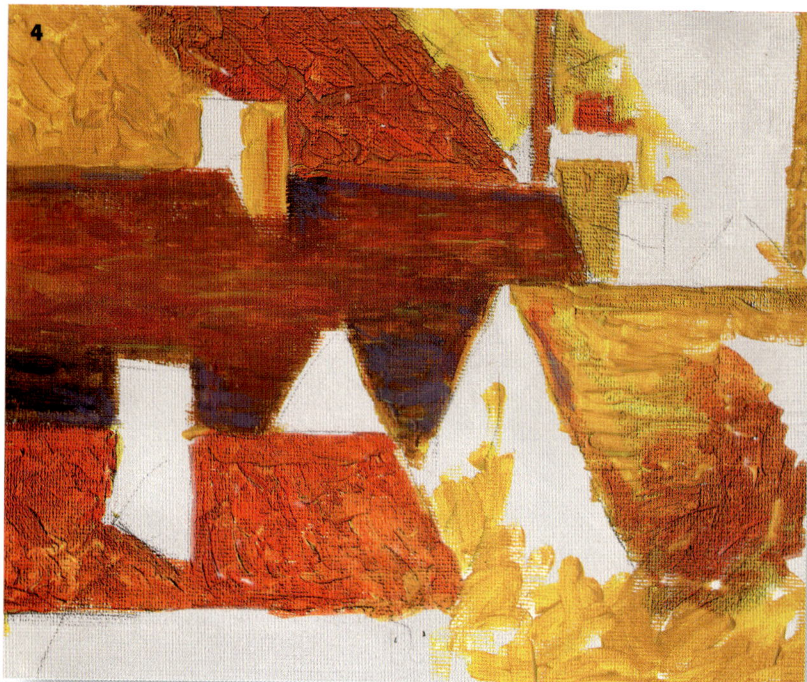

STEP 4 Using a small flat brush, add darker shadows with the addition of French Ultramarine to the right hand side of the chimneys. Remember the complementary contrasts that all the Impressionists practiced, so the dark blue shadows go next to the orange roofs. Although the roofs look like blocks of color, they are, in fact, made up of small, flat brush strokes.

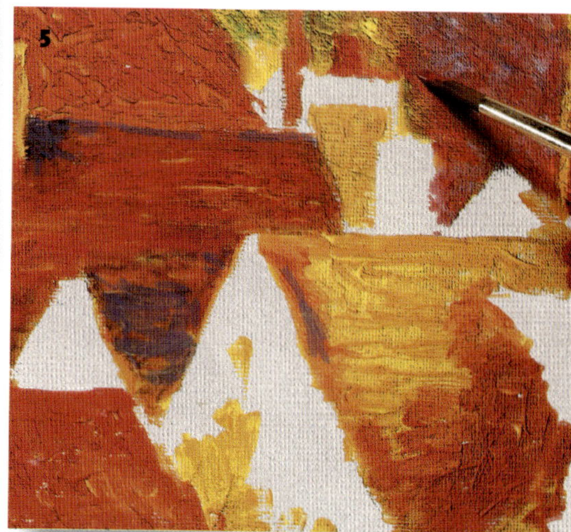

STEP 5 In broken diagonal marks, paint green (Viridian, French Ultramarine, and Cadmium Yellow) into the fields behind the houses. Make the russet plowed field out of Crimson Alizarin and Yellow Ocher.

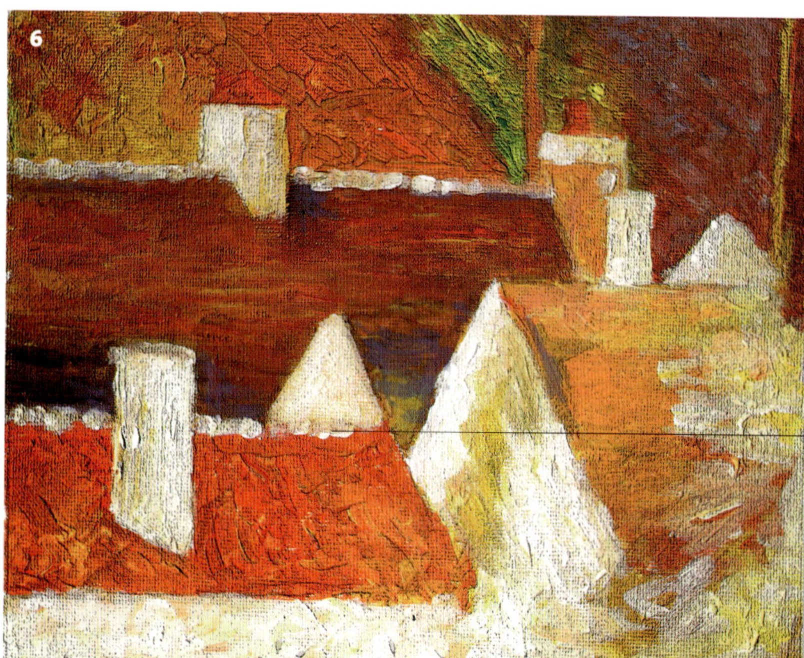

The layers of tiny strokes in multiple colors give the painting a slight relief in places. Add small dabs of impasted paint on the rooftops to indicate highlights from the sun.

STEP 6 Using a mixture of Zinc White with a touch of Cadmium Red and Yellow Ocher, paint the cream of the chimneys, the sides of the houses, and small dabs for highlights on the top of the two lefthand rooftops. Keep this color relatively stiff, and drag it across the canvas, using a relatively thin flat brush.

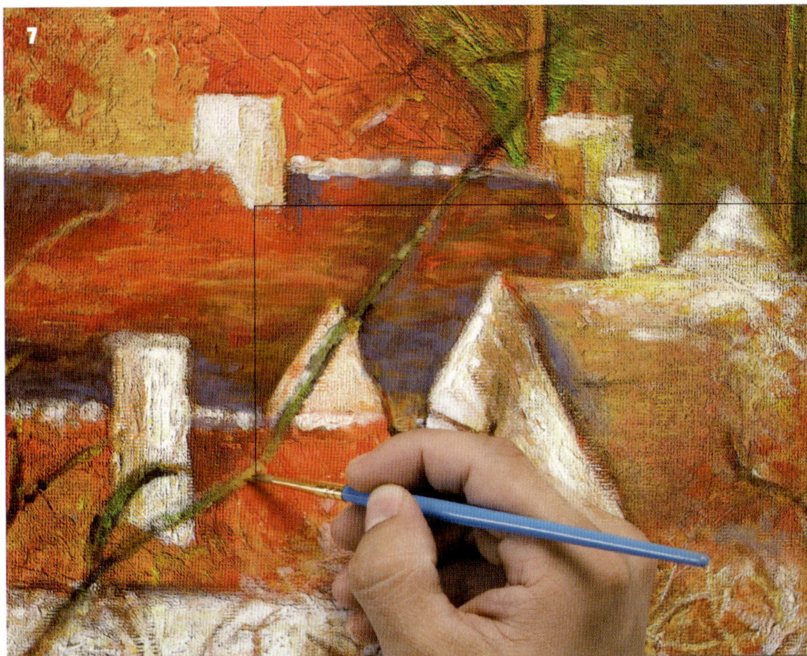

Continue the textural brush marks across the canvas, keeping within contours. Using a small round brush, apply small dabs of blended colors in browns, oranges, reds, and greens to the branches.

Place darker dabs of color under the branches and lighter dabs on top to give the impression of dappled sunlight.

STEP 7 Pissarro used long, thin strokes for the tree trunks and twigs and squarer, block-shaped marks for buildings and roofs. Shadows under the eaves should be a dusky violet to complement the yellowish-cream walls. There is evidence in Pissarro's work of relatively thick paints applied wet-over-dry and of thinner colors blurred and blended wet-in-wet, so, because you're working quickly, use both methods, always painting in small "taches." Be aware of the direction of light and layer the colors accordingly. Make up a variety of brown, fawn, and orange tints, using mixtures of yellow, red, and blue.

STEP 8 To finish the painting, use a brush with a fine point for the branches and use a variety of brush marks as you paint the branches across the roofs and background. Make these from Ceruleum Blue, Cadmium Yellow, and Cadmium Red. Keep to Pissarro's "two-dimensional brush marks" by placing chevronlike angular brush marks on the branches and roofs.

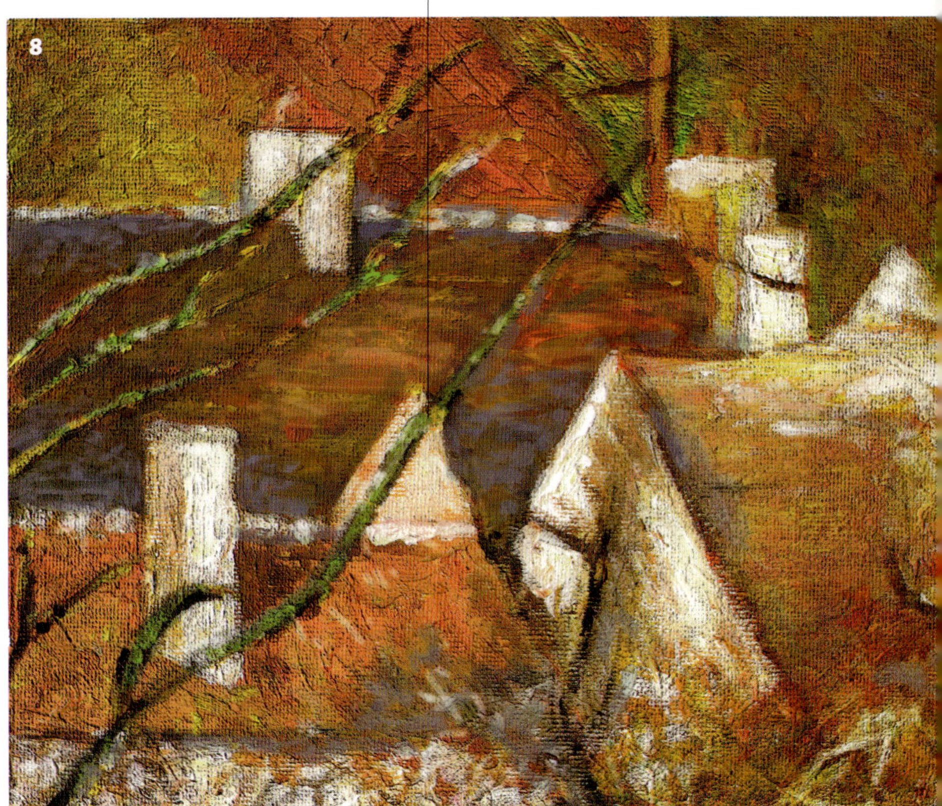

DEPICTING CITY VIEWS

BELOW
AVENUE DE L'OPÉRA, SUN ON A WINTER MORNING, 1898, oil on canvas, 29 x 36¼ inches (74 x 92 cm).
Pissarro painted a series of pictures looking up this avenue. He was interested in the way in which the weather both softened and sharpened the outlines of the city.

ALTHOUGH PISSARRO HAD strong moral and political views, he didn't let them interfere with his work. He believed that art shouldn't carry revolutionary messages and he also hated sentimental pictures. As a result, his paintings were never dramatic but often simply focused on such subjects as houses, factories, fields, laboring peasants, or river scenes. He had shown little interest in urban subjects early in his career, but, by the 1890s, his technical explorations developed into innovative series paintings. These series often concentrated on depicting town life in Paris, Rouen, Dieppe, Le Havre, and London. They were painted in the realistic and naturalistic style of Impressionism but were mixed with a Japanese influence that included angled, off-centered, or unusual viewpoints. These cityscapes are filled with light, color, and movement. The figures within them, although not detailed, are socially specific—there are workers in blue shirts, soldiers in uniform, and female workers in white caps.

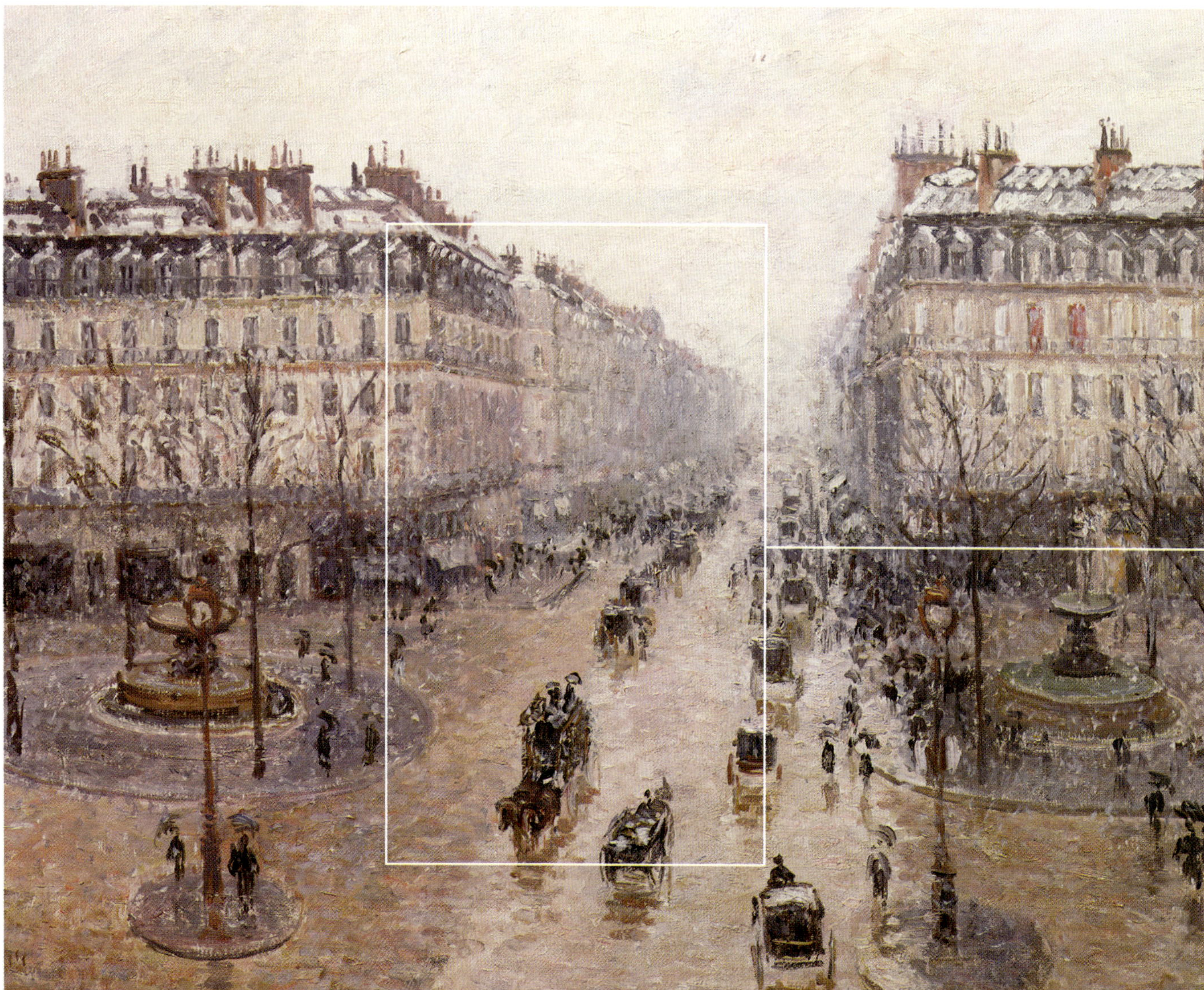

BELOW
AVENUE DE L'OPÉRA, detail.
In this painting, Pissarro applied the paint with regular brush strokes, returning to the more impressionistic techniques of his early career. The paint is built up to form an encrusted, opaque layer of pure colors, which are blended to give the overall impression of primarily blond and blue tones. The effect is to catch the brittle morning light of winter extremely well, particularly in the long, blue-violet shadows that it casts. Pissarro has built up the carriages and figures out of small, quick brush marks in pure colors, giving them a sense of movement.

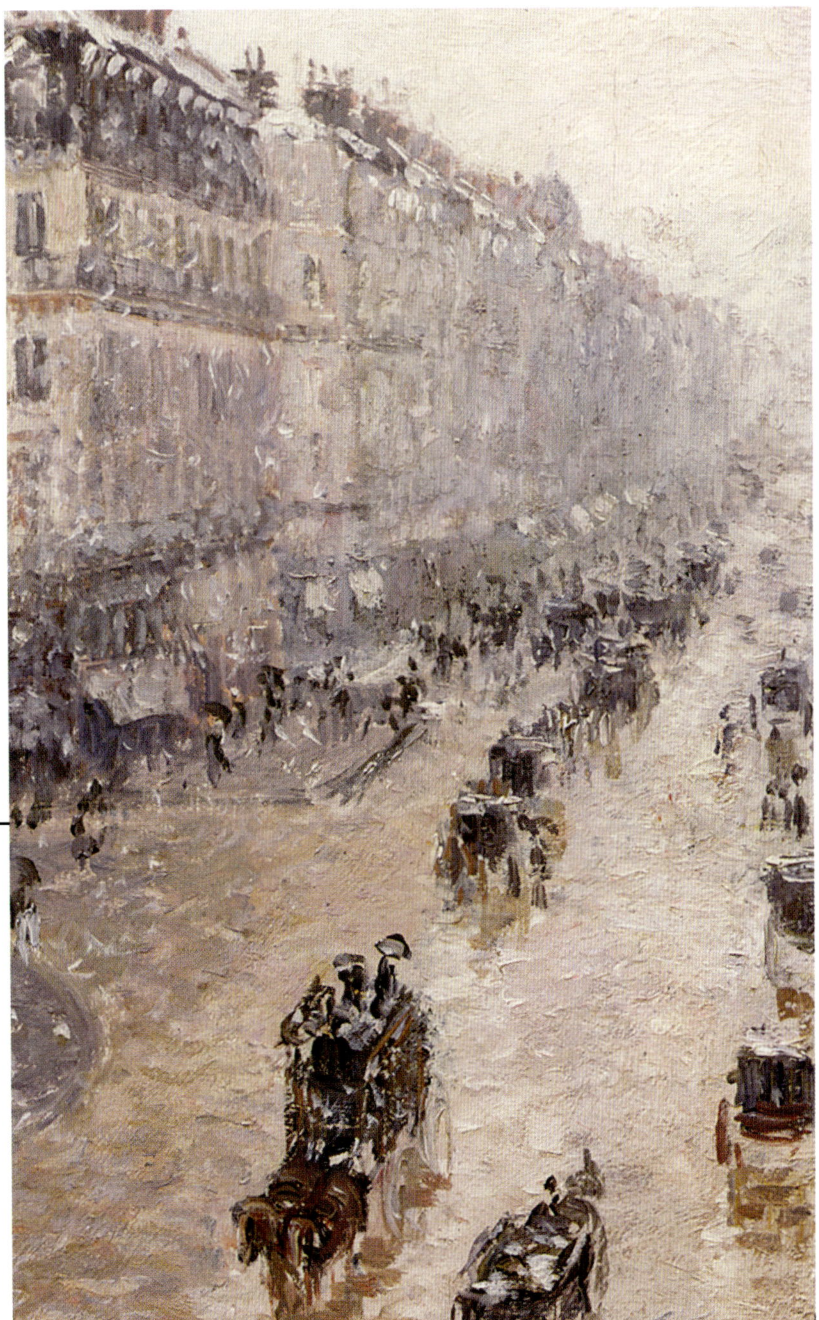

During the last 20 years of his life, Pisarro had problems with his eyesight, so he was more comfortable painting while indoors instead of outside in the open air. He mainly painted from the windows of hotels and apartments. In February 1897, for example, he took a room in Paris at the Hôtel de Russie on the corner of the Boulevard des Italiens and the Rue Drouot and produced a series of paintings of the Boulevard Montmartre at different times of the day. He was supposed to be resting his eyes during this trip, but the views were too good for him to ignore, and he made a large number of preparatory drawings, which he took back to his studio and turned into finished paintings.

Series paintings

Pissarro may have been inspired by the series of paintings on which Monet was engaged at this time (see page 31) and by Manet's earlier urban scenes. Whatever his reasons, he began working on his own city views after his brief experiments with pointillism. By this time, he was accomplished in the use of color, and his lightly handled compositions were carefully and accurately worked to record different times of the day, as well as different weather conditions. He started by producing careful outline drawings, with accurate linear perspective, then he applied paint, bringing out the effects of atmospheric perspective. The small brush strokes he used are dynamic, and, whether he painted day or night, sun, rain, fog, or snow, all the canvases are bathed in radiant light.

In his night scene, Pissarro created a dazzling effect using complementary contrasts of violets and yellows and blues and oranges. He then used toned-down colors in his daylight paintings of the same city streets.

During the last 10 years of his life, Pissarro painted over 300 urban views in 11 different series.

HOW TO DO IT

YOUR PALETTE

Believe it or not, your palette will consist of mainly yellows and blues, with just one red and white:

1 Zinc White
2 French Ultramarine
3 Lemon Yellow
4 Cadmium or Chrome Yellow
5 Crimson Alizarin
6 Cobalt Blue
7 Cobalt Violet
8 Yellow Ocher

Pissarro applied these paints in solid, bold strokes of color, creating patterns of luminous grays and blues on the road.

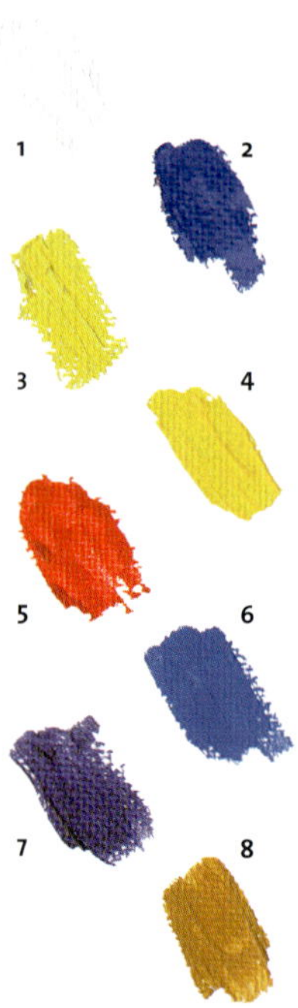

THE BOULEVARD MONTMARTRE was a new, airy, wide street in Paris that had modern gas street lamps and bright shop windows. Avoid specific outline and detail and concentrate instead on the essential shapes and colors. Try to focus particularly on Pissarro's textured brushwork and complementary contrasts. Apply the layers of paint in small dashes and dabs, using both wet-in-wet and wet-over-dry techniques.

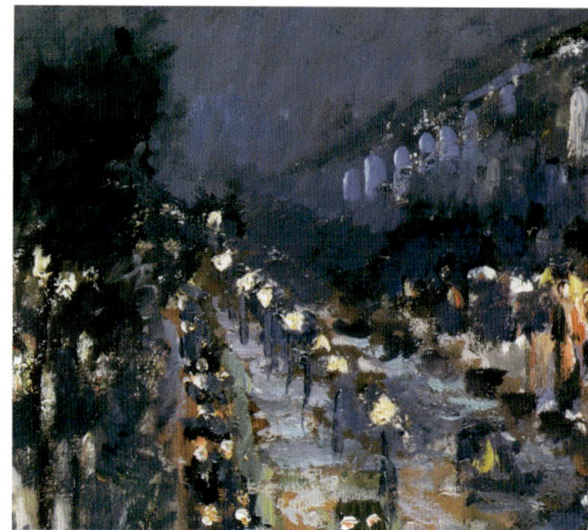

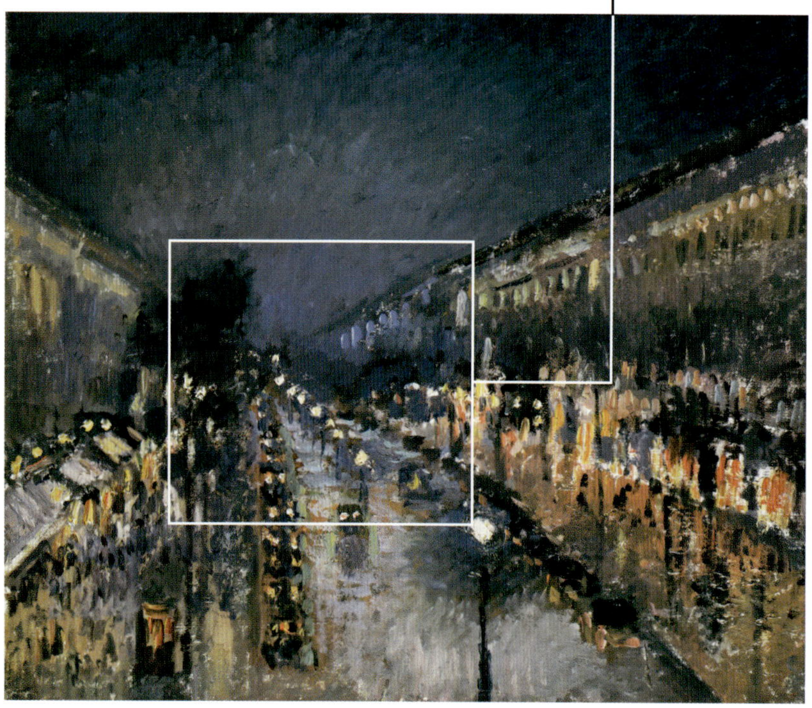

LEFT
BOULEVARD MONTMARTRE, NIGHT EFFECT, 1897, oil on canvas, 21 x 25½ inches (53.5 x 65 cm).
In 1897, Pissarro painted a series of paintings of the Boulevard Montmartre. This was one of the major boulevards created by Napoleon's architect Baron Haussmann, and it became instantly fashionable. For this night scene, he worked quickly but ensured he captured all the relevant details that reflected the weather conditions—for example, the street lamp in the foreground has a halo around it, created by the effect of rain in the air against the light.

The main techniques

Your first brush strokes should be larger than the later marks, and make sure you place them in different directions to cover the area loosely. Then apply the later, smaller strokes in directional layers over the top. You should paint the sky here using a fan effect with your brush strokes, and enhance the shimmering quality of reflected light on a rainy night by using contrasts of orange and violet and yellow and blue. Once you have a basic structure of loose perspective lines to describe the buildings and streets, work quickly—almost alla prima—to capture the lights, blurred reflections, trees, and storefronts in the wet street before the paint dries.

Note that the viewpoint is unusual—we are looking down on the street from above, which emphasizes the receding street lamps. You should apply the paint in directional marks, then add the horizontal shimmers of water on the road and pavement.

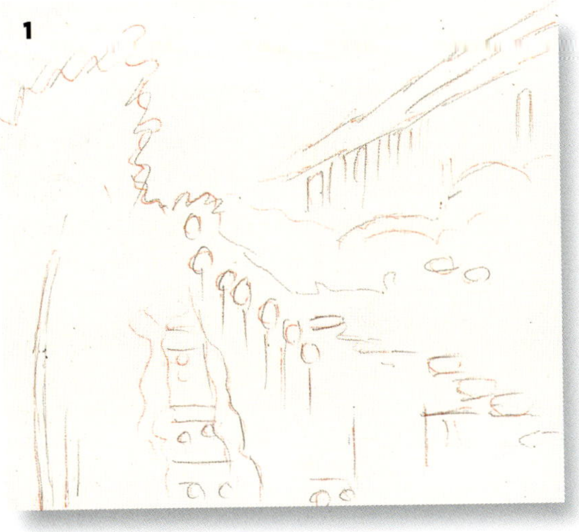

STEP 1 Begin with white priming on your canvas (or similar if you are using acrylics) and draw the one-point perspective view lightly in pencil. Note that the orthogonals meet to the left of this composition.

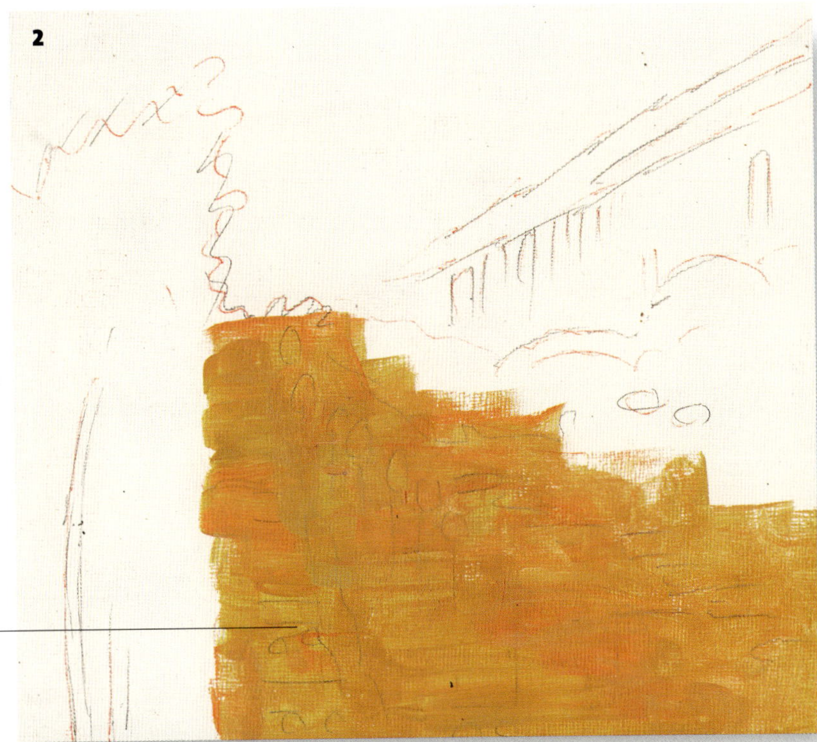

This is the only painting Pissarro did of night, and it is painted in a looser, more sketch-like way than the other paintings of the same series.

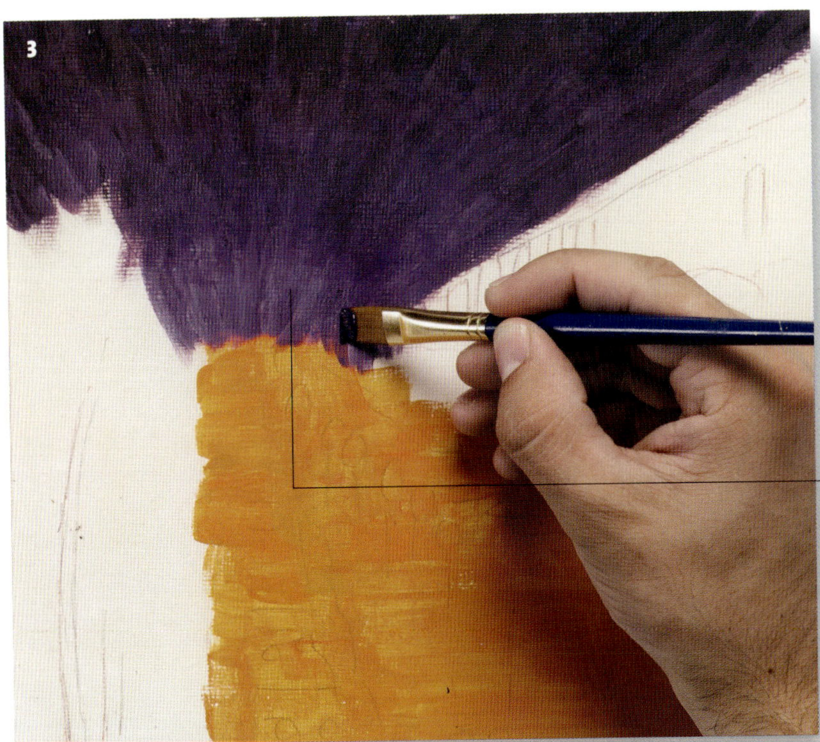

STEP 2 For this painting, Pissarro probably used a soft sable brush and thick liquid paint, which forms tiny blobs on the canvas in places. You should apply the paint in thick impasto to ensure that your brush marks are visible. For the road, make an underpainting of Yellow Ocher as a direct complement to the final covering of blue-gray.

STEP 3 Work on the sky, using fan-shaped brushwork radiating from the vanishing point with touches of French Ultramarine, Cobalt Violet, and Cobalt Blue. Begin with small brush marks within the "X" shape of the vanishing point and elongate them slightly as you move into the higher sky.

You may need to use a flat brush as well as the fan-shaped brush to ensure that the sky fills in the negative shapes between and around the buildings.

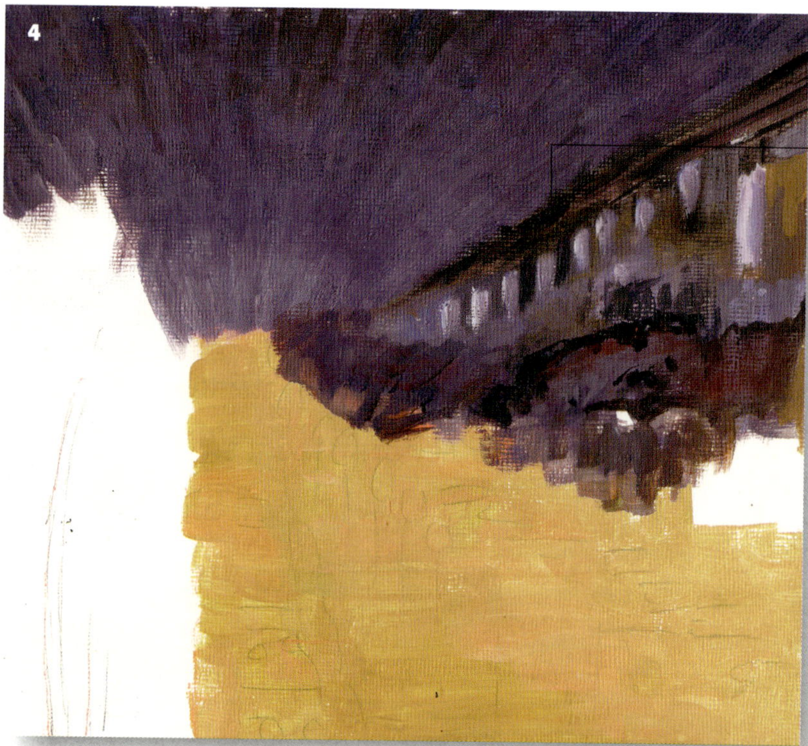

Working wet-over-dry, pick out the windows with the mixture of Cobalt Violet and Zinc White using a small, flat brush.

STEP 4 Create the roofline of the boulevard with Yellow Ocher and Cobalt Violet mixed with Zinc White, blended wet-in-wet. This should be lightly rendered, because the buildings are not definite but outlined against the sky. Add the windows using Cobalt Violet and Zinc White.

STEP 5 Begin making streaklike horizontal marks on the wet road and sidewalk in Cobalt Blue and French Ultramarine mixed with Zinc White.

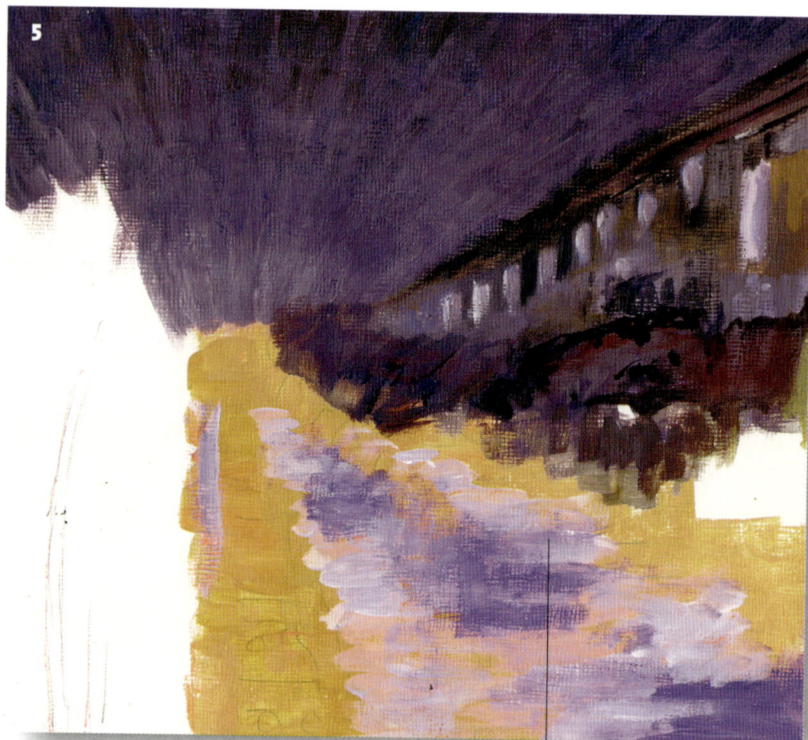

Add horizontal shimmers of water on the road and sidewalk, using French Ultramarine and Cobalt Blue mixed with Zinc White.

STEP 6 The line of carriages receding into the distance should be put in with relatively juicy paint and a small brush. Make this almost black color from French Ultramarine, Crimson Alizarin, and Yellow Ocher, with a touch of Cobalt Violet. For the headlamps, dab on Chrome Yellow mixed with a touch of Crimson Alizarin, and make shadows to the sides of the carriages from Cobalt Violet and Chrome Yellow.

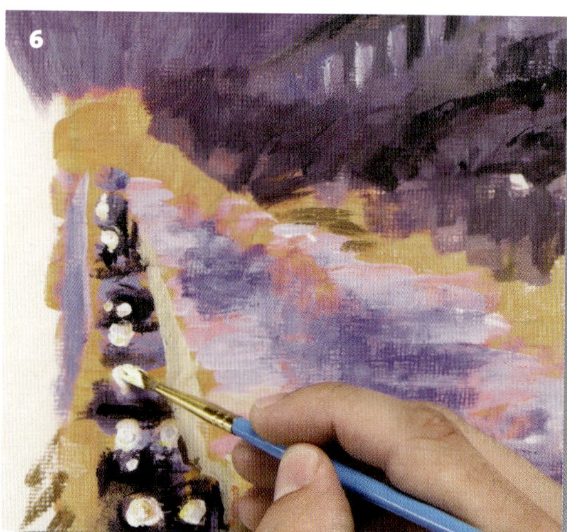

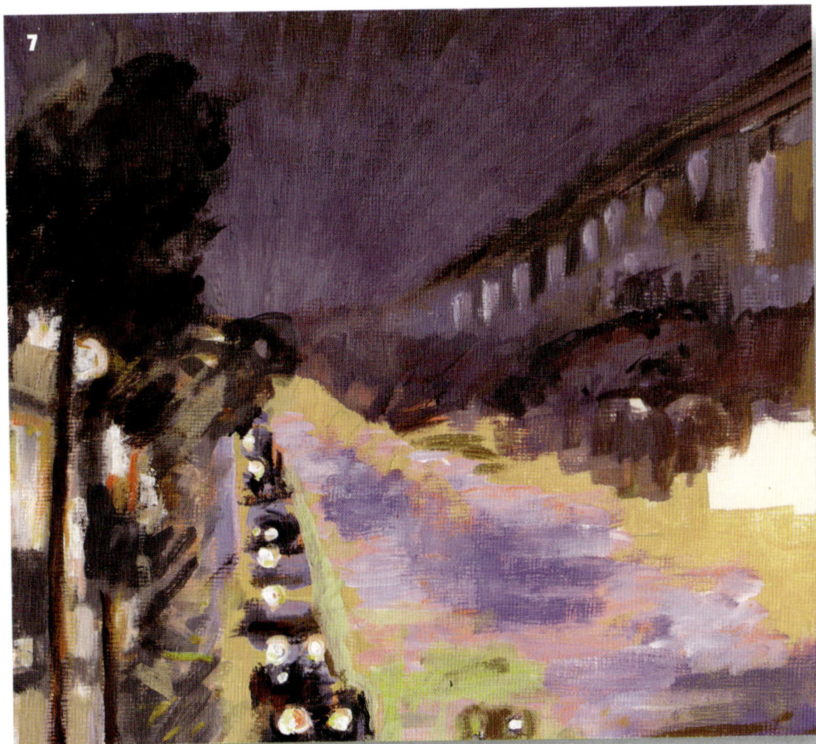

STEP 7 Next, begin to build up the trees and lights to the left of the canvas, using small dabs of French Ultramarine mixed with Cobalt Violet and a touch of Crimson Alizarin. Paint these in small vertical marks. Don't be too worried about mixing carefully—leave some of the color unmixed and visible. Dab on the lights with Zinc White and Lemon Yellow.

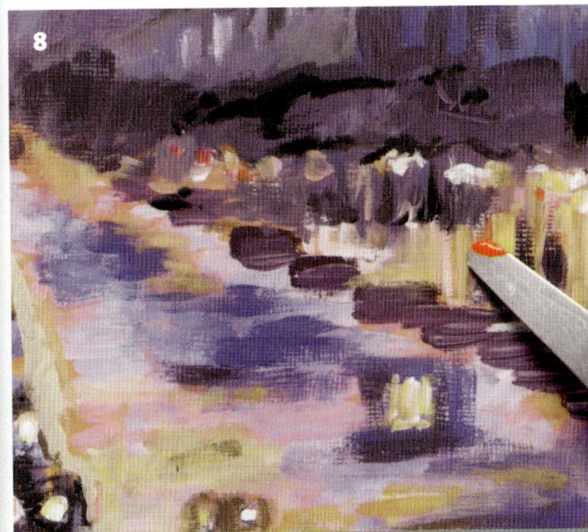

STEP 8 Mix together some more Zinc White with Lemon Yellow to create the hazy, fuzzy light emitting from the shimmering store windows. Mix some of these colors with Crimson Alizarin and Lemon Yellow while still wet on the canvas, and also make some darker marks to indicate the carriages on the righthand side of the road. Add some small squiggles of French Ultramarine next to the lighter reflections on the road.

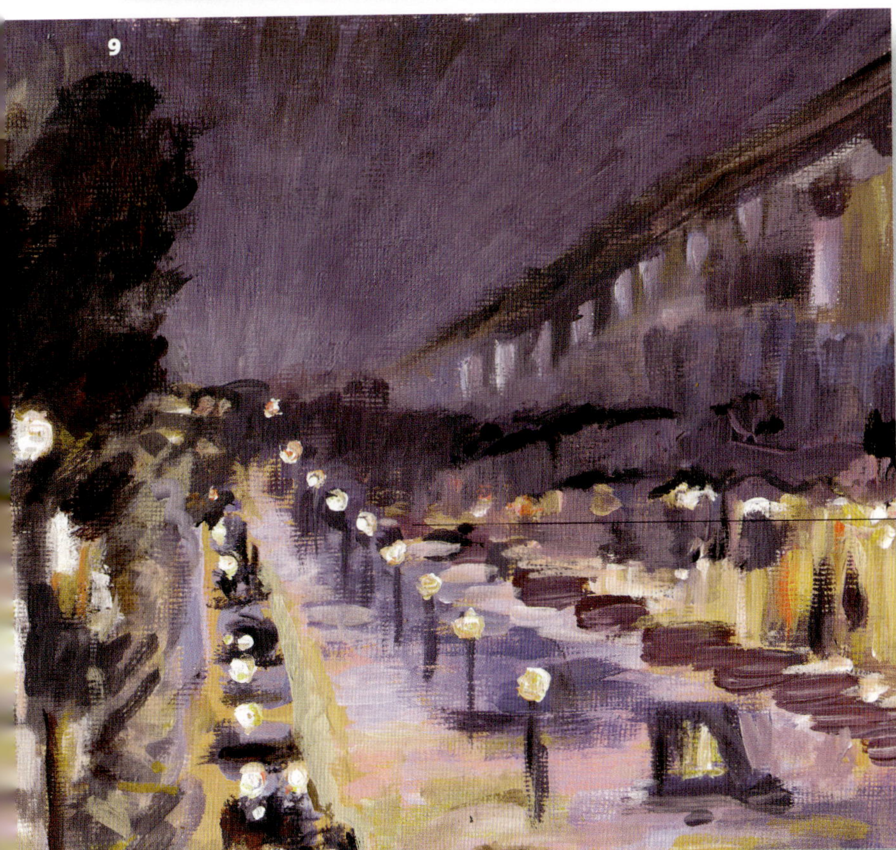

The wet sidewalks reflect the bright lights of the stores, cafés, and restaurants. The street lamps are made with dabs of pure Zinc White applied with a small round brush.

STEP 9 For the final step, paint the gas lamps down the center of the boulevard, using Ultramarine and Cobalt Violet for the posts and Lemon Yellow and White for the glowing lamps on top. Wait for the rest to dry, then add touches of pure White on the lamps with some extremely small touches in the reflections on the wet street. As with any painting, it's a good idea to look at it in a mirror to see if there are any mistakes.

Chapter seven

RENOIR

Whereas his friends were primarily landscapists, Renoir was first and foremost a figure painter. His figures were always happy, beautiful, and young. Indeed, few artists since have been able to capture the affable smiles, soft opalescent flesh, and sensuous, carefree enjoyment of life that he painted so well.

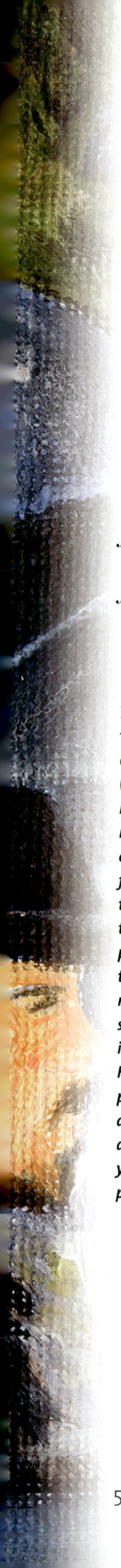

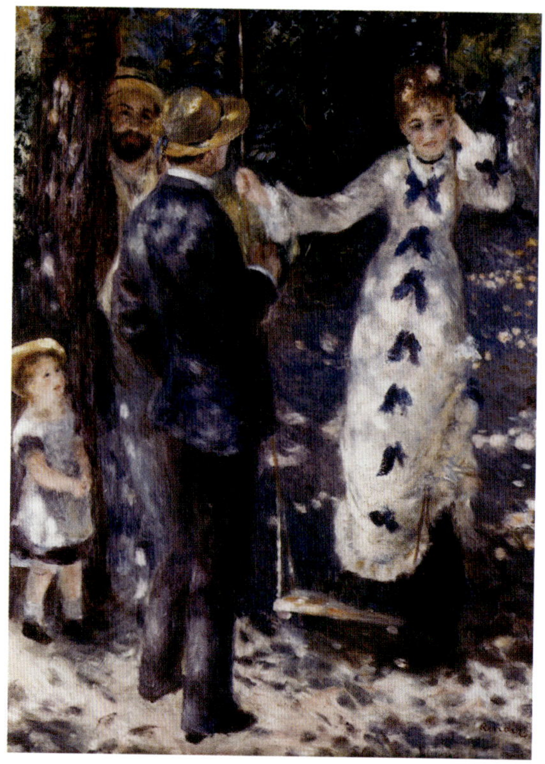

RIGHT
THE SWING, 1876, oil on canvas, 69 x 51½ inches (175.5 x 131 cm).
Here, Renoir combined movement with the effect of dappled sunlight filtering onto the figures through the overhanging trees. He worked on a preliminary oil sketch for this painting for several months, painting in situ, so he didn't lose the immediacy of the scene. He used mainly wet-in-wet paint across the canvas, and his vibrant contrasts are made up of mainly yellow-orange and blue-purple tones.

UNLIKE MANY OF HIS friends, who belonged to the middle or upper classes, Pierre-Auguste Renoir (1841–1919) came from a modest background. At the age of 13 he took his first job as a porcelain painter's apprentice, which gave him the experience of learning good craftsmanship. He also learned how to work with bright colors, something that later became a trademark in his paintings. When he decided on a career in the fine arts, his respect for tradition led him to enroll at the École des Beaux-Arts. Then, in 1862, he met Monet, Sisley, and Bazille at Charles Gleyre's (1808–86) independent studio.

Despite his close friendship with Monet, Renoir was never completely convinced about Impressionism. He did go on painting expeditions with Monet and did create *plein air* Impressionist paintings full of sparkling color and light. However, his approach to nature was always slightly different from the others in the group. He said, "Out of doors, one uses colors that one would never think of in weaker studio light. But landscape painting is a thankless job. You waste half the day for the sake of one hour's painting. You only finish 1 picture out of 10, because the weather keeps changing."

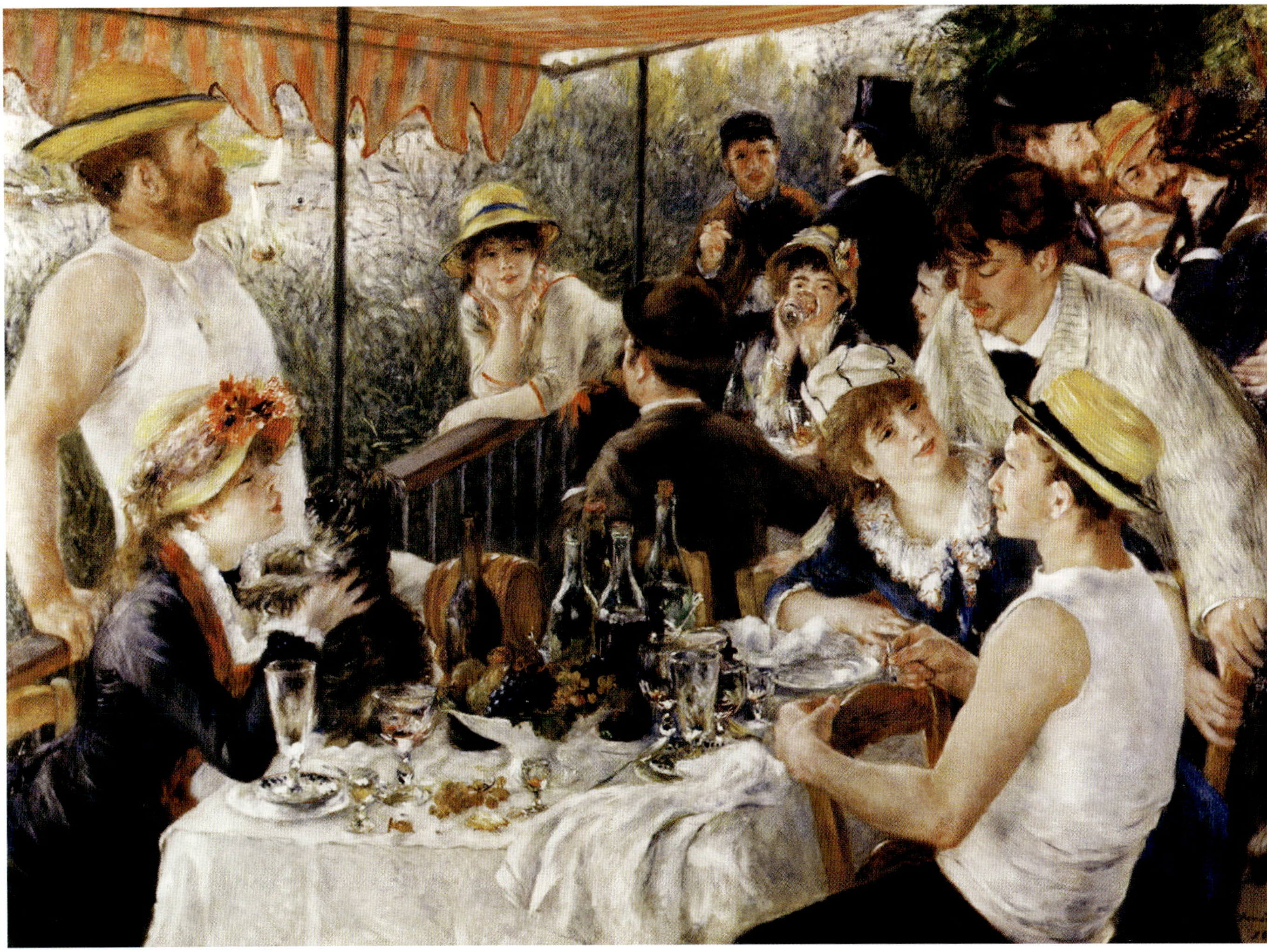

ABOVE
THE LUNCHEON OF THE BOATING PARTY, 1880–81, oil on canvas, 51¼ x 68 inches (130 x 173 cm).
This shows the first floor balcony of the Restaurant Fournaise, a favorite meeting place for Renoir and many of his friends. Aline Charigot, later to become Renoir's wife, is seated to the left. Most of the figures are concentrated in the lower half of the painting, while the striped awning and foliage in the top half holds the eye within the diagonal composition.

In the 1880s, after more than 20 years as an artist, he declared that he had "traveled as far as Impressionism could take me" and began a period of experimentation. He went to Italy to study the works of the Renaissance masters. By the mid-1880s, he was painting in a crisper, more precise technique, which he called his *manière aigre* (sour manner).

New themes

At the same time, Renoir turned from depicting contemporary themes to more timeless subjects, particularly portraits and figures. His preference for light-hearted themes was influenced by the great Rococo masters, such as Boucher, whose works he studied in the Louvre Museum. Unlike those masters, he observed real life instead of planned poses, and his portraits and pictures of people exert an unassuming and natural charm.

As a skilled draftsman, Renoir combined a richly textural style with a fluent manner of painting in many of his works. He usually began a picture by putting small dabs of thinned color over the whole canvas, which gave him an idea of color relationships, then he blended them together. When this was complete, he began to define each area, increasing the proportion of oil to turpentine.

Like most of the Impressionists, Renoir constantly experimented, and his methods and materials vary from painting to painting.

DEPICTING FLESH TONES

FIGURE PAINTING WAS always Renoir's greatest love. He told Berthe Morisot that the nude was one of the vital forms of art and he frequently copied from the works of Old Masters in the Louvre. During his life, he was influenced by eighteenth-century French painters, such as François Boucher (1703–70), Jean-Honoré Fragonard (1732–1806), and Jean August Dominque Ingres (1780–1867), and, as his career progressed, his admiration increased for the Spanish masters Goya (1746–1828) and Velásquez (1599–1660).

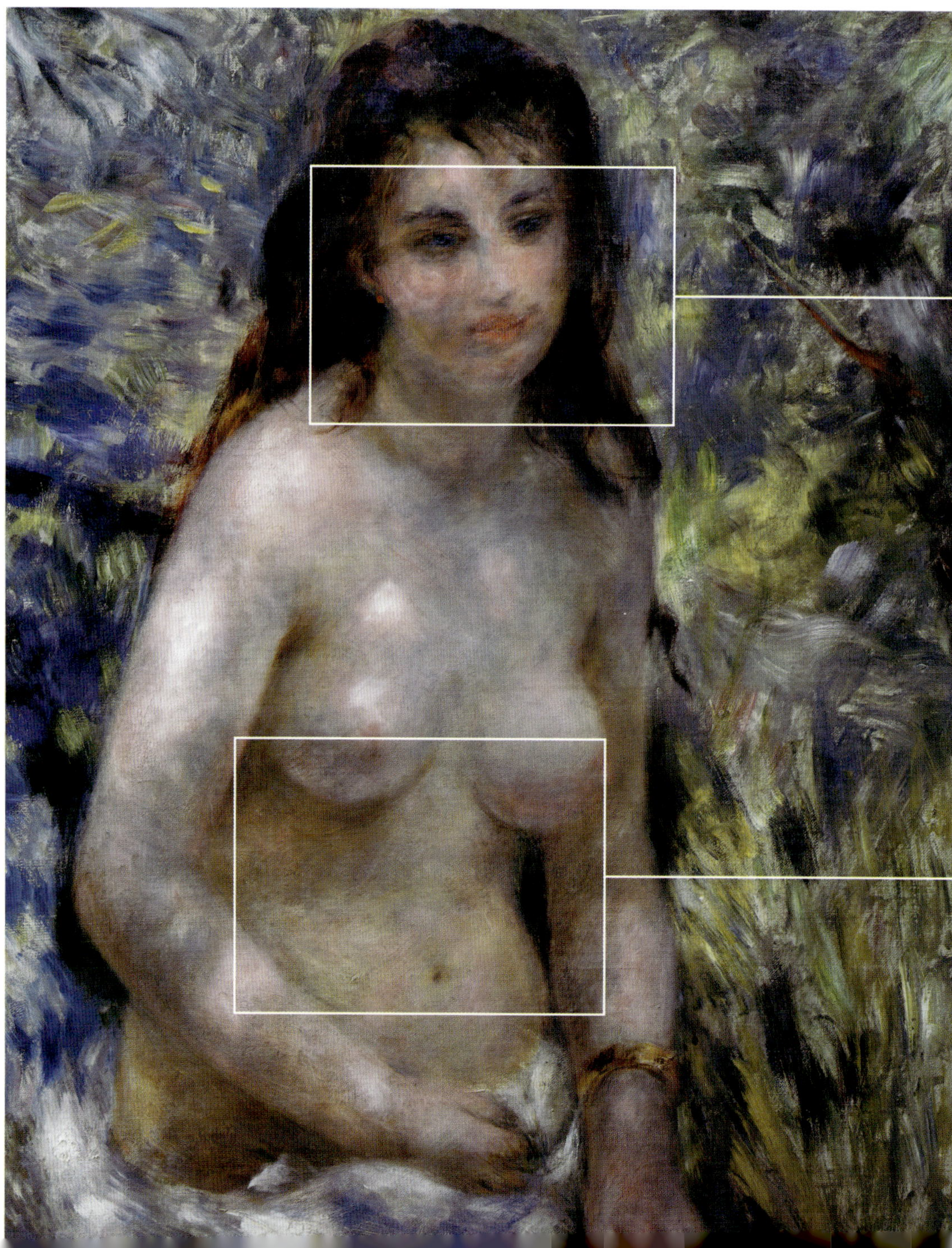

RIGHT
NUDE IN THE SUNLIGHT, 1875–76, oil on canvas, 32 x 25 inches (81 x 63.5 cm).
To create this painting, Renoir scumbled thin paint onto a pale gray background surface, then quickly worked wet-in-wet for the background, adding wet-over-dry layers to obscure the canvas texture. He used opaque colors for shadows on the body, including Naples and Chrome Yellow, Cobalt Blue, Crimson Alizarin, Viridian, Emerald Green, Vermilion, and Lead White. He applied impasted paint thickly to suggest the bulk of the woman's jewelry and built up the rich red hair color with wet-in-wet paint.

BELOW
NUDE IN THE SUNLIGHT, detail.
The paint has been applied loosely on the face, giving a blurred effect and softening the features.

BOTTOM
NUDE IN THE SUNLIGHT, detail.
The curves of the model's breasts have been emphasized with deep tones and bright highlights for greater sensuality.

He admired the strong tonal contrasts and smooth flesh tones created by these artists.

Renoir was never completely happy with the idea of being separate from the official art world in Paris, and, although he continued to paint with the Impressionists, he asked them to drop the name Independents, because he felt uncomfortable with the "revolutionary taint" that they were giving themselves.

Renoir's first nudes were tightly controlled, and often surrounded by dark tones to enhance their pale flesh. However, even during the early part of his career, his interest in observed light and color made his work freer and looser than many of the other figure painters of the day. He was fascinated with the contrasts of dark hair, eyebrows, and eyes against milky-white flesh, and he said that his flower paintings "... are experiments with flesh that I make for my nudes."

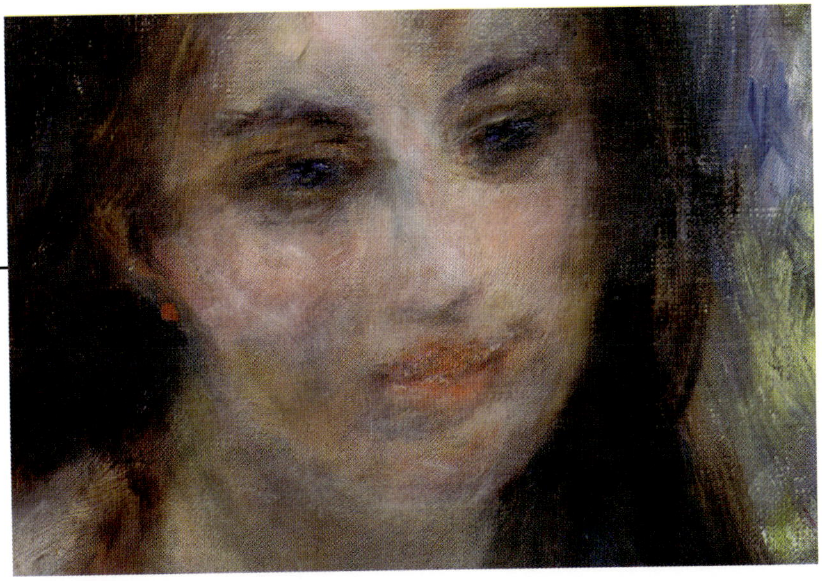

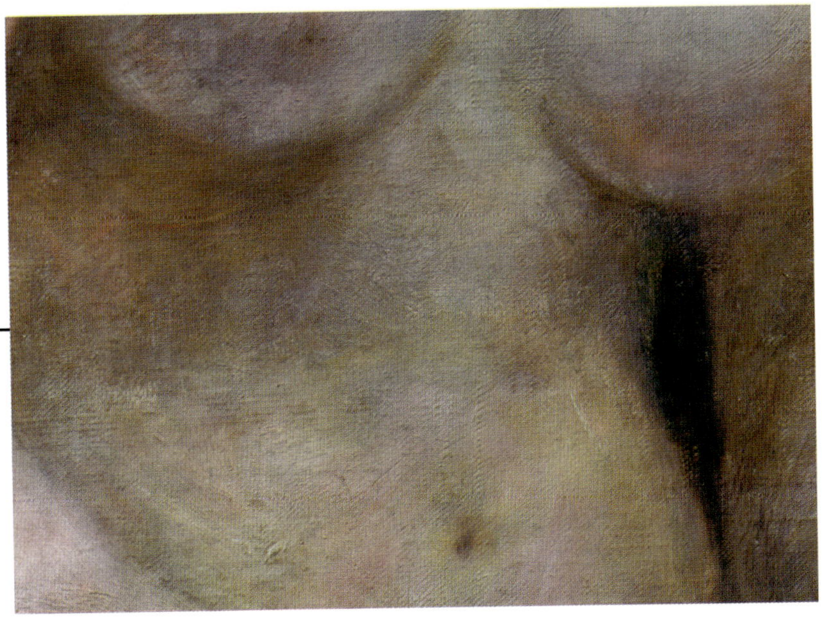

Luminosity and radiance

To give maximum luminosity to flesh tones and to enhance the radiance of the skin, Renoir primed smooth canvases with thick white paint to create a fresco effect. In portraits, he often used slightly broader strokes for clothing and smaller dabs for skin to bring out the delicacy of the face. Instead of gray or brown, he painted "soft complementaries" in shadows and crevices—for example, he used green next to pink, blue next to peach, and mauve next to cream.

It was not only the way in which he painted the actual skin that made the flesh on Renoir's figures so luminous and pearly. He became inspired by the brilliant light of Italy during his visit in 1881, and, afterward, he often set his peach-toned figures against a rich blue-green background, evocative of the Mediterranean Sea and in agreement with the color theory of complementary contrasts.

Renoir continued to paint nudes, and they were his favorite subjects during the latter part of his life. Combining Impressionist ideas with a more classical treatment of figures, by the 1890s he painted with rhythmic, sensual curving lines, using warm colors to contrast with cool flesh tones. He often echoed curving outlines of bodies by placing curved shapes in the background, explaining: "[The model] is only there to set me going, to permit me to dare things I should never have thought of inventing without her, and to put me on my feet again if I should venture too far."

HOW TO DO IT

YOUR PALETTE
To re-create Renoir's luminous flesh tones, your palette will need to include the following:

1. Zinc White
2. Naples Yellow
3. Yellow Ocher
4. Raw Sienna
5. Indian Red
6. Venetian Red
7. Terre Verte
8. Chrome Green
9. Cobalt Blue

Renoir applied many contrasts, so not only should you use warm and cool colors but also thick and thin paint across the entire painting.

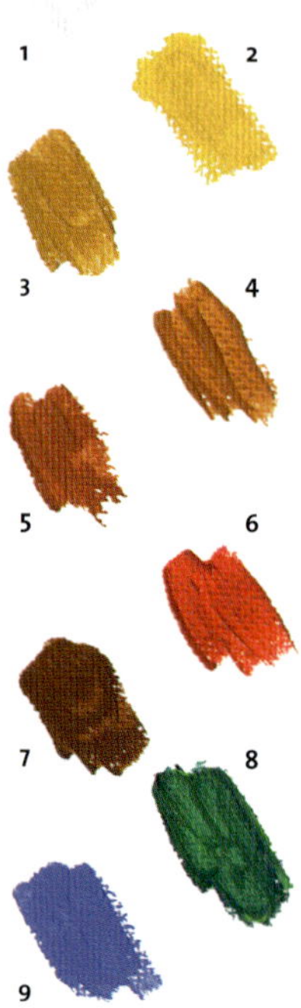

RENOIR ALWAYS PREFERRED a smooth white canvas to which he often added an extra priming of Flake (Lead) White mixed with one-third linseed oil and two-thirds turpentine. To achieve the required translucence of a Renoir painting, you will have to adopt a much more fluid manner of painting than Monet or Pissarro. To do this, you should blend in broken, moist brush marks as you work.

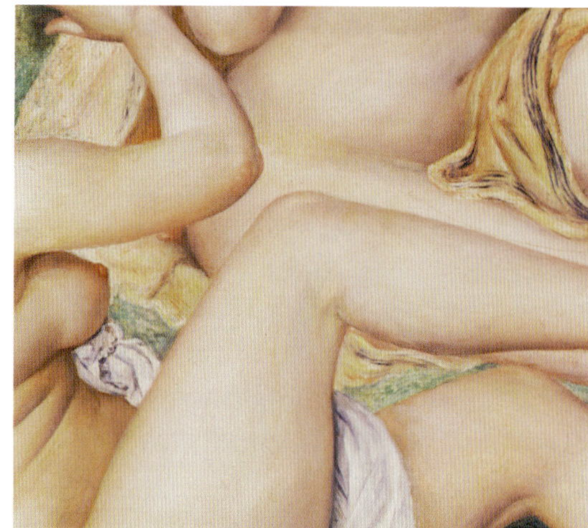

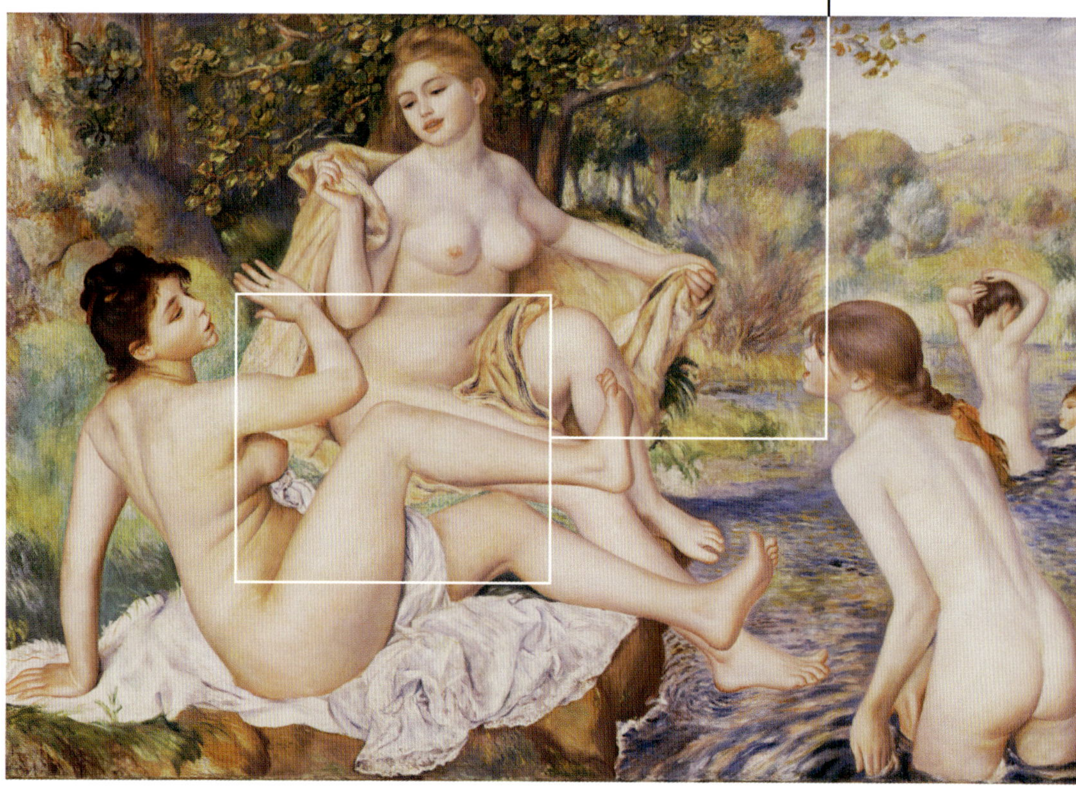

The main techniques

You will need at least a No. 14 brush for the initial wash, Nos. 8, 5, and 1 for the main painting, and a flat fan brush for blending. The tones should be soft but sure—cool colors complementing warm ones. Most of the work should be done wet-in-wet, with small touches of wet-over-dry to finish the painting off.

ABOVE
THE BATHERS, 1887, oil on canvas, 46½ x 67¼ inches (118 x 171 cm).
This painting has been called the masterpiece of Renoir's Mediterranean phase. He "borrowed" this composition from a classical source, then worked on the figures in the studio, later contrasting them with their landscape setting. Over four years, he made more than 20 preparatory studies for the work, then he painted the final picture on a specially prepared white background surface that enabled him to achieve a smooth, highly finished surface.

1

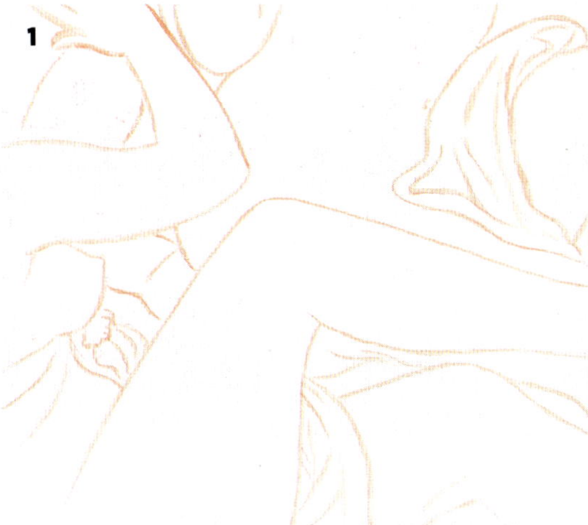

STEP 1 You should work on a relatively fine-weave canvas or similar support. Prepare this with at least three coats of white latex, acrylic, or gesso to create a thick, fresco-type covering, because the surface needs to be smooth and clear. Once this is dry, lightly sketch the outline of the composition; use the grid method if it helps (see page 95).

2

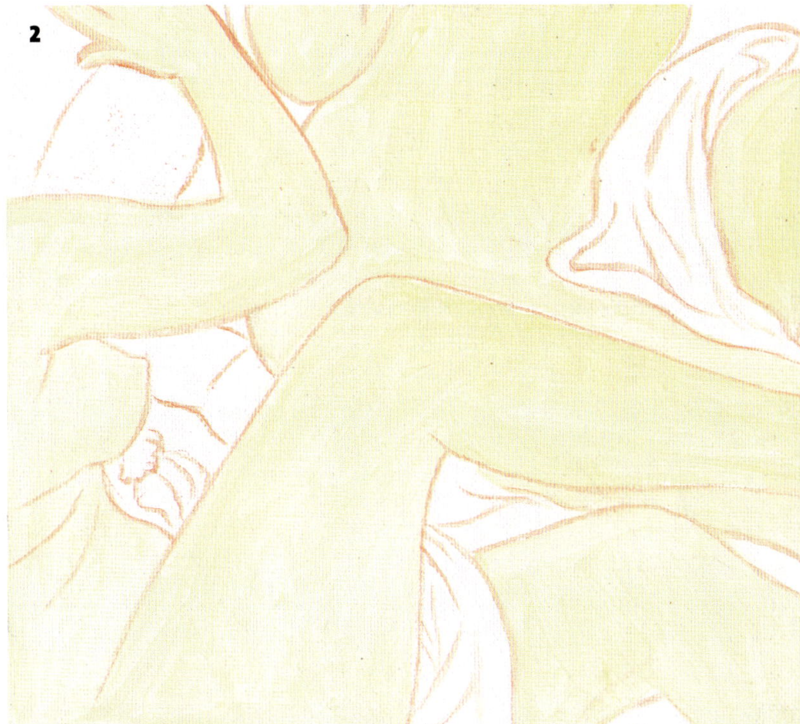

3

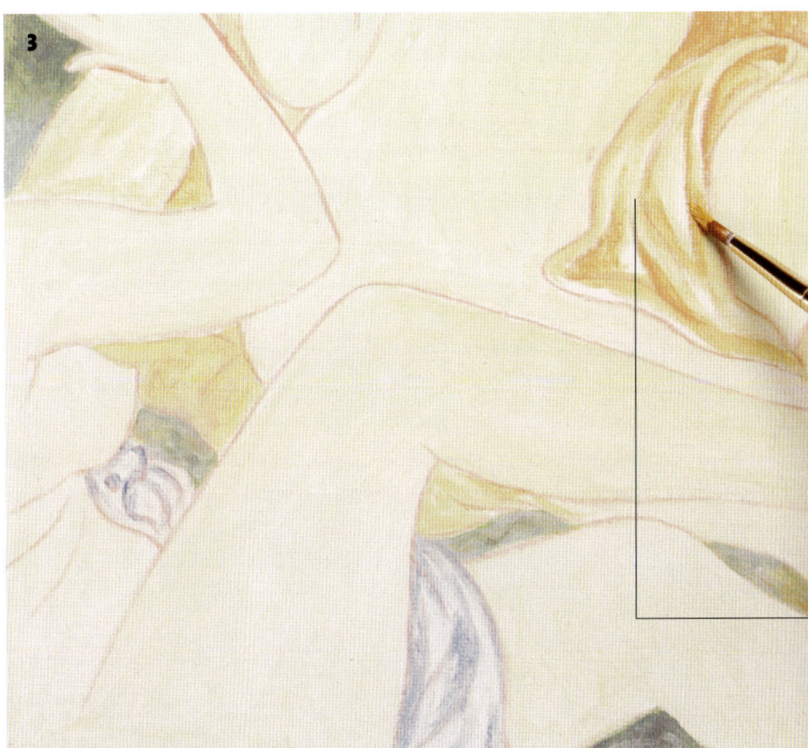

STEP 2 Before you start painting, double-check the proportions. Mix a thin pale pink wash using Zinc White and Raw Sienna. Brush this over the surface of the figures using a flat, stiff brush.

STEP 3 Renoir blended in the background in soft, vigorous strokes before painting the detail of the figures. In this particular section, there is hardly any background visible. With the No. 14 brush, rapidly work wet-in-wet with a little Cobalt Blue, Chrome Green, Naples Yellow, and Yellow Ocher in the background areas that can be seen. Use the fan brush to blend the colors until you create an "out-of-focus" finish. Don't worry about leaving a little of the canvas showing through here and there, because that is what the Impressionists themselves often did. Lightly apply some Cobalt Blue strokes to the fabric at the front and Yellow Ocher on the fabric at the back.

With the No. 1 brush, apply Yellow Ocher, Cobalt Blue, and Zinc White to build up a muted impression of the fabric draped over the leg. You will add strength to these tones later.

STEP 4 You should use a palette knife to smooth on the "flesh" paint in order to create a highly finished surface. Make up the three skin tones you will be using now—dark, medium, and light—by mixing various amounts of Raw Sienna, Venetian Red, Indian Red, and Yellow Ocher with touches of Terre Verte, Cobalt Blue, and plenty of Zinc White. You may need to make several different versions of these colors and modify them as you work. Apply the light to medium tones now.

STEP 5 Carry on applying the local colors, this time using all three tones, in thin scumbles. You should apply moist, medium-density layers to obliterate the canvas texture and evoke the quality of flesh. Build up the tones slowly and carefully, working wet-in-wet, then thin wet-over-dry to cover over any canvas texture that might still be apparent. Use brush Nos. 8 and 5 to make the small dabs on the skin.

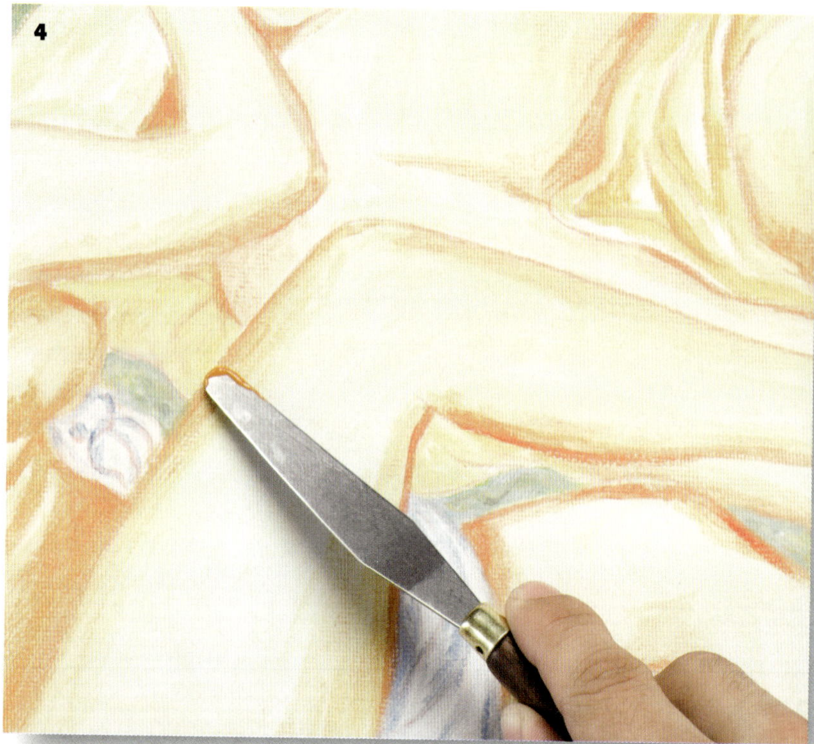

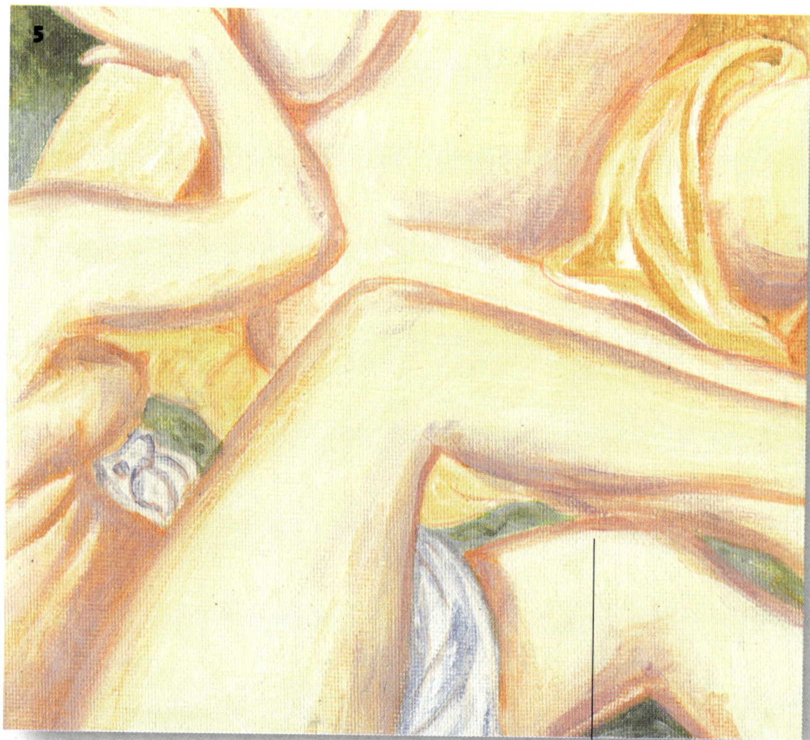

Apply the lightest flesh tones about one-third in from the top of the legs and blend this color into the darker areas smoothly.

STEP 6 Renoir was against using black at the time he painted this picture. This means you should create your darks using the deepest colors in your palette. Paint complementaries together and also juxtapose cool and warm colors. (You can mix some cool dark tones from Venetian Red, Naples Yellow, and Cobalt Blue, while warmer dark tones can be made from Raw Sienna, Cobalt Blue, and Yellow Ocher. Use some of these stronger hues to emphasize the draped fabrics.)

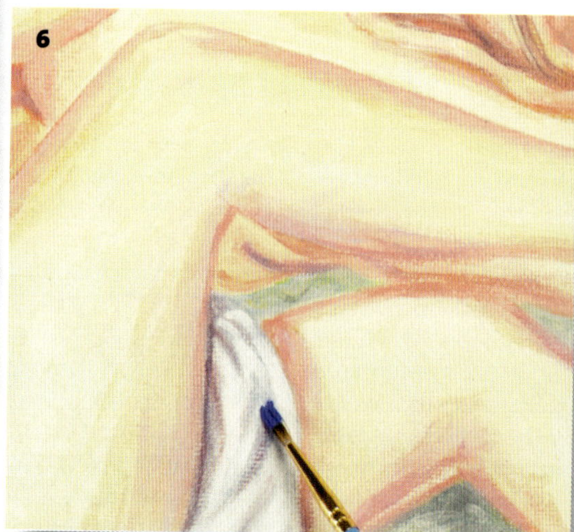

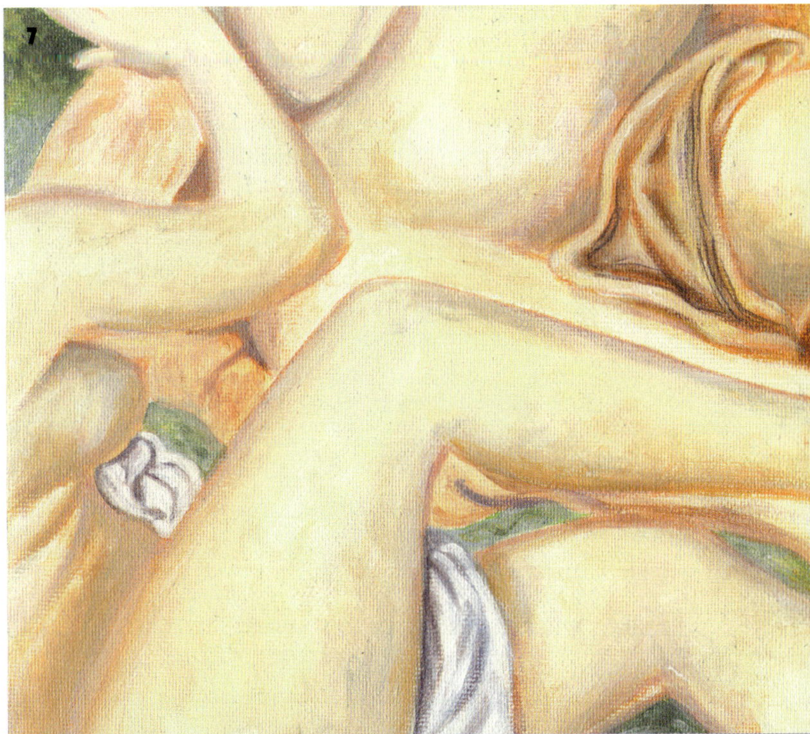

STEP 7 Once you have built up the impression of solidity by blocking in light and dark and cool and warm tones, add turpentine to your blends and paint with a thicker, juicier texture. Keep the strong tonal contrasts that you've established and use the small (No. 1) brush for details, particularly in the shadows around the figures.

STEP 8 Work a little more on the strong tonal contrasts of the two fabrics. The white should have blue-violet shadows, while the gold's shadows are made up of Yellow Ocher, Naples Yellow, Venetian Red, and a touch of White Zinc. Make the figures seem more definite with cream highlights and stronger shadows, using Cobalt Blue, Venetian Red, and Yellow Ocher. Balance the warm, peachy flesh tones with blue shadows, pinker tones with greenish shadows, and the cream highlights with cool violet hues.

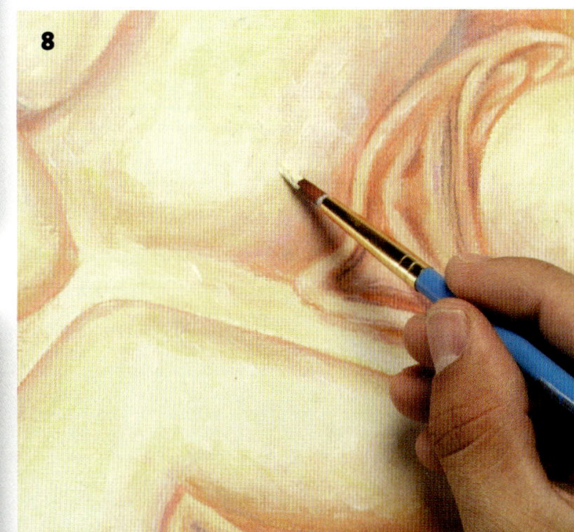

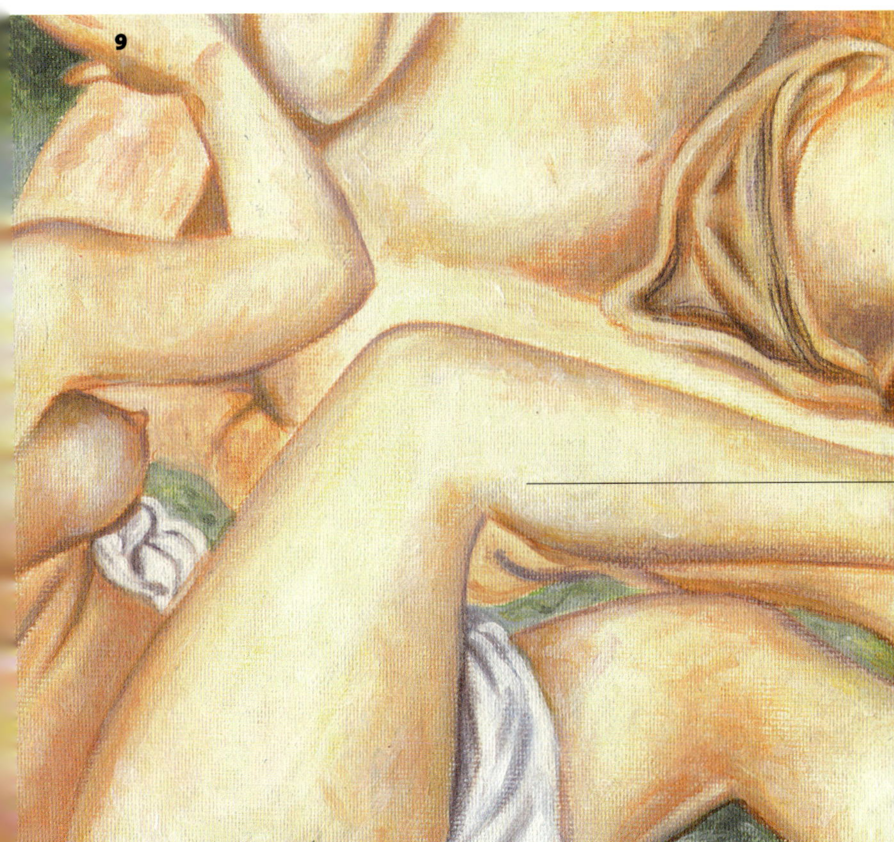

Add more density to your painting by deepening the mid-tones but keeping the lightest tones as bright as possible.

STEP 9 Now firm up the painting with stronger tones across it. With clean brushes, mix some of the deepest tones that you have been using, including the flesh tones and the darker shadows between the figures. Then with smooth fine strokes, shape and blend around some of the lower contours—that is, the forms that are in the most shadow, such as under the legs, breasts, and arms—to finish off the painting.

USING A LIMITED PALETTE

RIGHT

DANCE IN THE TOWN, 1883, oil on canvas, 70¾ x 35½ inches (180 x 90 cm). ***Throughout his career, Renoir used at the most only about 8 to 10 colors on any one painting. He preferred to work on fine-grained white primed canvases to give a lighter hue to his paintings. Renoir's friend Paul Lhote is the male dancer here, and the female model is Marie-Clémentine, later to become the painter Suzanne Valadon. Renoir used refined brush strokes on this painting, and his palette was restricted to white, yellow, red, green, and blue.***

BELOW

DANCE IN THE TOWN, detail. ***Thickly applied, strongly contrasting hues blended directly on the canvas build up the luxurious folds and drapes of the dress fabric.***

RENOIR'S EXPERIENCE AS a porcelain painter contributed to his method of using translucent color brushed thinly over pale background surfaces. To make his paint transparent, he diluted it with a mixture of oil and turpentine. This produced a smoother finish than the more obvious, textural brush marks of the other Impressionists. To avoid excessive mixing of colors and risking turning them muddy, he usually applied paint directly onto the canvas, wet-in-wet.

Renoir developed his own select palette through experiments and discussions with the other Impressionists. Even when he moved away from the *plein air* landscapes that he painted in the first years of Impressionism, he continued to use a restricted palette. He had several slightly different combinations of colors that he used for different subjects, and they evolved and changed over different periods. Overall, the palettes of premixed tints for depicting flesh were the most complex, while his palettes for *plein air* painting were the most limited.

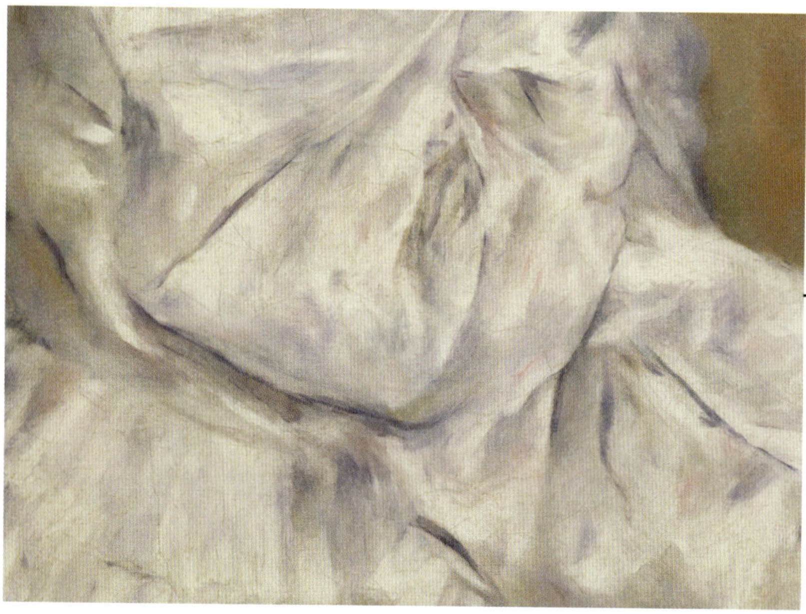

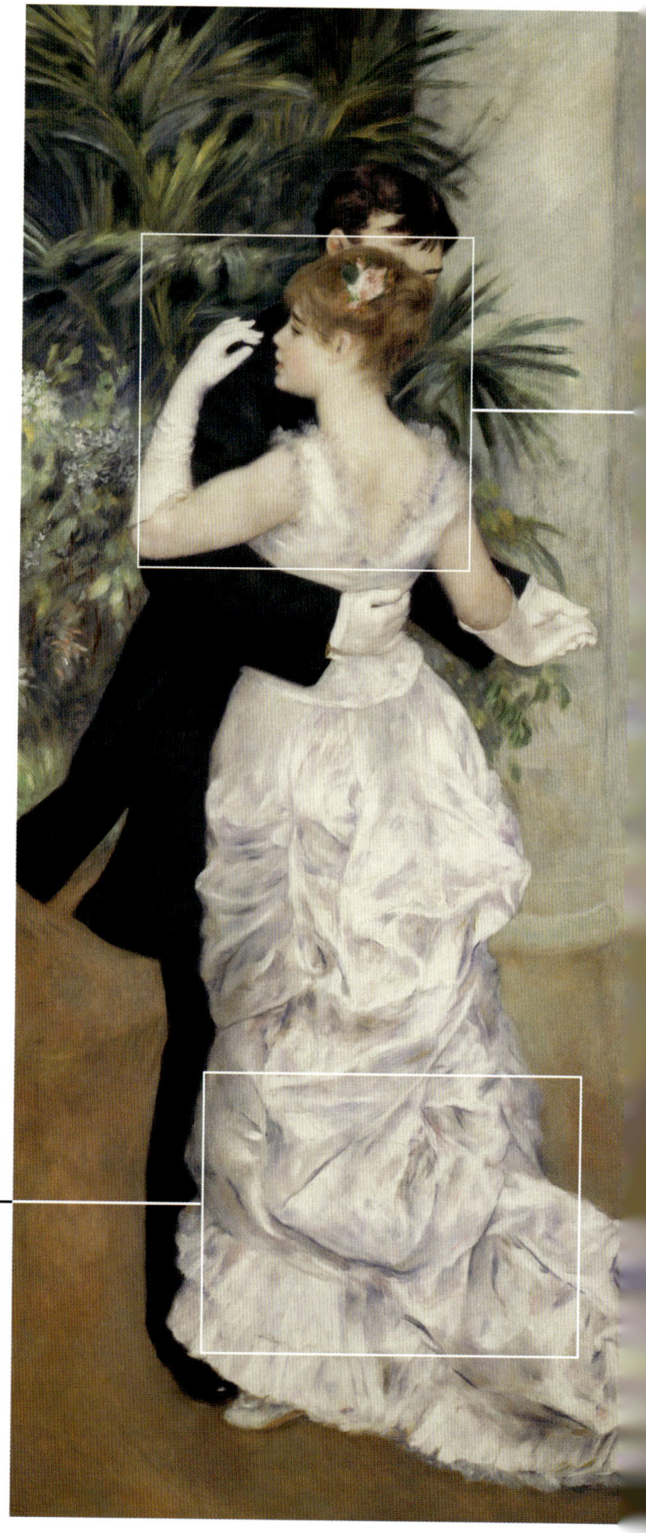

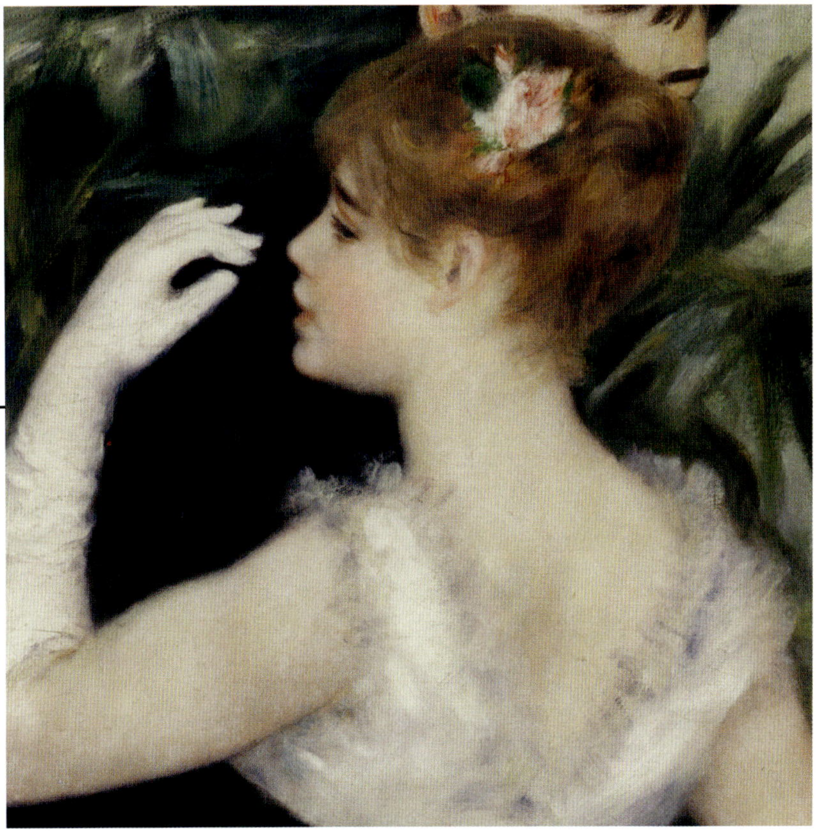

LEFT
DANCE IN THE TOWN, detail.
This painting has been executed with precise and delicate brush strokes to enhance the elegance of the subject. The careful brushwork on the hair and background foliage demonstrates Renoir's eye for detail, while the facial features are built up with wet-over-dry colors, mixed carefully on the palette before application.

Before the 1870s, Renoir included black, Sienna, and Umber in his palette, but, by the 1870s, he had rejected black and all earthy colors. Later, he occasionally used black for accents, but he never mixed it into colors because he believed it would deaden any resulting color. In the late 1870s and 1880s, Renoir added Ultramarine, Vert-de-gris, Yellow Ocher, and Naples Yellow to his palette. During his most intense Impressionist period, Renoir limited his palette to just two reds, two yellows, and two blues plus white. Later, he reintroduced greens. In his most restricted phase, Renoir confined his palette to only eight colors for each painting, although which eight colors these were varied, depending on the subject matter he was tackling.

Bright neutrals

Renoir's neutrals were never dull, and this was because he never mixed more than two colors together to create a neutral. Instead of blending those two colors, he juxtaposed or blurred and blended them together on the canvas. The two chosen colors always came from a close range on the color circle, never from opposite sides. In other parts of his paintings, Renoir used strokes of pure (diluted) pigment, such as Viridian, Cobalt Blue, and Cadmium Yellow.

As mentioned, to dilute his pigments, he used a mixture of linseed oil and turpentine in particular proportions because he liked the smooth texture achieved, although the high oil content made his paintings take longer to dry. By the 1880s, he used less oil, because he had become more interested in painting with precision and detail.

Renoir's careful application and handling of colors gave his paintings glowing and vivid radiance. Through a combination of mixed and unmixed colors laid next to each other, he injected a constant vitality and freshness into his work. He also applied translucent colors over opaque ones to give a juicy, jewel-bright finish.

HOW TO DO IT

YOUR PALETTE

To re-create this painting you will only need a limited palette, which should consist of just eight colors:

1 Ivory Black
2 Zinc White
3 French Ultramarine
4 Emerald Green
5 Yellow Ocher
6 Raw Sienna
7 Cobalt Blue
8 Scarlet Alizarin

Renoir applied Cobalt Blue straight from the tube, but blended the darker French Ultramarine with other hues to create a range of colored grays.

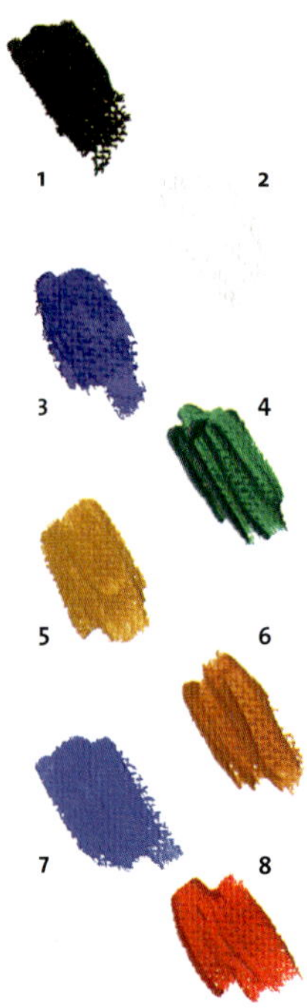

ALTHOUGH YOU'RE PAINTING with a limited palette for this picture, make sure you avoid blending too many of the colors. There is a range of complementary blues with a few peachy and brown tones for the skin and hair.

The main techniques

Try to use several colors in their pure state to create distinguishing accents. As you can see from this painting, by the early 1880s, Renoir was once again using black. He said, "Black is a very important color ... Nature abhors 'pure' colors ... we should use black but in a mixture as it is in Nature."

You should use feathery brush strokes to apply the warm blues and lavenders that predominate in this painting. It is these colors and strokes that give this picture a "soft-focus" charm. Keep the turpentine handy as you work, as well as plenty of rags or paper towels to smudge and thin the paint layers.

Instead of directly applying lights and darks to the picture, try to focus more on building up warm and cool hues to model form and allow the white background surface to glow through some thinner parts of the picture. Try to also vary your application between fine, transparent layers of paint to scumbled, opaque veils of color.

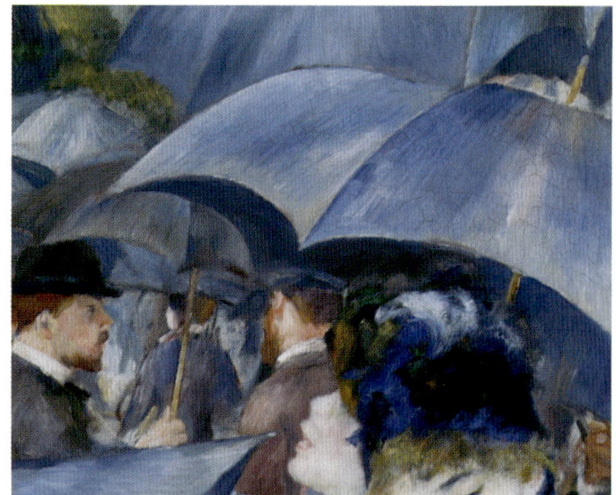

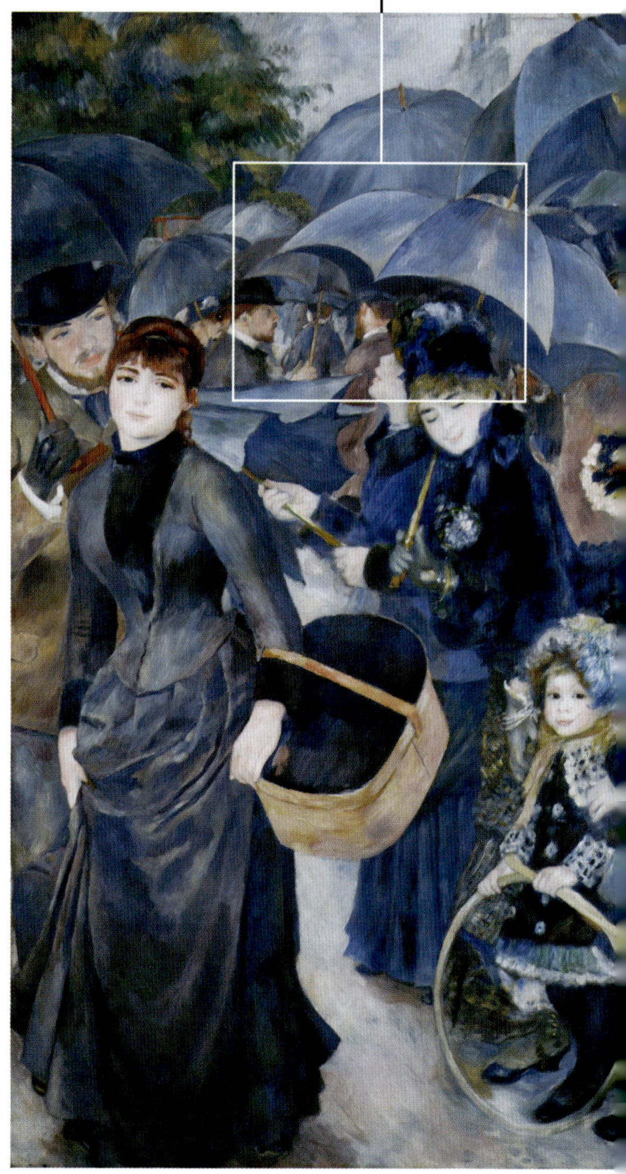

RIGHT
THE UMBRELLAS, 1881–86, oil on canvas, 70¾ x 45¼ inches (180 x 115 cm). *This painting shows the changes in Renoir's style that occurred from the early to mid-1880s. The girls on the right are in his Impressionist style, which he probably painted between 1881–82. Then Renoir began studying Ingres and Raphael; the woman on the right holding the basket shows his resulting preoccupation with line and form, and the style of her costume reveals that he painted this part of the picture in around 1885–86.*

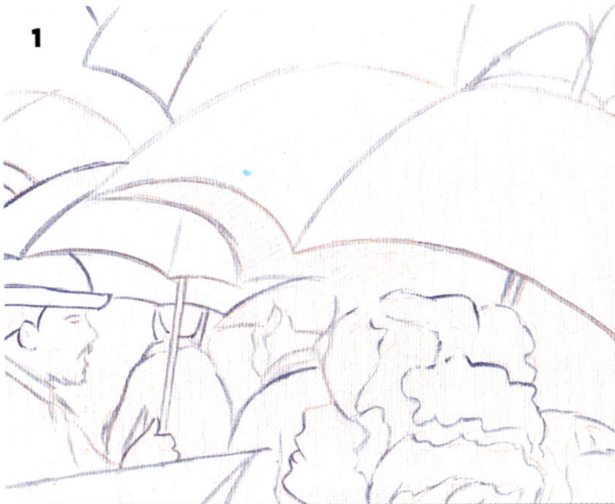

STEP 1 Use a fine-grained white primed canvas or board for this picture. Paint at least one layer of smooth Zinc White paint on your background surface. When this is dry, copy the outline of the painting onto your canvas. You may prefer to copy it upside down to make you more objective about what you are drawing—this should make you more accurate with proportions too.

Using a thin round brush, apply fluid, diluted Ultramarine paint smoothly under the umbrellas. You should work over this once the first layer is dry in order to re-create the look of deepest shadow.

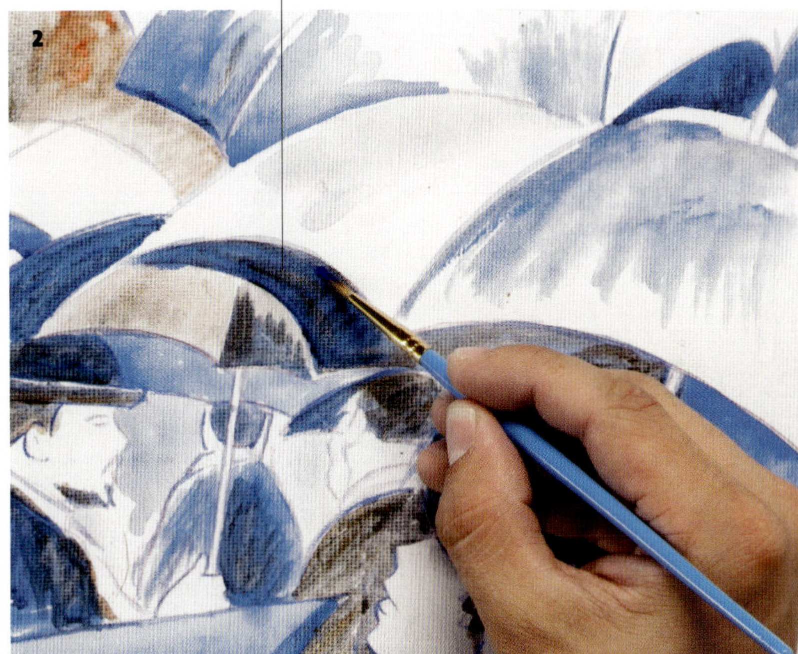

Mix Zinc White with Cobalt Blue for the lightest panels of the umbrellas, and blend this lighter color with unblended Cobalt Blue and with touches of French Ultramarine to create the ranges of shades necessary to show where the light catches the angles of the umbrellas.

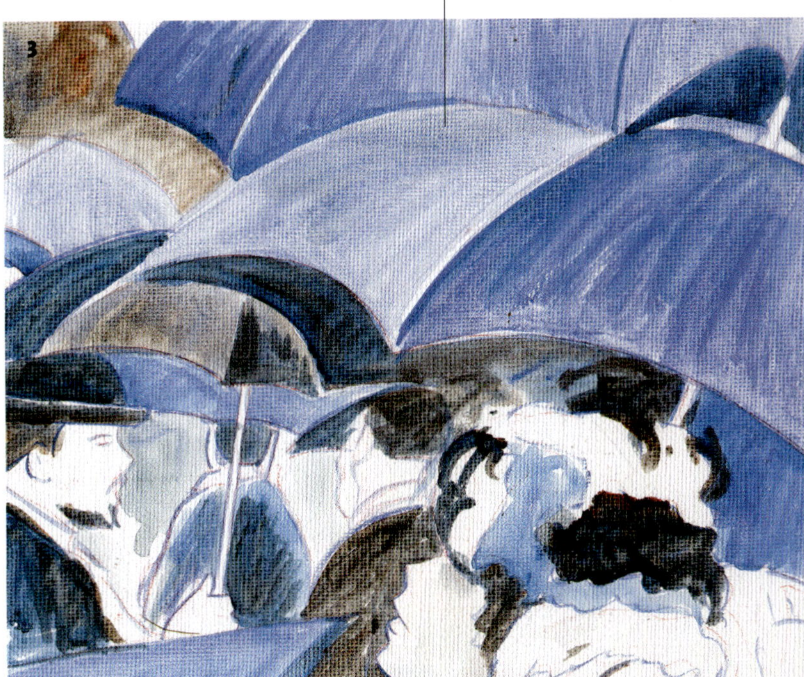

STEP 2 Dilute some French Ultramarine with turpentine and a little linseed oil. This will make the paint translucent and also give it an even finish when applied. Paint the color around the girl's hat, underneath the umbrellas, and on the distant man's hat. In small dabs, paint the two men's coats in French Ultramarine, Raw Sienna, and Yellow Ocher. Also use these colors on the men's hair and beards, in the top left-hand corner of the picture, and on the distant umbrella. Then add accents of Ivory Black on these darkest areas, including the flower on the girl's hat and the eyebrow on the cropped girl in the foreground. Use a thin round brush to apply these accents.

STEP 3 Using fairly unblended colors, paint directly onto the canvas wet-in-wet, still keeping the paints relatively thin and fluid. Apply Cobalt Blue onto the tops of the umbrellas, mixing this with French Ultramarine for the darkest areas. Make sure you leave fine lines of white primed canvas showing through.

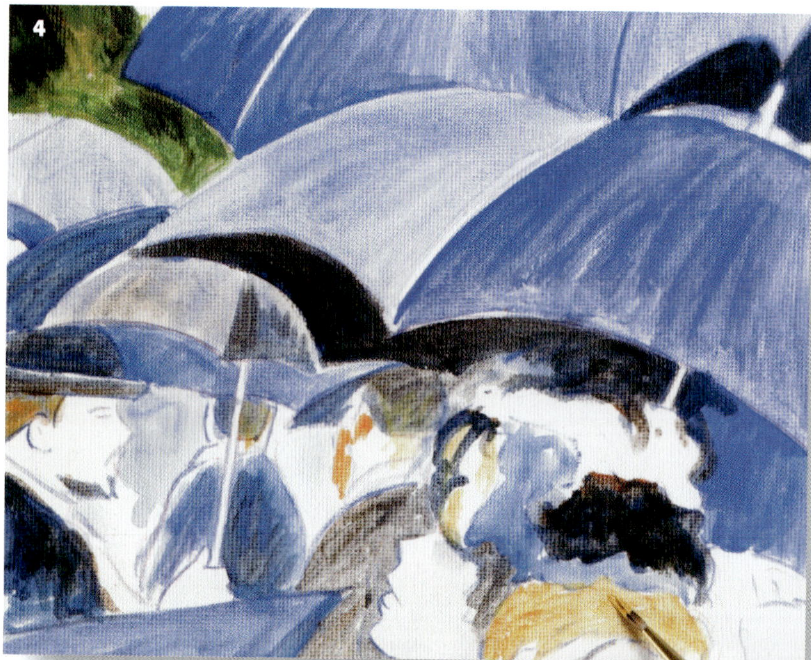

STEP 4 Continue blurring and blending the colors together on the canvas using small brush marks. Make the base of the girl's blonde hair out of Yellow Ocher with touches of Scarlet Alizarin. Mix this in the darker areas while the paint is still wet. Lightly and thinly paint the men's hair and beards in Yellow Ocher, Scarlet Alizarin and small amounts of Cobalt Blue and Zinc White.

STEP 5 Mix the flesh hues while the paint is still wet, using Zinc White, Raw Sienna, Yellow Ocher and a touch of Cobalt Blue. Add touches of Scarlet Alizarin mixed with Zinc White on the girl's lips (in profile) and add some Yellow Ocher to create some brighter tints on the men's faces. Darken the blonde woman's hair in the front with Cobalt Blue, Scarlet Alizarin and Yellow Ocher plus a little Zinc White.

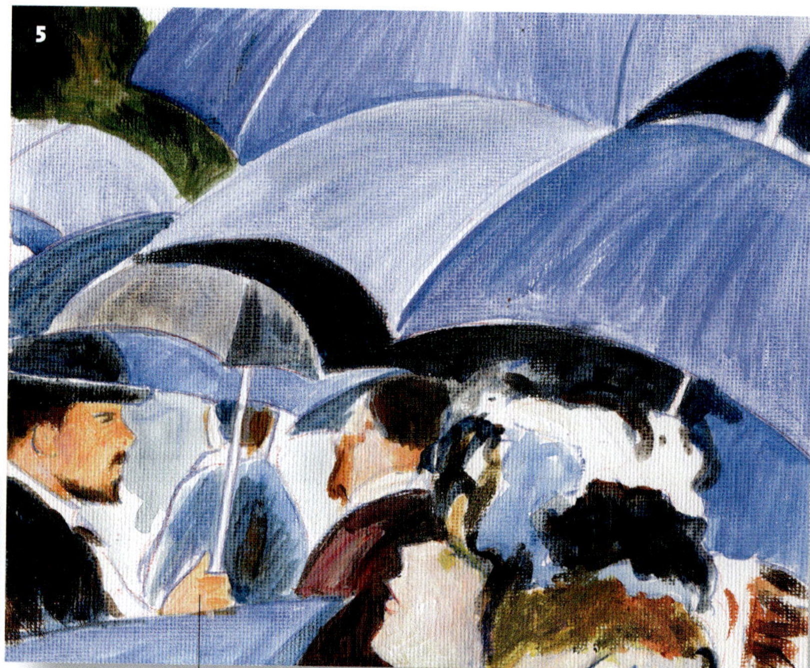

Make up some flesh tones using a blend of Zinc White, Raw Sienna, Yellow Ocher, and small amounts of Cobalt Blue. You should vary the amounts of each color in order to make the visible parts of flesh appear three-dimensional.

STEP 6 Using the tip of a small brush, paint two thin lines of Scarlet Alizarin for the umbrella handles. You may need to use masking tape to achieve the straightness required here. If so, first allow the paint from the previous steps to dry. Using feathered strokes, paint purplish shadows near the brown jackets, around the umbrellas, and on the hat near the black flower. Generally, try not to mix more than two colors together before applying them, but juxtapose or blur and blend colors next to each other on the canvas instead of on the palette.

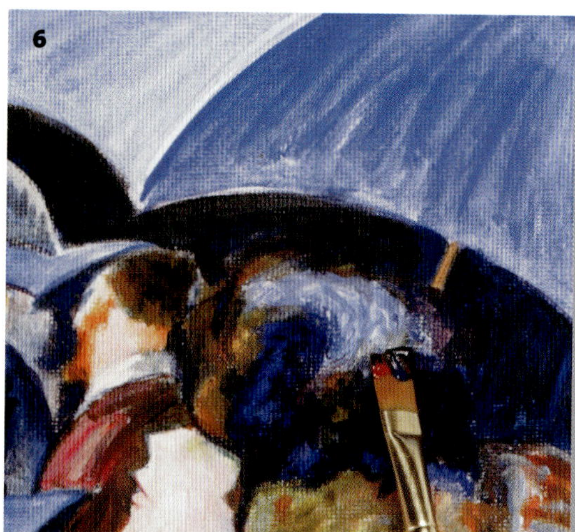

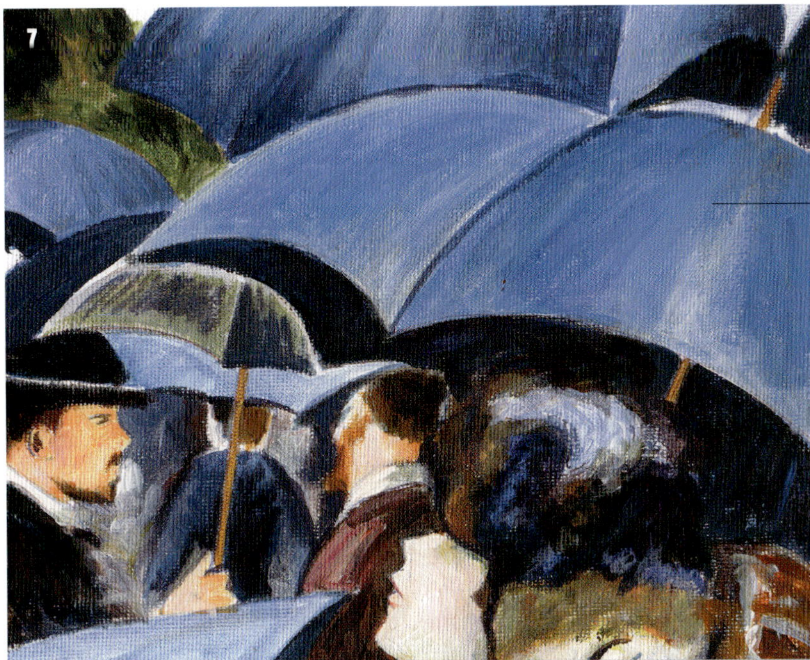

STEP 7 While the paint is still wet, blur and blend in deep violet (made from Cobalt Blue and Scarlet Alizarin) or French Ultramarine to make the shadows stronger and the lighter tops of the umbrellas stand out. Add small touches of Scarlet Alizarin where the blue looks too bright.

Working on the umbrellas once more, "firm up" any tones and deepen the colors with smooth, relatively thin paint, bearing in mind the direction of light and adding Zinc White where necessary.

STEP 8 To finish, add touches of Zinc White as a highlight and mix this in with color where necessary—such as on the umbrellas as the light catches them. Before adding these bright accents, squint your eyes at the painting to see where they are needed. Use small, vigorous brushwork and contrasting tones as you apply them.

The light is not strong in this picture because of the rain, but it is a cool light and comes from above. With this in mind, go over any details, painting in the darkest tones away from the light with a fine brush and smooth paint.

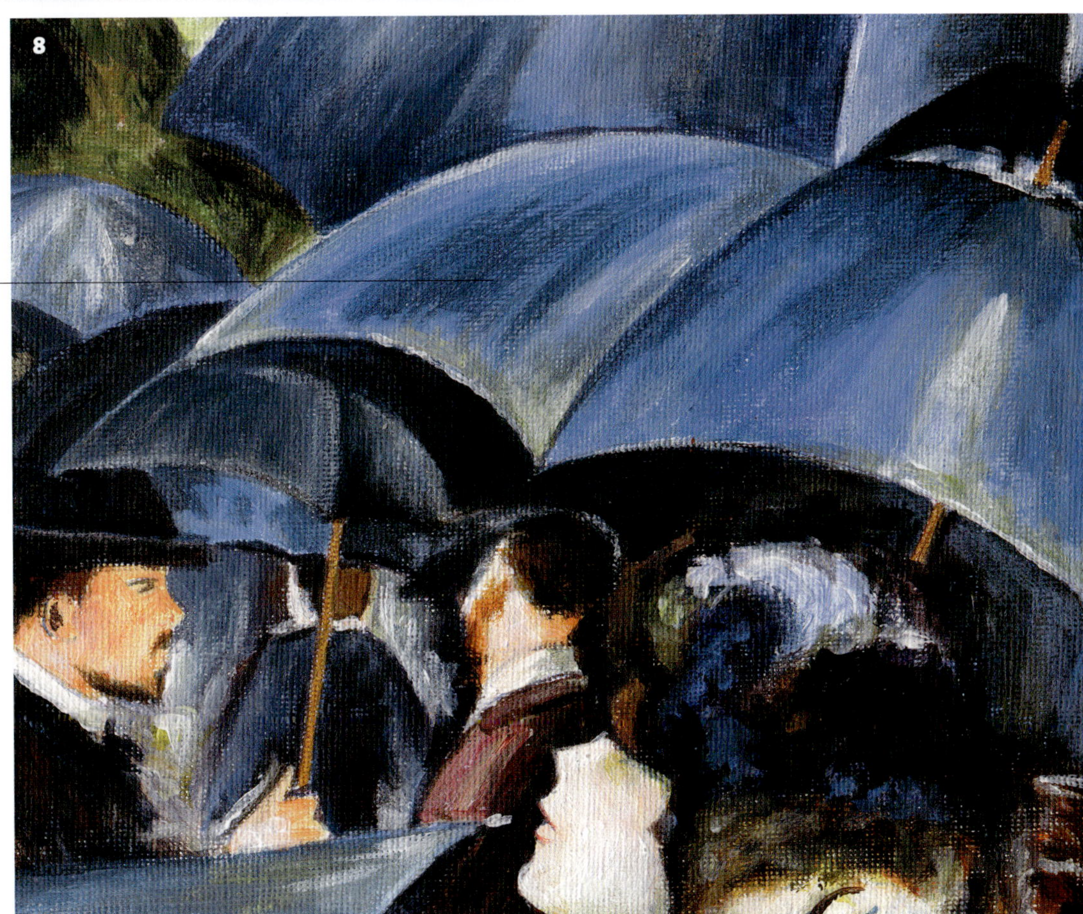

Chapter eight

CASSATT

It was unconventional for women of middle-class origins to have a profession at the time that Mary Cassatt become an artist. However, Cassatt was determined, and, after studying, she became a regular exhibitor with the Impressionists. She is best known for her intimate paintings of mothers and children.

MARY CASSATT (1844–1926) came from a wealthy family in Pittsburgh, Pennsylvania. She was spirited and independent-minded, and, although her family opposed, she studied to be an artist in Pennsylvania for four years. She then moved to Europe where a female artist was more readily accepted.

Cassatt traveled through Spain, Italy, Belgium, and Holland, studying and copying works by Old Masters. By 1873, she had settled in France and met Degas in 1877. He gave her advice and also invited her to exhibit with the Impressionists. She and Degas had a lot in common, and they became extremely good friends. Both studied and admired the disciplines of the Old Masters, and both also had a deliberate approach to design, line, and color.

Unlike the male Impressionists, Cassatt's range of subject matter was limited by social conventions. Women were not allowed to be alone in a room with a man unless he was a relative. Whereas the men worked with all kinds of models and moved freely to paint

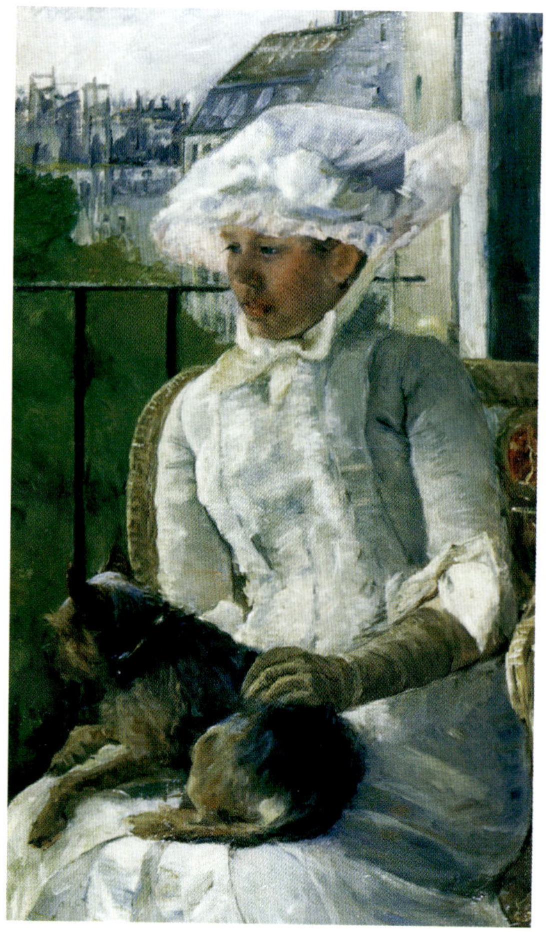

RIGHT
SUSAN ON A BALCONY HOLDING A DOG, 1883, oil on canvas, 39¾ x 25½ inches (101 x 65 cm).
This is one of the only paintings by Cassatt that includes urban views. The figure is pushed close to the viewer, framed by the middle tones of various greens, with the violet-hued town fading into the distance. Cassatt frequently dressed her models in white; here, it emphasizes the soft daylight on the girl's face as it filters through her hat. The vertical elements of the doorway, balcony railings, and the distant buildings contrast with the curves of the girl's hat and shoulders, the dog, and the back of the chair.

RIGHT
LYDIA IN A LOGE, WEARING A PEARL NECKLACE, 1879, oil on canvas, 31½ x 22¾ inches (80 x 58 cm). *Cassatt exhibited this painting of her sister in a "loge," or opera box, at the fourth Impressionist exhibition in April 1879. This is an evening performance, judging by the low-cut dress and pearls that Lydia is wearing. The rich harmonies of reds and golds show similarities to some of Renoir's works, while Degas possibly inspired the subject matter. The mirror behind Lydia extends the space and reveals other members of the audience to the viewer. The vigorous handling of the paint and firm modeling of the forms is derived from Cassatt's study of the works of the painter Manet.*

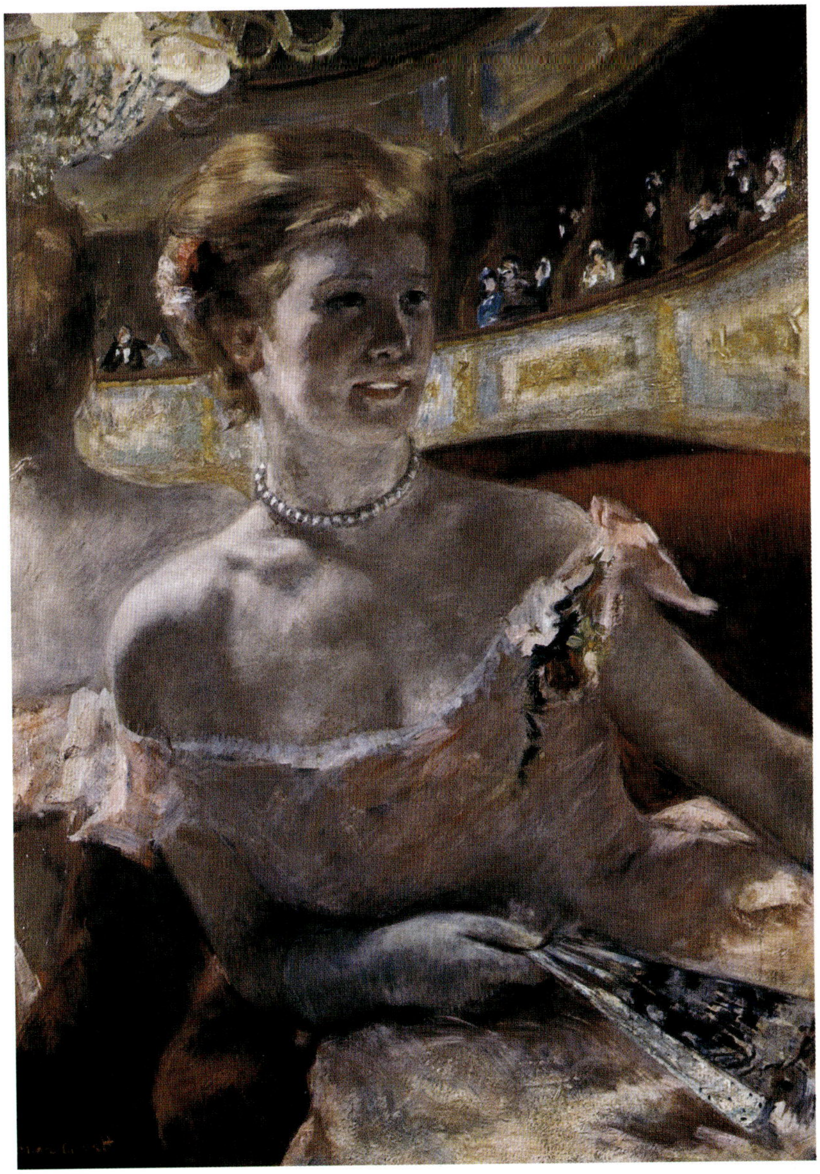

wherever they liked, Cassatt's chief subjects were relatives and their children in their domestic interiors, busying themselves at "feminine" activities. The difference between what she and her male contemporaries were allowed to paint made her acutely aware of the oppression of women, and she actively supported the women's suffrage movement back in her home country.

Linear approach

Cassatt's earliest techniques were somber with high contrasts, involving strong darks and dazzling lights and a few middle tones, reminiscent of Edouard Manet and Spanish paintings. As her style developed, she gradually abandoned the darker palette in favor of brighter colors, but, unlike Monet, Sisley, and Pissarro, she never stopped using black. Her most Impressionistic work was sketch-like and built up with broad strokes of thick or thinned paint, sometimes with colors mixed on the canvas. She utilized many of the techniques that she admired in Japanese art, such as a linear approach and asymmetrical compositions. As well as painting in oils, she worked with prints and pastels, eventually producing more of the latter.

Between 1879 and 1882, Cassatt showed her work at the annual Impressionist exhibitions and also exhibited in New York. After that, she focused almost exclusively on depictions of mothers and children, creating intimate images and revealing her acute awareness of the psychological aspects of these relationships. Her most well-known works were built up with fluid, rapid, and visible strokes of relatively unmixed color, which helped to retain the charm and freshness of the subject. Whatever she painted, her subjects appeared animated and often preoccupied with their own activities.

SKETCH-LIKE WORK

CENTER
THE SWIM, OR TWO MOTHERS AND THEIR CHILDREN ON A BOAT, 1910, oil on canvas, 39 x 50¾ inches (99 x 129 cm).
Here, Cassatt has set the viewer at an unusual angle in order to witness the exchange of glances between the women and their children at close hand. The painting gives the impression of a fleeting peaceful moment and the sketch-like quality adds to the immediacy. In her bold use of color, there is little attempt at naturalism. The pale tones of the figures' skin contrast with the pinkish-purple and yellow dresses and the green and blue water.

CASSATT'S MEETING WITH Degas was a turning point in her career. He played a crucial role in her artistic development, and, after meeting him, she decided never again to submit anything to an exhibition with a jury. Her paintings changed with this decision and seem almost unfinished by comparison to earlier works. She often began a painting with diluted color to position the main elements of the picture—including where the darkest tones would go. Her loose approach is perhaps a response to the restrictive life she was forced to lead as a female artist (Berthe Morisot's works have a similar sketch-like quality to them).

Cassatt's method of applying paint was to apply local color with thinned paint in loose, free strokes, sometimes premixing these on the palette and at other times mixing them directly on the canvas while the paint was still wet. She disliked the glossy surface produced by oil paints, which was why she thinned them or used pastels. She especially liked the idea of being able to rework pastels rapidly. Whatever material she used, the overriding

BELOW
THE SWIM, OR TWO MOTHERS AND THEIR CHILDREN ON A BOAT, detail.
The little girl is caught in a restful pose, with darkish tones added in broken brush strokes and contrasting hues. Cassatt's images of people have a unique charm. The atmosphere and impression of a transient moment in time comes across as strongly as any more precise painting.

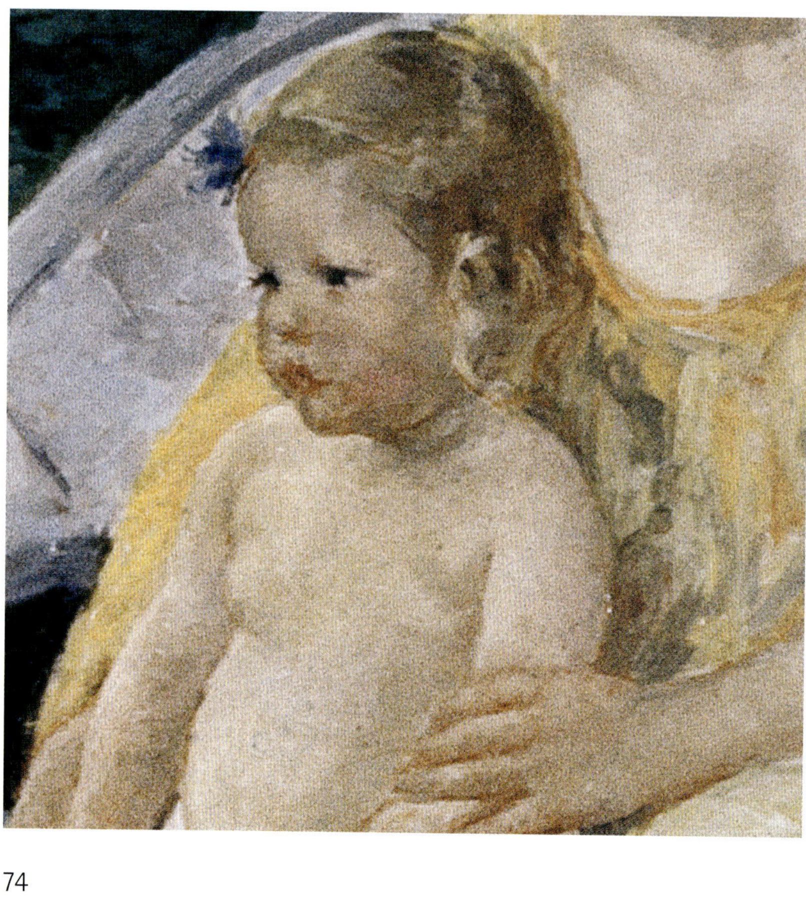

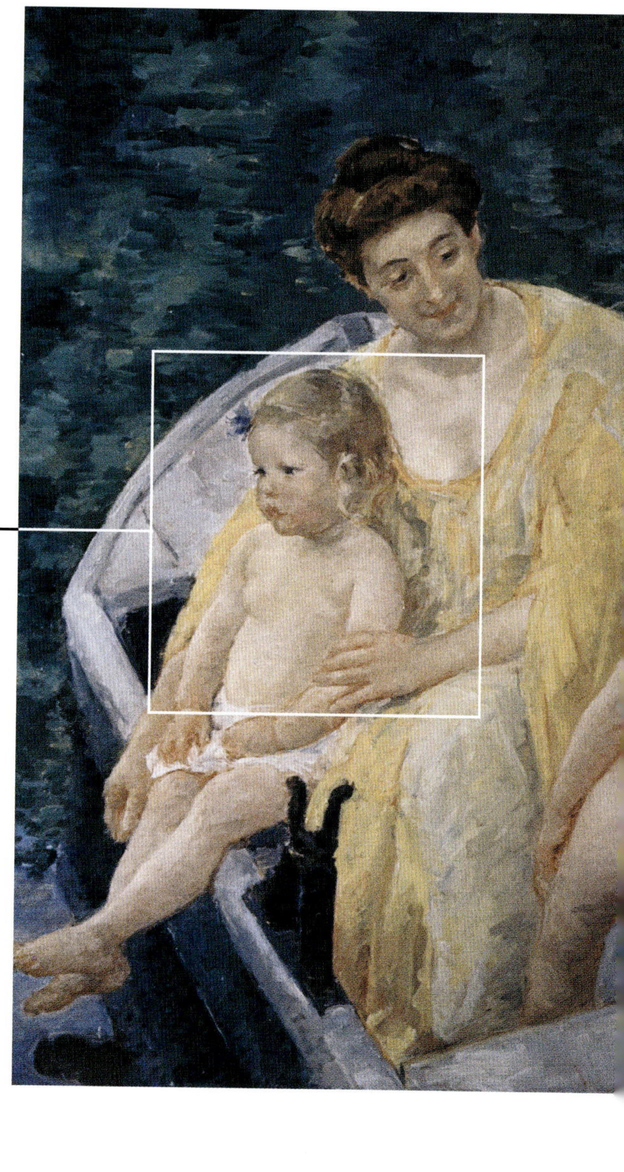

feature of her work was her lightness of touch and skillful rendering of people and facial expressions. To create these portraits of people, she used subtle tones and a range of delicate marks that were hatched, dragged, blurred, smudged, and blended across the canvas.

Cassatt often used a finely grained canvas and preferred neutral background surfaces, such as oatmeal or beige. Parts of these canvases were frequently left to show through the paintings. She achieved her "unfinished" look by using dry and fluid lines laid rapidly on the main aspects of the subject, while the background was often loosely summarized by color dragged hastily across the surface.

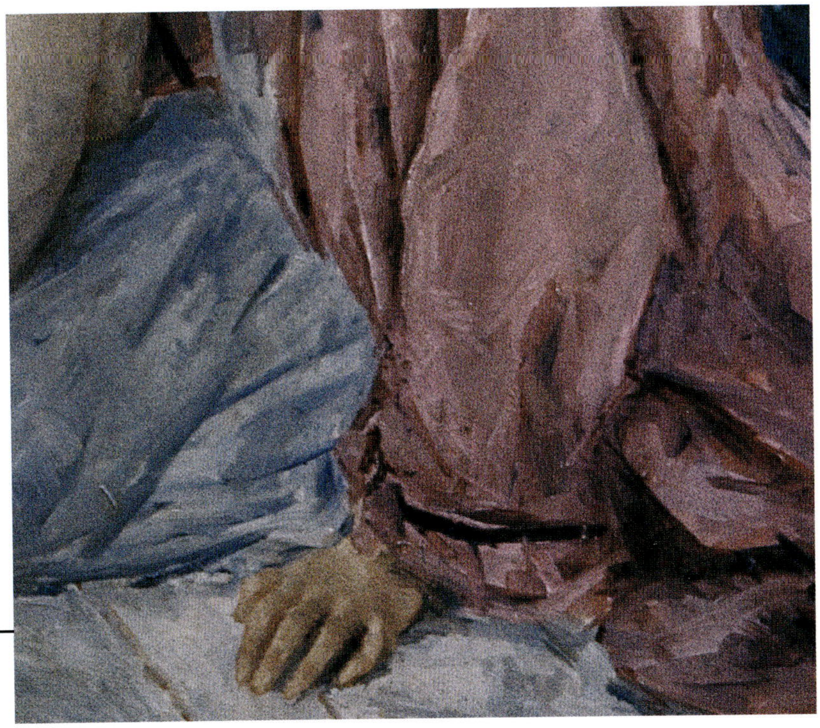

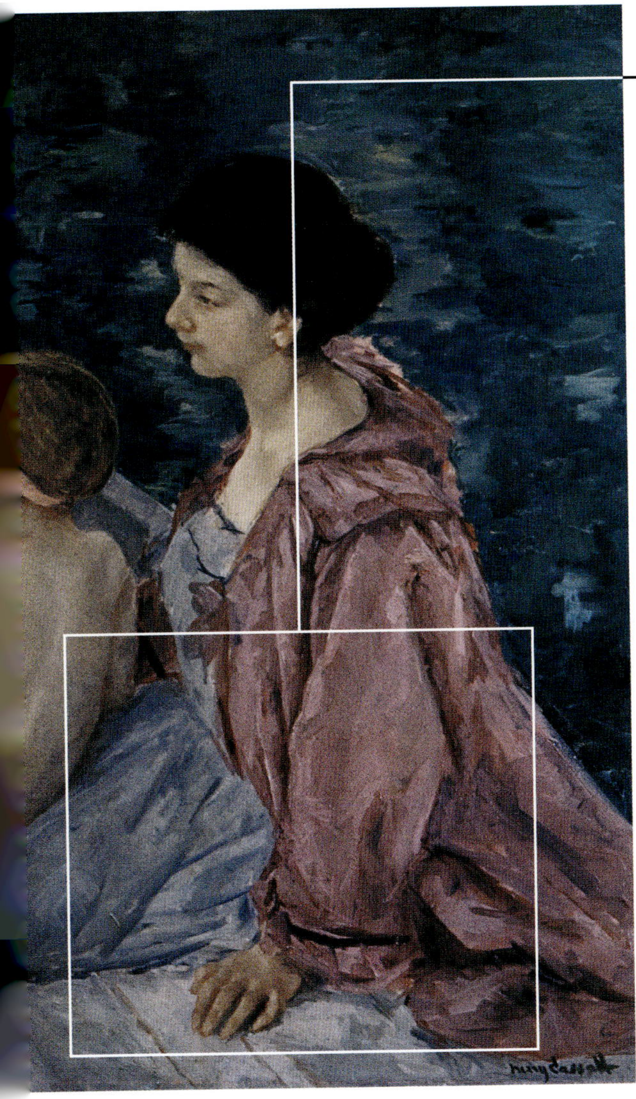

ABOVE
THE SWIM, OR TWO MOTHERS AND THEIR CHILDREN ON A BOAT, detail.
The way in which Cassatt has painted the fabrics with flat, loose applications of color looks haphazard on close inspection, but captures the essence of the clothing from viewing distance.

Cassatt's brushwork is broad and decisive and her paint thickness varied considerably from painting to painting. She used both wet-in-wet and wet-over-dry and sometimes even dry brush strokes over wet paint, which pushed around the paint that was underneath. This approach softened any crisp technique that she might have started with and also gave the desired unfinished look.

Negative space

Cassatt's awareness of negative space was apparent in many of her paintings. These were utilized effectively, just as all the other seemingly unplanned elements were. Although she was striving for a feeling of spontaneity in her painting, there was nothing spontaneous about how she created them. She shared Degas' opinion that "it is essential to do the same subject over again, 10 times, 100 times. Nothing in art must be left to chance, not even movement."

HOW TO DO IT

YOUR PALETTE

Your basic palette should be:

1 French Ultramarine
2 Burnt Sienna
3 Warm Gray
4 White
5 Rose Madder
6 Vermilion Hue
7 Yellow Ocher
8 Sap Green
9 Raw Umber
10 Cadmium Yellow Hue
11 Crimson Lake

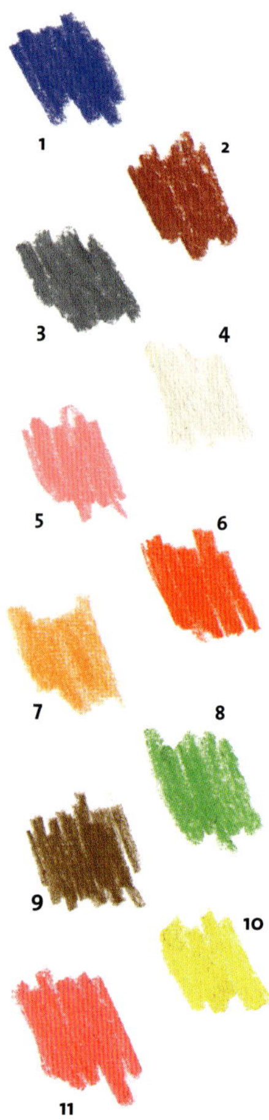

Although the sketch-like, loose approach looks as if it is spontaneous and free, Cassatt's pictures were carefully planned. She developed a discerning eye when viewing relationships between people, and this detail shows how her seemingly capricious application was in fact deliberate. Be aware of the general tones and tensions that you are aiming for in the picture, then begin with a light outline.

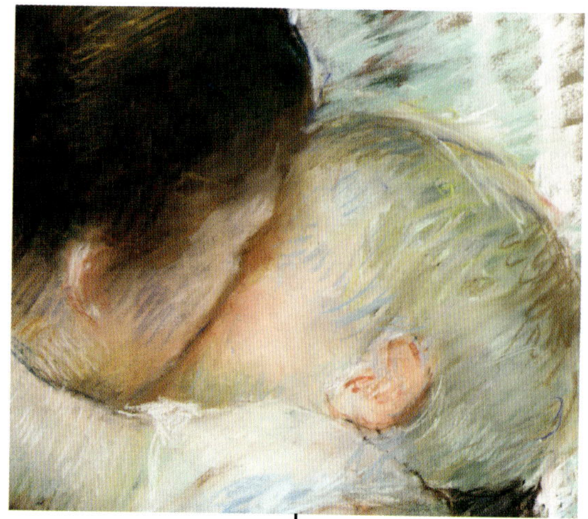

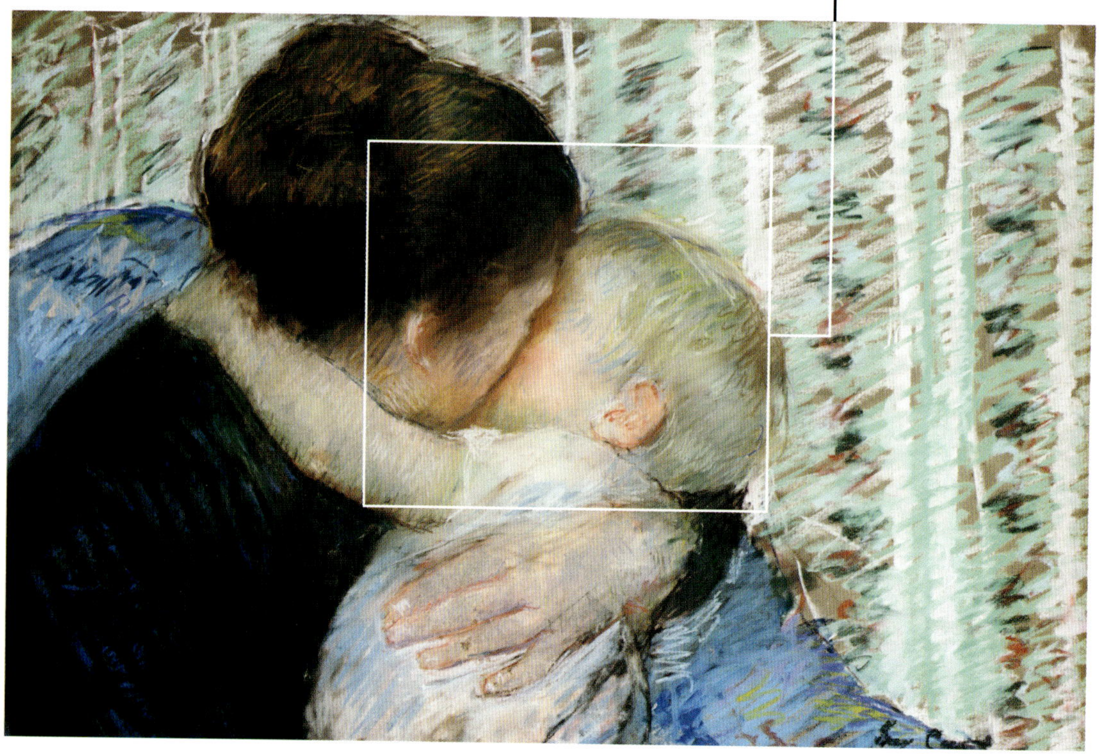

The main techniques

Pastels have an immediate effect and vigorous handling will give the best results. Some areas should be layered with successive reworkings, while others should be lightly handled in one layer. Try not to rub or smudge too often, so that you allow the textural marks to show through. If you are not happy with a color or area, simply modify the colors and tones with further layers over the first one.

ABOVE
A GOODNIGHT HUG, 1880, pastel on paper, 16½ x 24 inches (42 x 61 cm).
Both faces here are obscured—the picture is created by our recognition of the gesture's emotional intensity. Short, sketch-like strokes of pastel define the body of the mother and her child, while the wallpaper in the background is rendered with almost scribbled hatching. Cassatt loosely layered the colors, which is a technique reminiscent of Degas' pastels, building up delicate webs of colors and leaving some showing through from beneath each other.

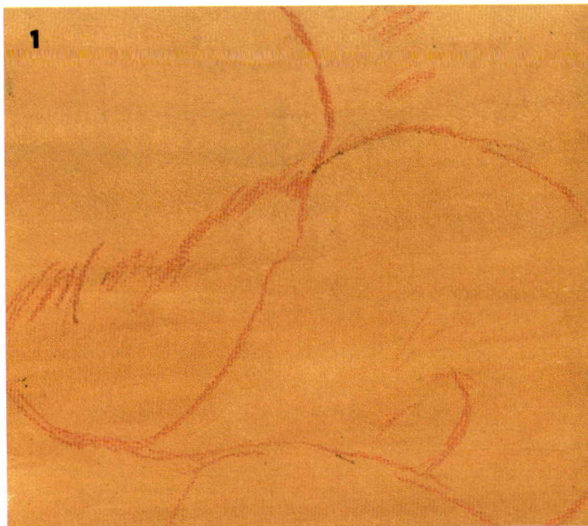

STEP 1 Use a brown- or tan-tinted paper or board. If you only have a white or cream surface to work on, give it a light wash of brown gouache first. Cassatt's picture was created with a combination of soft and hard pastels, but use whatever suits you. Lightly draw the outlines of the figures in dark red or a neutral-colored pastel, carefully measuring the proportions as you do so.

Use loose, rapid strokes to describe the skin of the mother and child, working a blend of White, Rose Madder, and Yellow Ocher into the shapes of their faces, ears, and the child's arm.

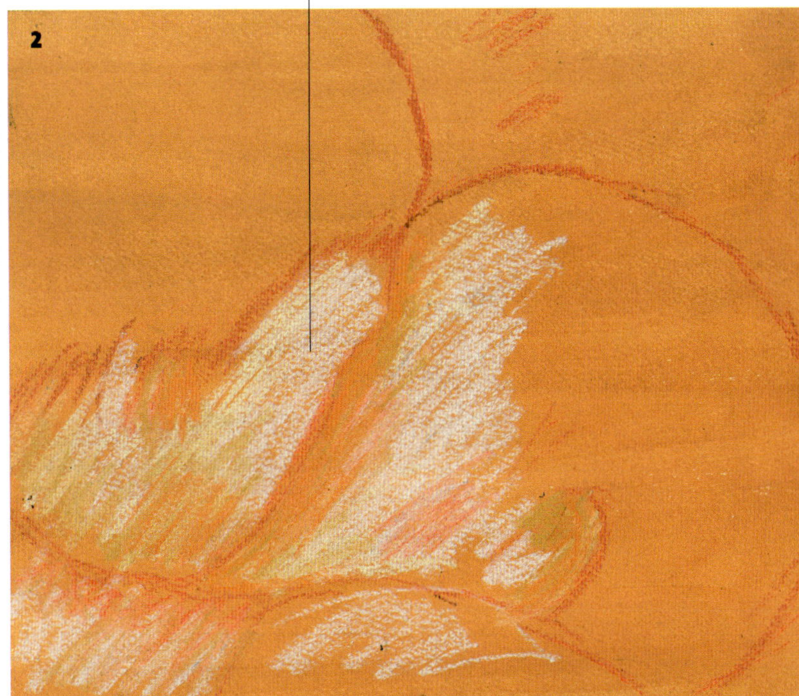

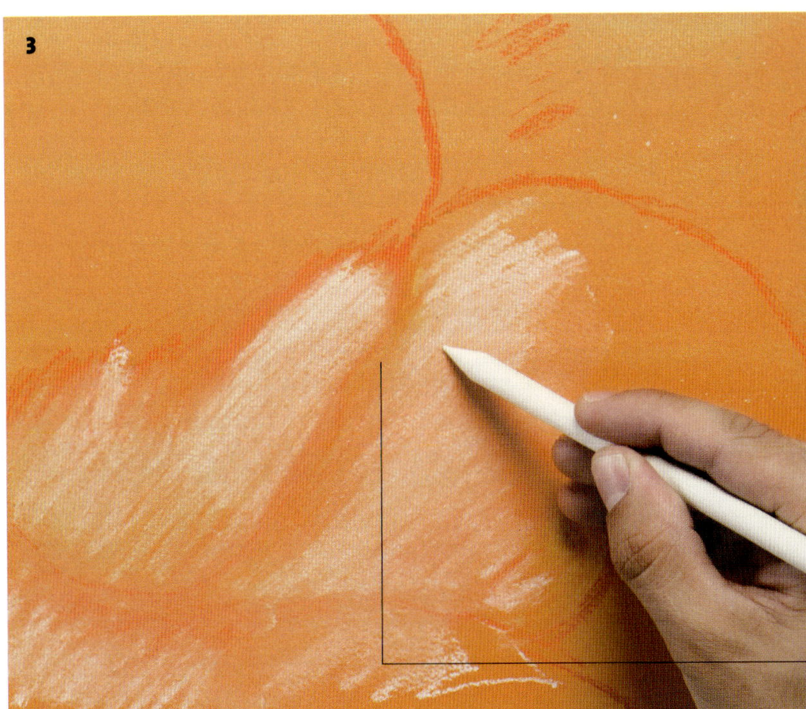

STEP 2 Begin to establish color foundations. Although the whole treatment of this image should be sketch-like, the background should be even looser than the faces. Start by adding some directional strokes in White, Rose Madder, Cadmium Yellow Hue, Yellow Ocher, and Crimson Lake for the skin of both mother and child. Layer these quickly into the general shapes of the ears, foreheads, and cheeks, and add some color to the child's arm.

STEP 3 Cassatt's choice of pinks and blues is perfect for the mother and baby image she builds up. With small, directional marks, continue using blues and pinks on the faces using short, diagonal strokes. Then use your finger or a torchon to blur and blend the tones together.

If you're not happy with a color or area, simply modify the colors and tones with further layers or hatchings over the first colors. Use a torchon to blend and merge the marks you have made with the pastels.

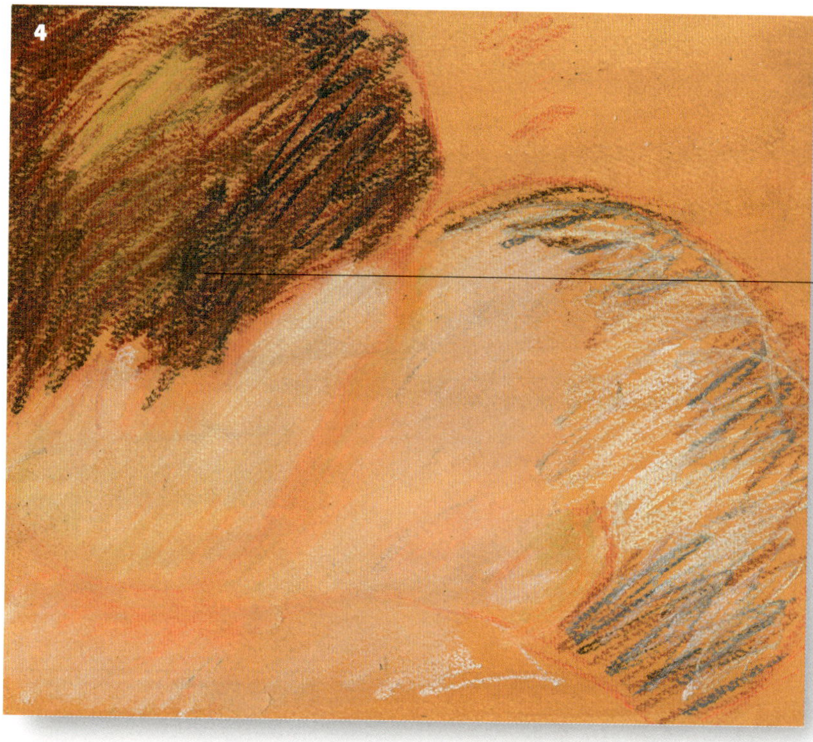

STEP 4 Establish the darker hair tones now, working from dark to light. Build up the mother's hair with Raw Umber, Burnt Sienna, and French Ultramarine. Once you've drawn in the blues and browns of the child's hair, add some cooler, lighter highlights with White and Warm Gray pastels.

Build up layers for the darkest areas of hair out of Raw Umber. Continue to apply this relatively quickly and vigorously.

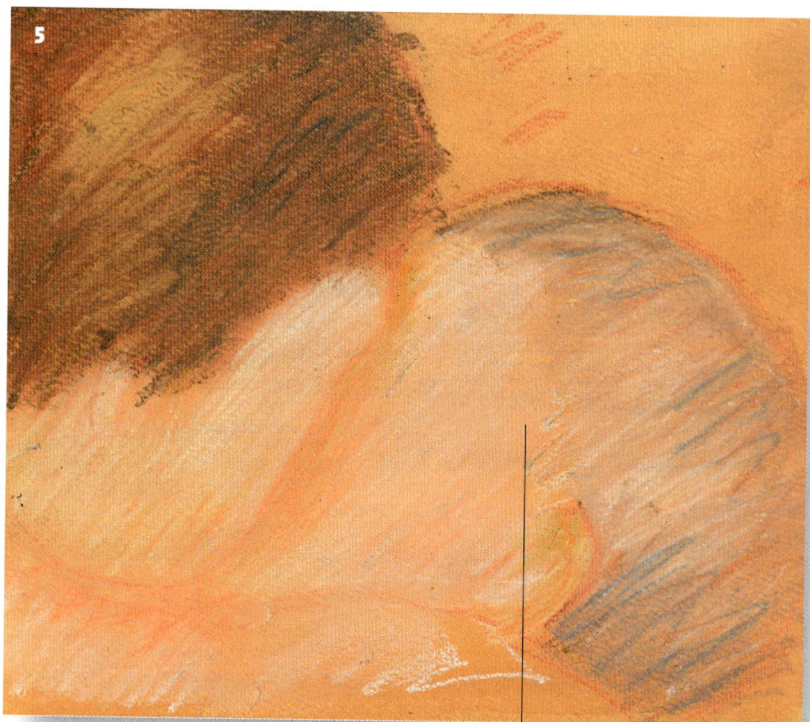

Although you are working vigorously, the baby's head must seem soft and smooth, so apply color with rapid strokes, then blend, then use rapid strokes again.

STEP 5 While you should still be generally building up and layering the tones, textures, and colors at this point, it is important not to be too precise but to keep things loose. Use the side of the Vermilion Hue pastel to add color to the baby's face. The grain of the paper or board will be evident. Now start to smooth and blend the colors with the torchon or your finger.

STEP 6 Work the background wallpaper with loose strokes of White, Sap Green, Crimson Lake, and French Ultramarine. This must be rendered very loosely in order to make the background appear to recede. This will also help the foreground appear to come forward. Blend the wallpaper with a torchon or your finger.

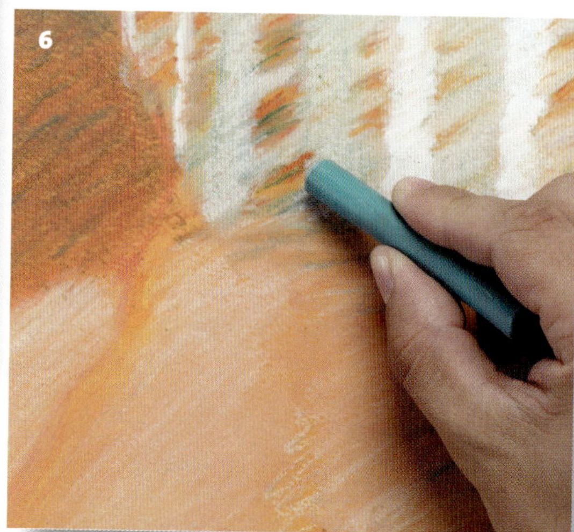

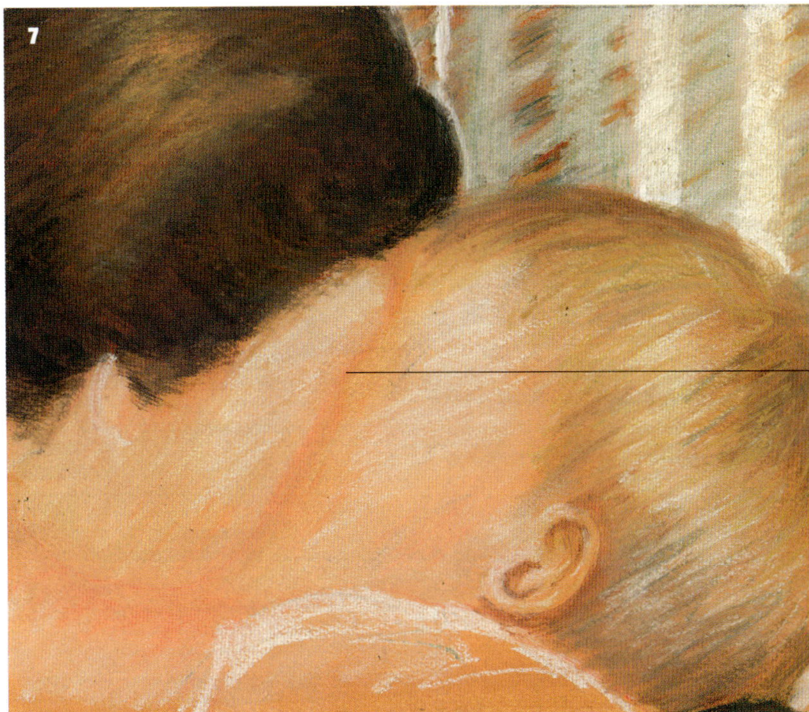

STEP 7 Clarify the child's arm, clothing, and face using mainly White directional strokes. Define the details in the hair, the ears, and the shadow between the two faces. Use French Ultramarine, Burnt Sienna, and Raw Umber for the darkest parts.

Begin to show the contours of the faces to differentiate them. Use broken lines of Warm Gray, layered with Raw Umber, ensuring that the hard line is on the mother's side and the softer shadow is on the child's face.

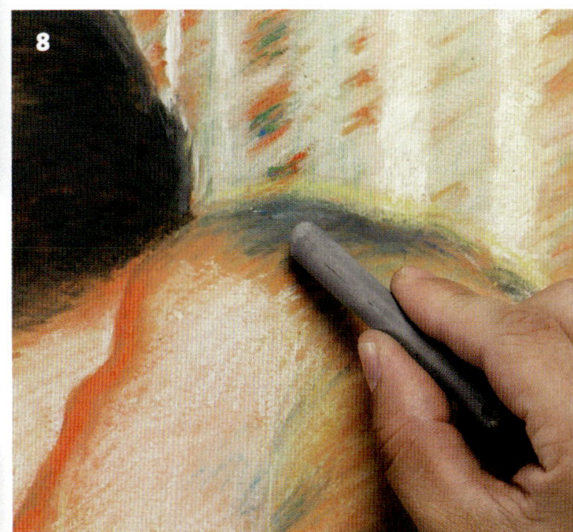

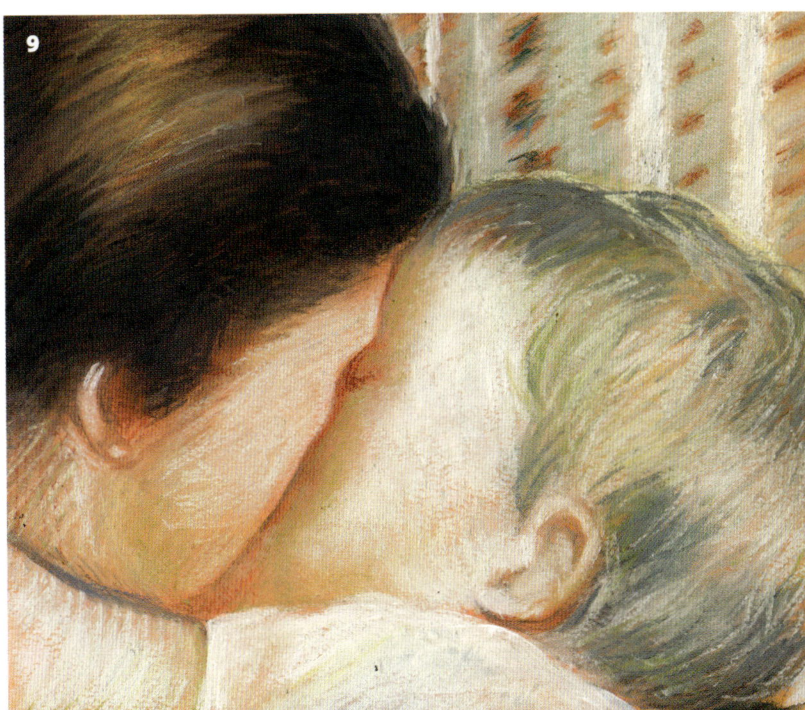

STEP 8 Darken the hair tones on the mother's hair with Burnt Sienna, and use French Ultramarine and Raw Umber on the child's hair. Use hatched lines over the first applications of pastel to increase the density of both value and color. Keep the directional aspect of the hatching and crosshatching visible.

STEP 9 Scumble White highlights onto the clothes, faces, child's arm, and hair (particularly the child's). (To scumble pastels, apply them with the side of the stick and drag the color lightly over the under layers, never completely covering them.) Blend and layer with hatched strokes to add further details where necessary. For example, ensure that the tones on the faces are completely blended and that there are obvious individual strokes within the hair. To complete the picture, indicate the child's eye with Raw Sienna.

CREATING SOFT TONES

As Cassatt's technique matured, she stopped using the brilliant colors of her earlier years and began using white and grays for the soft tones that were necessary for her paintings of mothers and children. This was a recurring subject for her and the one that brought her fame. At a time when men's paintings of women and children focused principally on their physical beauty, she captured the beauty that shines from within. At first she painted pictures of children, using her nephews and nieces as models. The subject had intrigued her after she had studied Antonio Allegri da Correggio's (1489–1534) paintings of the Madonna and Jesus in Italy. When the theme experienced a surge of popularity in the United States she decided to explore it further.

Working with a variety of materials and techniques—pastels, oil, and etching—Cassatt

RIGHT
REINE LEFEBVRE HOLDING A BABY, 1902, oil on canvas, 27 x 22½ inches (69 x 57 cm).
This tightly knit unit of mother and child dominating a flat, enclosed space was characteristic of Cassatt's work throughout the 1880s, 1890s, and early 1900s. The interlocked figures create a flowing, curving rhythm of line and form and the subtle color scheme adds to this rhythm. She limited her palette here mainly to shades of Raw Sienna, Burnt Sienna, and flashes of red-orange.

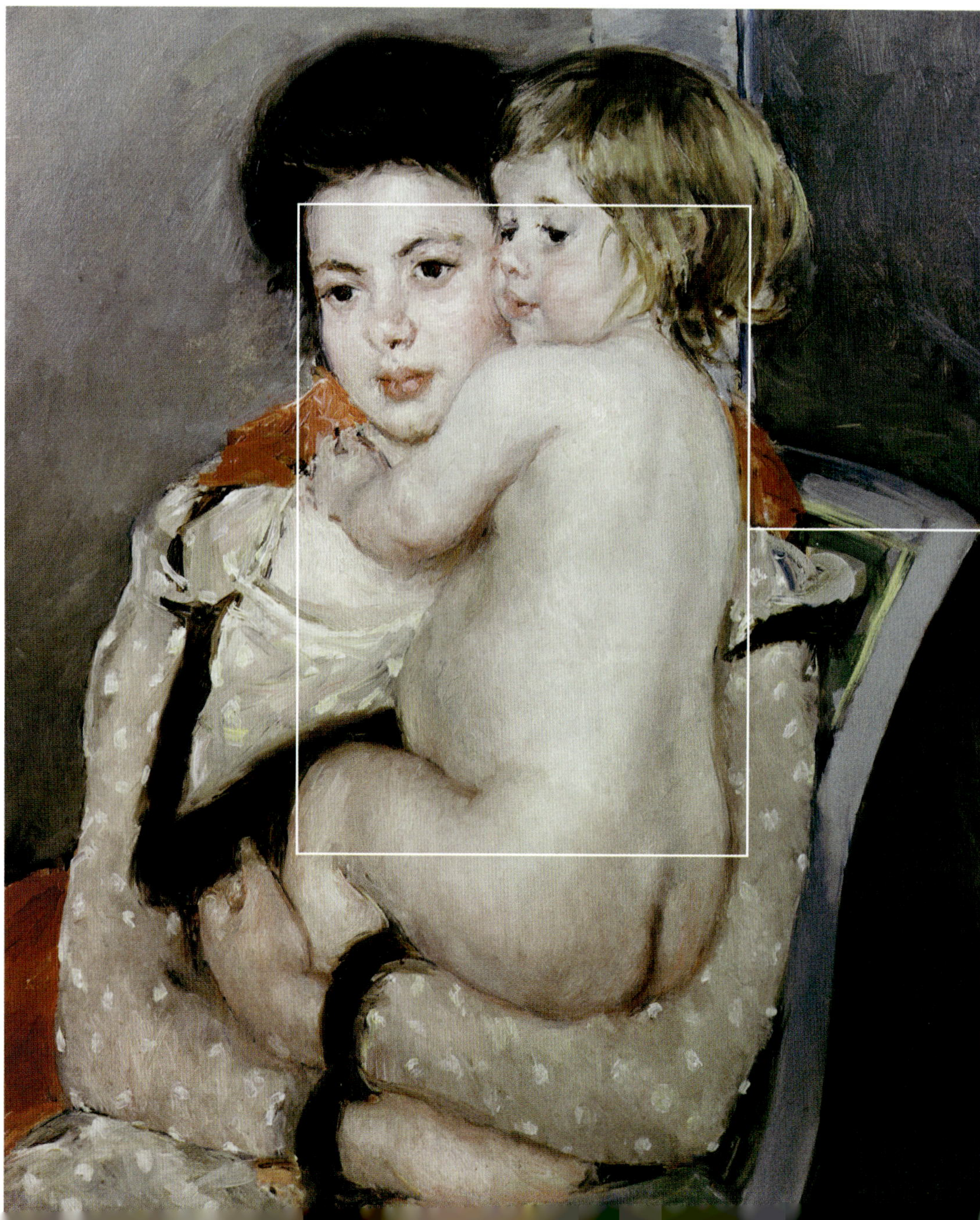

BELOW
REINE LEFEBVRE HOLDING A BABY, detail.
Cassatt created soft, almost touchable tones with her gentle handling of the brush and knowledge of her subject. Curves pervade every image—each one part of an intricate pattern used to emphasize intimacy within the composition.

tried several compositions with each mother and child that modeled for her, although none of the resulting pictures were repetitive. Her paintings of mothers and children always have a secure, relaxed feel, and the intimate bond shown between them is instantly recognizable. They touch each other, sitting closely, often with the mother holding the child gently.

These paintings were an instant success when they were first exhibited at the Durand-Ruel Gallery in Paris. Even the critics loved them, although one annoyed Cassatt by alluding to the fact that she was bound to produce sensitive pictures of this particular subject since she was a woman. Nevertheless, none of the paintings unduly flatter her sitters; they are simply treated, as all her subjects were. Her works all give the impression of being informal, passing moments. The mothers and children never seem posed and, while the scenes are always warm and affectionate, they are never overly sentimental.

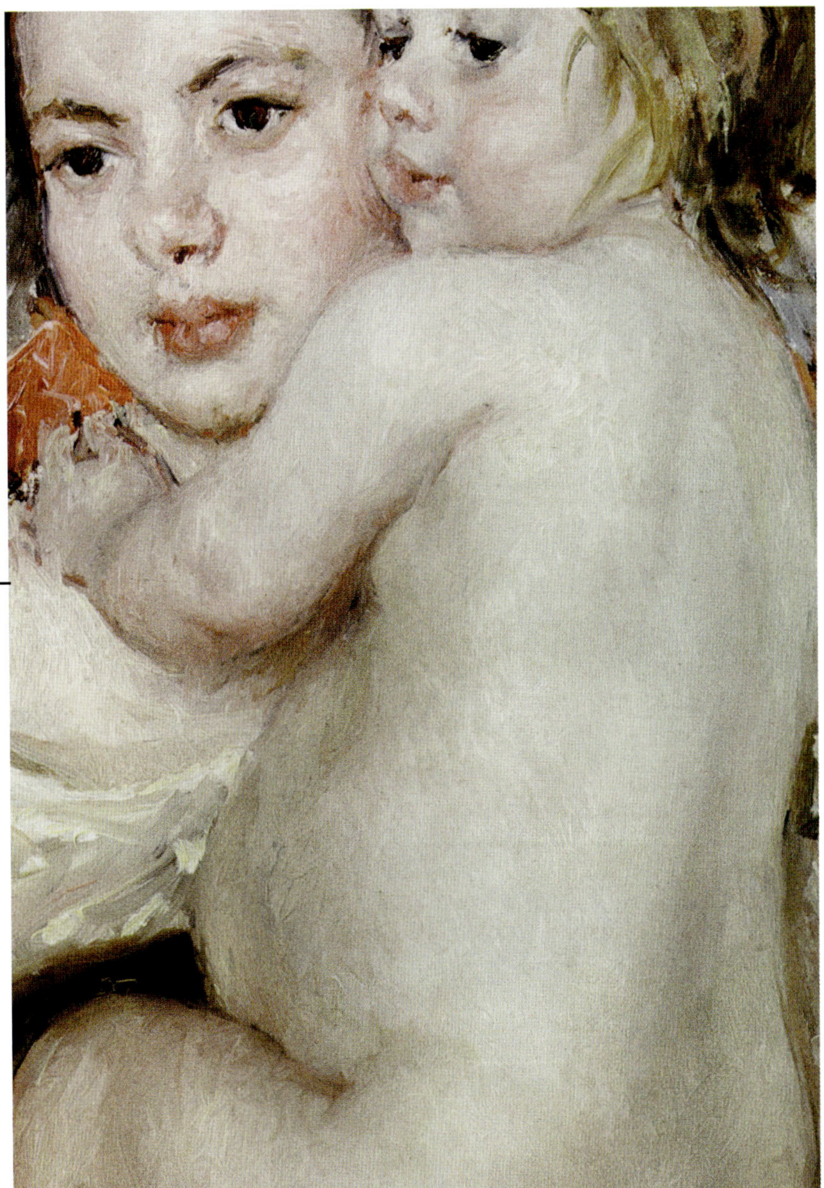

Three main influences

Cassatt's skill at capturing the essence of the relationship between mother and child came from a mixture of three main influences: Impressionism, traditional Italian images of Mary and Jesus, and Japanese art. She fused the three styles together successfully to create bold compositions, using fresh colors and a lack of fussy details.

The children she painted were of all ages, and she captured each one's distinct persona. This approach was almost revolutionary at a time when few people thought of children as having their own personalities. In 1902, her painting of a mother and two daughters, *The Caress*, was selected for a prize by the Pennsylvania Academy of the Fine Arts, but she turned it down in order to remain true to her principles of "no jury, no awards." Eventually, she did accept it, as well as the ultimate accolade—the distinguished Légion d'honneur.

Toward the end of her life, poor eyesight meant that Cassatt turned more to pastels and almost gave up oils. She loved the directness of pastels and the intense colors that she could layer. Her later pictures of mothers with children became more vivid, almost as bright as the work of the Neo-Impressionists, but she retained her ability to create soft tones with a few effective techniques.

HOW TO DO IT

YOUR PALETTE
To re-create this detail, you should enhance the tonal contrasts, using:

1 White
2 Ivory Black
3 Burnt Umber
4 French Ultramarine
5 Burnt Sienna
6 Vermilion Hue
7 Rose Madder
8 Sap Green
9 Yellow Ocher
10 Warm Gray
11 Cadmium Yellow Hue
12 Cadmium Tangerine Hue

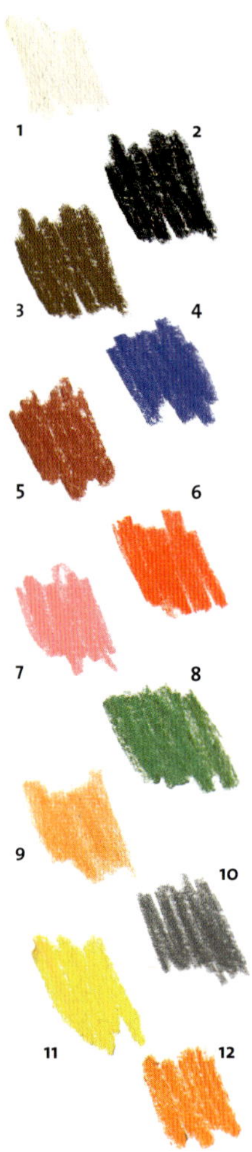

Often in Cassatt's mother and child paintings, one or both of the figures are looking away from the viewer, engrossed in their own world and their relationship with each other. The relationships speak to the viewer as much through the way Cassatt placed the figures within the frame as with their body language. Concentration on scale and positioning will enable you to build up interlocked gestures that are both intimate and informal.

The main techniques

In order to create a soft, natural, and sensitive image, keep the outlines firm but blend the tones softly and subtly. Use broken lines for the outlines and smudge any that begin to give your picture a "cartoon" feel. Create subtle facial expressions, especially around the eyes. By only partially blending, dragging, or smearing your medium without adding too much finish, the resulting slightly out-of-focus effect will suggest the movement and softness that gives the subject its appeal.

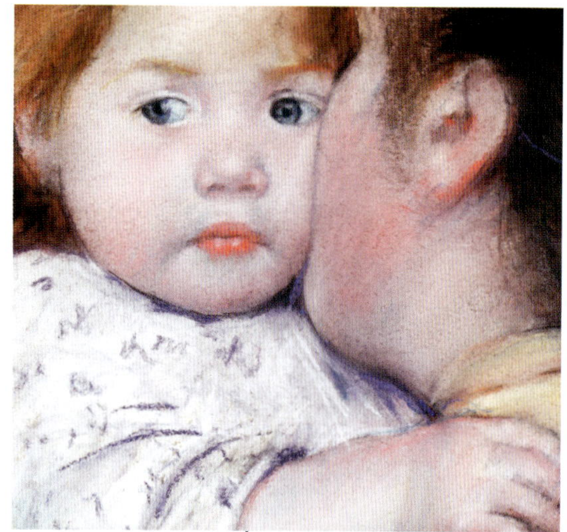

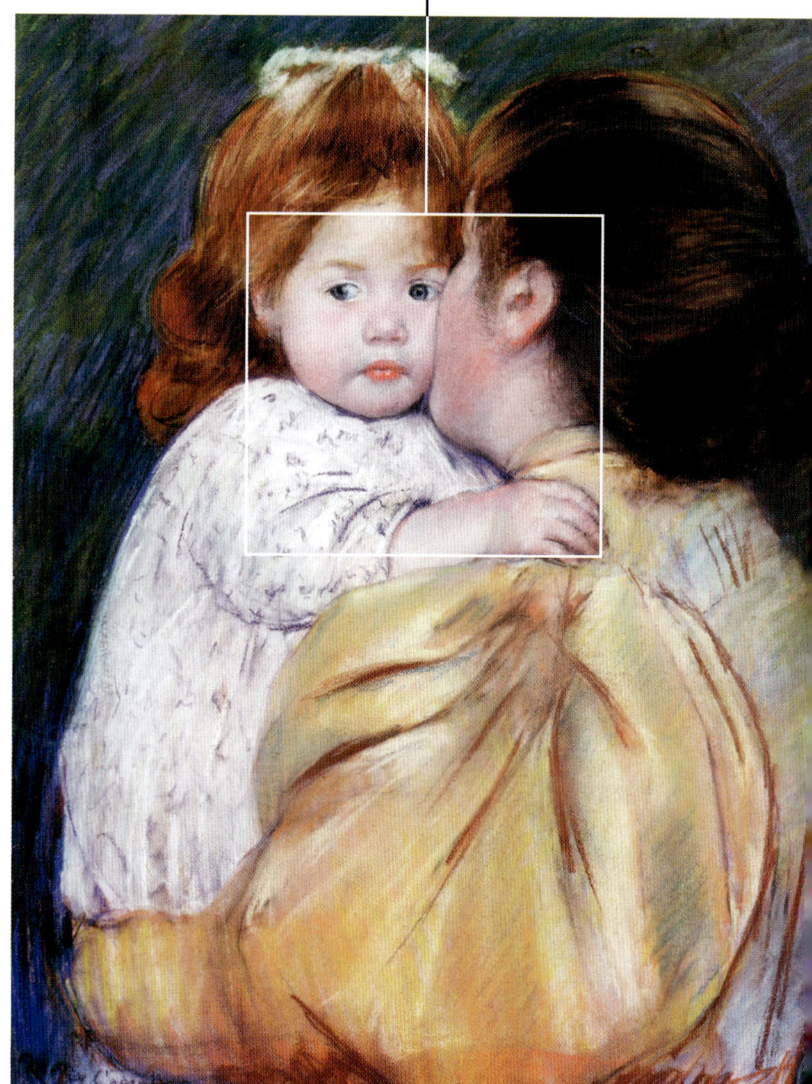

RIGHT
MATERNAL KISS, 1897, pastel on paper, 22 x 18 inches (56 x 46 cm).
The child's small hands rest on her mother's shoulders with trust and love. Most of the negative space surrounds the two figures, making them almost into one shape, and the background is flat and almost incidental. The curving shapes of the connected figures are echoed within the shapes of their clothes, hair, and heads.

STEP 1 Use pastel paper, board, or watercolor paper. If you are using colored paper or board, select a pale brown. If using white paper or board, lay a wash of Umber gouache. Gouache or poster paint is better for this initial layer than acrylic, because they are matte and, therefore, the pastel adheres well to them.

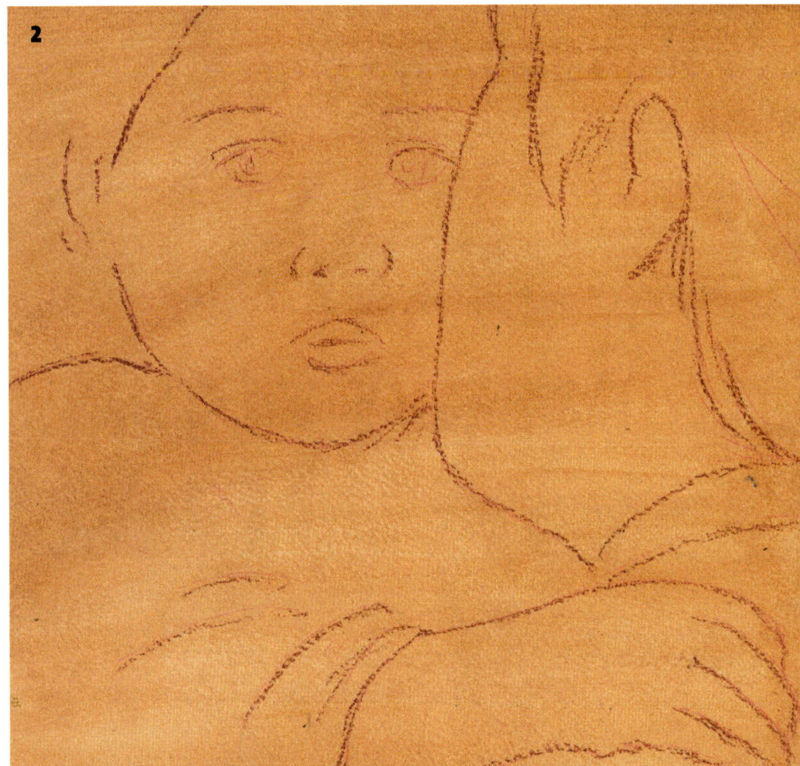

STEP 2 With a Burnt Sienna pastel, lightly outline the section of the little girl's face and the profile of the mother. Draw the child's small hand on the mother's shoulder too.

STEP 3 Cassatt firmly modeled the heads and limbs, and her color scheme was limited and direct. Introduce the flesh tones here, making them out of White, Rose Madder, and Vermilion Hue, and the shadows with French Ultramarine. Blend these colors relatively rapidly to create solid color.

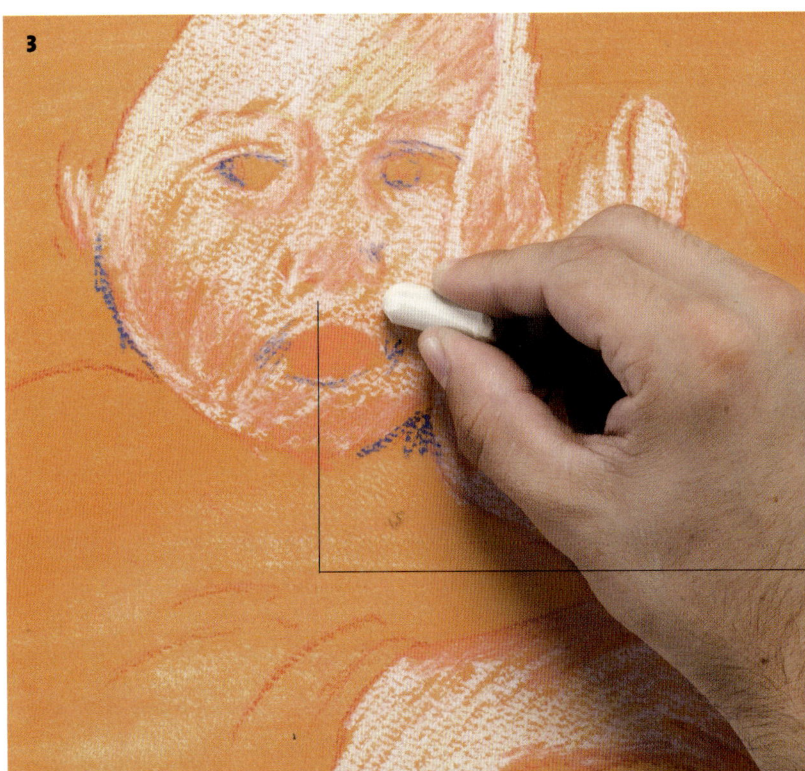

The pale pink and white colors that you are applying here will not remain so chalky, so don't try to adjust them at this point—more natural tones will be added later.

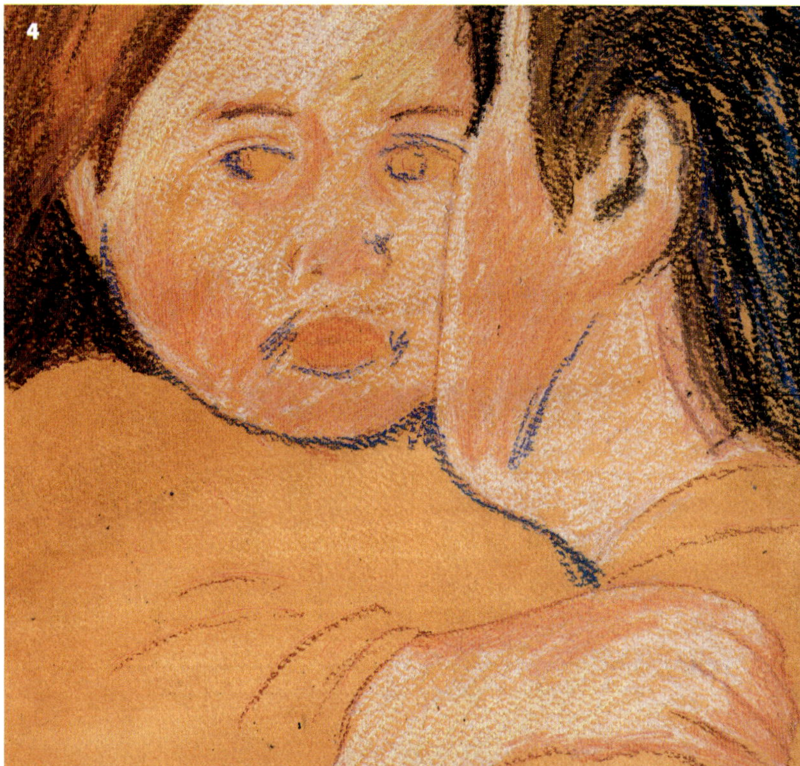

STEP 4 This drawing is more controlled and finished than much of Cassatt's earlier work. To scumble pastels, apply them with the side of the stick and drag the color lightly over under layers, never completely covering that color. Scumble the darker areas of the hair with Burnt Sienna, Burnt Umber, and Ivory Black, and add a deeper line of Ultramarine under the chins of both mother and child.

Use directional marks to create the hair, allowing the lines that you make to show clearly. Layer darker colors on top of lighter colors to indicate individual strands of hair.

STEP 5 Cassatt also used the feathering technique in this picture. Do this by swinging the pastel loosely on the diagonal, going back and forth, barely touching the surface but letting the background surface just catch the pigment. Use this technique on the clothing to give a translucent quality, using White, Cadmium Yellow Hue, Cadmium Tangerine Hue, and French Ultramarine.

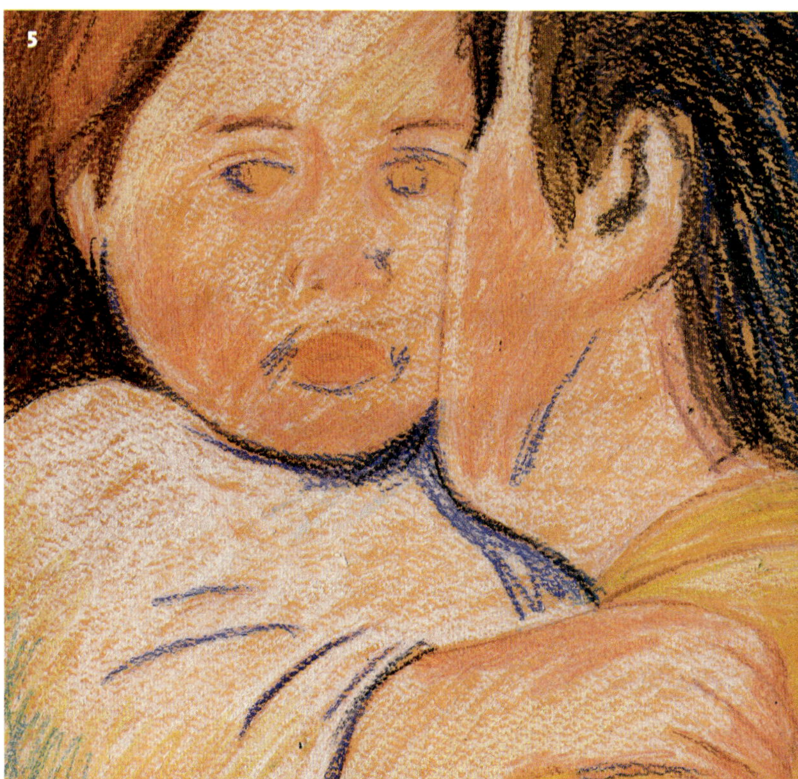

STEP 6 Begin to set down areas of cross-hatching, then smooth and blend the pastels with your finger or a torchon. Do this on the faces and hand, adding more color where necessary. Try to incorporate cool/warm and complementary contrasts—layer Warm Gray, Burnt Umber, and French Ultramarine for the dark shadows close to the warm flesh tones of Yellow Ocher, White, Vermilion Hue, and Sap Green. Form the whites of the eyes and use Ivory Black for the pupils. Use French Ultramarine for the irises.

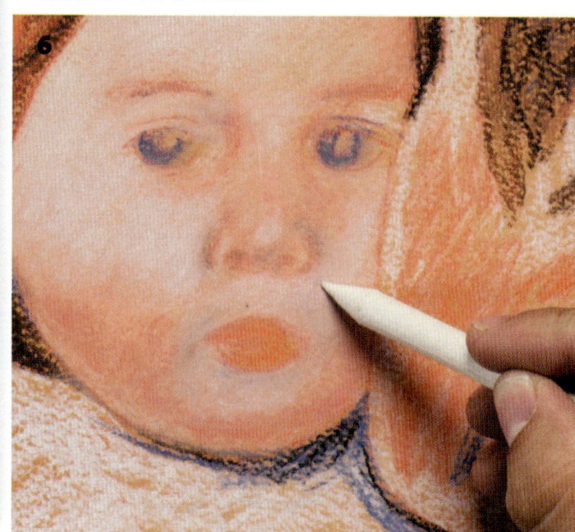

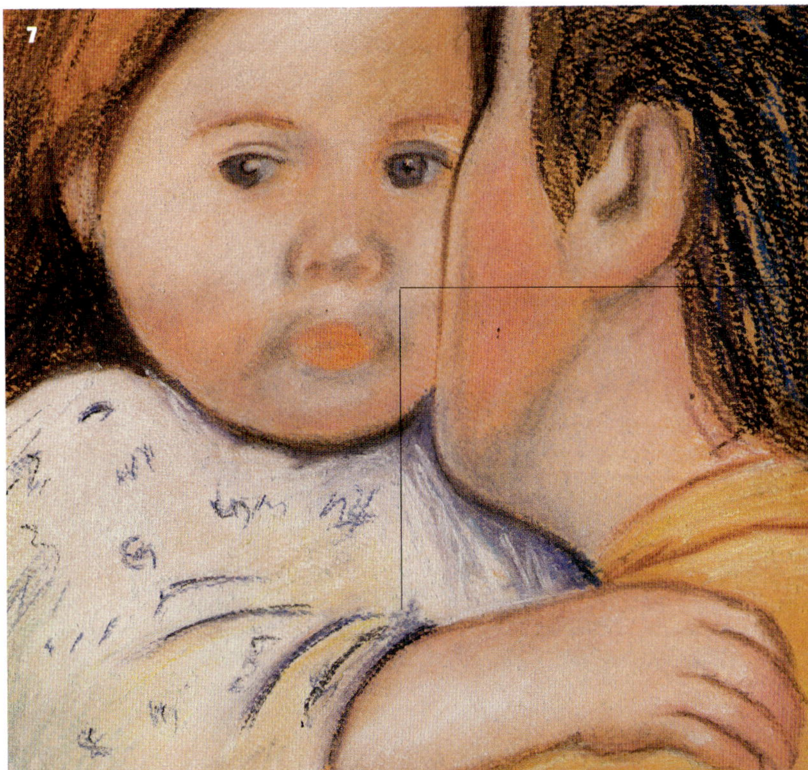

STEP 7 Strengthen the White and yellows on the clothing and work in the patterns and folds of the fabrics with French Ultramarine. Begin to add details to the facial features. Do this by echoing colors around the whole composition. For example, add some orange tones in the child's hair, as well as to her lips, arm, and eyebrows and around the mother's clothing.

The light brown background surface helps to establish the mid-tones of the skin and clothing, so use highlights and darker tones to express subtle volumes.

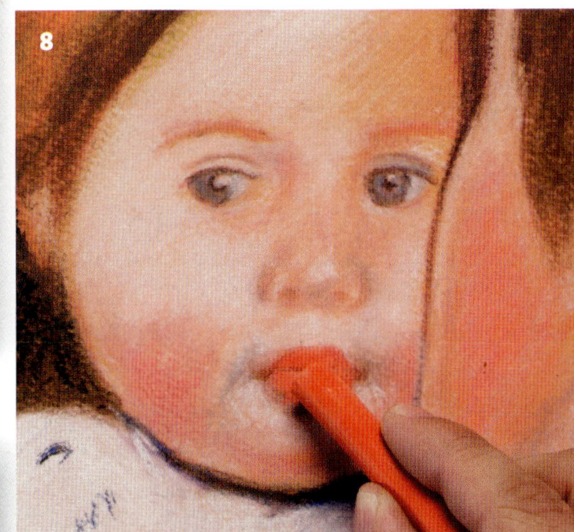

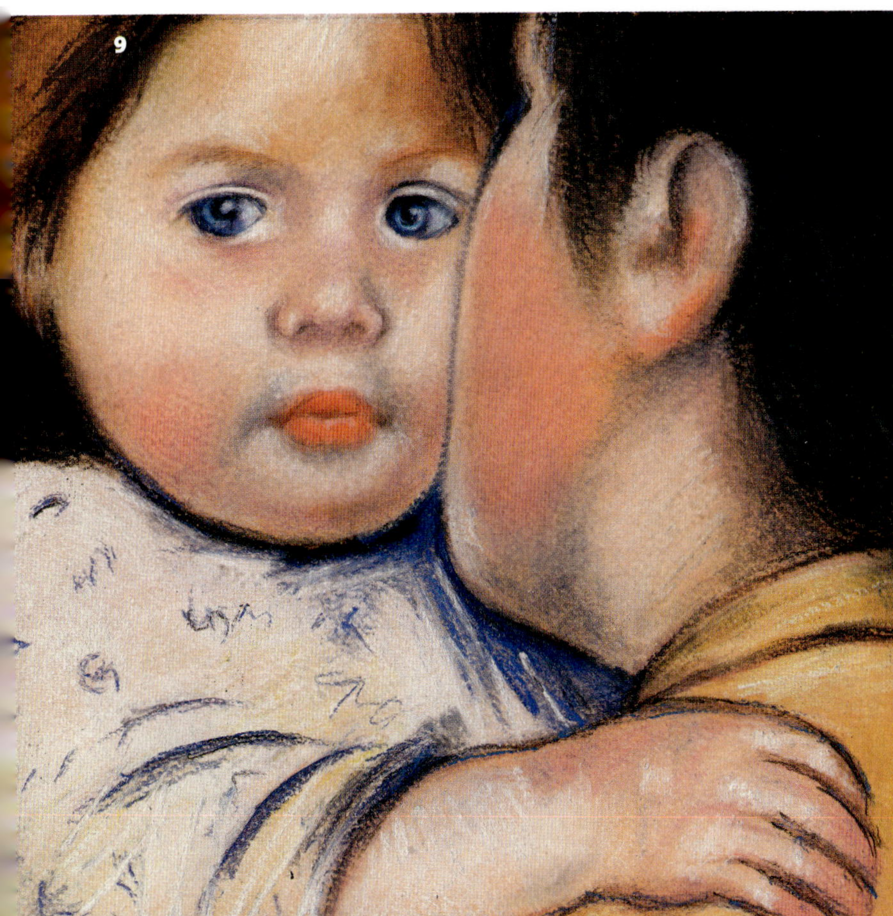

STEP 8 Mix some of the French Ultramarine with the Burnt Umber to make up the dark tones around the mother's ear. Using the point of the pastels, firm the lips using Warm Gray, Burnt Umber, White, Vermilion Hue, and Rose Madder. Create hair details using Burnt Sienna, Cadmium Tangerine Hue, French Ultramarine, and Ivory Black. Add shadow with Warm Gray and Burnt Sienna.

STEP 9 Strengthen the small details and the shadows. Refine the flesh tones and check that your background surface is not "clogged" with excessive layers of pastel. Do this by snapping your fingers against the paper or board surface to jolt the pastel and reestablish the tooth. Use the point of the French Ultramarine and White pastels to create details in the eyes and add a little white in the corners of the eyes, on the skin. Add an orange highlight around the mother's ear and White highlights on the girls' face, arm, hand, and clothes. Strengthen the small details—in particular, the French Ultramarine shadows under the chins, between the faces, and at the back of the mother's neck.

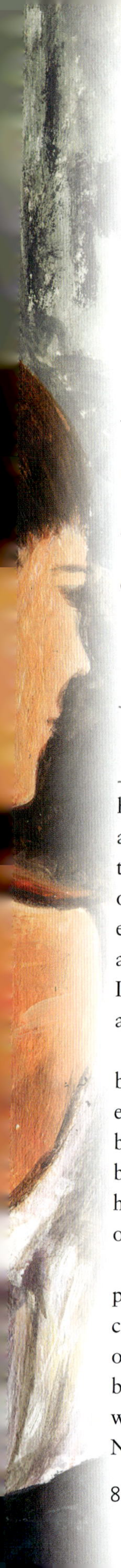

Chapter nine

DEGAS

Degas was not a typical Impressionist. He was more interested in line and composition than color and experimented with various techniques and materials. His paintings and drawings of women, particularly his paintings of ballet dancers, are probably the best-known examples of his work.

EDGAR DEGAS (1834–1917) never painted *en plein air*, and if he had not exhibited with the Impressionists he would probably never have been classed as one. His aims and ambitions differed from theirs, and he always worked in the studio, often from memory. He also preferred the effects of artificial lighting to natural light, although much of his later work exploits Impressionistic objectives, such as fleeting aspects of daily life from unusual viewpoints.

Degas came from a wealthy French banking family with connections in Italy. He entered law school—the expected path for a bourgeois young man—but two years later he began studying art. In the spring of 1855, he met Ingres who told him, "Draw lines, lots of lines, either from memory or from nature."

Although other young artists of the period thought that Ingres was rigid and conservative, Degas admired his emphasis on the importance of draftsmanship. Degas began painting family portraits and copying works in the Louvre, the Bibliothèque Nationale, and in the Ingres retrospective

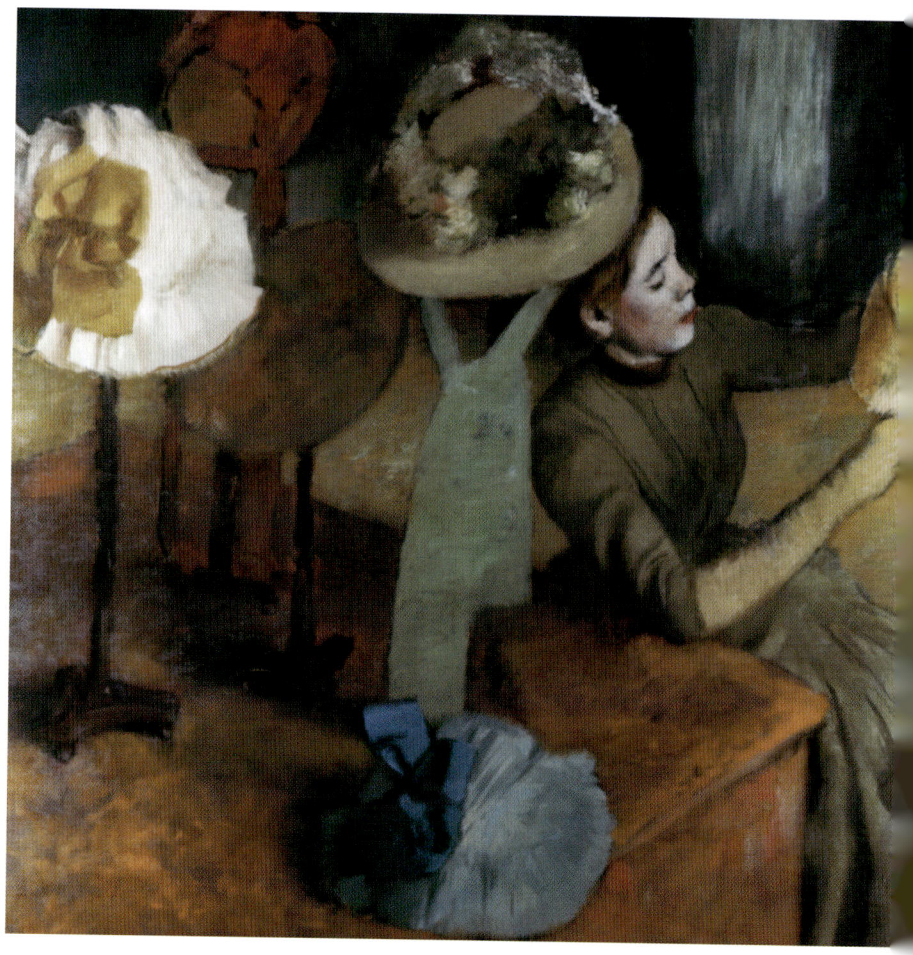

RIGHT
THE COTTON EXCHANGE, 1873, oil on canvas, $28\frac{3}{4}$ x $36\frac{1}{4}$ inches (73 x 92 cm).
The foreground is in deep perspective and the viewpoint is slightly raised, so that we can see everyone individually absorbed in his or her work. The strong contrasts of dark browns, grays, and blacks against the pale greens, ochers, creams, and white are carefully placed across the painting. They are suggestive of black-and-white wood engravings of the period. Although it depicts a passing moment, it shows Degas' interest in line and tone.

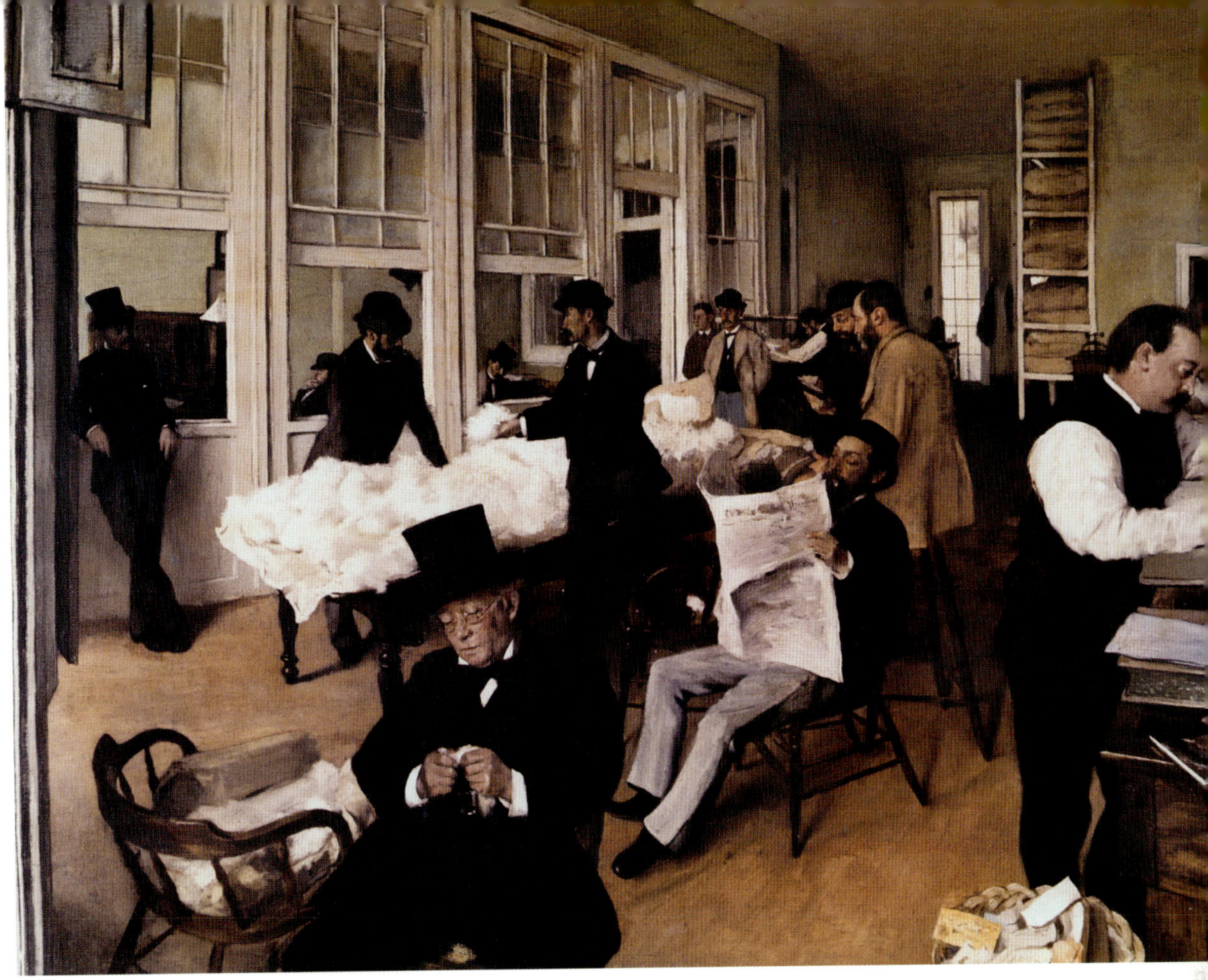

LEFT
THE MILLINERY SHOP, c.1882–86, oil on canvas, $39\frac{1}{2}$ x $43\frac{1}{2}$ inches (100 x 110.5 cm).
The photographic quality of Degas' work is apparent in many of his paintings of women at work and grooming themselves. Like many of the Impressionists, he was fascinated by Japanese wood-block prints, and their effect is apparent here in the diagonal composition. This is the largest of a series of millinery store paintings, which are characterized by their unusual and unexpected viewpoints that draw the eye into the frame.

at the Paris Exposition. He also spent time in Italy, studying early Renaissance masters. On his return to Paris, in 1859, he became inspired by the trend for Japanese prints, admiring their unusual viewpoints and informal glimpses into everyday life. When he met Manet in 1865, he began painting scenes of contemporary life instead of his usual history paintings. After that, the whole of Paris became his subject.

Drawing and experimenting

Above all, the female form fascinated Degas, and he painted women dancing, singing, ironing, washing, combing their hair, and even sleeping. He painted some landscapes, but he preferred the man-made over the natural world and always emphasized the importance of drawing over color. He said, "They [the other Impressionists] are all exploiting the possibilities of color. And I am always begging them to exploit the possibilities of drawing. It is the richer field." Even so, he used a bright, restricted palette similar to the other Impressionists. He experimented with various techniques, trying different background surfaces, including unprimed canvases, and he sometimes mixed gouache, charcoal, and printing ink into his paintings. Unlike Monet and Renoir, he built up his paint in relatively uniform layers and applied his pastels in layers of hatched and crosshatched color. He sometimes sprayed a thin mist of water over his pastels and worked the resulting paste with his fingers or a stiff brush.

Degas also experimented with printing, sculpture, and photography, developing each to his exacting standards. For him, art had a strong intellectual basis; he said, "What I do is the result of reflection and study ... of inspiration, spontaneity, temperament, I know nothing."

USING PASTELS

DEGAS' EYESIGHT STARTED declining in the 1870s and, by the early 1890s, he could scarcely see. He began using pastels more often for their instantaneous results and their matte, sketch-like finish that contrasted with the glossy effect of oils. In addition, he could feel what he was doing with them, which he couldn't do when using a brush.

By the early 1890s, Degas was creating unusual landscapes in monotype and pastel. Unlike other Impressionist landscapes, these were carefully planned explorations of solid forms and aerial perspective. Pastels enabled him to work quickly, switching from one color to another without having to wait for paint to dry or to change brushes. He applied them lightly with a loose, semitransparent look, allowing the background surface to show through in parts. These surfaces were

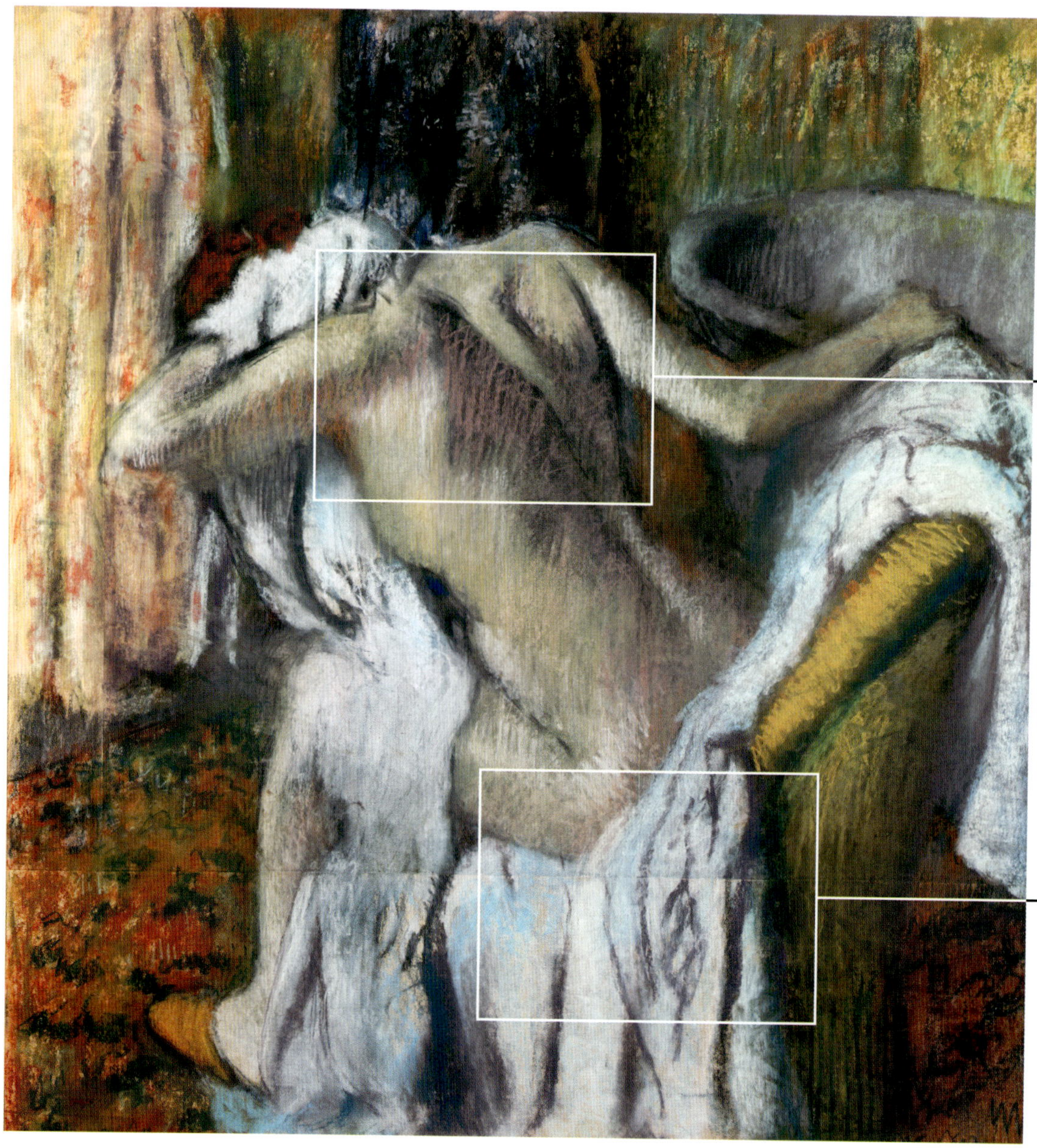

RIGHT
AFTER THE BATH, WOMAN DRYING HERSELF, 1880, pastel on cardboard, 41 x 38¾ inches (104 x 98.5 cm).
Degas produced many pictures of women in their private daily routines, seemingly unaware of anyone watching them. Here, he cut off the bathtub and towel at the edges to give the look of a photograph. Pastels gave him an ideal combination of line and color, which he built up in hatched layers. He used a bold palette, placing colors on top of each other, sometimes blending them together with a stiff brush.

BELOW
AFTER THE BATH, WOMAN DRYING HERSELF, detail.
Degas used a textured, cream-colored background surface and first drew the image in charcoal. Then he worked the colors across the picture at once with broken strokes. French Ultramarine, Cadmium Tangerine Hue, Purple, and White are among the colors used. The woman's back has been densely colored in dark tones and overlaid with pale flesh-colored vertical strokes.

BOTTOM
AFTER THE BATH, WOMAN DRYING HERSELF, detail.
Many colors have been left unblended to keep the picture vibrant and fresh. The cloth has been worked more densely to show its texture.

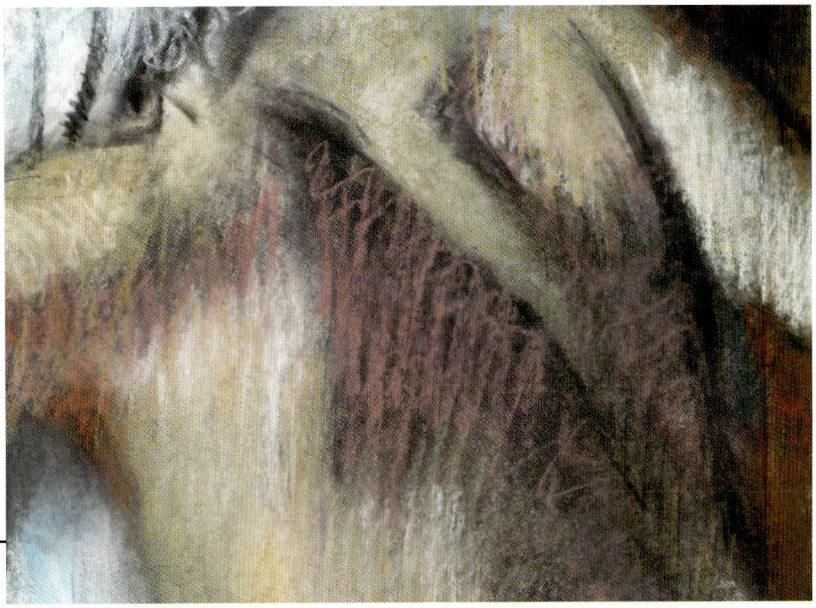

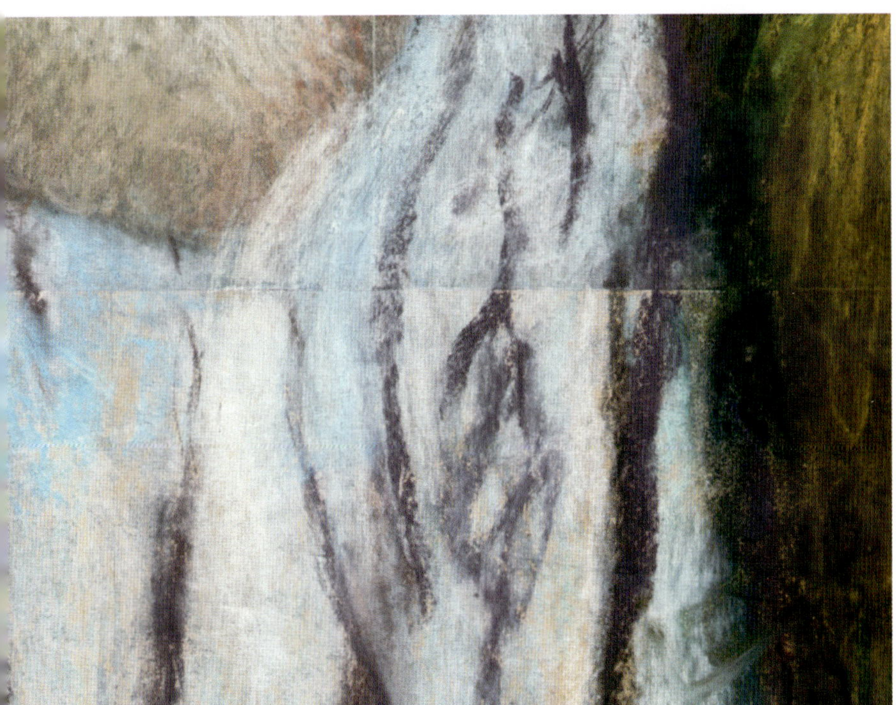

usually canvases that he had left unprimed or painted with distemper. He had exacting standards for the textures he liked to work with and experimented with various types of pastels. In the end, he made his own out of a combination of pigment and gum, which he rolled into sticks.

Webs of color

Probably best known for his paintings and pastel drawings of dancers, horse-racing scenes, and women preparing themselves to be seen, Degas excelled at depicting expressive movement. These were moments in time that should be captured quickly without losing any of their ambience, and pastels were the perfect material to do this. He handled his pastels lightly, creating webs of color and layering lines in different directions.

In the last Impressionist exhibition in 1886, Degas exhibited a group of 10 pastels, which he called *Series of Female Nudes, bathing, washing, and drying themselves, combing their hair, or having their hair combed*. Although these were intensely criticized at the time for being obscene representations of prostitutes, lewd visions of nakedness, and evidence of his misogyny, they have gone on to be considered some of the most admired intimate and expressive images of women. By this time, he was applying his pastels in even more delicate layers. Directional strokes produced a range of different finishes and textures, such as a feathery approach for hair and soft fabrics and a gleaming, pearly finish for flesh.

Degas began his pastel drawings by marking the contours of the main objects, then he applied layers of dark and light and cool and warm colors. Toward the end of his life, his strokes became broader and the colors more vibrant and intense. At this time, the scale of his pastels became much greater than his earlier work.

HOW TO DO IT

YOUR PALETTE

For this picture, you will need three shades of blue within your palette:

1 French Ultramarine
2 Cobalt Blue
3 Ceruleum or Phthalo Blue
4 Hooker's Green
5 Olive Green
6 Vermilion Hue
7 Vandyke Brown Hue
8 Raw Umber
9 White
10 Burnt Sienna
11 Ivory Black

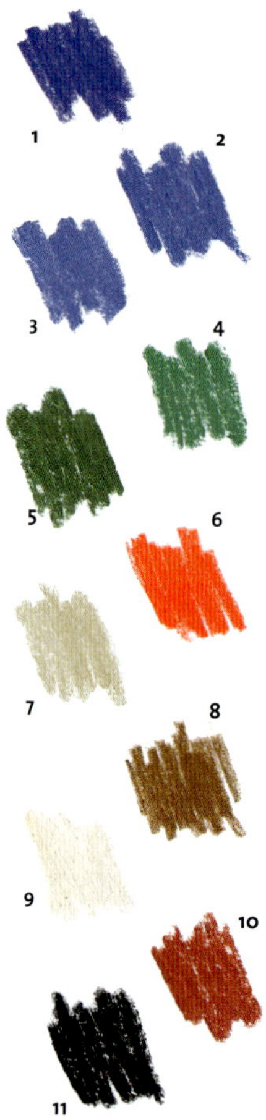

DEGAS BELIEVED THAT all paintings require some mystery or vagueness. Something should always be left to the viewers' imaginations instead of everything being immediately apparent. This fits with the Impressionists' idea of keeping paintings looking spontaneous—and pastels are the ideal medium to this. Degas used them by contrasting sharp edges against soft ones and light color against heavy hatching.

The main techniques

Immediacy is one of the positive qualities of pastels, so, whether you're using textured, colored pastel paper, painted watercolor paper, or board, handle your pastels lightly and rapidly. Either mix colors in layers or build up networks of vibrant colors and textures, using different directional strokes without overly blending. Make sure you keep your handling delicate, because the aim is to keep everything light and the colors as pure as possible. To intensify the vibrancy of color and impressions of spontaneity, work colors into each other to create additional tints and broken colors. For this picture, the tone of the background surface gives the image depth and allows the brighter colors to gleam.

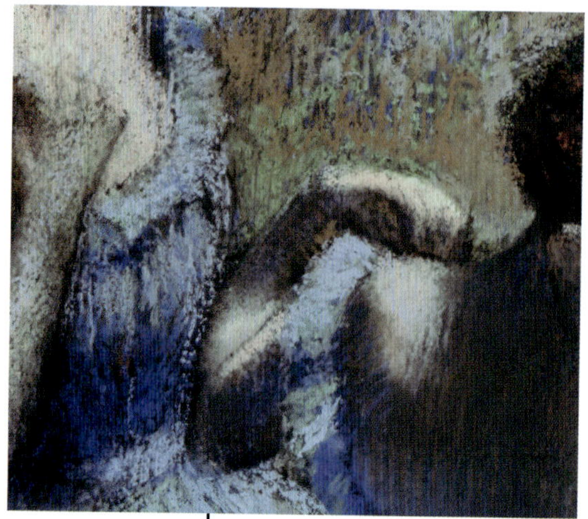

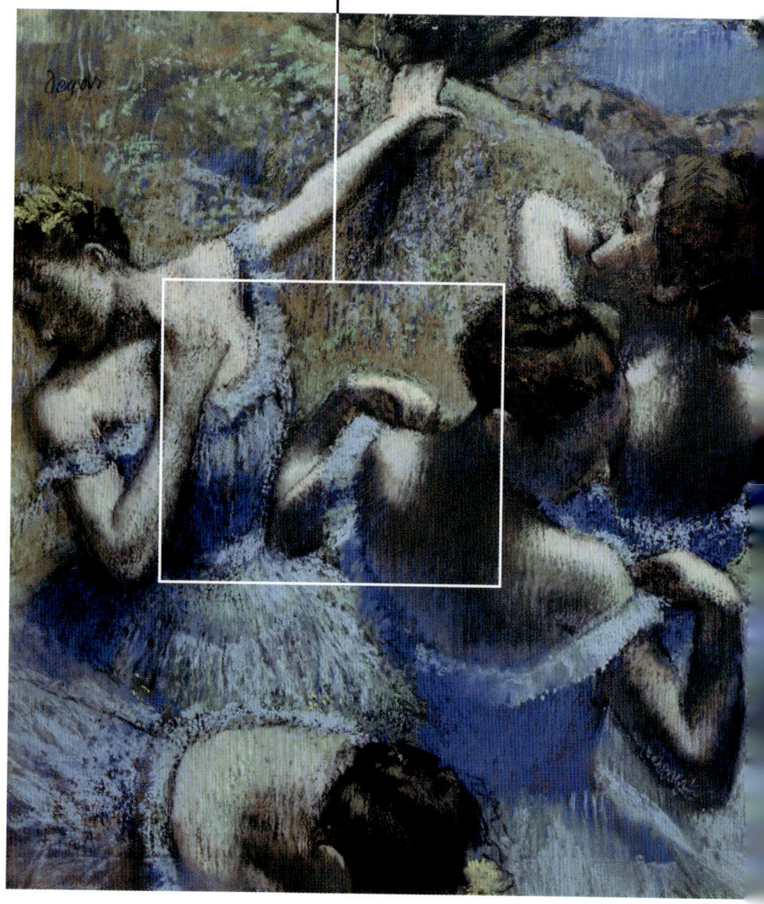

ABOVE
BLUE DANCERS, 1898, pastel on paper, 26 x 26¼ inches (66 x 67 cm).
This composition was worked out directly from three photographs.

Degas often used photos as an alternative or supplement to sketches and tracing. He combined the photographs and used an unusual viewpoint—looking down in close-up.

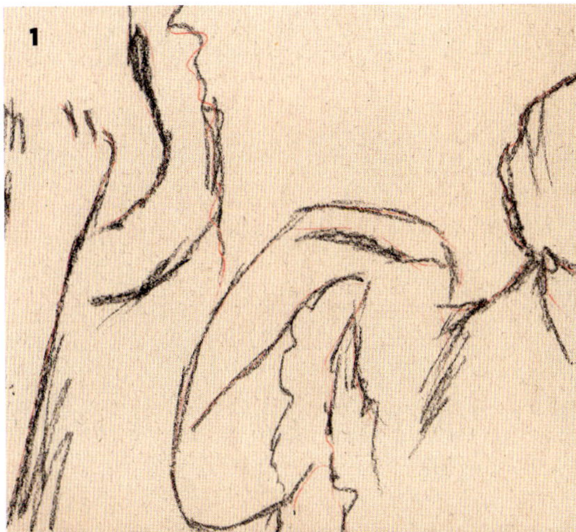

STEP 1 Use heavy white paper tinted with a watercolor wash of Burnt Sienna. Alternatively, you could use colored pastel paper or board. Start by drawing the outlines with charcoal.

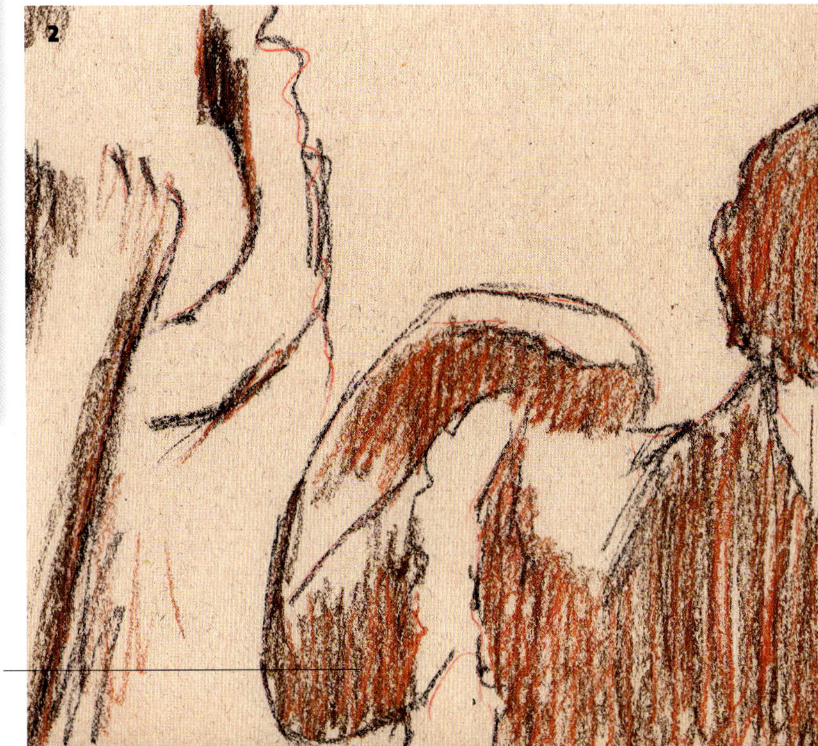

Use the evanescent quality of pastels to emphasize the darkest tones without applying heavy pressure. The dancers' arms and shoulders form a pattern, giving the composition balance and dynamism.

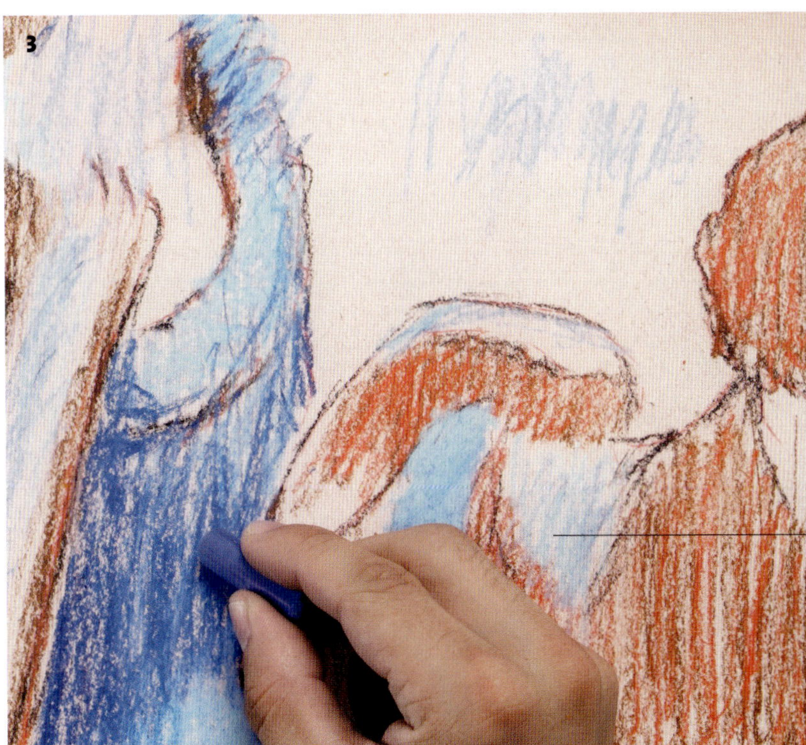

STEP 2 Degas called the trying out of techniques his "recipes" or "cooking." The pastel marks vary greatly in this picture and were used for both decorative and textural effects. Using Raw Umber and Burnt Sienna, begin to build the shadow areas of the flesh and hair, using vertical strokes and just a little finger or torchon smudging.

STEP 3 On the highlighted areas of the flesh and background, stroke in some blue. Introduce the blue tones of the dresses using Cobalt Blue and French Ultramarine. Degas' pastel marks were calculated to define or emphasize the changing planes and angles of each form. Be aware of this as you layer and blend the blues, using a torchon or your finger.

Work in the same directional marks that you see here. They help to stress the dramatic effects created by artificial light shining up at the dancers, instead of down on them as natural light does.

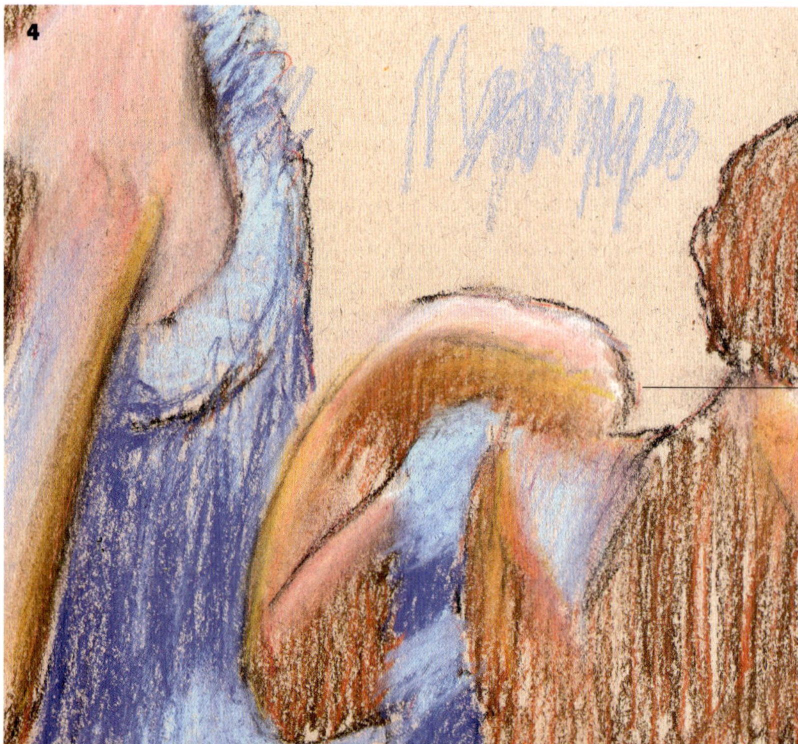

STEP 4 Gradually build up the tonal contrasts on the figures. Create lighter flesh tones with White and Vermilion Hue, blurred and blended with a little Yellow Ocher. Work these flesh tones into the light blue tones, and blend them together with a torchon or your finger. Work across the figures, laying in darker tones on the arms and back.

Soften the flesh tones as you work by smudging them lightly. Make sure that you blend in some pure White where the highlights fall—in particular, on the shoulders and the top of the hand.

STEP 5 Establish the background colors with Burnt Umber. Blend lightly with a torchon or your fingertips, then add another layer. The background must not look detailed or sharp, so leave it looking unfinished.

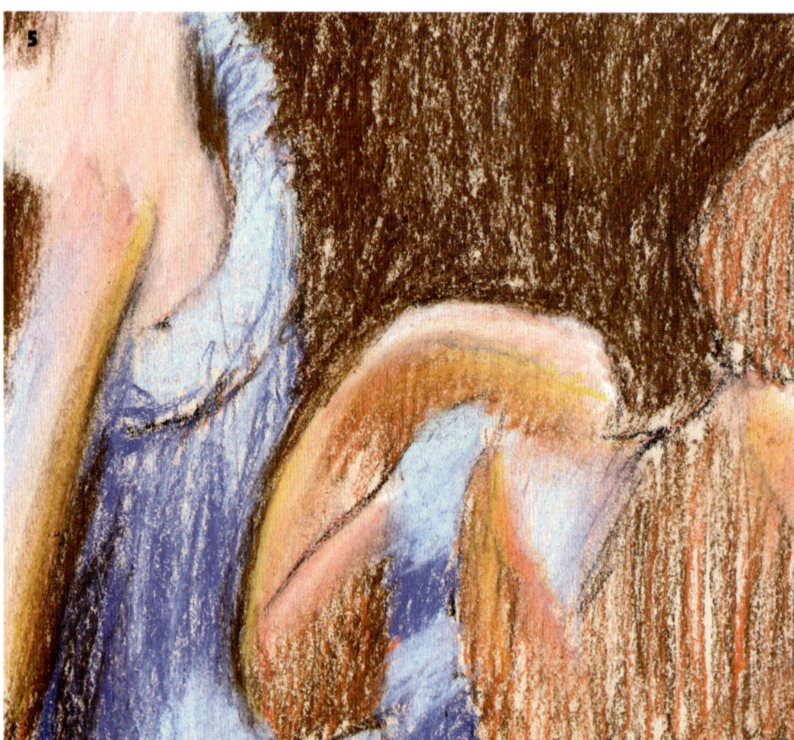

STEP 6 Overlay the Burnt Umber background with some Cadmium Tangerine Hue, Hooker's Green, and Cobalt Blue in vertical smudges and scumbles. Build darker tones on the foreground figure with Burnt Umber, Burnt Sienna, Yellow Ocher, and a little Ivory Black and Cobalt Blue. The skin should be light and the darkest shadows extremely dark.

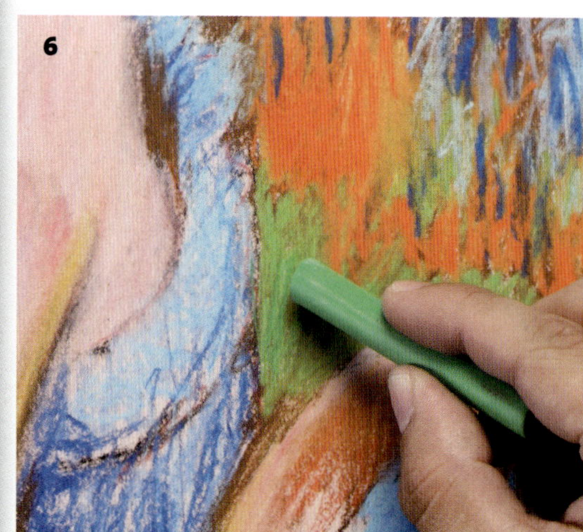

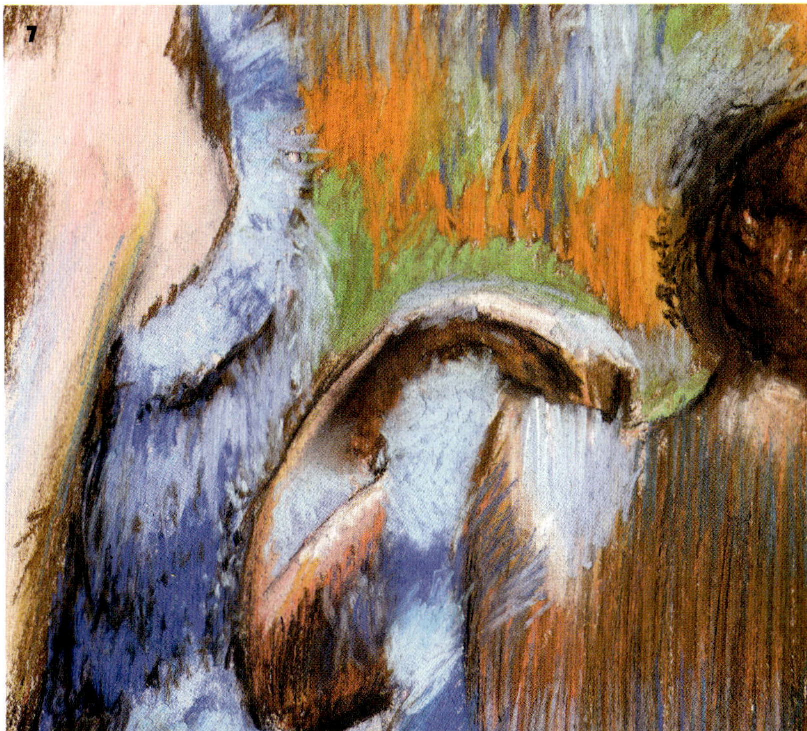

STEP 7 Establish the rear figure's flesh tones with vertical strokes of Cobalt Blue, Hooker's Green, and Burnt Umber. Strengthen the folds and creases of the clothing with light strokes of French Ultramarine and White mixed with Cobalt or Ceruleum Blue. Add details to the outlines of the dancers with a thin or pointed end of the French Ultramarine and Burnt Sienna.

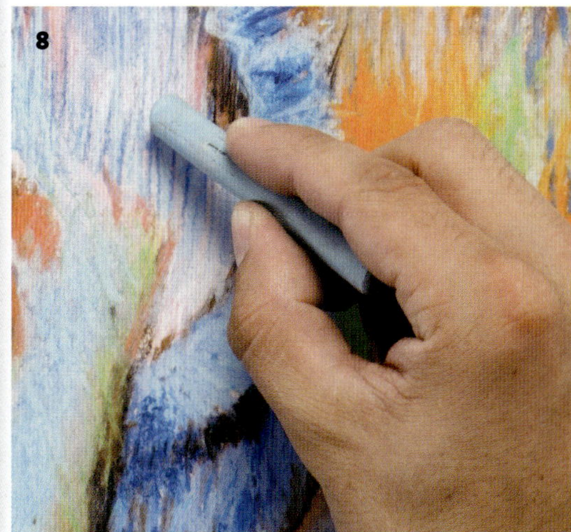

STEP 8 Continue to build on the flesh tones, layering more colors. Do the same with the blues on the dresses until the tones are smooth and subtle. Adjust the tones accordingly, then blend and strengthen the rear figure's dress even more.

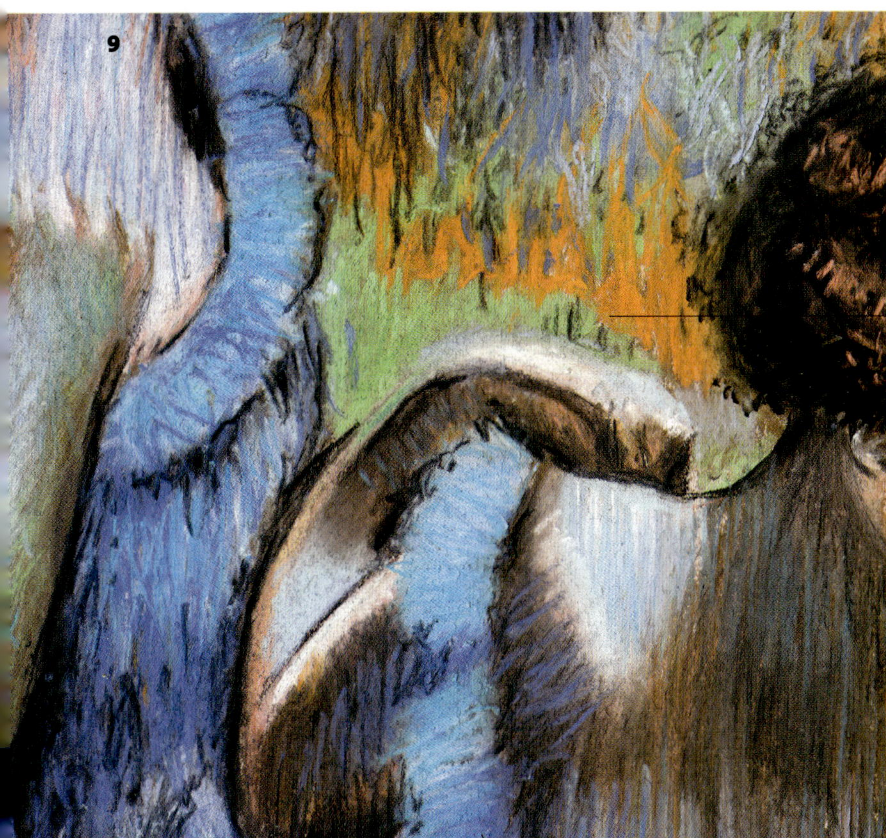

Soften the background by roughly smudging the colors into each other. Don't overdo this, because you should leave some directional marks showing. Go over the lightest parts with your White and the darkest parts with your French Ultramarine pastels.

STEP 9 Firm up the outline detail of the dancers. Blend tones by smudging and scumbling small strokes of pure colors on the figures and their dresses. Finally, to finish the painting, use the French Ultramarine pastel to scumble on the dresses and a little Ivory Black to define the contours. Use Ivory Black in the background space too.

CAUGHT ON CAMERA

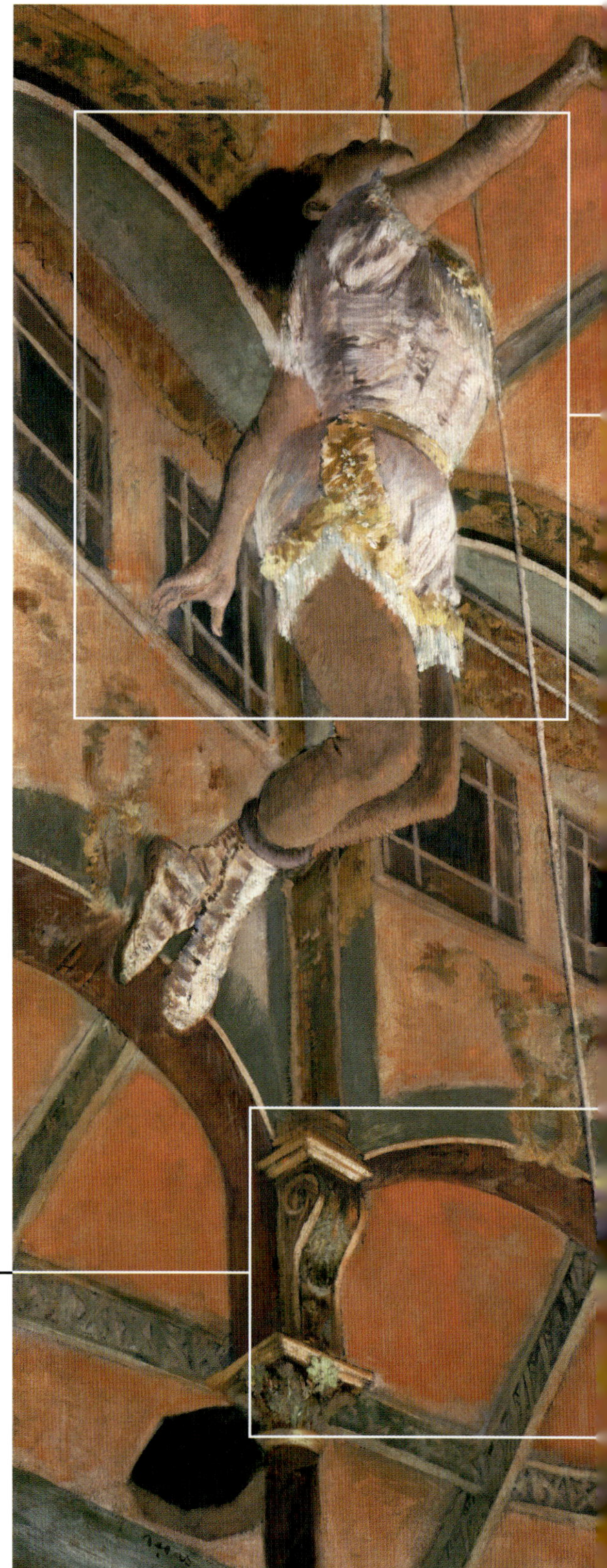

CENTER
MADEMOISELLE LA LA AT THE CIRQUE FERNANDO, 1879, oil on canvas, 46 x 30½ inches (117 x 77.5 cm).
This picture was produced with an awareness of the camera, because there is no conventional background surface to give viewers an anchoring horizon. Miss La La's body is suspended in the top lefthand quarter of the picture, as if in a snapshot. Degas used the Venetian technique of warm colors over cold and cold colors over warm. His interest was the figure's position and the emotions her body expressed.

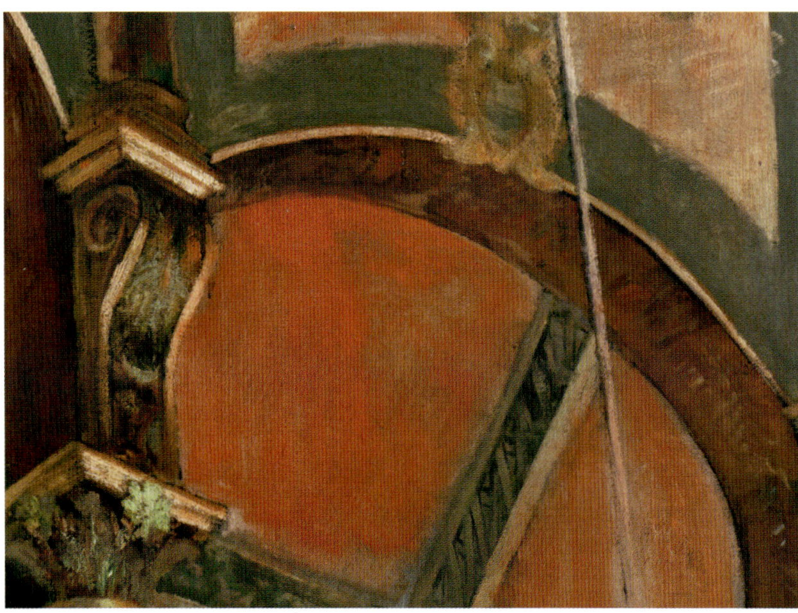

BELOW
MADEMOISELLE LA LA AT THE CIRQUE FERNANDO, detail.
Degas painted the roof bright orange to convey the danger and excitement of Miss La La's performance.

FROM THE MOMENT it was invented in 1839, photography had a potent effect on the visual arts. Some artists saw it as a useful tool, while others considered it a threat. Chevreul's influential book on color was published in the same year and had about the same impact on artists' practice. Degas became particularly interested in the work of Eadweard Muybridge (1830–1904), who took freeze-framed photographs of humans and animals in motion. This revolutionized the way artists depicted movement. Muybridge's multiple photographs had a huge influence on Degas' portrayal of movement, particularly in his racehorse and dancer pictures.

Degas' curiosity about photography is evident in many of his works, from their snapshotlike viewpoints to their seemingly informal compositions and vivid contrasts. He became interested in photography in 1860 and eventually bought himself a camera in 1895. Using a tripod and glass plates, he created photographs of people in poses that he'd positioned carefully to look as if they were

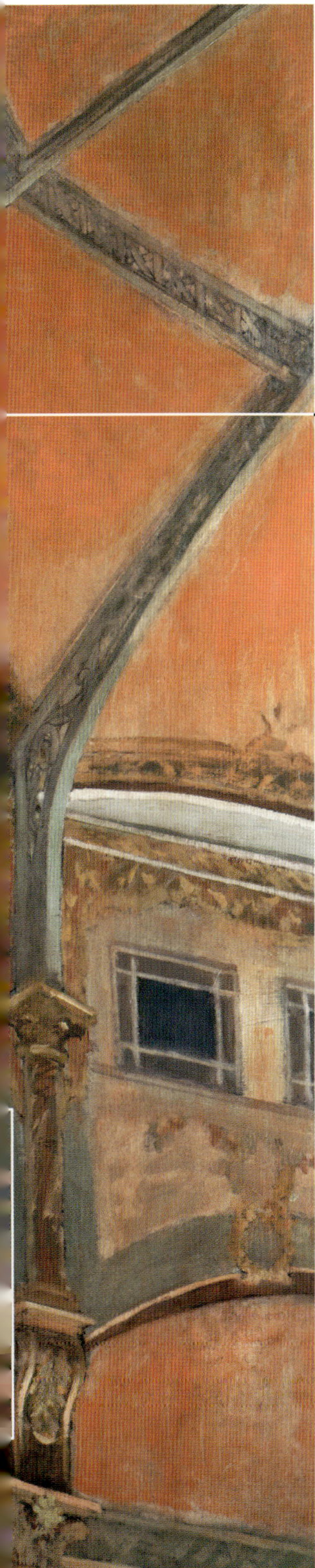

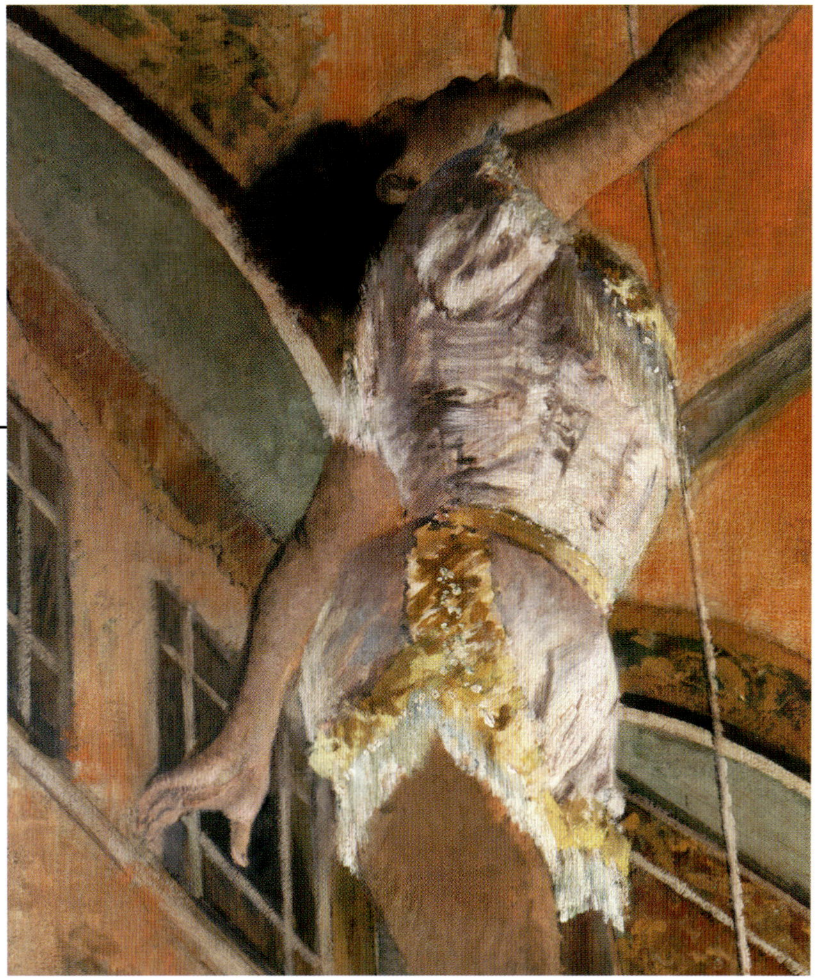

LEFT
MADEMOISELLE LA LA AT THE CIRQUE FERNANDO, detail.
Degas began this painting by making a pencil sketch at the circus, then he used the grid method to enlarge the sketch onto canvas. You can see his attention to detail and the almost photographic reproduction of the architectural ornaments. The dramatic and crisp tones, the fluid and smooth handling of the paint, and the thoroughness with which he has re-created this scene are all indications of his fascination with the camera.

incidental. He had no lessons in photography and took photos at night because he spent the days painting. He played with contrasts and light effects, because he wanted to explore the "atmosphere of lamps or moonlight" and he took numerous portraits of his friends, as well as photographs of nudes, which he frequently transferred onto canvas. Photographs helped Degas to work out various visual puzzles and to reproduce frozen moments in time.

Powerful compositions

Degas always recognized the camera's limitations, so he used drawings, as well as photographs, to prepare for final paintings. To transfer photographic images onto canvas, he used the grid technique of laying a sheet of tracing paper onto a photograph and ruling a grid of squares on it. Then he transferred what he saw in each square into a larger-sized grid on a canvas.

In 1874, Degas painted one of his most famous paintings, *The Ballet Class*. He took photographs and made sketches from life in charcoal, pastel, and Conté crayon. The final picture was made of figures from his sketchbook, his photographs, and his memory of the scene. Photography allowed Degas to experiment with compositions. It also helped him use cropping, where parts of people and objects are cut off at the edges of pictures. It gradually became recognized (although not necessarily accepted) that viewers should "finish" these pictures in their own minds.

HOW TO DO IT

YOUR PALETTE

Your palette should follow Degas' method of using only primary colors, one green, and white:

1 Silver White
2 Yellow Ocher
3 Lemon Yellow
4 Venetian Red
5 Prussian Blue
6 Chrome Green
7 Vermilion
8 Cobalt Blue

By mixing these in different orders, you will find you can make a range of dark, medium, and light colors in varying degrees of brilliance.

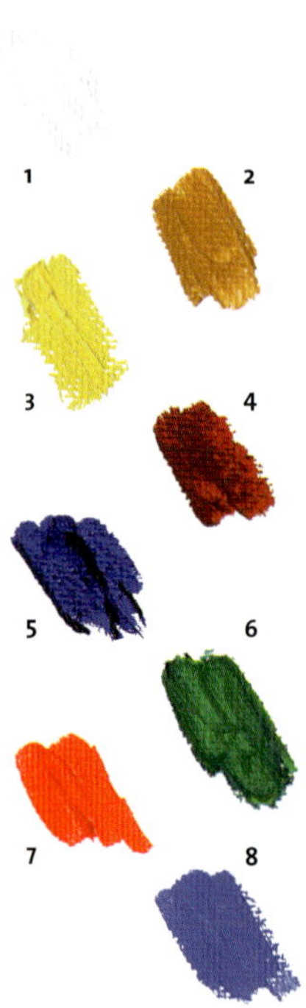

PAINTERS OFTEN OVERLOOK interior scenes, because it can be difficult to set up an easel in the center of someone else's activities. In such situations, photographs can be helpful visual notes. They enable you to move about with your camera, taking shots from different viewpoints. You can then select parts of the images to create a final painting. This is just what Degas did for *The Dance Class*.

The main techniques

Choose a smooth canvas or board, because you should make the brush marks as even as you can. To re-create the subtle quality of Degas' scraped-down paint surfaces, you should apply the paint thickly, then scrape it down with a palette knife to produce a flatter surface. You can apply more paint over this, but use a creamy consistency so that you avoid drawing attention to its texture. Compositions inspired by photography are usually relatively dramatic. Watch out for foreshortening and unusual angles. With so many people in the picture, Degas avoided an overcrowded and congested feeling by arranging the figures around an empty area to draw the viewer's eye into and around the picture.

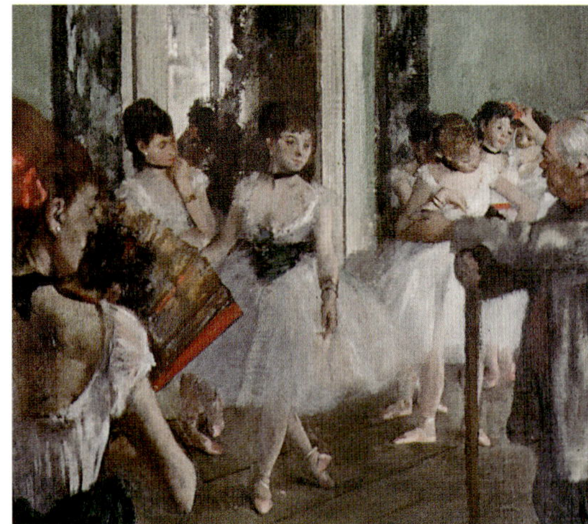

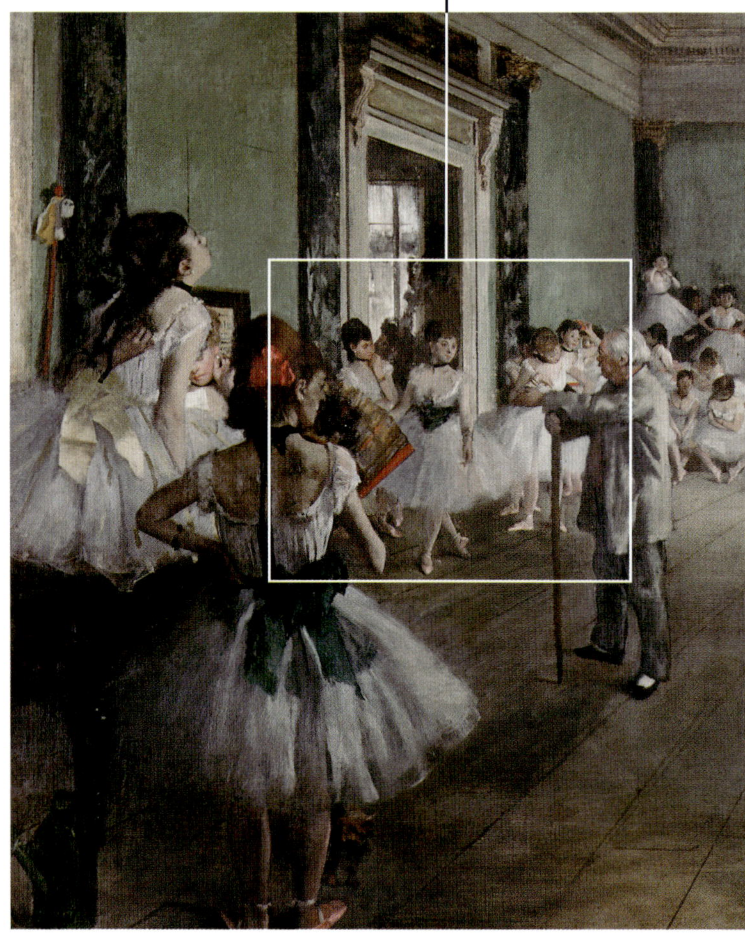

ABOVE
THE DANCE CLASS, 1874, oil on canvas, 32¾ x 31¼ inches (83.5 x 79.5 cm). ***Degas painted two versions of this picture. His knowledge of photography is evident in the clarity between black and white, the dramatic viewpoint, and the cropping at the edges of the picture.***

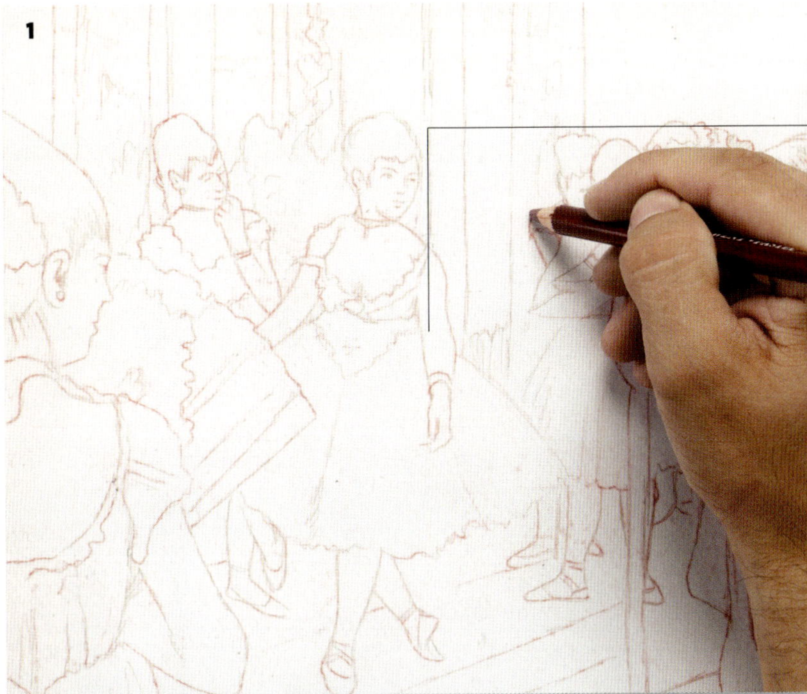

Be aware of the foreshortening in this picture, for example, the central dancer's arm and foot.

STEP 1 Prime your canvas or board with cream paint. Degas often used gouache for its opacity and was happy to allow some of it to show through the finished painting. When the paint is dry, lightly sketch the outlines in pencil, noting the spaces between the figures, which help to strengthen the composition and bring the viewers' attention to the figures. You can use the grid method to do this if you want.

STEP 2 The verticals in this section pull the composition together, as do the strong contrasts of the dark shadows and white highlights. Paint the floor with a mixture of Venetian Red, Yellow Ocher, and Prussian Blue. Block in some background tones using Yellow Ocher, Cobalt Blue, and Venetian Red with touches of Chrome Green and Vermilion.

STEP 3 Degas made the most of the glazing technique here. Glazing is the oldest of all painting techniques and involves thin, transparent layers of paint being applied over other layers of paint. Using thinned paint, develop the figure of the dancing master using Venetian Red, Chrome Green, Silver White, Cobalt Blue, and a little Yellow Ocher. Build it up, applying a bright mixture of Yellow Ocher, Vermilion, and Cobalt Blue as the base and adding Silver White to this blend for the face and hands.

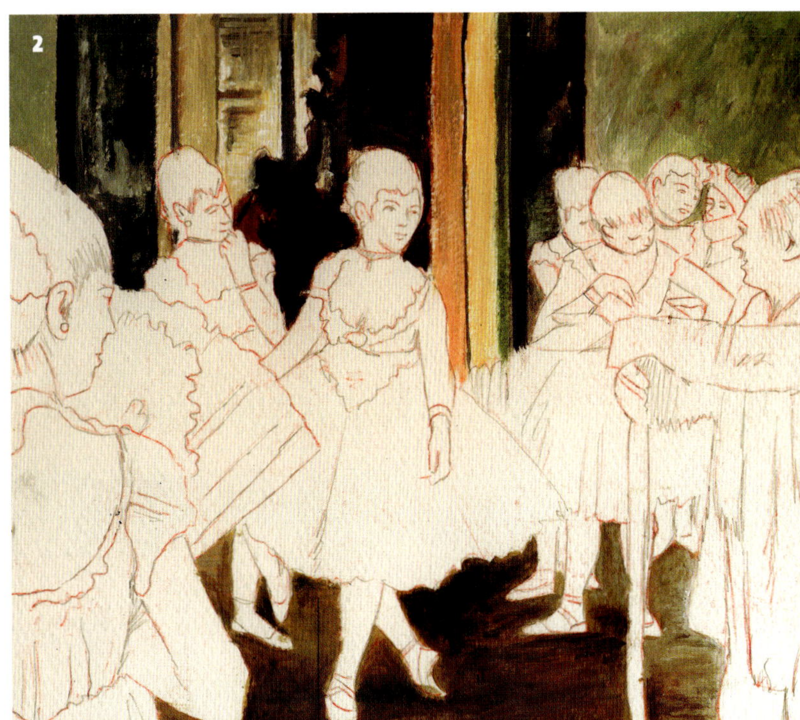

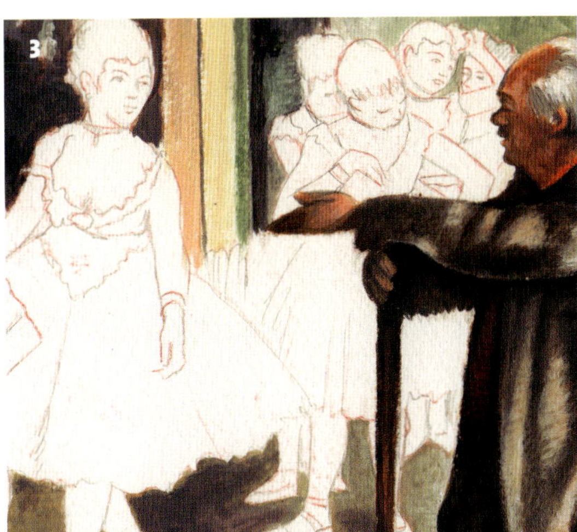

Paint the floor in longish horizontal brush strokes. It should be a little darker around the dancers' feet and at the base of their dresses. If it seems too dark, either thin the color with turpentine or add a touch of Silver White.

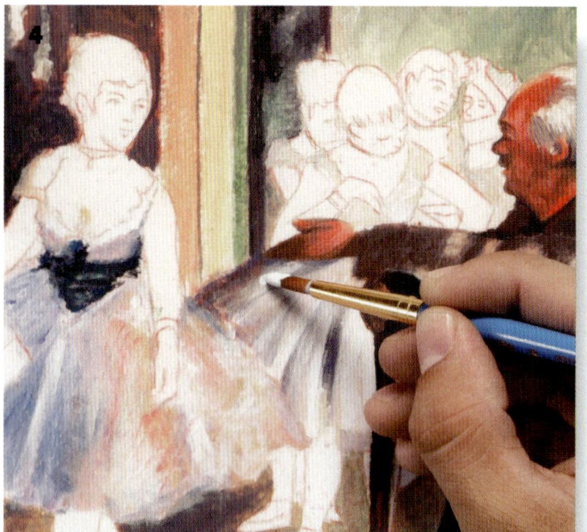

Create smooth flesh tones using Silver White, Yellow Ocher, and small touches of Venetian Red and Cobalt Blue where necessary. Add shadows under the chin and on the back with the same mixture, omitting white.

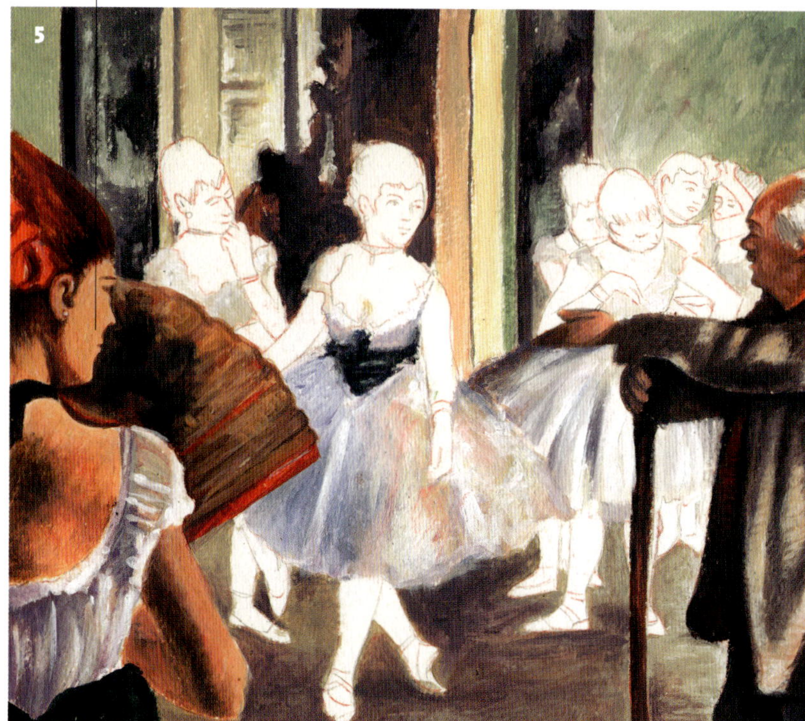

STEP 4 Build up the central dancers' dresses in Silver White, Vermilion, Cobalt Blue, Venetian Red, and a touch of Lemon Yellow. On top of this, paint streaks of Silver White, Cobalt Blue, and Prussian Blue. Paint the bodice with a blend of Prussian Blue and Chrome Green. To create the highlights on these figures, apply Silver White by dragging relatively stiff paint over some dry Yellow Ocher. This will give the impression of translucency.

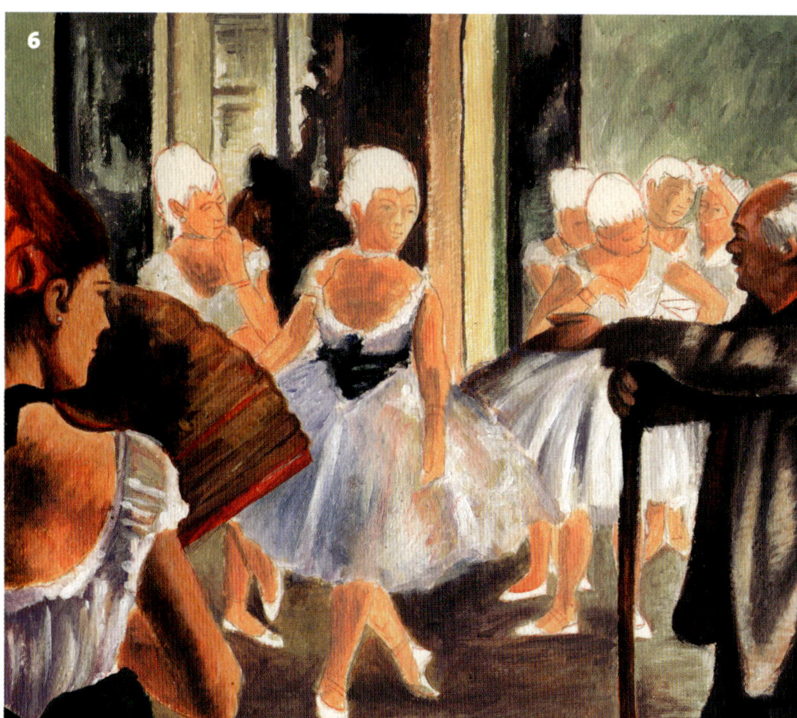

STEP 5 Using a small, flat brush, establish the foreground dancer with blends of Silver White, Vermilion, Cobalt Blue, Lemon Yellow, Venetian Red, and Yellow Ocher. Apply the paint relatively thickly, then scrape some of it off with a palette knife. Reapply the paint in a creamy consistency to develop the smooth look of a photograph. Create the black ribbon around the neck and sash from Prussian Blue, Venetian Red, and Chrome Green. Make the red rose in the hair and the edge of the fan using Vermilion straight from the tube.

STEP 6 Apply the darker skin tones to the other figures using a blend of Yellow Ocher, Venetian Red, a touch of Chrome Green, and an even smaller touch of Silver White. This should be applied to the creases and shadows. For the lighter skin tones, mix Yellow Ocher, Vermilion, and Silver White. As you do this, note the direction of the light and add the darker shadows accordingly.

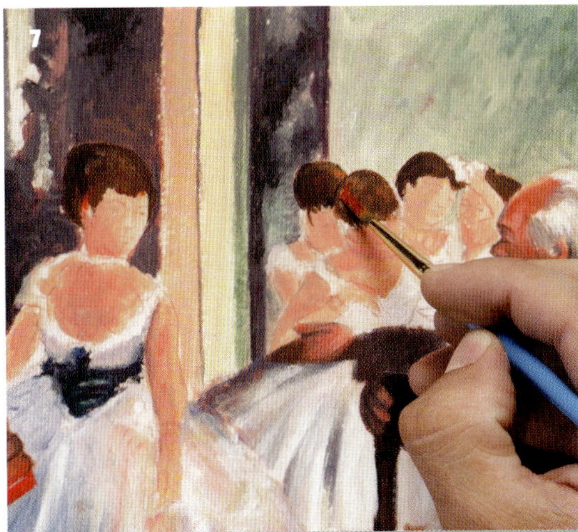

STEP 7 Now apply the hair to these dancers. Use Prussian Blue, Chrome Green, Vermilion, and Yellow Ocher in differing proportions and blend the darkest areas behind the ears. Don't forget to apply these tones roughly behind the two central figures too.

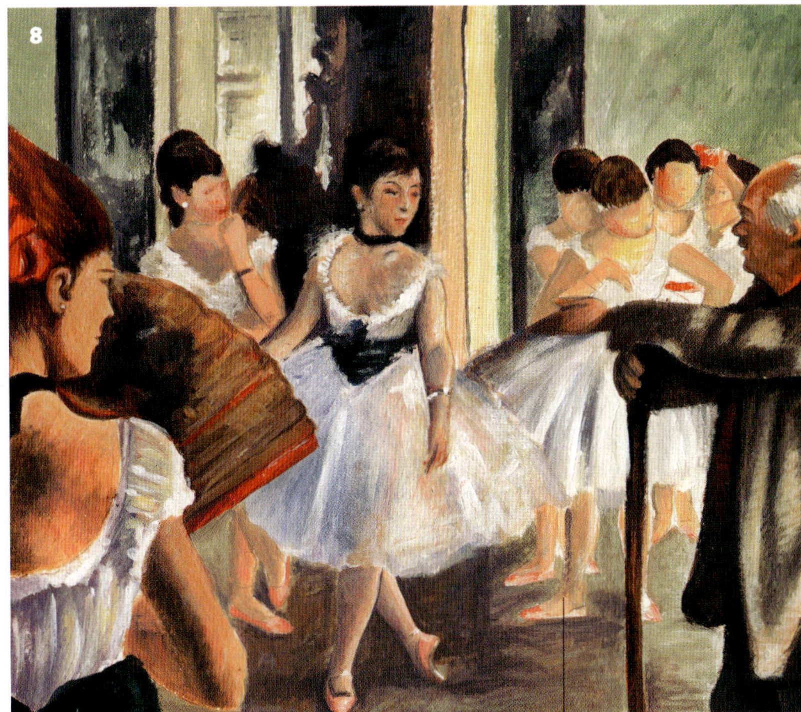

To give the impression of the shiny satin ballet shoes, make sure that your contrasts are definite and strong. Pure Silver White for highlights contrasts with some tiny touches of pure Vermilion.

STEP 8 Make refinements to the figures, blending tones and shadows using a little Cobalt Blue and gray made from Venetian Red, Chrome Green, and Lemon Yellow, as well as the previous flesh colors. Paint the ballet shoes lightly with broken marks of pink paint, leaving some of the canvas showing through. Add the pure Vermilion highlights to the dancers, the flowers in the hair, the lips, on the fan, and in the shadows on the skin. Give the central figure a black ribbon around her neck, using a fine brush loaded with a mixture of Prussian Blue, Chrome Green, and Venetian Red.

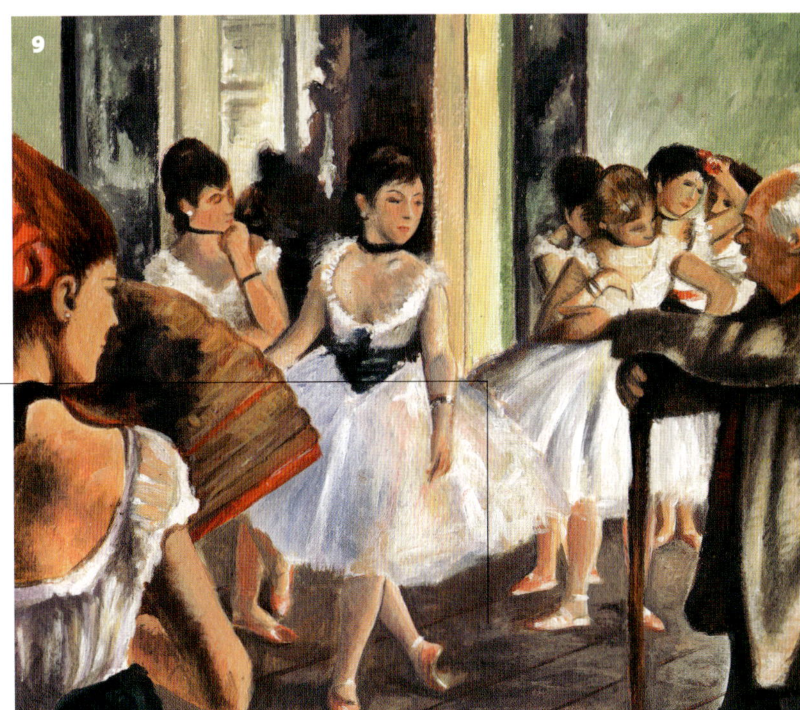

Pick out the grooves between the floorboards in straight lines with the point of a small brush or filbert brush and the dark brown mixture you began with.

STEP 9 Now create the final details, such as the floorboards, with a fine brush, picking out shadows and lighter areas. Add further highlights to the dresses with pure Silver White. Adjust any tones as necessary and, still using the fine brush, define the edges of the figures using Prussian Blue, Yellow Ocher, and Venetian Red.

Chapter ten

CÉZANNE

Paul Cézanne has been called the father of modern art. Fascinated with the techniques of both the Old Masters and the Impressionists, he began working and exhibiting with the latter group. An innovative painter, Cézanne paved the way for the movements that came after Impressionism.

RIGHT
ROCKS AND TREES, C.1904, oil on canvas, 31½ x 25¼ inches (80 x 64 cm). ***Throughout his life, Cézanne felt an affinity with his native Provence. The 1880s onward has been called his "classical" period. Here, he has broken down his natural surroundings into fundamental structures of form and color. The painting is stunningly bright, and the contrast of warm and cool colors in almost crosshatched brushwork gives the entire canvas a look of solidity. Cézanne painted this in careful, relatively thin strokes, covering the whole canvas in the first sitting and applying a few layers later.***

PAUL CÉZANNE (1839–1906) grew up in Aix-en-Provence and went to school with the novelist Emile Zola. He enrolled at the University of Aix to study law, but his heart wasn't in it, and, by the time he moved to Paris in 1861, his father reluctantly agreed that he could study art. He joined an independent studio where he met other young painters, including Pissarro, who introduced him to painting outdoors, as well as working with a brighter palette. He and Pissarro painted alla prima together daily during 1872, and his work became noticeably more Impressionistic during that time. Both artists used small brush strokes and snapshot techniques, such as cropping the edges of scenes, in a similar way to Degas.

Until about 1870, Cézanne's work varied dramatically. In some works, he applied paint expressively with a knife or thick impasto, and, in others, he used more traditional, finer brushwork. He studied Old Masters, particularly Peter Paul Rubens (1577–1640) and Delacroix, and also became fascinated with the Impressionists' ideas. Through

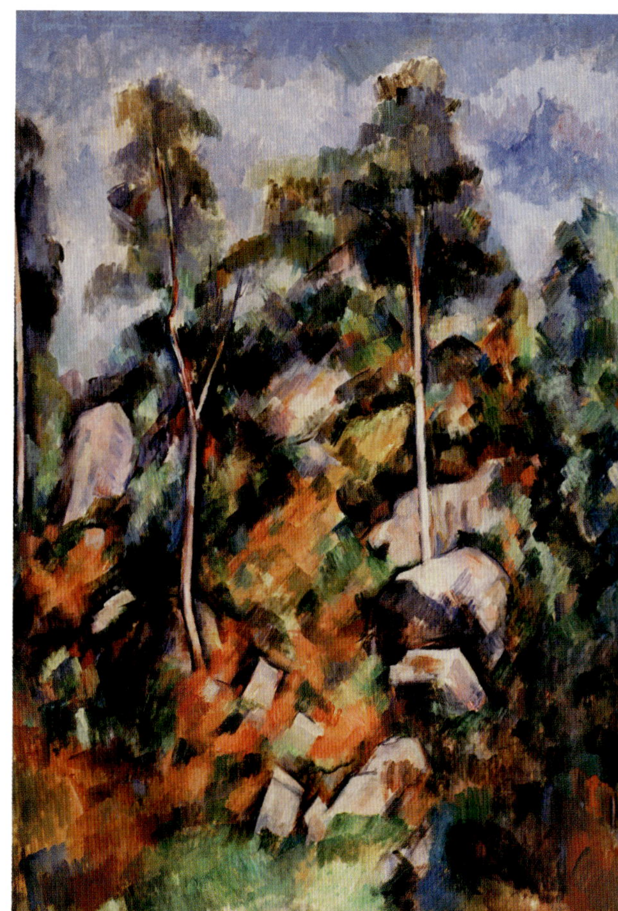

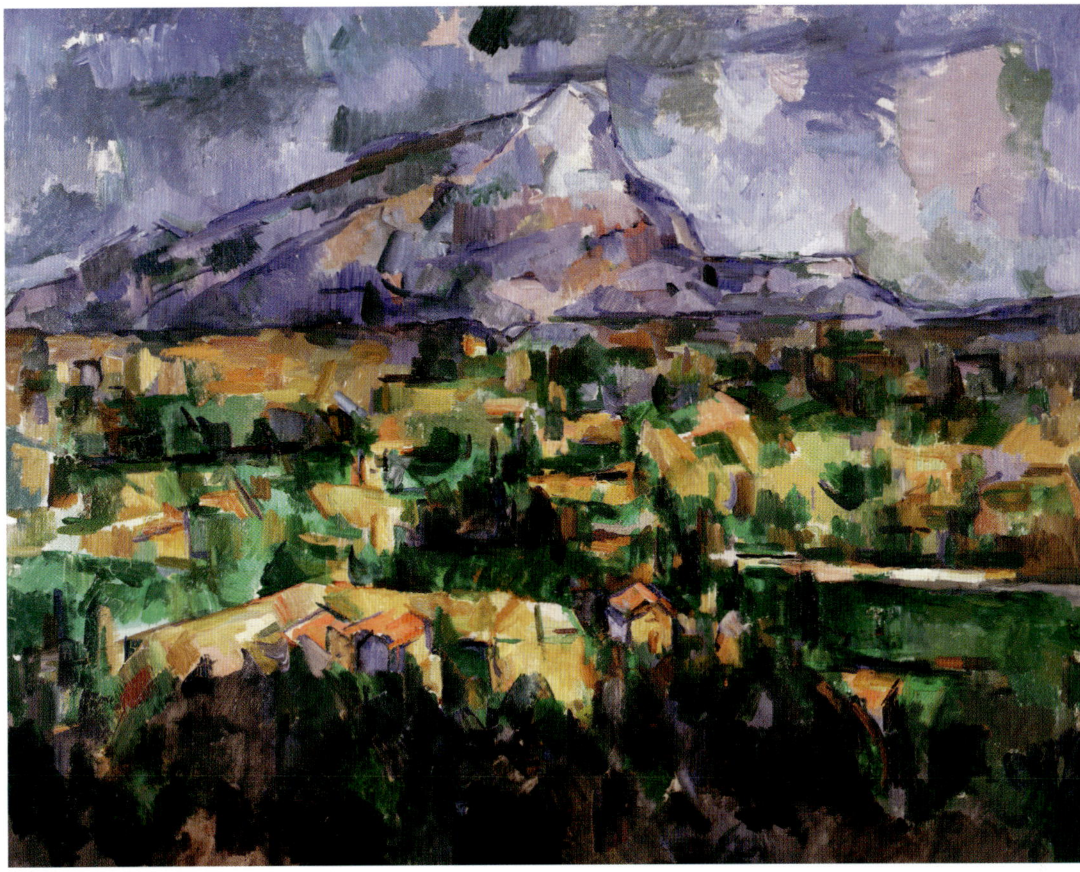

RIGHT
MONT SAINTE-VICTOIRE, 1904–1906, oil on canvas, 28¾ x 35¾ inches (73 x 91 cm).
Cézanne revisited this subject many times from the early 1880s until his death, trying to imbue each painting with the emotions he felt for the area. Although he was painting what he saw, he never intended to paint replicas of any image, but used expressive brushwork to create paintings that expressed his emotions at the sight of it. He never seemed to tire of this view, and he painted it so often in different lights and materials that it has become synonymous with his name.

Pissarro, he took part in the first Impressionist exhibition and began to consider how he could unite Impressionist ideas with the traditions of the masters. By the 1880s, Cézanne began traveling back and forth between Paris and Aix-en-Provence and started developing a way of painting that he spent the rest of his life refining. He applied paint with separate, overlapping brush strokes to produce patterned, almost woven, structural effects. In his own way, he was trying to resolve the contradiction of creating three-dimensional illusions on two-dimensional picture surfaces.

Searching for structure

Unlike many of the Impressionists, Cézanne practiced still-life painting throughout his career. He repeatedly painted the same objects, trying to work out their underlying structures. His way of working tended to isolate him from society, and he usually worked alone.

Toward the end of the nineteenth century, he had established a completely new approach to painting—images from different viewpoints painted onto one, flat canvas. The rules of perspective that had been handed down from the Renaissance were no longer appropriate or necessary to him. He had worked out a fresh approach to representation that tried to uncover the essence of nature. This meant that his paintings were made up of relatively complex structures, instead of direct illusions. Artists that came after him picked up this idea when they moved toward Cubism. Despite the obvious differences, Cézanne was in accord with the aims of the Impressionists, and his commitment to recording his visual sensations stayed with him for the rest of his life.

CREATING MASS AND SOLID FORM

BELOW
THE CARD PLAYERS, c.1893, oil on canvas, 17¾ x 22½ inches (45 x 57 cm).
Cézanne was not interested in painting an emotional scene here but a deliberate combination of shapes and colors. The symmetrical composition, emphasized by the shadows on the wall, the bottle on the table, the chair back, and the table legs, gives the picture a solid stillness.

ONE OF THE MOST noticeable and unique aspects of Cézanne's paintings is the appearance of solidity. He was not concerned with representing short-lived impressions and light effects. Instead, he was more interested, as he said, in making "something solid and enduring, like the art of the museums." He worked in a slow, methodical way, often spending years on one painting, leaving it and returning to it later to make adjustments.

Cézanne aimed to achieve depth and density on his canvases and his determination paid off. Often applying relatively thick, almost buttery, paint with a palette knife, or overlaying oil paints with transparent watercolors, he produced remarkable effects. He often layered his oil paints while the paint surface was still wet in order to create interlocking planes of contrasting colors.

In 1872, the paintings that Cézanne produced with Pissarro were more Impressionistic due to the way he used thin, flexible palette knives and small dabs of color. Even then, he was focusing on

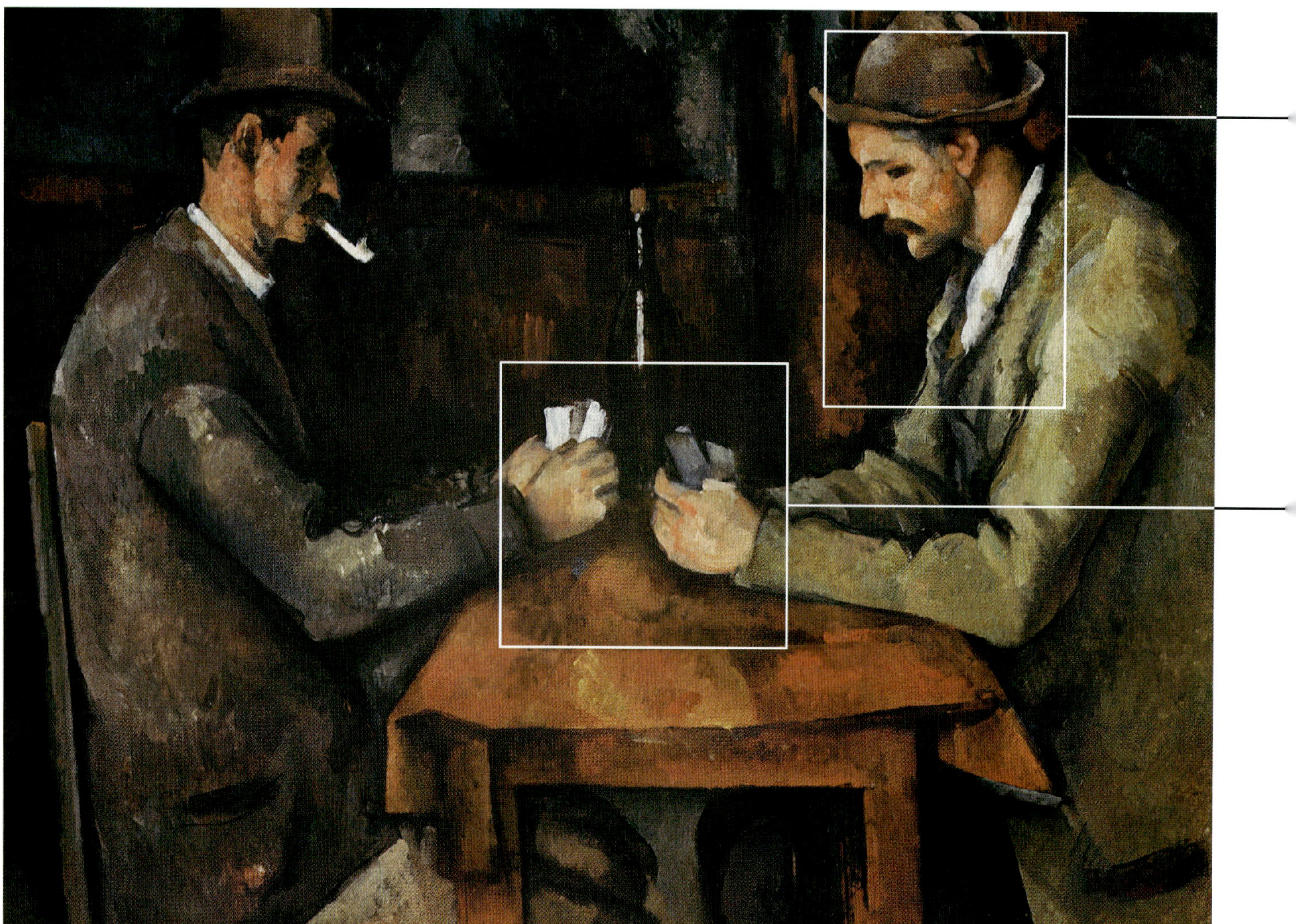

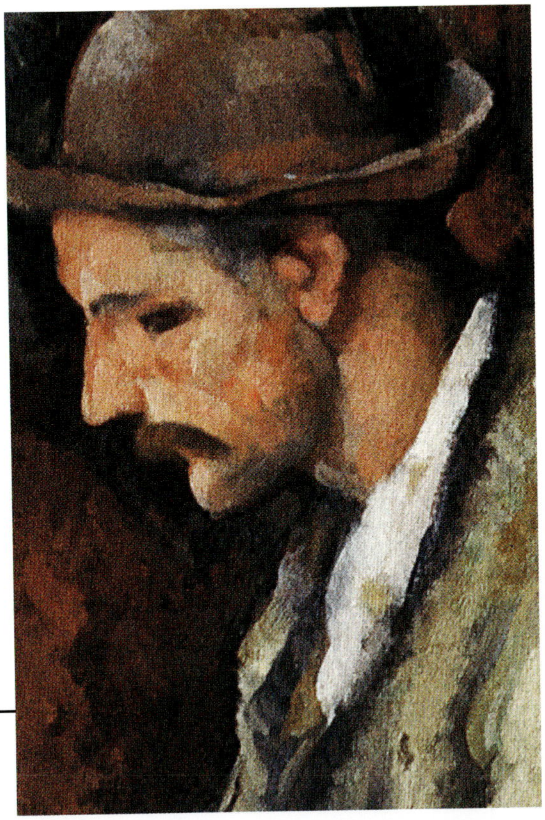

LEFT
THE CARD PLAYERS, detail.
The paint is applied in thin brush marks, layered and overlapped to build up the smooth, opaque shapes on the canvas that convey the image in a patchwork of forms and patterns. Cézanne insisted that each small brush stroke was significant.

how forms are constructed, instead of how they appear. All his paintings have dense, intricate modeling and every object is painted carefully and individually.

Relationships between elements

Because Cézanne came from a successful family and was, therefore, relatively wealthy, he didn't have to make a living out of his art. This allowed him to experiment and spend time striving for a new approach to painting. He was mainly concerned with two things, which he described as his motif and his "*petite sensation.*" The motif was the identity of the subject and the *petite sensation* was its individual special quality. No scene or image was reproduced simply for its own sake. All component parts of each picture, whether the negative spaces, shadows, or objects themselves, had their own relationships to each other. Even the backgrounds he created were of critical importance to the overall image of solidity.

Cézanne's ideas about mass and solidity didn't mean his paintings were heavy. Indeed, many of his works are painted so lightly that the canvas shows through the paint. He painted slowly, carefully considering each brush stroke before applying it. He often layered cool over warm colors, and redrew contours several times in the course of a painting to ensure that the composition didn't "slip." He usually kept to a palette of four reds, four yellows, two browns, three blues, a green, and black and white. The resulting bright but earthy tones helped to give weight to his works.

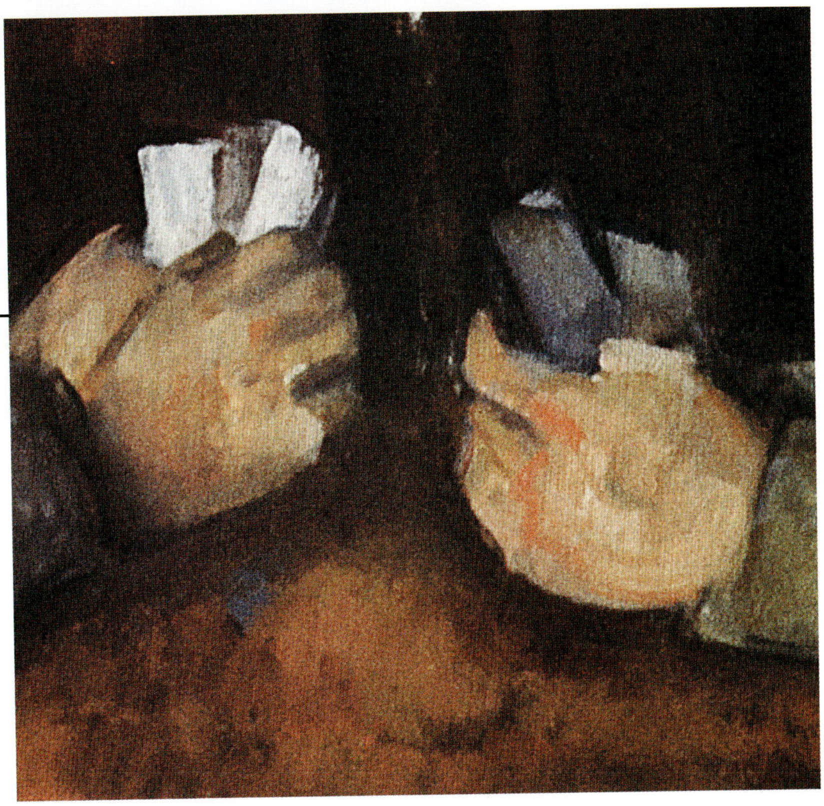

LEFT
THE CARD PLAYERS, detail.
Cézanne began lightly with almost neutral colors, then layered further colors on top. The jacket and hands have been worked rapidly.

HOW TO DO IT

YOUR PALETTE

Cézanne used a bright, fresh palette of colors:

1 Raw Umber
2 Zinc White
3 Cobalt Blue
4 Yellow Ocher
5 Chrome Yellow
6 Vermilion
7 French Ultramarine
8 Emerald Green
9 Viridian
10 Ceruleum Blue

As you work, keep the paint in a relatively fluid, creamy consistency and don't overblend. Use small marks in pure colors blended together on the canvas.

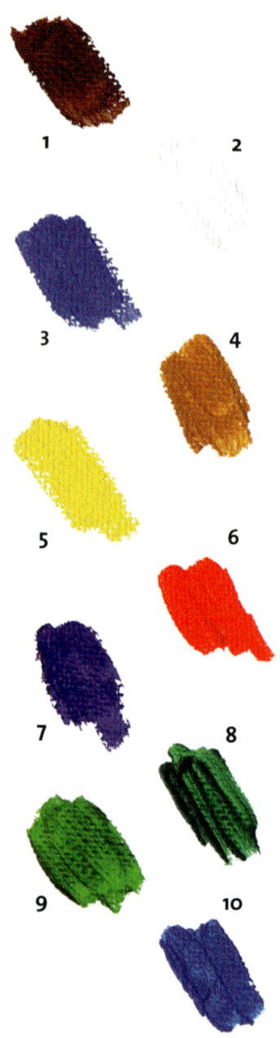

Compared to Monet's or Sisley's trees, Cézanne's look solid and immobile. This is partly because of the effects of light and color. The light and color in Paris, where the majority of the Impressionists painted, was different from the light and color found in Provence. This is because south light reflects an almost gaudy color. In this painting, the light is both diffused and reflected, which amplifies the colors.

The main techniques

As well as intensifying and brightening the colors that appear in the light, you should strengthen the shadows—both cast and reflected—to create the impression of solidity. The idea here is not to see the image as a whole, but to examine it piece by piece. Allow your sense of perspective to continuously change and exaggerate the effects as you paint. Although Cézanne's brushwork is not apparent, the sense of the direction of his paint applications is characteristic of his work and is something that you should focus on as you re-create this painting.

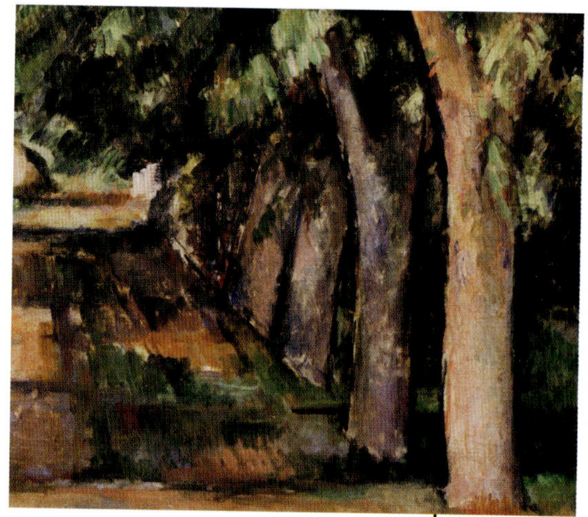

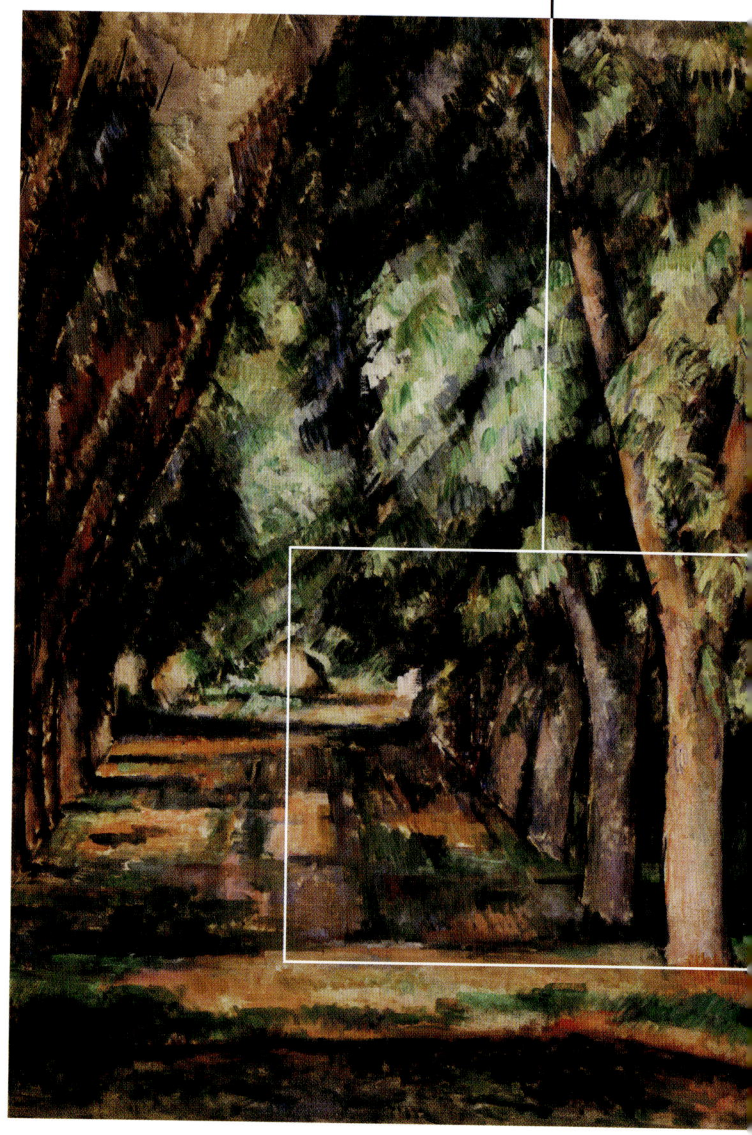

RIGHT

APPROACH TO JAS DE BOUFFAN, c.1888, oil on canvas, 31½ x 25¼ inches (80 x 64 cm). ***The Jas de Bouffan was an eighteenth-century country house owned by Cézanne's father and was one of his favorite retreats. The picture shows part of the chestnut tree-lined driveway that was behind the house. He wanted to capture the serenity and pleasure he felt when walking along that road to the house and created a taut network of trees that rise up to a dense and radiant leafy green canopy above.***

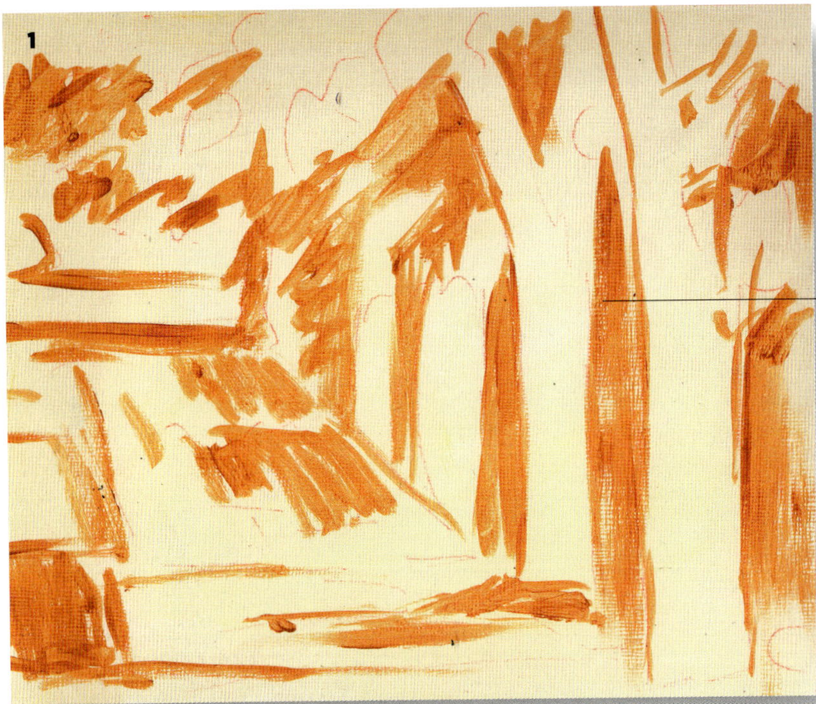

STEP 1 Prepare your canvas with a coat of cream acrylic, then sketch the outlines of the composition with pencil, graphite, or charcoal. Use a light wash of Raw Umber to indicate the shapes of the trees and their shadows.

This thin underpainting has been made out of Raw Umber, diluted with turpentine and applied with a relatively small brush.

STEP 2 Mix up about three shades of green, using the yellows, blues, and greens of the palette in varying amounts. Apply these in thin scumbles, using relatively wide brushes, to create the foliage and grass.

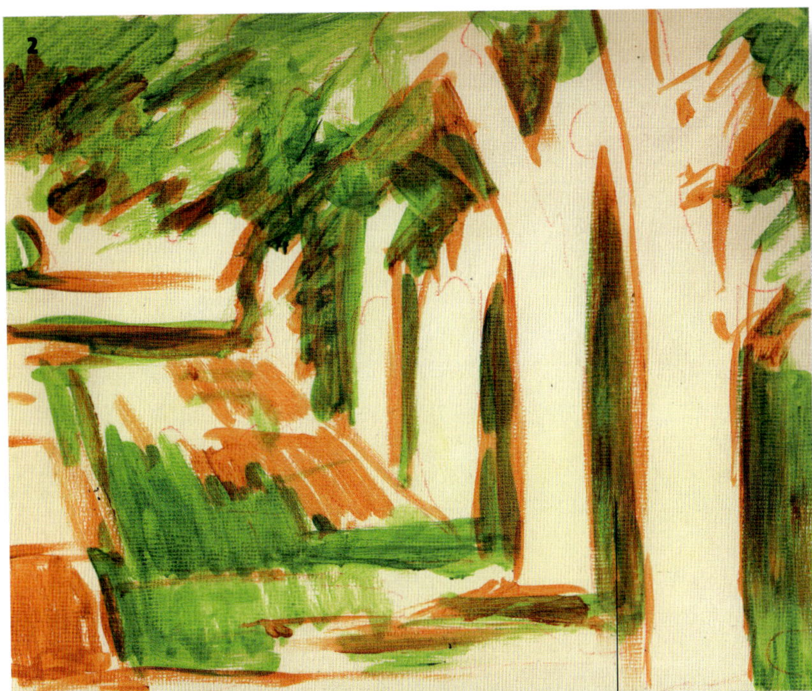

The depth and density of the foliage is carefully worked in contrasting colors, so apply the paint in thin, opaque layers.

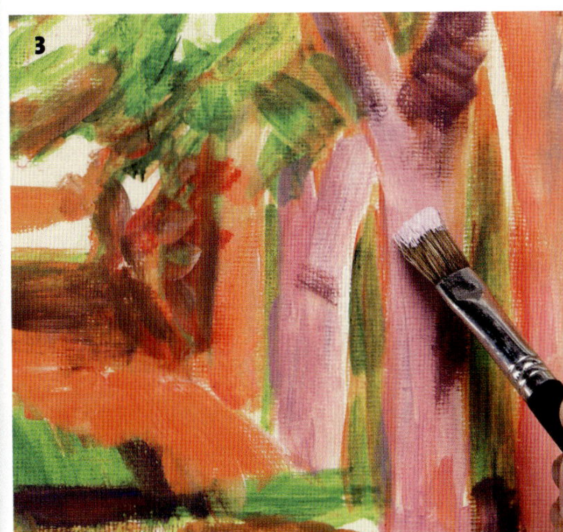

STEP 3 Using a bristle brush, apply color loosely to the tree trunks. For this, you should use a mixture of Vermilion, Zinc White, Cobalt Blue, and Yellow Ocher. You should not worry about being neat as you do this, but try to keep your touch light and the paint relatively thin. Also allow the canvas to show through here and there. Indicate shadow areas using Viridian, Chrome Yellow and French Ultramarine.

STEP 4 Using a smaller brush and thicker paint, work on small sections of the painting—beginning with the tree in the foreground to the right and moving on to add in the darkest tones to the whole picture. Use mixtures of Yellow Ocher, Vermilion, Zinc White, Cobalt Blue, Viridian, French Ultramarine, and Ceruleum Blue. Squint as you do this to ensure you create the darkest areas of color in the right places. Add shadows to the base of the trees using French Ultramarine, Vermilion, and Yellow Ocher.

STEP 5 The monumentality of this painting comes from the tonal contrasts and the layers of heavy-looking paint. So, working wet-in-wet, use a knife to enhance the tactile surface quality of the picture, concentrating mainly on the extreme darks and lights. Continue working on the trunks of the trees, and merge them with the distant foliage, blending this into the ground at the base of the trees.

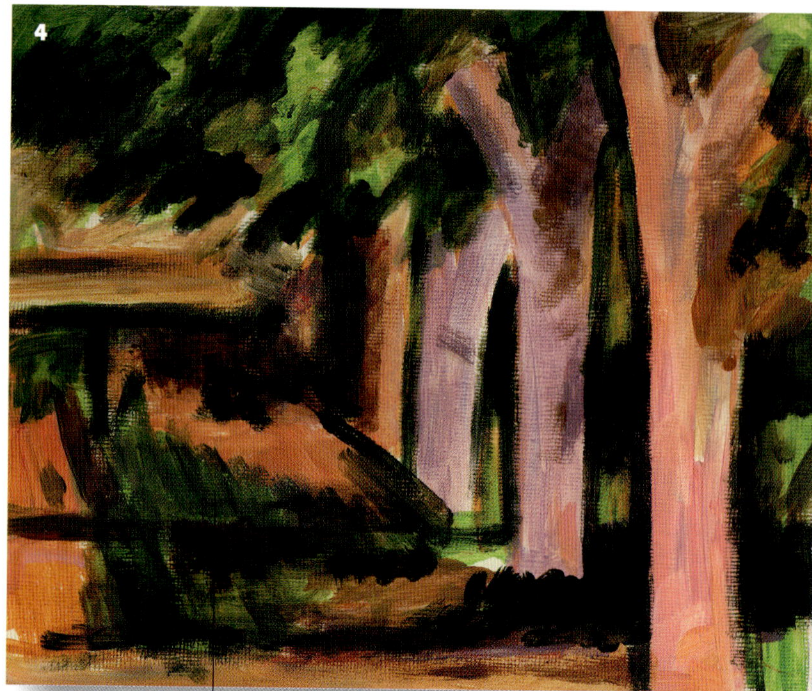

Layer the paint in thin applications without worrying too much about neatness at this stage—just ensure that your colors remain distinctive and bright.

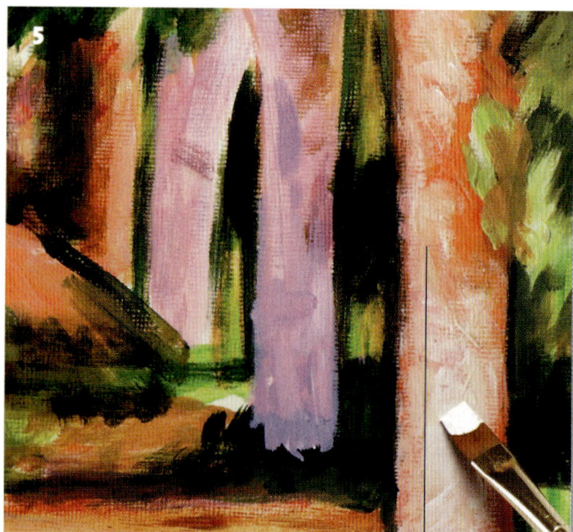

Your paint should be creamy, but not too thick or impasted. Exaggerate the tones here—they will be softened and merge as you continue.

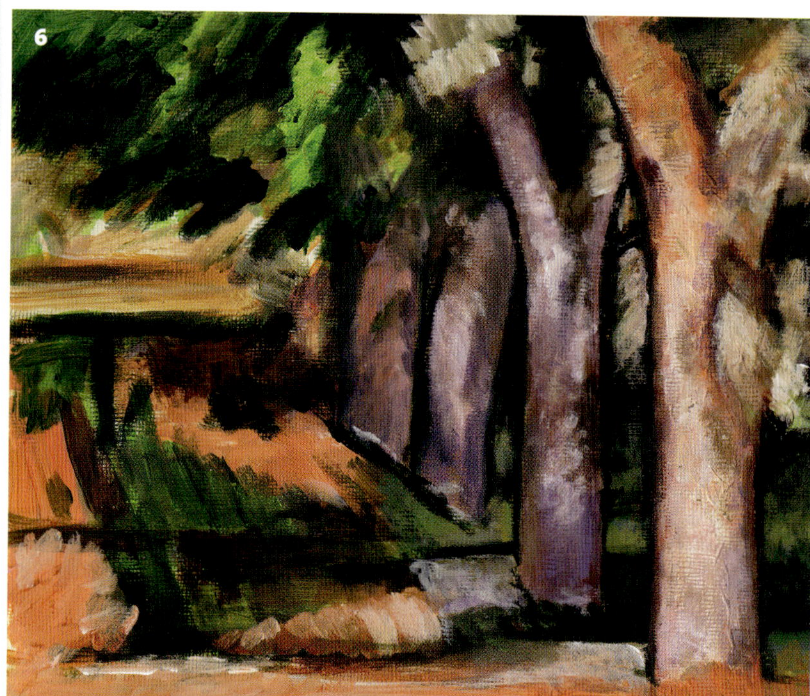

STEP 6 Block in the road tones with flat strokes to give the impression that the road is receding, using Viridian, Emerald Green, Yellow Ocher, Vermilion, Ceruleum Blue, and French Ultramarine. Also blur and blend these colors, wet-in-wet, onto the tree trunks and foreground.

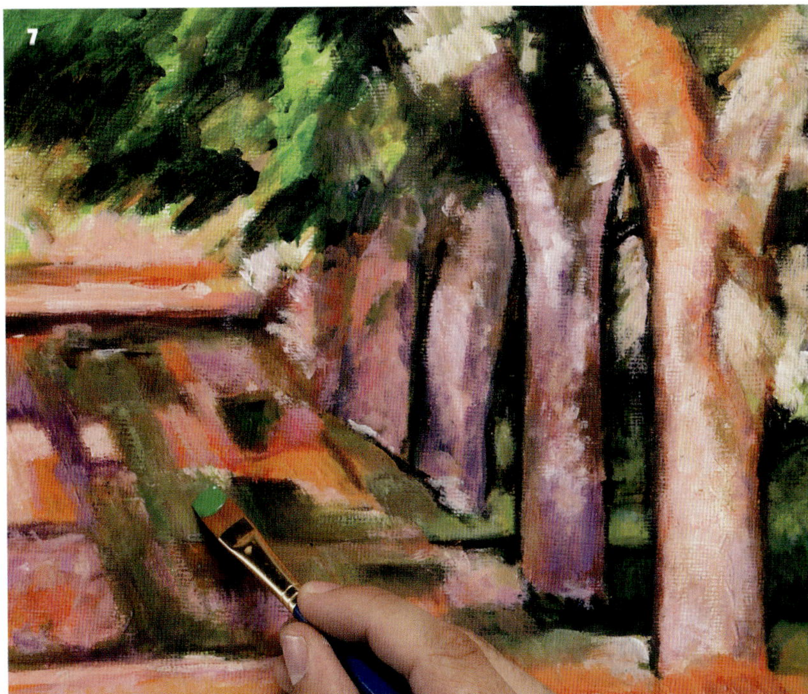

STEP 7 Using a small flat brush and keeping the paint in the same creamy consistency that you have been working with, lighten the areas where the sunlight has managed to touch. This includes the road and some of the foliage. Work with directional brush marks to aid the impression of perspective and the same colors as in Step 6, only with the addition of Zinc White.

STEP 8 For the final step, work on the foliage on the trees using angled, flat brush strokes. Add brighter accents to them with Viridian mixed with Ceruleum Blue and Chrome Yellow. Hold the painting up to a mirror to ensure that you've included the right amount of dark and light tones and make any necessary adjustments.

Although you have been applying lighter colors predominantly in the last couple of steps, don't go over the darkest tones. If this happens, simply reinforce them with further thin layers of paint.

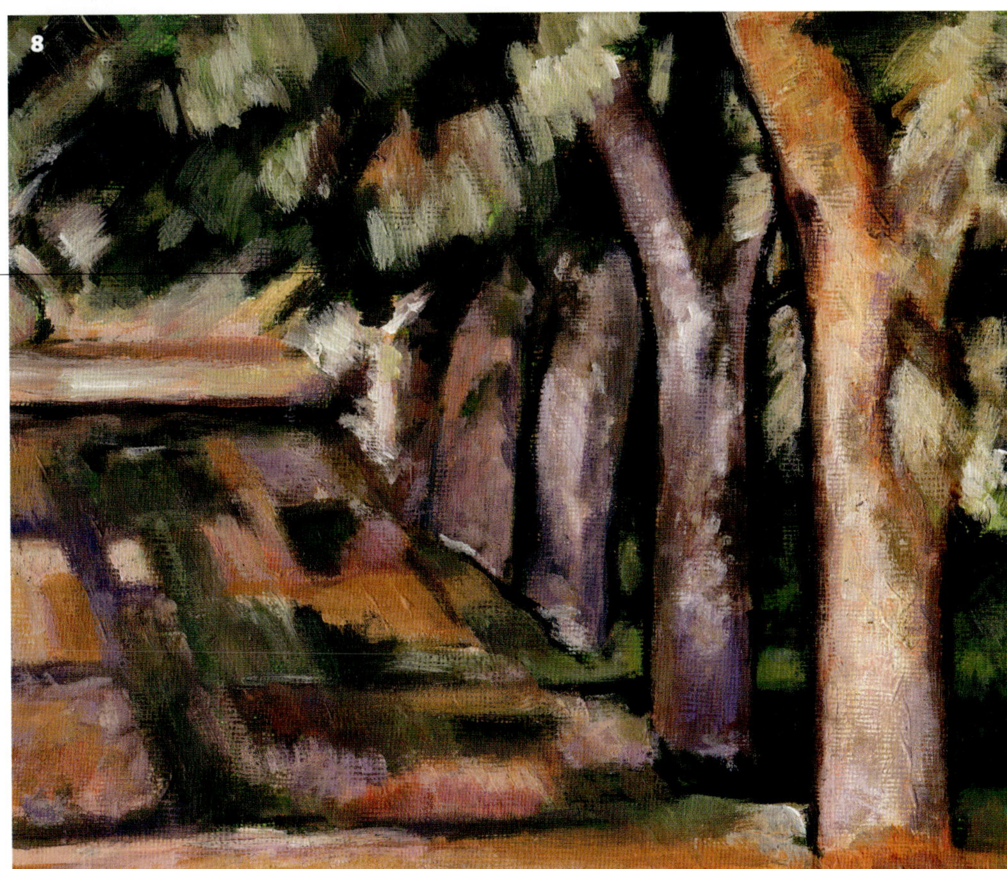

PAINTING STILL LIFE

During the early nineteenth century, the still life declined in popularity. It was Cézanne's explorations into it that were largely responsible for rekindling artists' interest. However, since he applied the same methodical analysis to his still-life paintings as he did to his landscapes, his still lifes were unlike anything that had been painted before. He painted simple shapes of fruits, jugs, and bowls as if he was trying to analyze their fundamental forms of spheres, cubes, and cylinders. He also arranged them carefully before beginning work, in such a way that he could concentrate on the contrasts and contradictions of round and angular forms.

Cézanne often spent ages in front of the canvas without painting a single brush stroke, just contemplating what he was going to do. In his lifetime, he completed over 200 still-life paintings, creating an infinitely varied series of compositions and repeatedly including the same household objects along with everyday fruits and vegetables.

The main ingredients of Cézanne's still lifes were not the objects themselves, but the fact that he painted them from several different angles at once, avoiding conventional linear perspective. The objects may appear to have been arranged at random, but Cézanne planned every composition carefully to ensure it would be full of dynamism and tension. He admired the Spanish painter Francisco de Zurbarán (1598–1664), who,

BELOW
PEARS AND PEACHES, detail.
Cézanne experimented with still life to explore how color contrasts can create the impression of three-dimensional forms. His use of bright, clear colors, contrasting with the deepest tones and tints, emphasize the solid forms of the fruits.

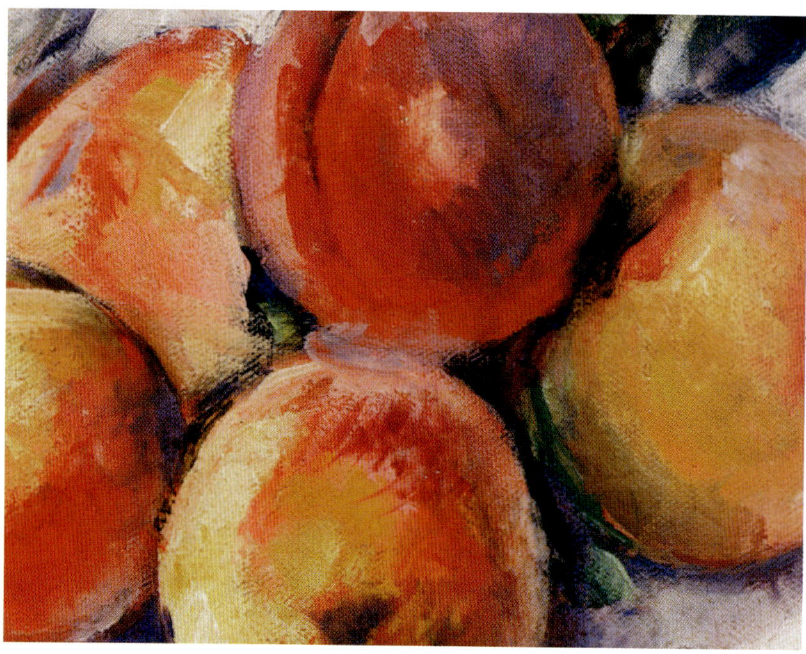

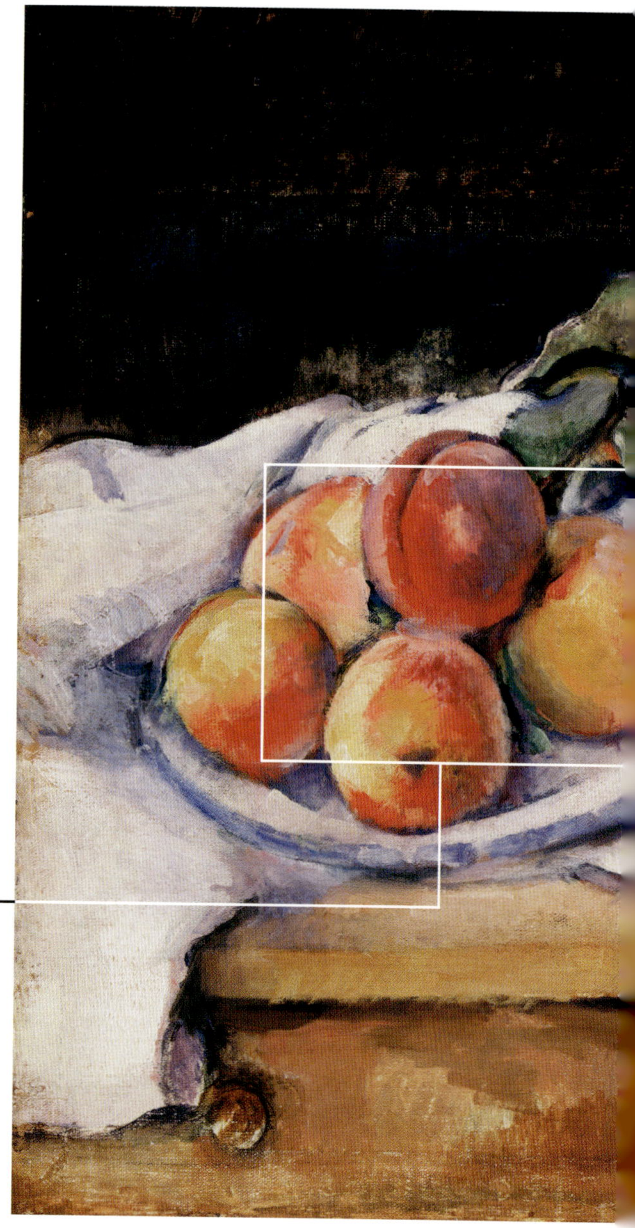

BELOW
PEARS AND PEACHES, 1890–93, oil on canvas, 14¾ x 17¼ inches (37.5 x 44 cm). *Cézanne often painted the same fruits over and over again, and his constant rearranging of them was his way of understanding structure. Note how the curves of the fruits and certain colors are echoed across the painting. Cézanne's contrasts are strong and the shadows do not deepen continuously but are a patchwork of blues and complementaries, applied in brush strokes that echo the shapes of the cloth and the fruits.*

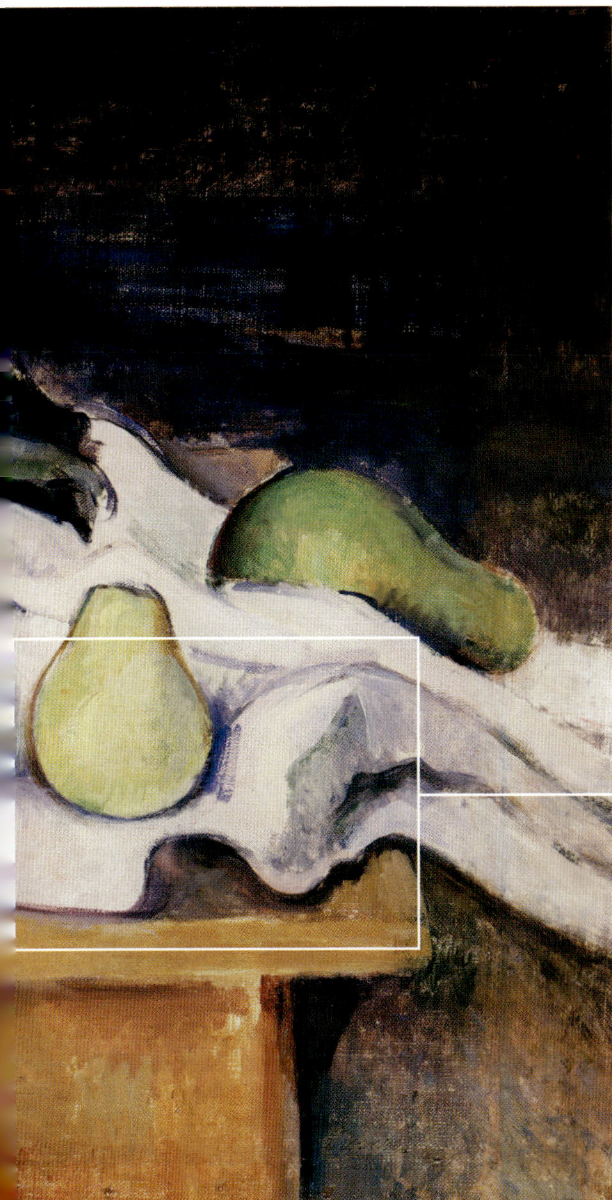

among other things, painted dramatically modeled still lifes. Many of Cézanne's paintings included gleaming white cloths, relatively plain containers, and spherical fruits and vegetables—such as onions, oranges, apples, cherries, pears, and peaches. He used neutral foregrounds to make the colors of the objects appear more intense.

Because all the colors were tonally balanced with one another, the paintings required a slow and careful style of working. He developed each picture with small areas of paint placed across the whole of the canvas—a method he had developed when painting alla prima. Later in life, Cézanne used base washes of pale cream, and he occasionally left these washes showing through gaps in the paint layer. He also sometimes experimented with transparent layers of watercolor over several oil paintings. Cézanne included complementary contrasts in his shadows and painted with mainly square, blunt brush strokes, following the curves of each object. Several of Cézanne's objects were painted from such close proximity that they appear to be dramatically foreshortened.

BELOW
PEARS AND PEACHES, detail. *Cézanne said that all shadow is darkest at its source and that reflective color bounces off local color. In this painting, the white cloth and rounded fruits are built up from what he called "little planes" of color.*

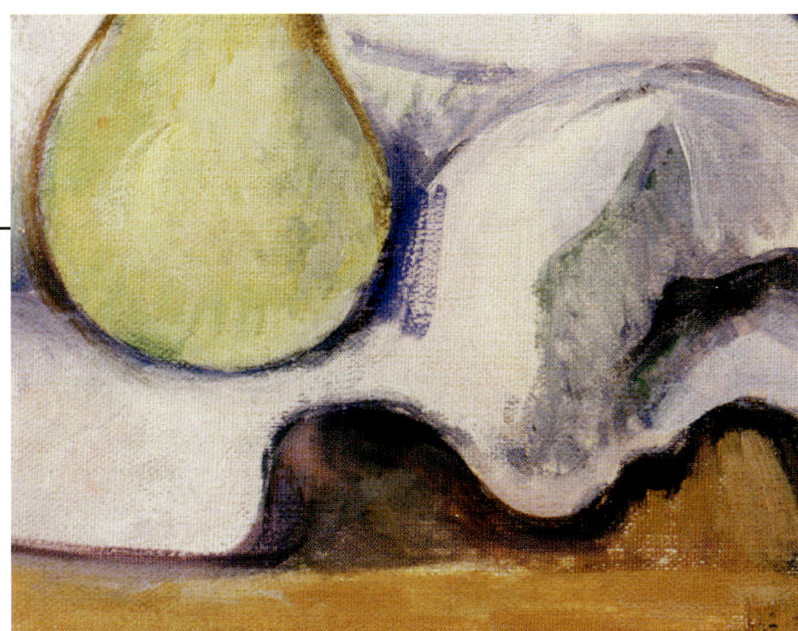

HOW TO DO IT

YOUR PALETTE
You should use a selection of pure colors and make the necessary varieties of hues and tones from them:

1 Zinc White
2 Yellow Ocher
3 Chrome Yellow
4 Vermilion
5 French Ultramarine
6 Emerald Green
7 Viridian

Be bold and confident in your use of these colors as you build up the painting.

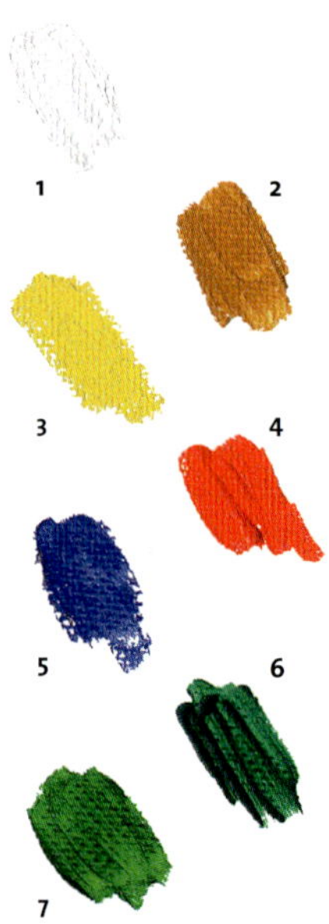

TO ACHIEVE CÉZANNE'S still-life style, you should paint contrasting edges between one color and another or apply white between colors. You might also want to begin with an underpainting in tan, which is something Cézanne often did.

Try to emphasize where a curve balances a straight line and contrast shiny surfaces against matte ones. In a similar way, place cool colors (such as Cobalt) in close proximity to warm ones (such as Vermilion).

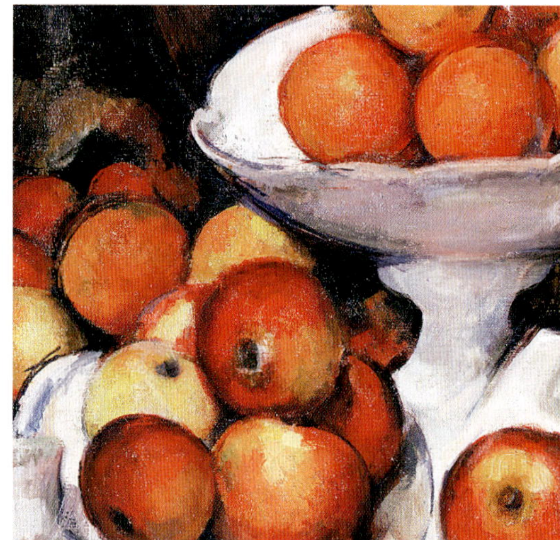

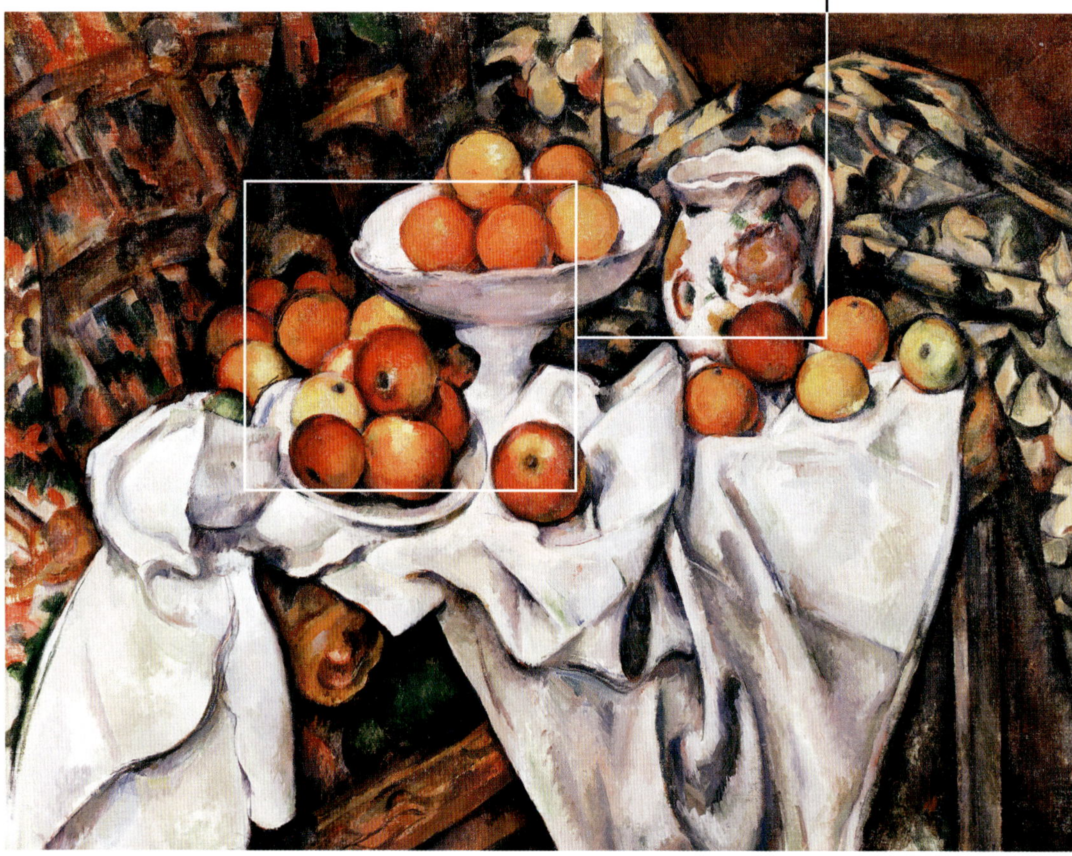

The main techniques

Juxtapose complementary colors and echo and complement shapes across the canvas, picking up a curve here and a sharp angle there. Be aware of this as you apply your paint, as well as the changing perspective.

ABOVE
STILL LIFE WITH APPLES AND ORANGES, c.1898–99, oil on canvas, 29 x $36\frac{1}{2}$ inches (74 x 93 cm).
The simple forms and polished surfaces of the apples and earthenware contrast with the soft folds of the white cloth. These elements emphasize Cézanne's commitment to composition and shape, instead of light or movement.

STEP 1 Prepare your canvas or board with a cream wash, using a large brush and thin paint. Use opaque gouache, thinned oil paint, latex paint, or acrylic paint.

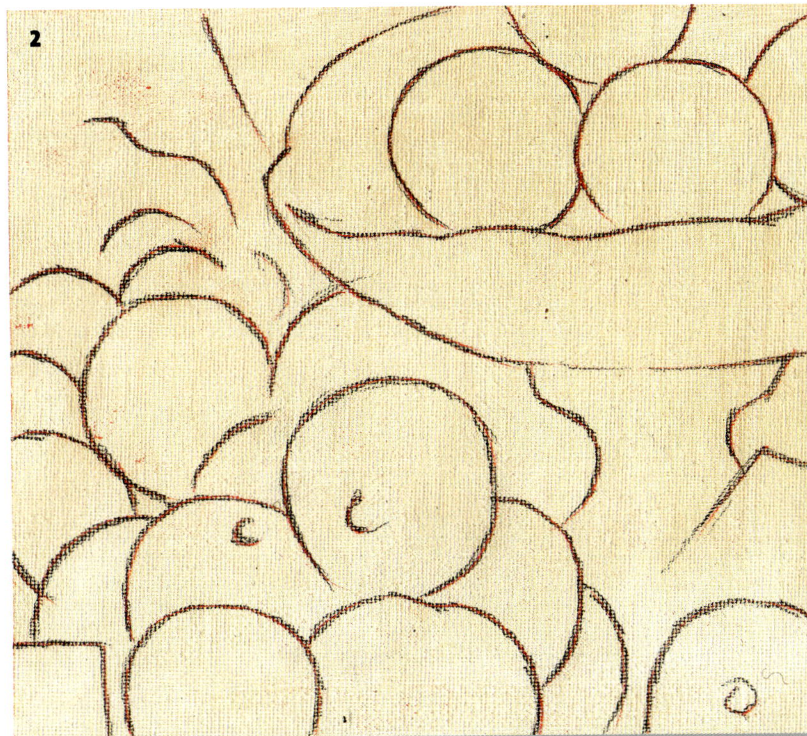

STEP 2 Draw the initial outlines of the fruits and dishes using a soft 2B pencil. As you do this, pay attention to the curving shapes that echo one another, and create the two different viewing angles.

STEP 3 Continue to work on the drawn shapes, outlining them with a thin wash of French Ultramarine paint. Apply this lightly and sketchily and fill in the background with the same color.

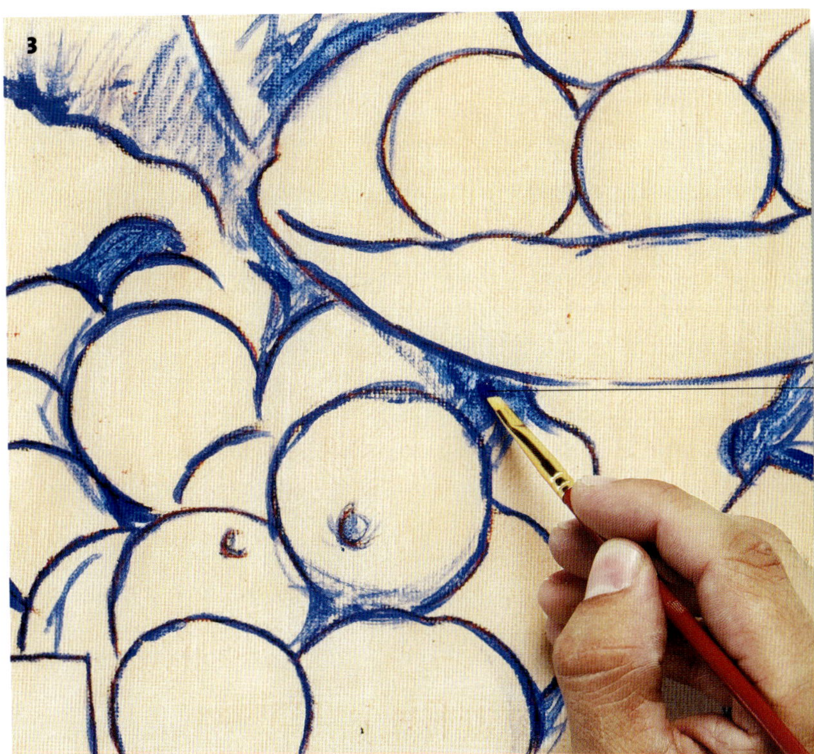

Apply the Ultramarine paint with a No. 4 filbert brush and lightly fill in the background color.

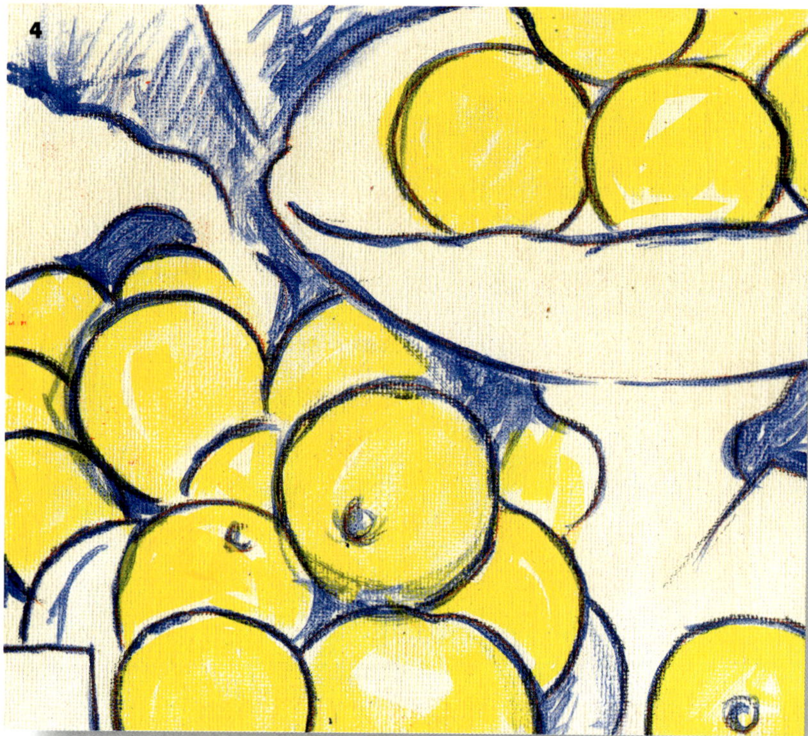

STEP 4 Instead of modeling the three-dimensional shapes by gradually blending shades from dark to light, Cézanne gave them form by juxtaposing colors. Use a small to medium flat brush to fill in the fruits with a thin wash of Chrome Yellow, being careful to follow the contours of the shapes. Allow the canvas to show through in places.

STEP 5 Using pure, unblended Zinc White, block in the dishes and cloth. Cézanne used both color contrasts and a variety of brush strokes to describe the objects. Begin using slightly thicker, more fluid paint to make the darker tones in the background and around the fruits with Vermilion, French Ultramarine, and Emerald Green. Remember to use complementaries next to each other, so, for example, next to the brightest red-orange apply dark, green-blue shadows.

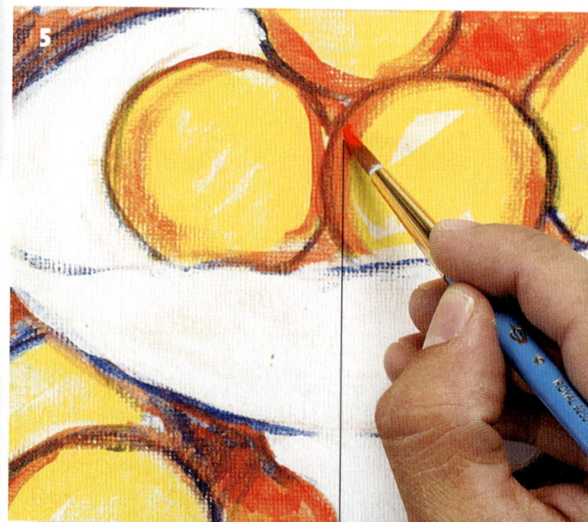

Apply Vermilion to the apples with a No. 6 round brush.

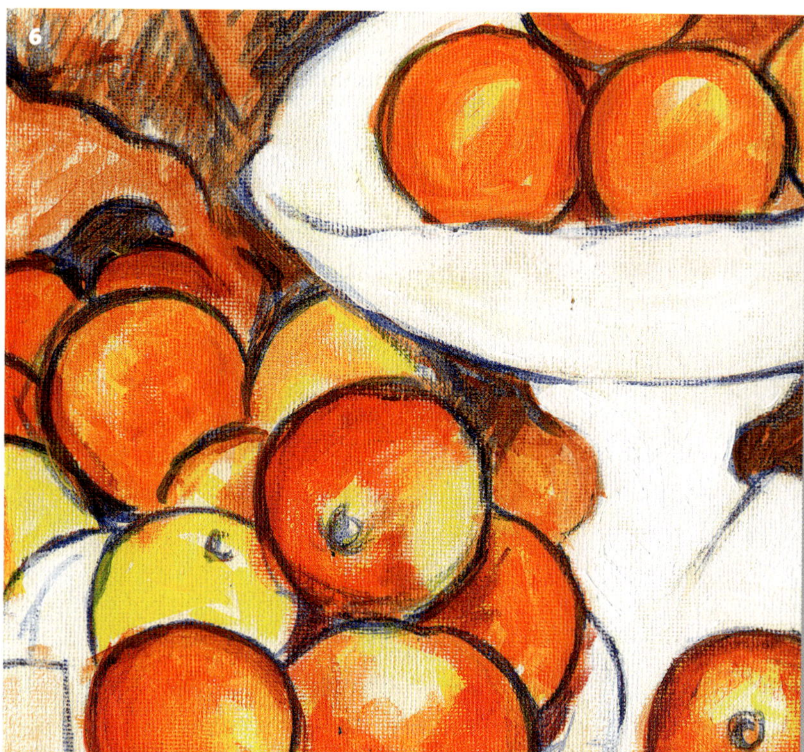

STEP 6 Add accents of reds and oranges with Vermilion and Chrome Yellow. Work wet-in-wet for this and make adjustments continuously as needed. Using blue under orange, as you have done here, is known as the Venetian technique. Many of the Impressionists employed this method of using cool colors under warm or vice versa. Here, it deepens and enriches the look of the fruits.

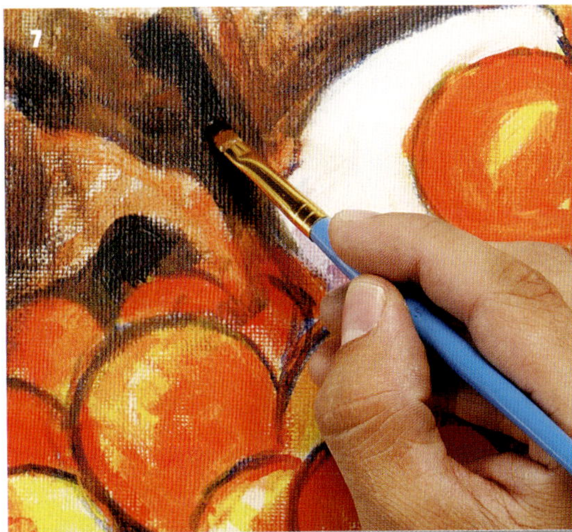

STEP 7 Apply pinkish tones to the underneath of the tall dish, using Vermilion, French Ultramarine, and Zinc White. Strengthen the shadows in the background with a mixture of French Ultramarine, Viridian, Chrome Yellow, and Vermilion.

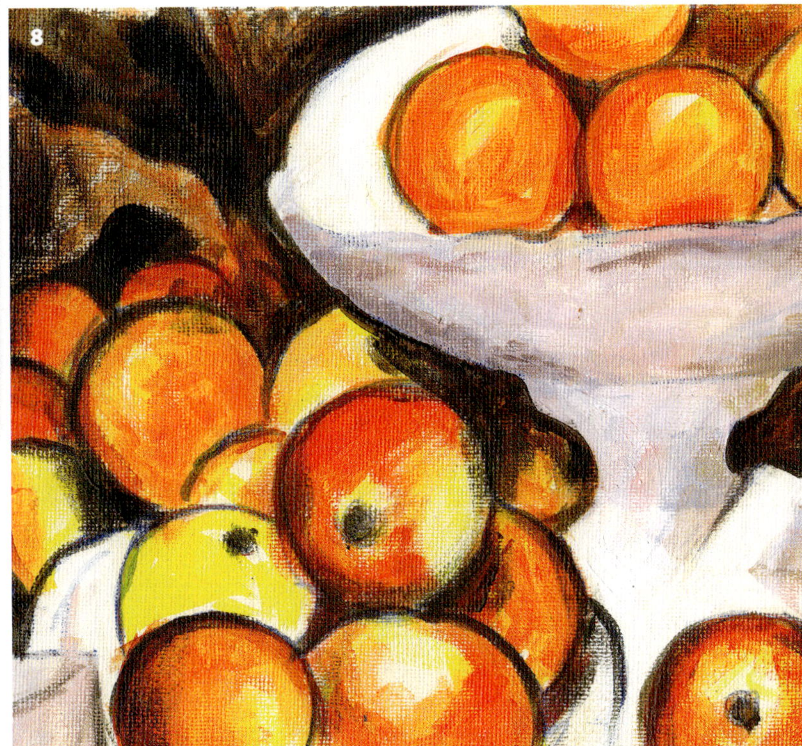

STEP 8 Blend and refine the apples and oranges using Chrome Yellow, Vermilion, and Zinc White with touches of French Ultramarine, Viridian, and Chrome Yellow added in the shadows. Create mid-tones, and begin to apply these between the objects.

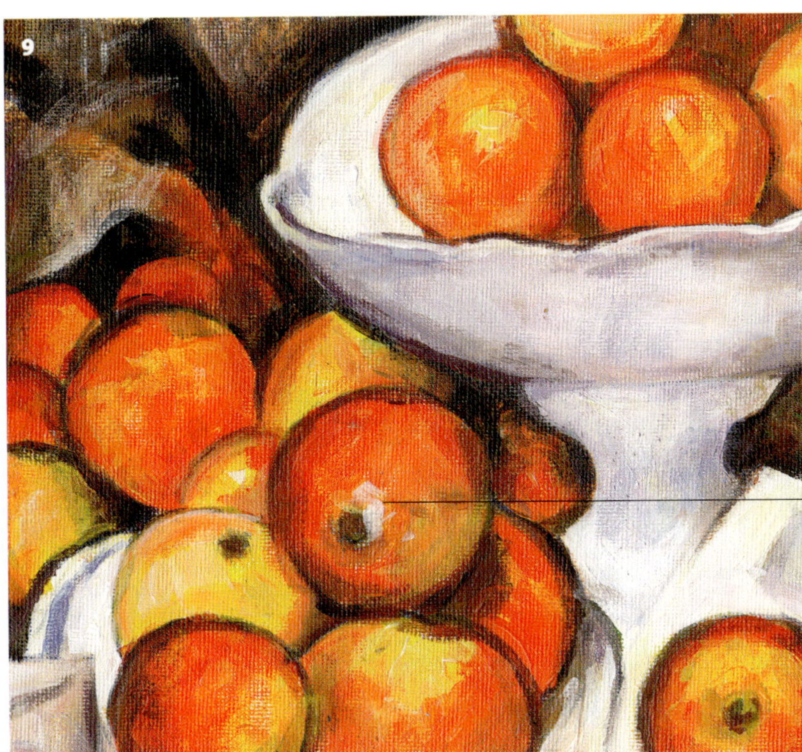

The brightest highlights have been achieved using pure white.

STEP 9 Enrich and deepen the colors on the fruits using pure colors straight from the tubes where necessary. Also use pure Zinc White to add the brightest highlights. To finish, using the point of a fine brush on the top rim and lefthand side of the tall dish, paint a dark outline with French Ultramarine, Yellow Ocher, and Vermilion. These finishing touches will complete your painting.

Chapter eleven

SEURAT

Seurat was younger than the Impressionists but saw their fourth exhibition in 1879. He was interested in what he saw and adopted many of the Impressionists' ideas, even exhibiting with them later on. However, he took his painting in a different direction and eventually developed the style known as pointillism.

RIGHT
YOUNG WOMAN POWDERING HERSELF, 1888–90, oil on canvas, 37½ x 31¼ inches (95.5 x 79.5 cm).
This portrait of Seurat's mistress was his only large portrait. Painted in his meticulous pointillist style, she is laced into a tight corset and dabs herself with a dainty powder puff. Seurat believed that, as with different sounds and tempos in music, the directions of lines and warmth and coolness of colors had an effect on the viewers' moods. The mood he was expressing here, with his swirling dots and happy colors, was happiness. (This adheres to the theories of a scientist named Charles Henry [1858–1951] who declared that rotation from right to left indicates pleasure.)

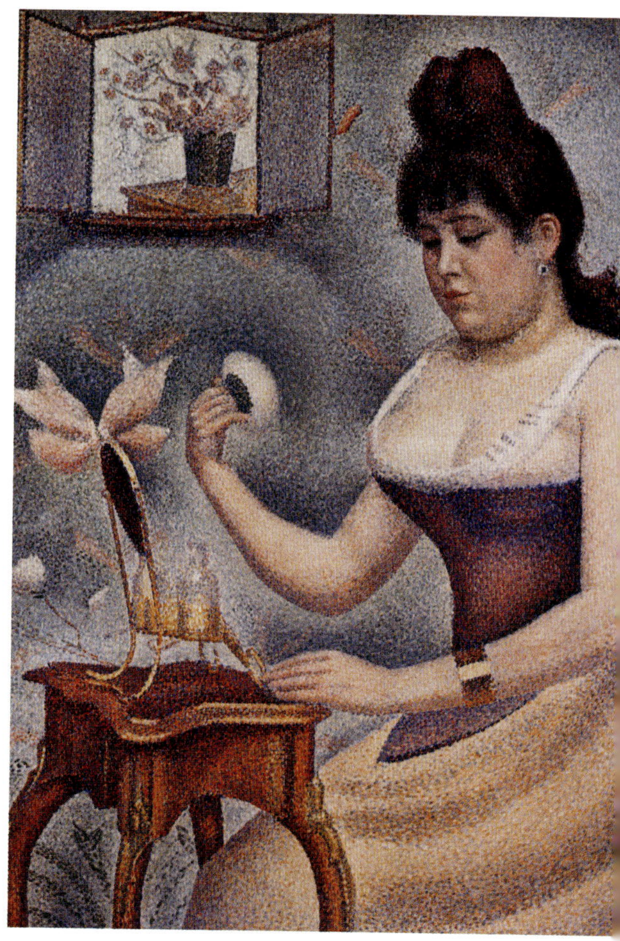

GEORGES SEURAT (1859–91) was reserved, highly intelligent, and methodical. He trained in the conventional French artistic tradition with a pupil of Ingres and began painting in about 1881. As a skilled, classical draftsman, he concentrated on drawing at first, and many of his early drawings were in the style of the Old Masters. From these artists, he evolved his own style of subtle tonal contrasts through the use of Conté crayon on textured paper. By varying the pressure and handling of the Conté, he created varying tonal effects.

Seurat's scientific interest in color theory began as early as 1878, when he read the work of Delacroix and the color theorists, including Chevreul, Blanc, and Rood. From 1884, he abandoned his usual earth colors for brighter pigments and never used dull colors again. In the early 1880s, he began making studies in oils outdoors and, with Pissarro's support, exhibited with the Impressionists in 1886. He started using some of their ideas, such as working on a white or light-colored canvas, instead of the

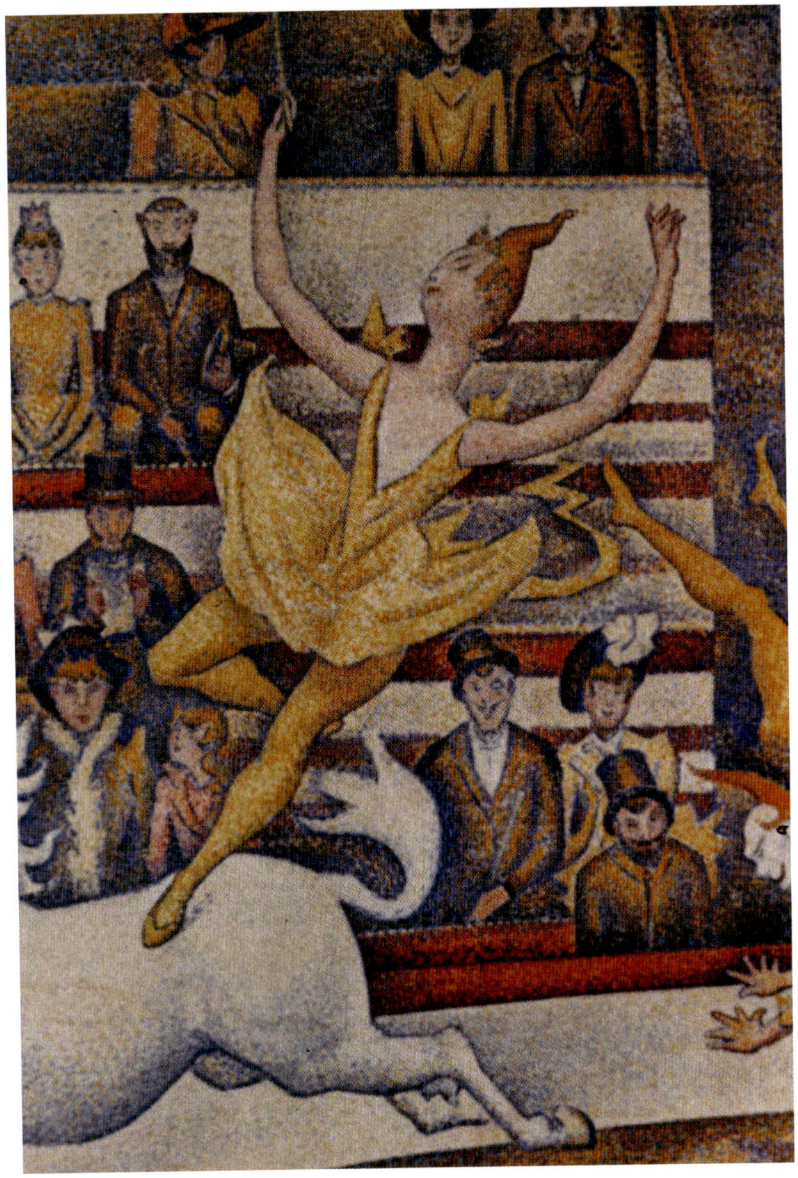

RIGHT
THE CIRCUS, 1891, oil on canvas, 73 x 60 inches (185.5 x 152.5 cm). *Although unfinished, this shows how Seurat built up his paintings in layers of colors. He began with blue, followed by yellow, then red. Circles, ellipses, curves, and horizontals are balanced like a pattern across the canvas. Unlike most of his paintings, the picture conveys excitement and movement. The circus was a favorite attraction for many artists, and Seurat enjoyed painting not only the performers, but also the class differences of the audience. You can see the richer viewers in the front and the less well off in the background.*

brown background surfaces that he had been taught to work on. The Impressionists' choices of subject matter also appealed to him, but he was always looking for new ways of working and Impressionism didn't answer all his questions. After years of experimenting, he developed pointillism, which exploits contrasts of warm and cool colors, light and dark tones, and the optical reactions we get from looking at juxtaposed colors. The Impressionists had done a similar thing before him, but he took the ideas even further.

Planned palette and procedure

From the early 1880s, Seurat carefully and deliberately applied 11 colors in a particular order on each painting. He sometimes omitted a few of them but never added any others. White was crucial for him, and he mixed it with most of his colors to create a light, opaque finish. By 1885, he had replaced his hatched brushwork with tiny dots of paint, which he placed side by side to create the impression, from a distance, of areas of solid color.

As well as canvases, Seurat painted on small wooden panels, such as cigar box lids, which he left unprimed so that the warm nut-colored wood could play a part in the painting. These wood paintings were simple studies from nature that could be translated later into controlled studio paintings.

Seurat's images contrast with the freer works of the Impressionists—he didn't aim for a look of spontaneity. He referred to the way he worked as a scientific, methodical procedure, which he called "my method."

TONAL CONTRASTS

CENTER
SHORE AT THE BAS-BUTIN, HONFLEUR, 1886, oil on canvas, 26¼ x 30¾ inches (67 x 78 cm).
The angle of this view directs the viewer's gaze out to the open sea, where two sailing boats and a steamer are moving by. There is a calm and harmonious balance and close scrutiny reveals Seurat's diversity of brush strokes and the contrasts of warm and cool, light and dark, and complementary colors.

SEURAT'S CONTÉ CRAYON drawings are soft and subtle and do not have any obvious lines. He spent two years drawing in black and white, just trying to understand tone. Although there are no harsh lines in his work, the tones are dramatic. The darkest tones are black and the lightest white, reflecting the strongest chiaroscuro effects (the dramatic use of light and dark to create atmosphere and depth) of those artists he admired most, namely Holbein and Ingres.

When Seurat painted, he used a similar set of values but, because he handled and applied paint so differently from Conté, it has a completely different effect. Instead of large areas of one color using a relatively broad application, his paintings are made up of hundreds of tiny variations of color, whether hatched brush marks or precise dots.

The secret to Seurat's success with tonal contrast in both his drawings and paintings was the fact that he relied on tones instead of lines to model form, and he exaggerated those tones with strong lights and darks. This is what gives his work the appealing, soft, undulating shapes.

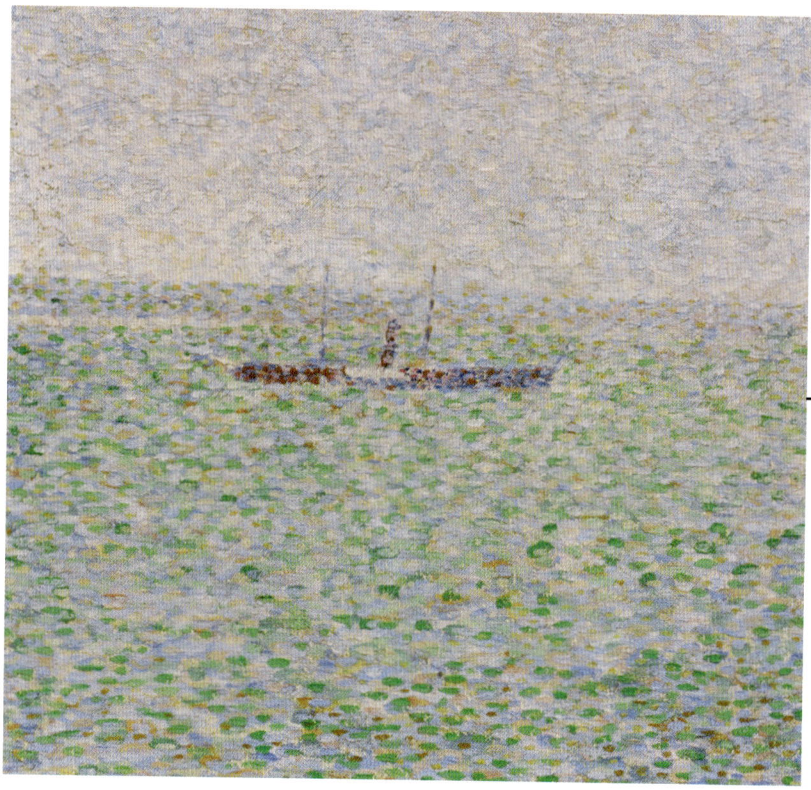

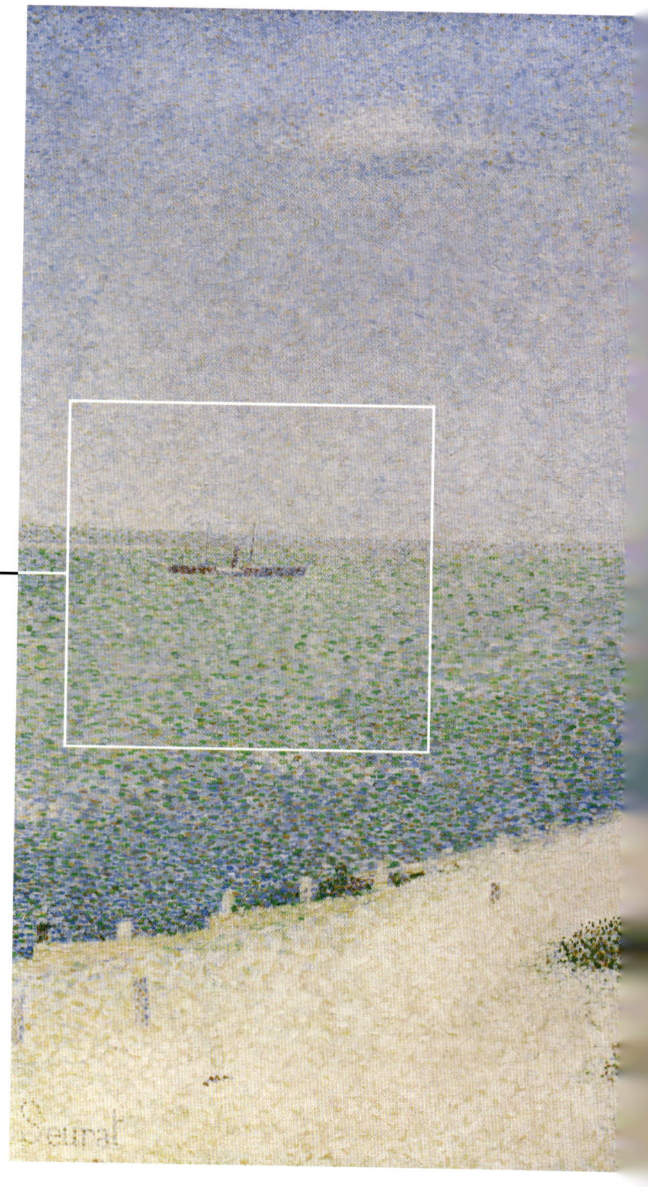

ABOVE
SHORE AT THE BAS-BUTIN, HONFLEUR, detail.
Seurat painted this picture while on vacation. Tone, shape, and color contrasts built up with tiny brush marks give an image of balance and harmony. The ship silently traveling along the calm water can be picked out in the sea.

Opposing color

Seurat created forms with contrasts in color, warmth, and complementaries instead of using black for depth. For example, in *Young Woman Powdering Herself,* he placed cool, dark blue shadows on her skin next to the warm, pale peach flesh. In *Shore at the Bas-Butin, Honfleur,* the pale cream sand was placed directly between the dark blue sea and dark green foliage. This gave the impression of soft, undulating forms without rigidity. Not only did Seurat use strong tonal contrasts to model form, he also contrasted them against their backgrounds, using complementary colors, to make the main subjects stand out within a picture. For example, in *The Circus,* the yellow figures of the acrobats are almost outlined by the blue shadows of the background surrounding them.

Seurat's painting methods may have been inspired not only by color theorists, but also by printing methods. Modern technology and images of popular culture fascinated him. Also, contemporary printing strongly emphasized dark and light tones to give the clearest possible image. By using small brush marks, Seurat could note subtle gradations of tone, building up from extremely light to extremely dark, with variations in between. He was careful to use layers of transparent colors in his shadows too, often applying wet-over-dry paint to keep the colors clear and fresh.

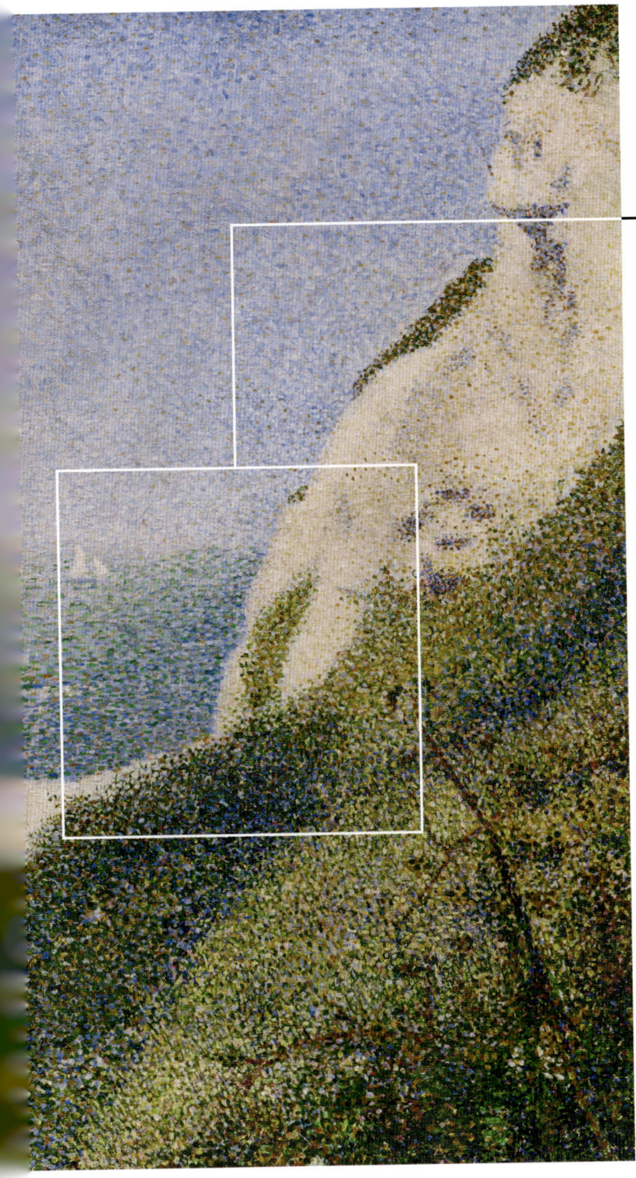

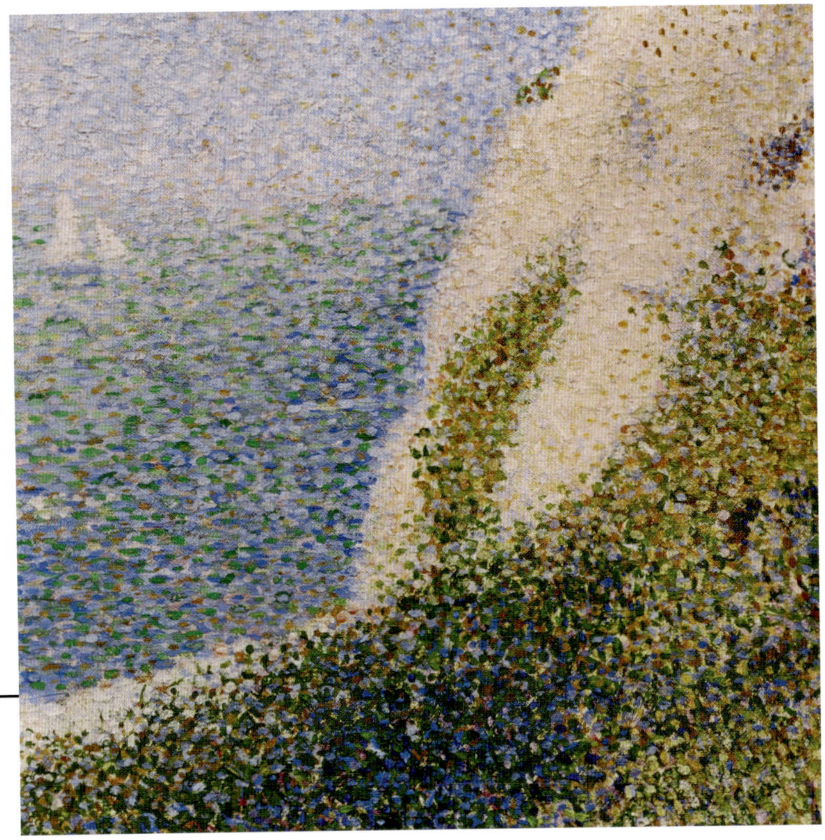

ABOVE
SHORE AT THE BAS-BUTIN, HONFLEUR, detail.
In this detail, the pale ecru of the boats' sails are echoed in the cream sand. By exploring color and tonal contrasts, Seurat has created the effects of both solid form and hazy, shimmering light.

HOW TO DO IT

YOUR PALETTE

For this picture you need:

1 Chrome Orange
2 Raw Sienna
3 Crimson Alizarin
4 French Ultramarine
5 Cobalt Blue
6 Vermilion
7 Emerald Green
8 Viridian
9 Cadmium Yellow
10 Yellow Ocher
11 Zinc White

You will also need a lot of violet to contrast with the yellows.

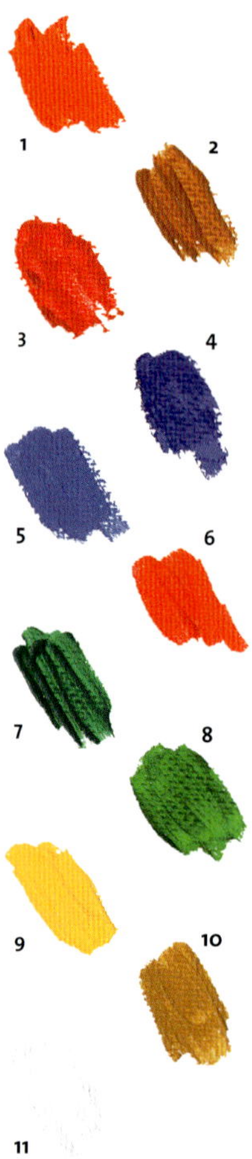

ONE OF THE WAYS in which Seurat created sharp contours without lines was to contrast background tones with no regard to optical reality. This can be seen where the water looks dark behind highlighted skin and vice versa. By employing this technique, you should be able to re-create the calming effect of Seurat's painting. The composition of this painting is based on a grid, as were most of Seurat's works.

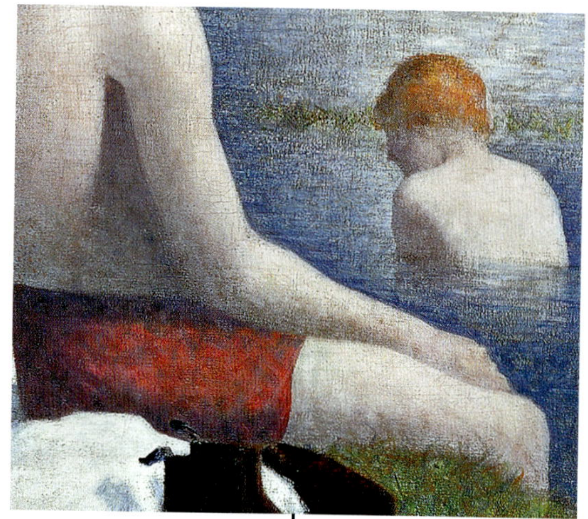

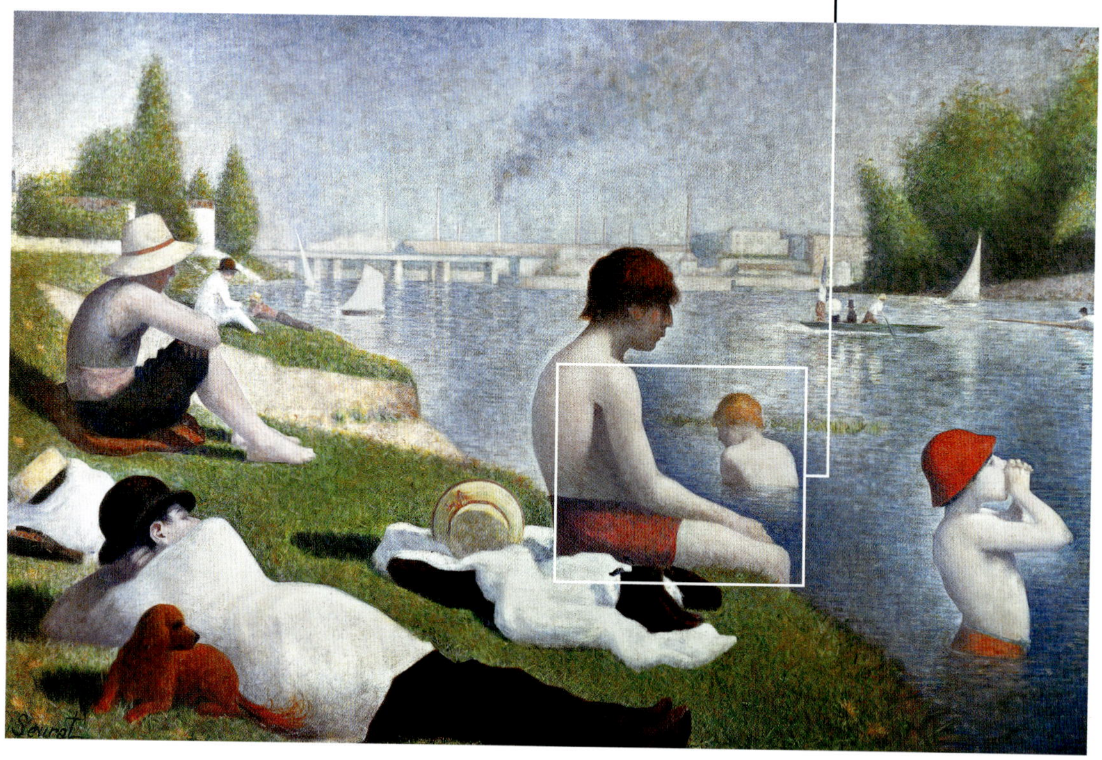

The main techniques

Virtually "ignoring" line, you should make clear distinctions between objects by placing dark next to light. For example, the darker tones on the swimmers' pale skin should be contrasted with a white shimmer on the adjacent water. Also, the figures and garments in the foreground must be heavily worked in opaque layers, while the background needs a thinner, softer application.

ABOVE
BATHERS AT ASNIÈRES, 1883–84, oil on canvas, 79 x 118¾ inches (201 x 301.5 cm). *This large canvas first brought Seurat to the attention of the Paris public. It was painted completely in the studio, although he made many preparatory studies outdoors. Seurat adhered closely to the laws of contrast and reworked parts of the painting later by adding touches of pure color here and there.*

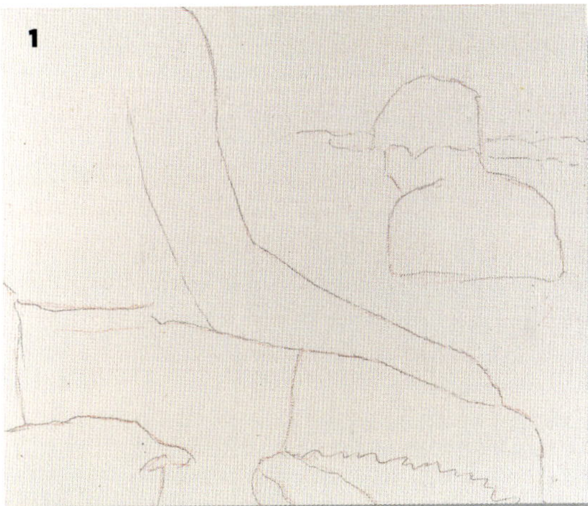

STEP 1 Using a firm canvas or board, apply a wash of white or off-white priming, as Seurat did, to enhance the luminosity of the picture. Allow it to dry, then lightly draw the outlines of the shapes.

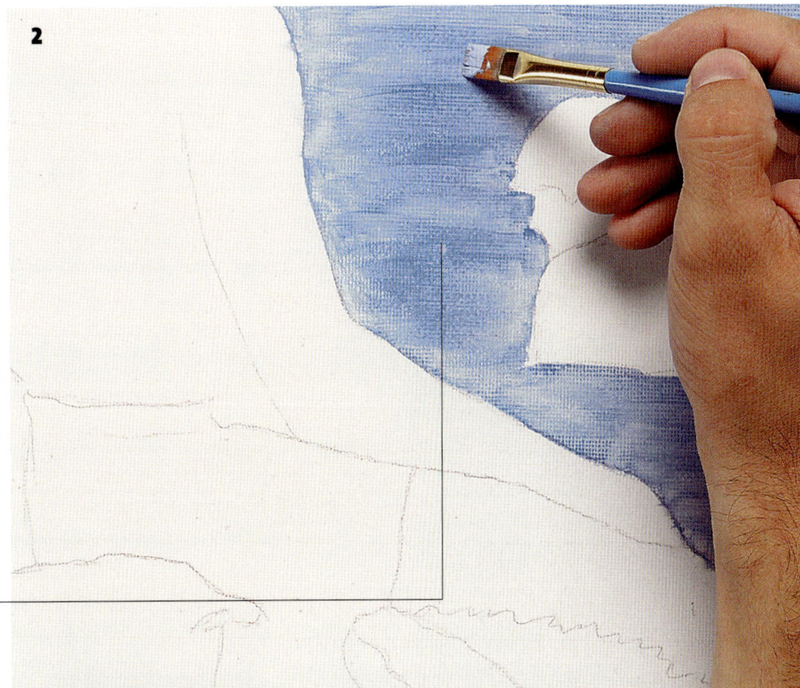

Dilute the paint for this first blocking in and paint it on, almost as if it's watercolor.

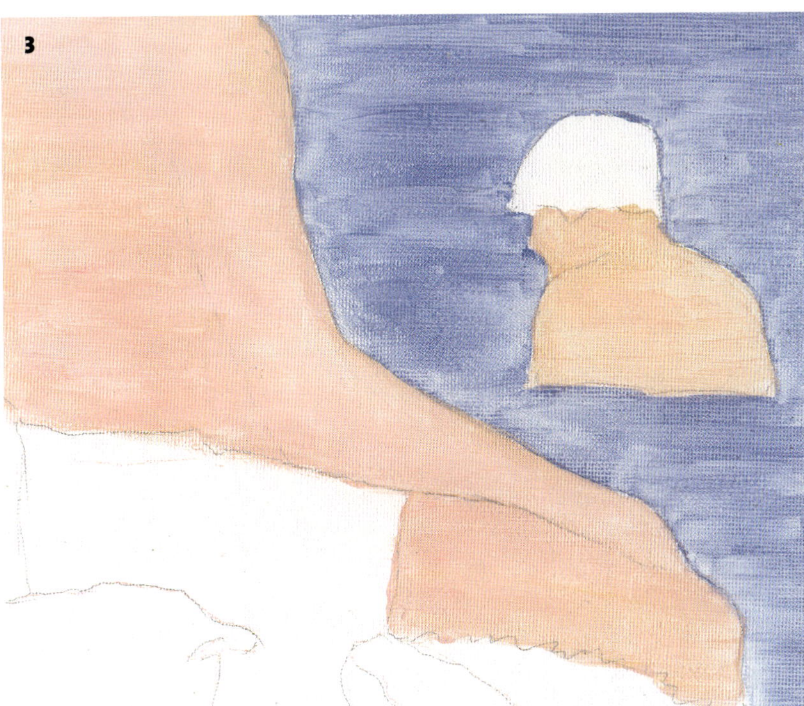

STEP 2 With a thin paint, lightly block in broad areas of local color, starting with the river, using Cobalt Blue and Zinc White.

STEP 3 Build up the paint carefully, mainly using the wet-over-dry method to retain the purity of the colors. Block in the flesh tones using a wash of Crimson Alizarin, plus a little Yellow Ocher and Zinc White. You should paint mainly with broad, smooth brush strokes placed on top of each other, adding Zinc White to the lighter colors to create a brilliance to them. Use opaque layers to build up the figures.

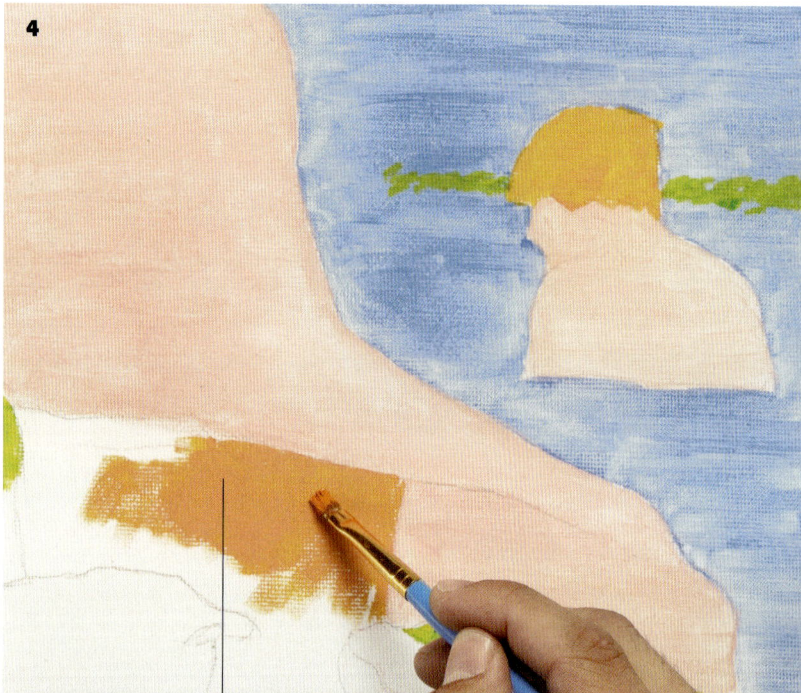

STEP 4 Again, using opaque layers, paint Chrome Orange for the shorts and swimmer's hair, making your brushwork follow the folds in the fabric and curves of the hair. Paint the grass with dry, hatched strokes of Cadmium Yellow and Emerald Green, and dab a bit of this on the water, horizontally behind the hair.

STEP 5 Seurat varied between using thick Impressionist brush strokes and fine criss-crossed lines. Tonal contrasts are not simply light and dark, but a blend of darks, mediums, and lights. Therefore, introduce darker shades on the figures to aid form, using French Ultramarine and Vermilion in small strokes of pure color over a lighter wash. Paint the clothes in the foreground, making the brown from Yellow Ocher, Vermilion, and Emerald Green.

Using a thin brush, block in the orange shorts and swimmer's hair without adding any tones yet. The aim at this stage is simply to lay down the main blocks of color.

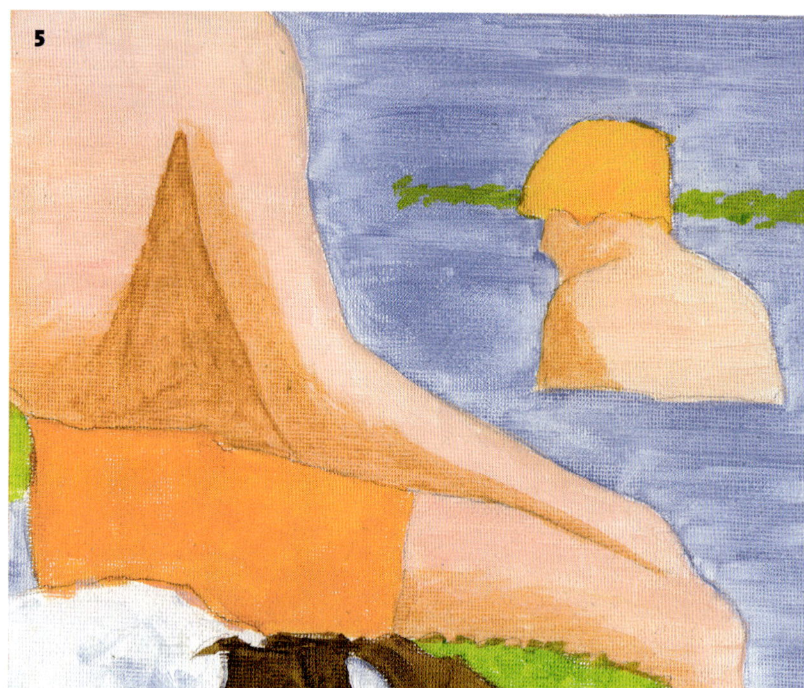

STEP 6 Extend shading to the boy's shorts, both figures, and the hair of the swimmer with French Ultramarine, Zinc White, Yellow Ocher, and Raw Sienna.

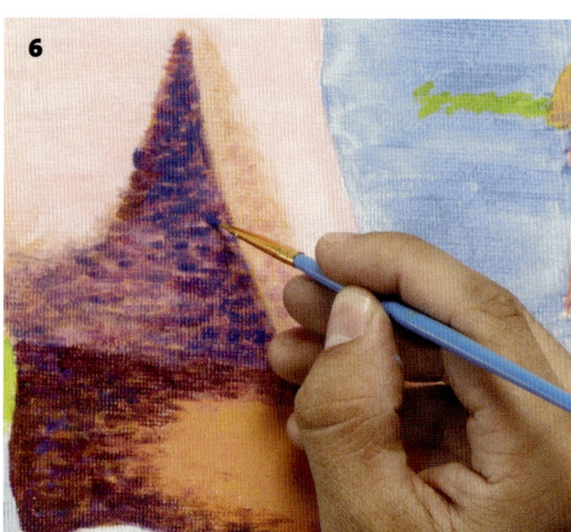

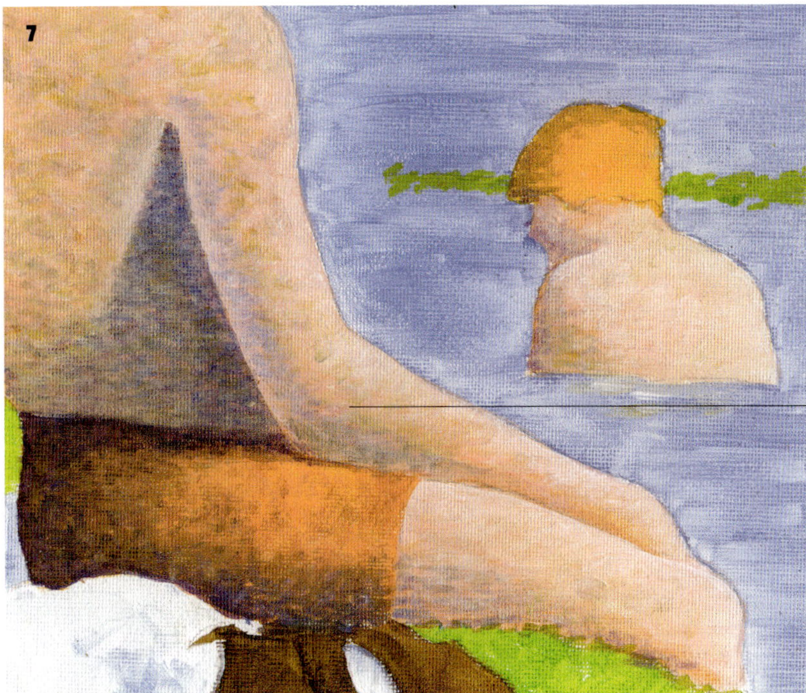

STEP 7 Establish the mid- and light tones of the figures, and merge them on the canvas with Zinc White, Yellow Ocher, Crimson Alizarin, and Cobalt Blue. To do this, build up stiff paint over thin, opaque layers of local color with complementary shades worked in. Use violet, mixed from Alizarin Red and Cobalt Blue, in small dabs for the shadows around the foreground figure.

The light colors indicate the heat of a sweltering summer afternoon and the parts of the body exposed to the sun appear flatter than the areas in shadow.

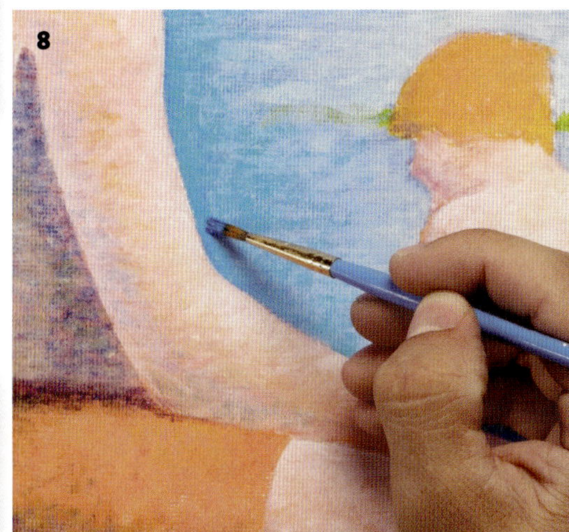

STEP 8 Blur in the colors using the wet-in-wet method, so that there are no harsh lines. The water is mainly a blurred mixture of Cobalt Blue, French Ultramarine, and Zinc White, with a little Emerald Green.

Paint the swimmer's thick hair in reddish brown dabs. Make this color with Raw Sienna, Chrome Orange, and touches of French Ultramarine in the darkest areas.

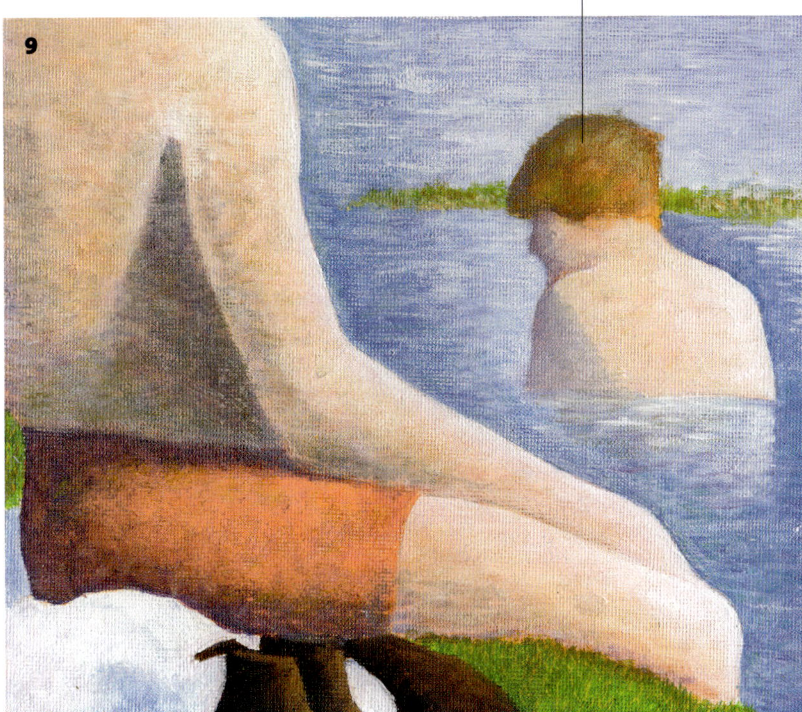

STEP 9 To finish the painting, strengthen the clothes in the foreground with Raw Sienna, Yellow Ocher, Viridian, Cobalt Blue, Cadmium Yellow, and Zinc White. Also work on the hair of the swimmer and add deeper tones to the water where necessary. With short, fine vertical marks, build up the grass with Viridian, Emerald Green, and French Ultramarine interspersed with Chrome Yellow and Cobalt Blue. Add final highlights and harmonize the tones with Zinc White and small individual dots of pure color in selected areas.

POINTILLISM

CENTER
THE BRIDGE AT COURBEVOIE, c.1887, oil on canvas, 18¼ x 21¾ inches (46.5 x 55.5 cm).
For this painting, Seurat used his finest pointillist technique. The dots are tiny and precise, placed carefully to allow more light into the picture and to show his scientifically based approach. The small, individual dots beside each other tend to merge together when viewed from a distance.

BELOW
THE BRIDGE AT COURBEVOIE, detail.
The overall tone of the picture is predominantly blue and mauve, while details have been emphasized with darker, more complex colors.

THE ART CRITIC FÉLIX FÉNÉON first used the term pointillism to describe *La Grande Jatte* in 1886. Since then, it has become the most accepted name for Seurat's technique. Optical mixing and Divisionism also describe the general idea of separating colors, but pointillism refers specifically to the use of dots. The intention of the method was to give paintings greater iridescence, as well as creating a shimmering sensation when viewed from a distance. (The appropriate viewing distance was thought to be three times the length of the picture's diagonal.)

There has been a lot of debate over who actually "invented" the technique of dividing colors on canvas, because Seurat, Pissarro, and Signac all developed their unique techniques at around the same time. However, it is generally accepted that Seurat pushed the idea to its limit. His idea was to avoid any muddiness and produce the maximum brilliance of color by systematically painting small dots of pure color side by side. Fénéon wrote a detailed analysis of Seurat's work in 1886, and in it described several of the "types" of colors that Seurat used, including local color, directly and indirectly reflected light, color reflections from neighboring objects, and complementaries. Seurat believed that by using his method, just before the viewer's eye blends two of his juxtaposing colors, the paint surface seems to flicker and become luminous.

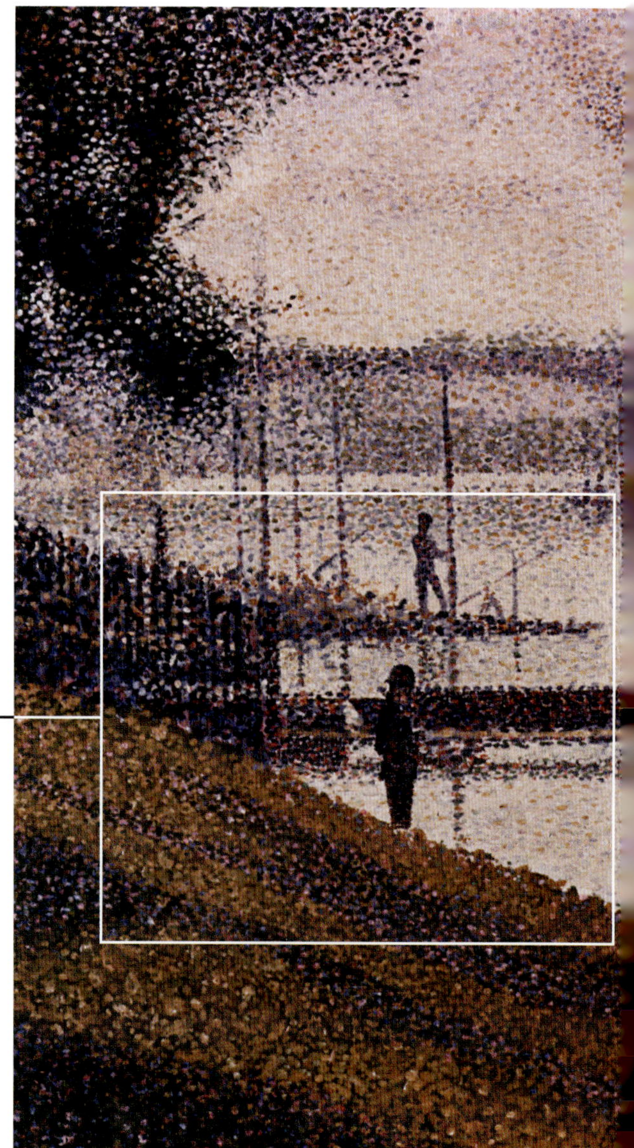

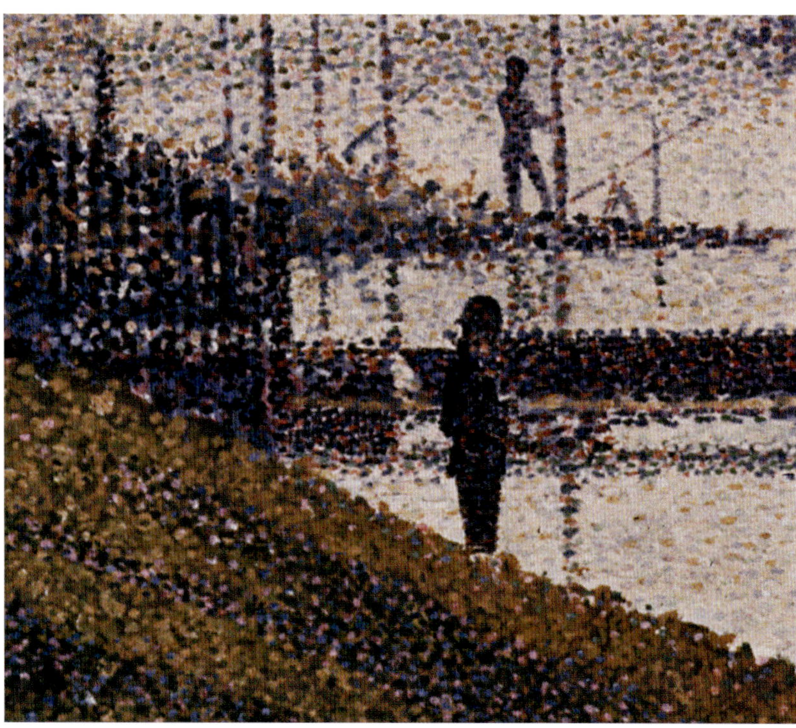

Mosaic-type application

Seurat's life's work stretched over just 11 years, and it is often divided into three phases. Between 1880 to 1883, he concentrated exclusively on drawing in black and white, focusing his attention on the problem of shadow and light, or contrasting values. Between 1883 to 1884, he painted a series of pictures in which he continued the exploration of tonal contrast and also tackled the problems of color contrasts. Lastly, between 1884 to 1891, he concentrated on large compositions using his exacting pointillist technique. In each successive period, he extended the activities of the previous one. His work became progressively detached from nature up to the point where he thought he could re-create nature in his studio, which was the opposite of the Impressionists' methods of alla prima and *en plein air*. His early death at the age of 31 ended the pointillist explorations.

Seurat's paintings are of people using the manners and customs of his age, but the way that the pictures were planned and produced makes them seem timeless and silent—almost unreal. In close-up, his pointillist paintings are a brilliant mass of contrasting colored dots, like mosaics, and, at a distance, the colors seem to fuse together to create soft, calm, classic forms.

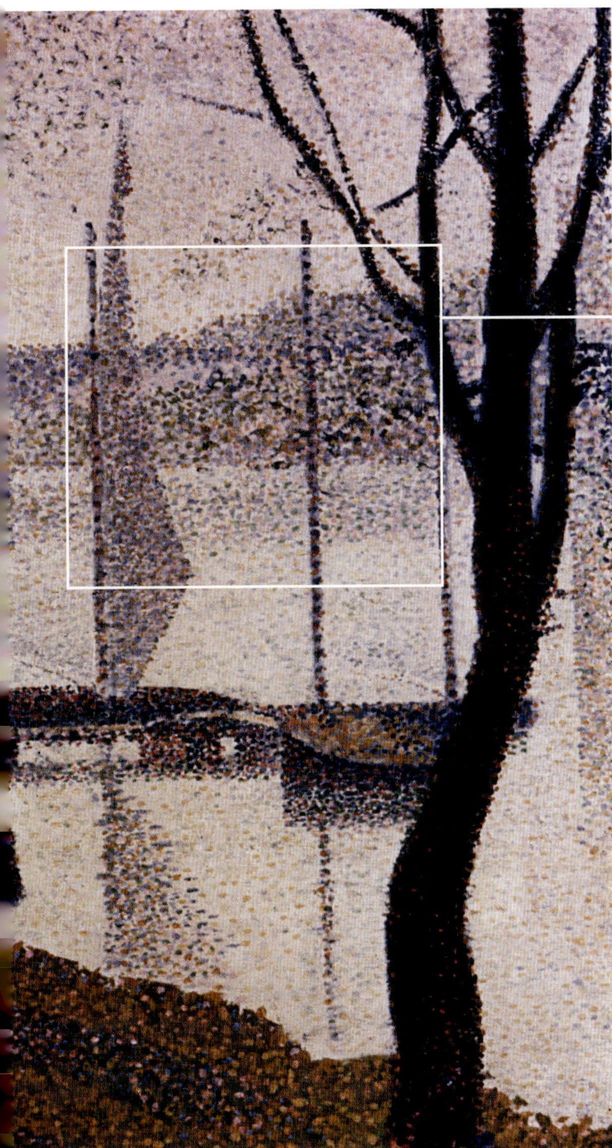

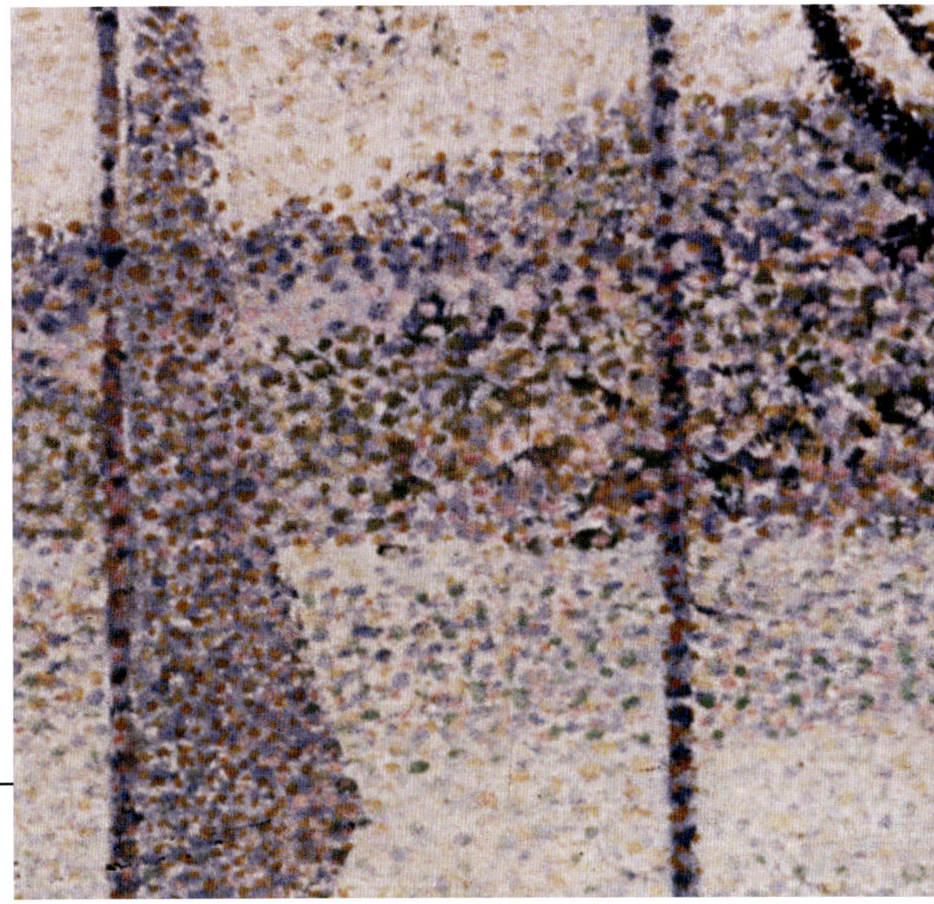

ABOVE
THE BRIDGE AT COURBEVOIE, detail.
The vertical and horizontal lines in this painting create a rhythm across the canvas. The sail is enlivened with pink and orange tones.

HOW TO DO IT

YOUR PALETTE

As well as the systemized application of paint for pointillism, Seurat also organized his palette carefully into the following colors:

1 Zinc White
2 Cadmium Yellow Pale
3 Cadmium Yellow Deep
4 Vermilion
5 Crimson Alizarin
6 Cobalt Violet
7 Cobalt Blue
8 Ceruleum Blue
9 Viridian
10 Chrome Green

The dots produce a subtle "optical vibration," which is known technically as "luster."

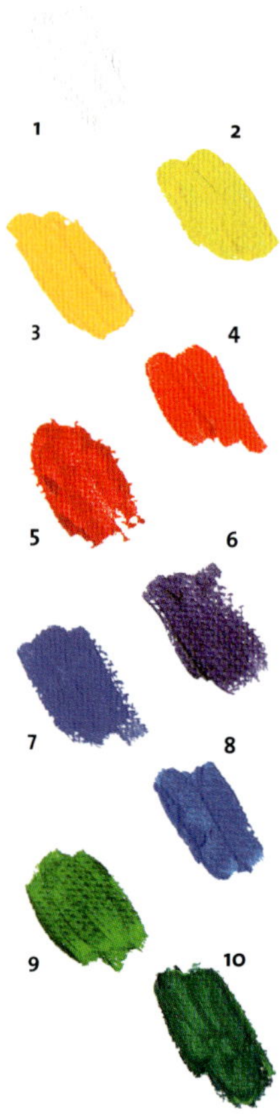

ALTHOUGH SO FAR the size of the canvas you should use for the re-created paintings hasn't been dictated, you will find it easier to interpret Seurat's pointillist style if you work on a relatively large scale, because the dots and colors will merge and blend well. The final painting is made up of several layers of dots, and much of the work done in the initial stages will be altered by subsequent applications of paint.

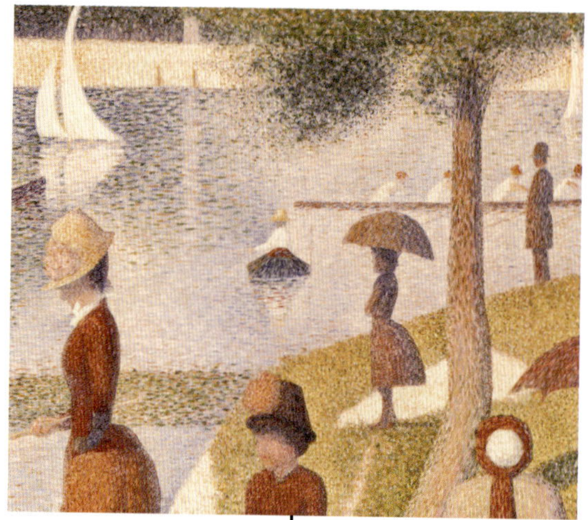

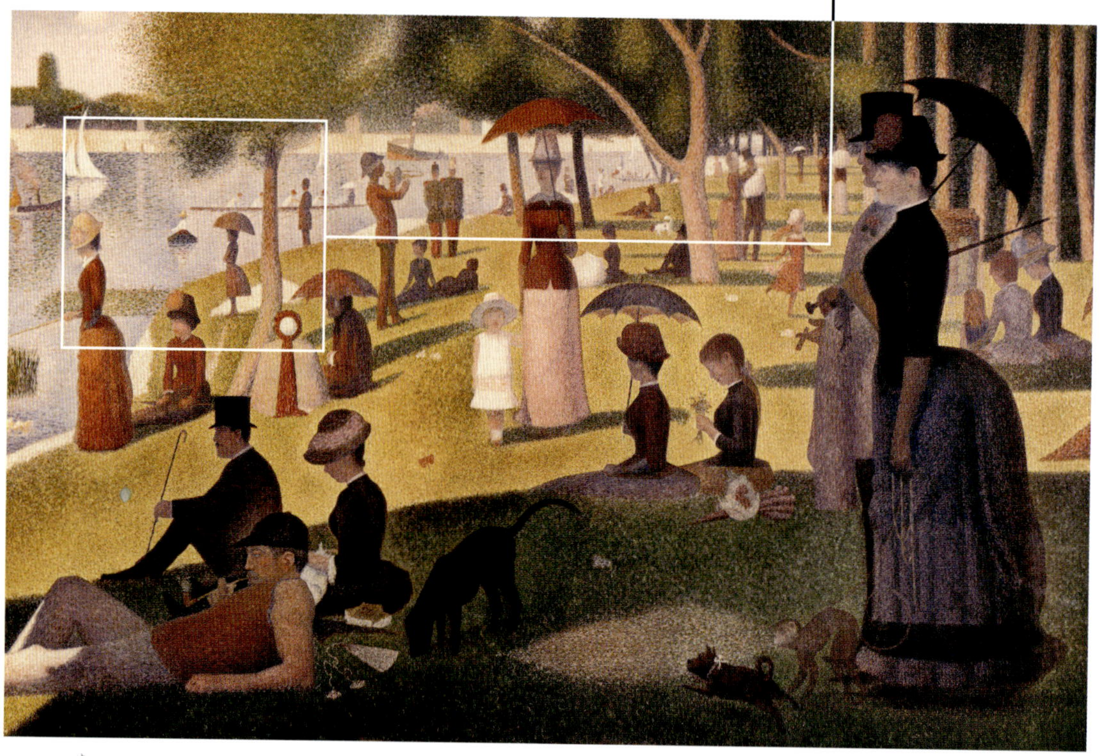

The main techniques

As well as concentrating on applying dots in neat arrangements across the canvas, you should focus on the harmony and unity that Seurat attained in all his works. By working on a large format, you will be able to build up the clarity and also the balance that pointillism evoked. You will also find that using small brushes on a large format will naturally make dots appear smaller by comparison.

ABOVE
SUNDAY AFTERNOON AT THE ISLAND OF LA GRANDE JATTE, 1884–86, oil on canvas, 82½ x 121¼ inches (210 x 308 cm).
Soon after completing Bathers at Asnières, *Seurat began work on a second large painting of a recreational spot popular with Parisians. The entire painting was planned on a geometric grid, which turned the composition into a pattern of repeated verticals, horizontals, and arcs, occasionally intersected by diagonals. Each person in the picture is positioned where he or she can be seen, and the figures seem motionless and monumental.*

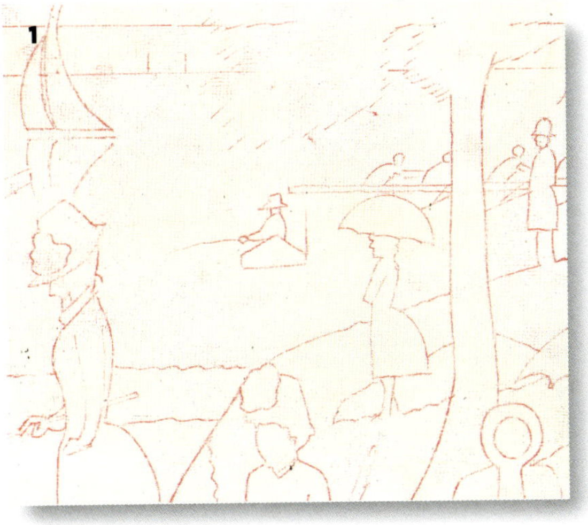

STEP 1 Prepare your canvas or board with white or cream paint and lightly indicate the broad outlines of the figures with red chalk or Conté crayon. Use the grid method if this helps you to map out the picture.

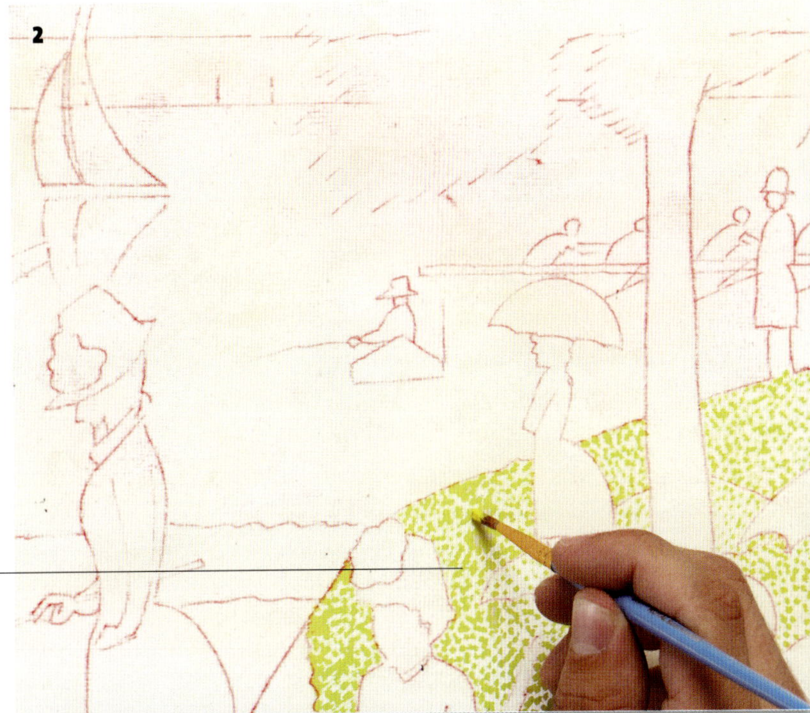

This is built up from a series of preliminary studies to give the appearance of a passing moment. To apply the dots, hold the brush relatively far back and almost at a right angle to the canvas.

STEP 2 Using the paint in a relatively dry consistency, build up layers of color slowly and carefully, wet-over-dry, using a moderately stiff brush to create a hazy-edged effect. Start this by using Cadmium Yellow (Pale and Deep) dots around the righthand figures to indicate the grass.

STEP 3 Place Vermilion dots in the shadow areas beneath the trees. If you find your arm begins to feel weary as you apply the dots, hold it or rest it across your other arm as you hold the brush.

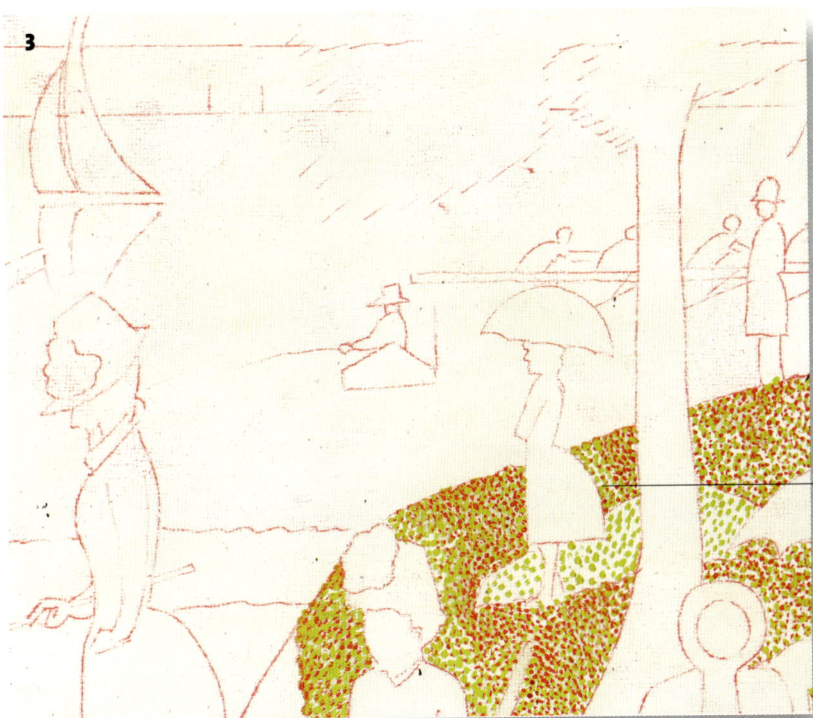

To make the figure stand out from the background, deep-colored dots of Cobalt Violet have been placed on this back edge of the skirt, and Pale Cadmium Yellow dots were used on the grass.

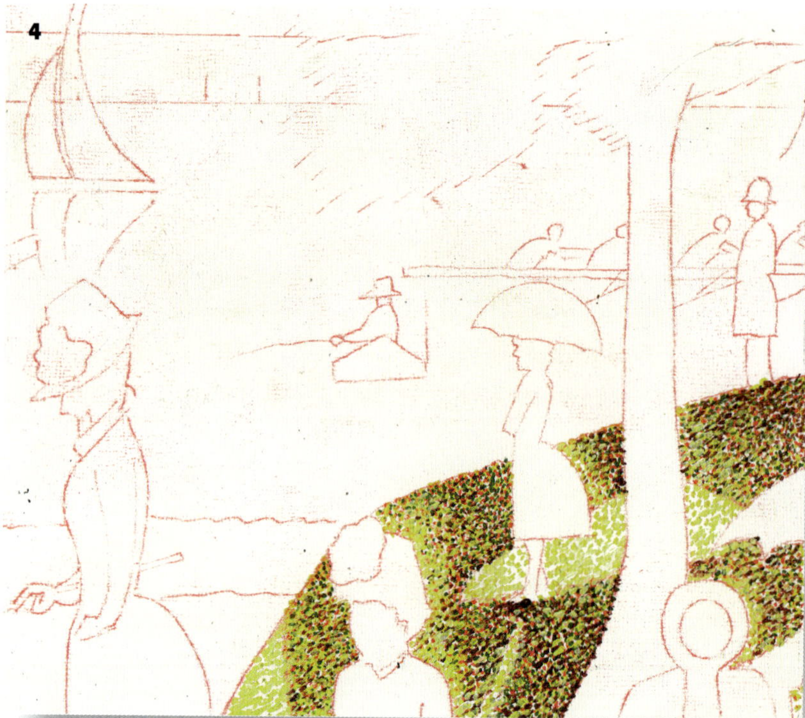

STEP 4 Few brushes are needed for this painting, because the dots are of uniform size. Place complementary Chrome Green dots next to the Vermilion dots without merging them. Use Crimson Alizarin to reinforce the shadows and Pale Cadmium Yellow for the highlights.

STEP 5 Seurat only mixed adjacent colors from the color wheel—never complementaries as this would have destroyed the vibrancy of the hues. Be sure to do the same; for example, mix Cobalt Blue and Cobalt Violet for the cool shadows. Juxtapose the darkest tones with the brightest, such as light green grass against a dark red skirt. Work on the main figures using this technique.

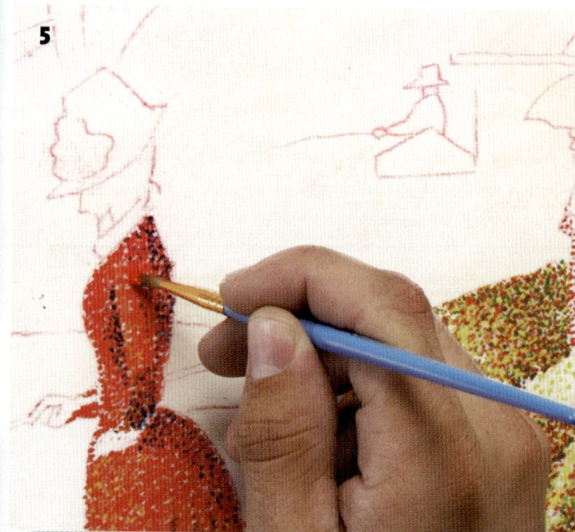

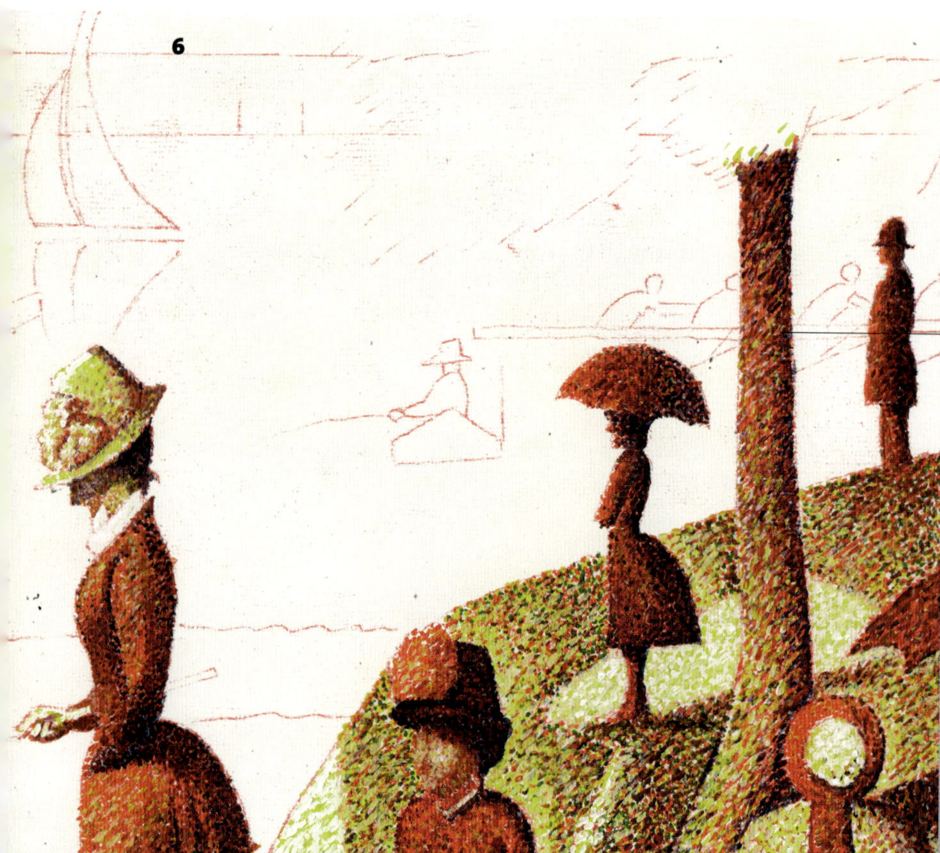

To develop form, overlay dark colors and light tones, such as in the water, on the tree trunk, and on the figures.

STEP 6 Begin to build up the clothing on the figures, using Crimson Alizarin, Cadmium Yellow Deep, Vermilion and Cobalt Violet, and Chrome Green in the darkest areas. This is painstaking but persevere, being particularly careful on such things as the circular hat, the parasol, and the figure in the background. Also build up the tree trunk, paying attention to the direction of light and shade. Put in darker tones, such as cool Cobalt Violet and warm browns from Crimson Alizarin and Viridian, and concentrate on building up a network of cool/warm, dark/light, and complementary contrasts across the canvas.

STEP 7 Build up the foliage on the tree with dots of pure Cobalt Blue layered with pure Cadmium Yellow Deep. On the underside of the leaves, add in some dots of Vermilion.

Define the outline of the parasol with dots in close proximity. Avoid the look of a continuous outline, but still make it look solid and separate from the background.

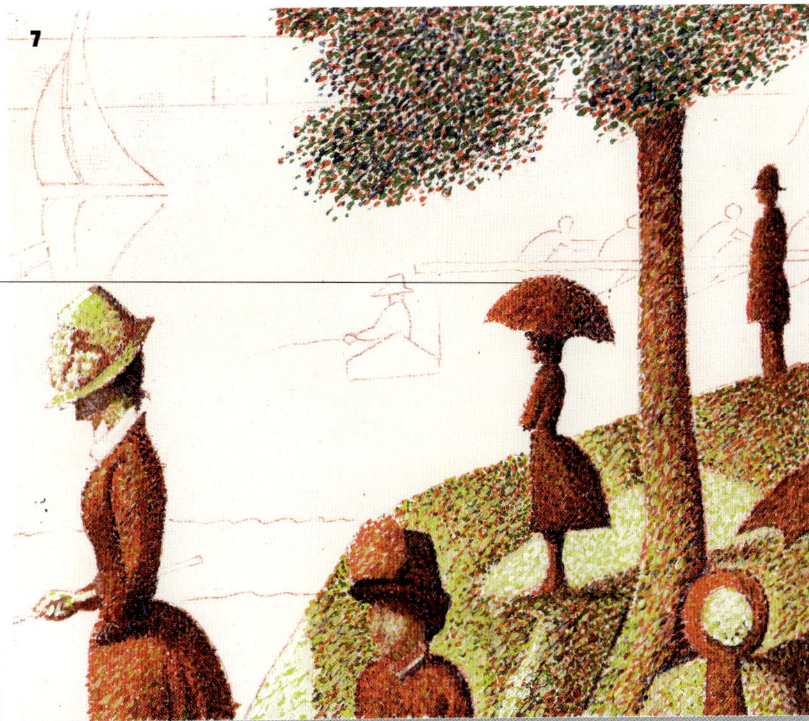

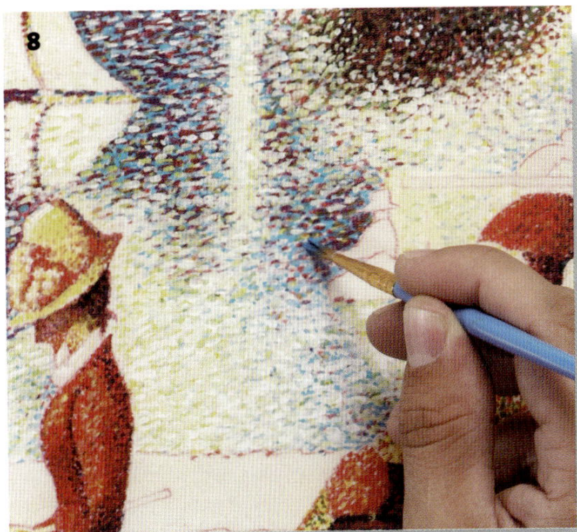

STEP 8 Begin to establish the river tones using Ceruleum Blue, Cobalt Blue, and Cobalt Violet, as well as tiny and subtle dots in reds and yellows. Work horizontally across the water. Apply dots of Viridian where the light shimmers on the water, and use plenty of Zinc White for the yacht and to indicate highlights.

STEP 9 To finish, apply blue dots for the shaded water and the bands of dark green in the water behind the woman in the foreground and further in the distance. To create this dark color, apply dots of Chrome Green, Viridian, Crimson Alizarin, Cobalt Blue ,and Cobalt Violet. Develop the figures on the water and the boats in dots of Cadmium Yellow Deep, Crimson Alizarin, and Cobalt Blue. Add Cobalt Violet and Chrome Green for the boats, allowing some of the background surface to show through. Apply some of the colors almost straight from the tube.

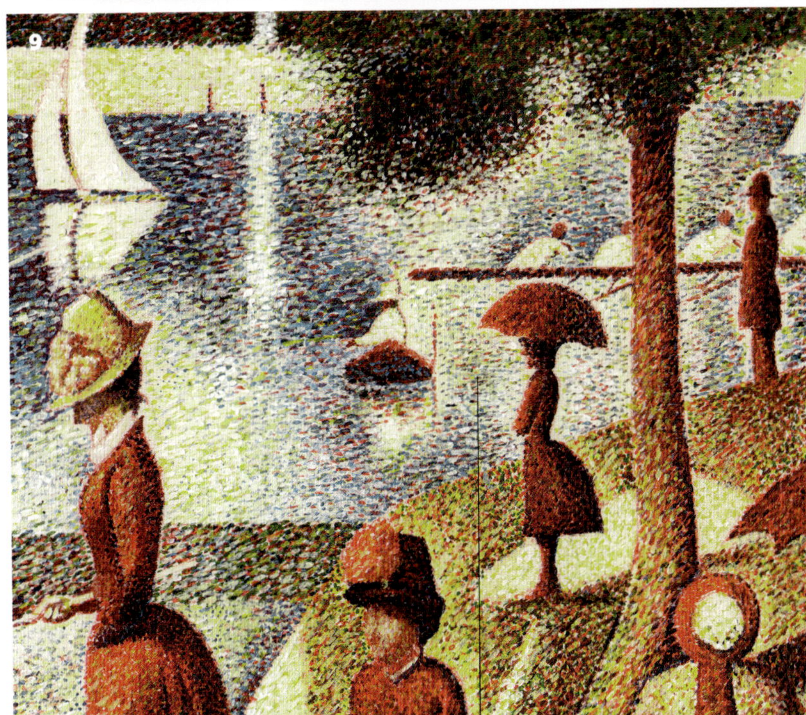

For the final touches, try using a filbert brush, because these long brushes allow a good deal of control.

Chapter twelve

VAN GOGH

Vincent van Gogh had a short, turbulent life, and in many ways he has become what we perceive as the archetypal artist—poor, lonely, misunderstood, and suffering for his art. His work sells for millions now, yet he only sold one painting during his lifetime.

BELOW
IRISES, 1889, oil on canvas, 28 x 37 inches (71 x 94 cm). ***The bold colors and sinuous design show links with both Art Nouveau and Japanese design. He began this painting shortly after admission to the mental hospital in Saint-Rémy.***

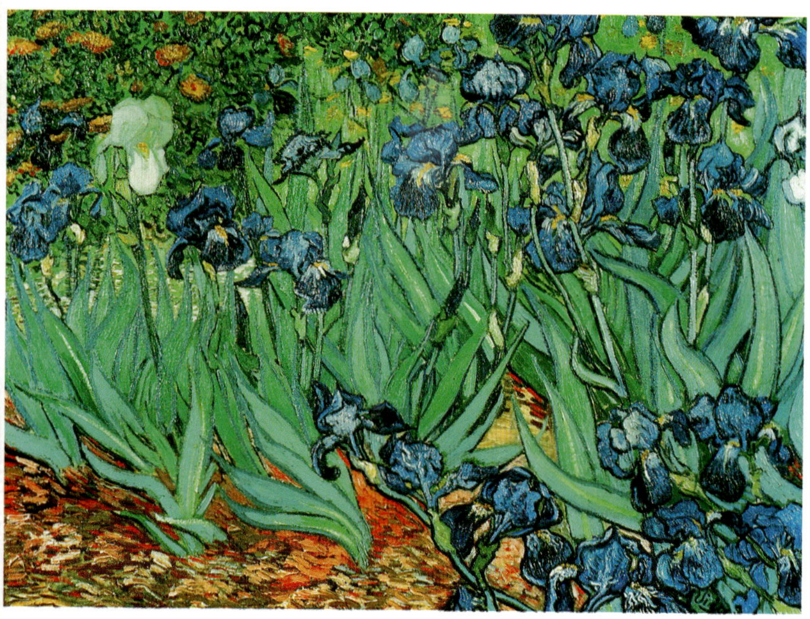

VINCENT VAN GOGH (1853–90) WAS born in Holland, the eldest son of six children, to a Protestant pastor. Before realizing that art was his true vocation, he tried out several careers, including art dealing, teaching, and preaching. Finally, at the age of 27 van Gogh decided on his future—he would become an artist.

Eventually, he moved to Paris to live with his closest ally and supporter, his younger brother Theo. There, like the Impressionists, he admired and studied Delacroix and became intrigued by the idea of simultaneous contrast and complementary colors.

Initially, Vincent, as he called himself and signed his canvases, did not feel particularly attracted to the Impressionists' works. He thought that they were: "... ugly, sloppily and badly painted, badly drawn, of a poor color, everything that is miserable." However, Theo believed that his brother would benefit from their example and introduced him to Pissarro, who later said that he had felt that van Gogh "would either go mad or leave the Impressionists far behind."

Van Gogh's earliest influences were the Dutch Old Masters and contemporary Dutch Realist painters. In keeping with academic practice, he focused on drawing, producing strong contrasts of dark and light tones. When he painted, he stayed close to the traditions of his native country, focusing on tonal and linear images in dark colors.

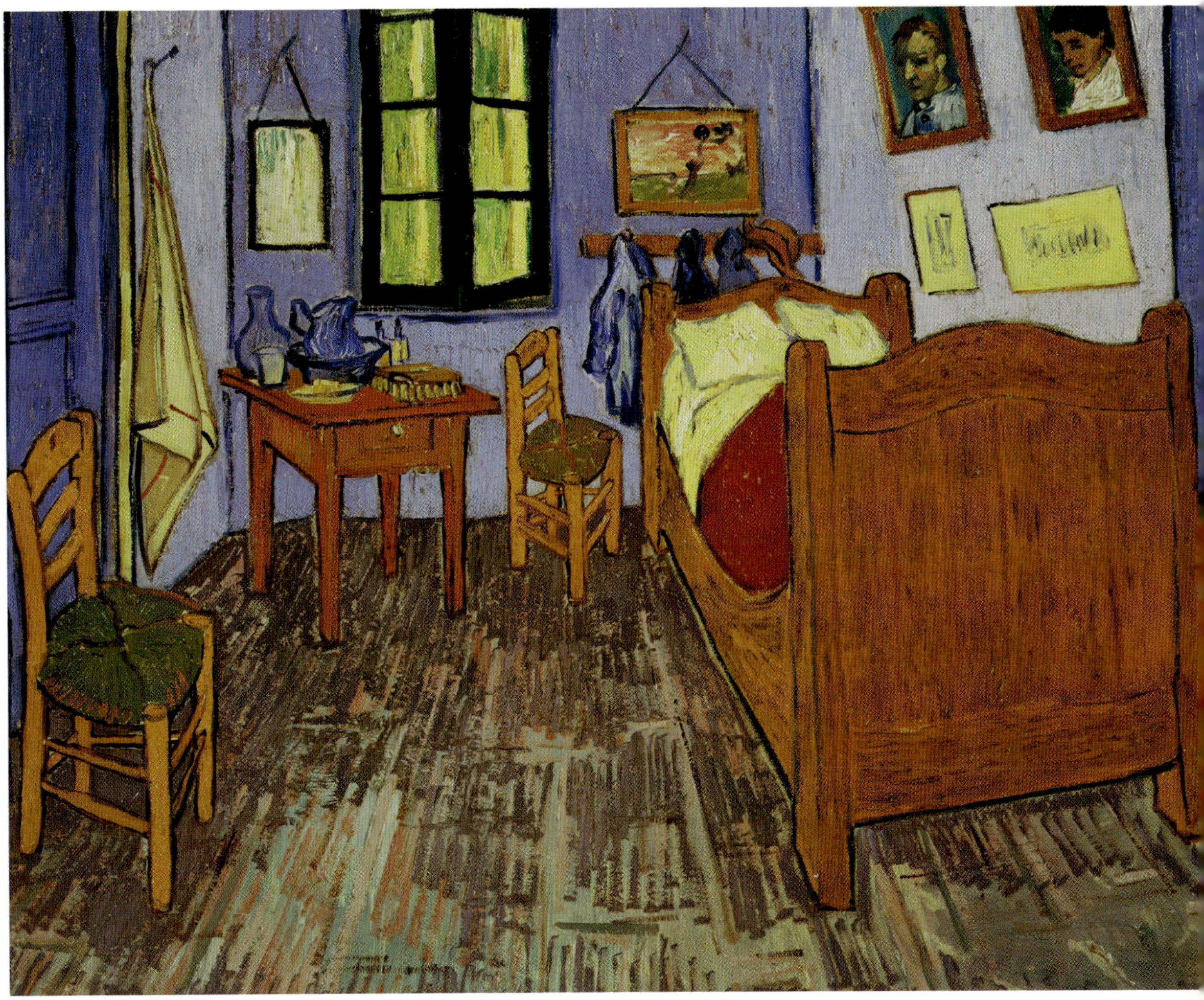

RIGHT
THE ARTIST'S BEDROOM, 1888, oil on canvas, 29 x 36¼ inches (74 x 92 cm).
Painted in anticipation of Gauguin coming to stay, at first glance it seems an objective image, but there are symbols within it that were deliberately included. For example, on the table stand two jugs of water, two bottles, and two brushes. On either side of the table stand two chairs, and on the walls are two portraits, two prints, and two other pictures. These pairs imply the close bond of friendship that he believed he and Gauguin would share. Van Gogh had abandoned the strict rules of linear perspective by this time, because they were no longer important to his aims. Instead, he sought to create harmonies and textures.

Brighter palette

By 1887, after meeting Toulouse-Lautrec, Gauguin, Emile Bernard (1868–1941), and Signac, van Gogh began painting outdoors. He began to lighten his palette and use complementary color contrasts, and, probably through Signac, he briefly adopted the broken touch of pointillism—however, he wasn't happy with the results, so this style didn't last long. He then began using broader, denser, expressive brush strokes.

Van Gogh experimented enthusiastically with new techniques. He tried Japanese reed pens and various other media. Japanese prints and their use of asymmetrical compositions, bright colors, and "busy" and "quiet" parts of a picture fascinated him. He worked on light colored supports, often using commercially prepared canvases or even unprimed ones.

Attracted to the warmth and light of the south, in 1888 he moved to Arles, where his paintings became even more expressive. "This world of colors is completely new to me and thrills me extraordinarily," he wrote to Theo. Vivid colors now completely replaced his earlier strong, dark, contrasting tones. On his canvas surfaces, he created swirling patterns in thick, impasted paint, deliberately expressing emotions and moods. Now he used only vibrant colors and brilliant contrasts in small, angled brush strokes.

THICK, DIRECTIONAL BRUSH STROKES

IN 1887, VAN GOGH THREW himself into Impressionism, painting with a fresh, bright palette and with quick, short brush strokes. Later, he gave up Impressionism for his own ideas, but he never reverted back to the smoother brush strokes and dark colors of his early paintings.

He's known now, of course, for his thick impasto work, his swirling and expressive brush strokes, and his clear, vivid colors. His technique varied enormously throughout his life, and he often applied paint with stabbing, criss-cross strokes—allowing the thickness of the paint to create textures. Slabs of paint in

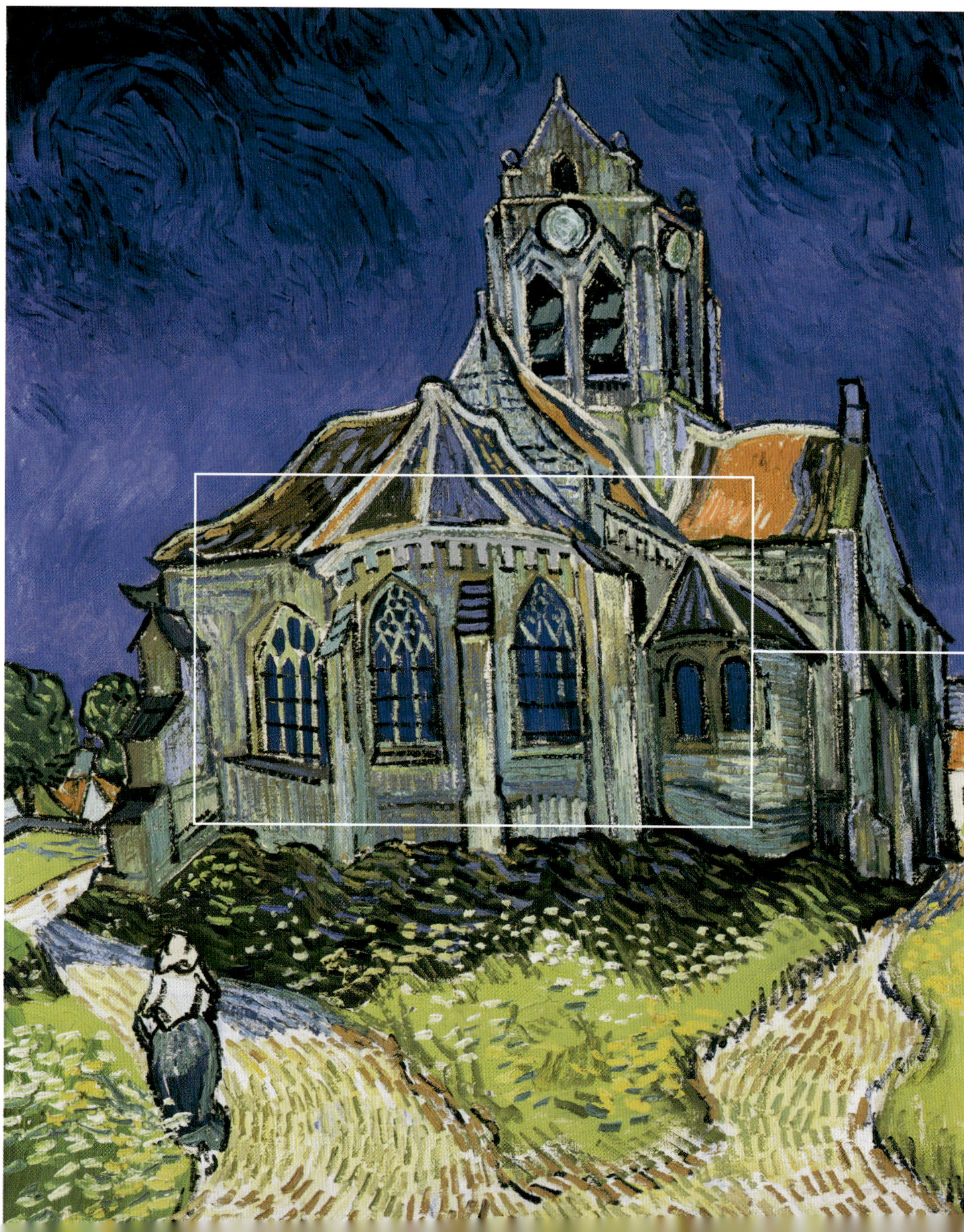

RIGHT
THE CHURCH AT AUVERS, 1890, oil on canvas, 37 x 29 inches (94 x 74 cm).
Vincent spent the last 13 days of his life at Auvers-sur-Oise. There, he produced one finished painting each day and eventually took his life in a field behind this church. The contrast of deep dark sky, strong sunlight, and shadow indicates his troubled mind, which is also implied by the two paths on either side of the church. The thick impasto paint is applied in curving and descriptive directions, and the lone figure in the foreground is emotive of the isolation he felt.

directional strokes built up forms and echoed textures. Some of these vigorous strokes were crudely painted. His way of painting also seemed to be affected by his mood—quick, short marks when happy and slow, longer marks when sad.

Venetian technique

Like some of the Impressionists, he used the Venetian technique of laying complementary colors over each other. For example, he applied a blue-purple wash under his orange-yellow sunflowers. He aimed to paint every picture alla prima, because this was considered the way "real" artists worked, and he usually managed this while imprinting his own personality into each work.

His brushwork described more than just an image—it described texture, emotions, distance, and form. For texture, he followed the contours of whatever he was depicting; for example, making the marks rougher and more obvious when painting a cypress tree or wheat field and smoother and subtler for skin or soft clothes. For emotions, he applied the same thick textured paint in patterns, as in his famous *Starry Night*, where the swirling sky represents an all-powerful God looking down on the world. Distance and form are shown through sensitive handling of color.

Sometimes he worked on unprimed, textured canvases, rough sacking, or stretched, raw burlap, which absorbed the oil binder in the paint. Or he used white or gray commercially primed canvases. He began with washes of undiluted paint, then often worked wet-in-wet to achieve a smooth, buttery effect. The paint is usually at its thinnest near the contours of the objects, and it is smeared, blurred and blended, or applied with a palette knife on parts of the painting that he wanted to be noticed more. Where he wanted more detail, he used narrow, small brushes and painted in careful, curved or hatched strokes. At times, his ruggedly applied paint is almost in relief, and, at other times, it is smooth and even. Despite the myths about him, he was always lucid when he painted and the final results were always rationally intended.

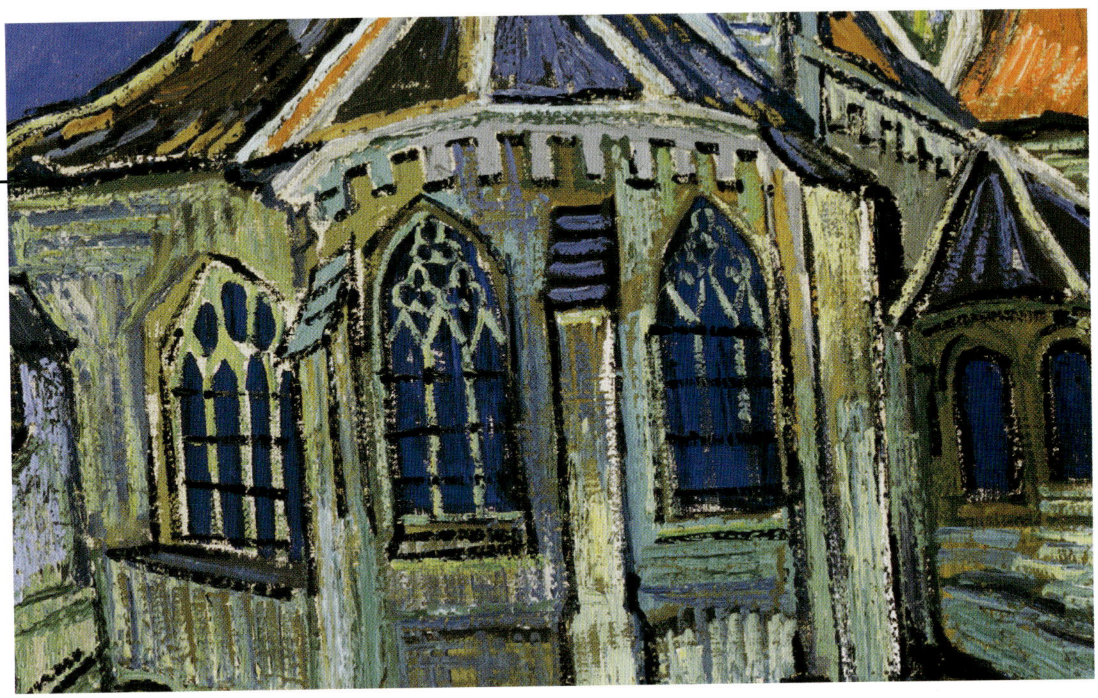

LEFT
THE CHURCH AT AUVERS, detail.
This is painted in fluid lines and juicy paint often squeezed straight from the tubes on to the canvas. Despite the way that van Gogh has made the church walls seem to undulate, the painting captures the appearance of the church extremely well. The use of rich colors, including Ultramarine on the windows and Cobalt Blue with Chrome Orange for the roof slates, adds to the vibrancy of the image.

HOW TO DO IT

YOUR PALETTE

In order to create the brightness and richness of this detail, you will need:

1 Chrome Yellow
2 Titanium White
3 Ceruleum Blue
4 Raw Umber
5 Cadmium Red
6 Ivory Black
7 Viridian
8 Yellow Ocher
9 Sap Green
10 Cobalt Blue

Use smaller strokes as the picture recedes to create perspective.

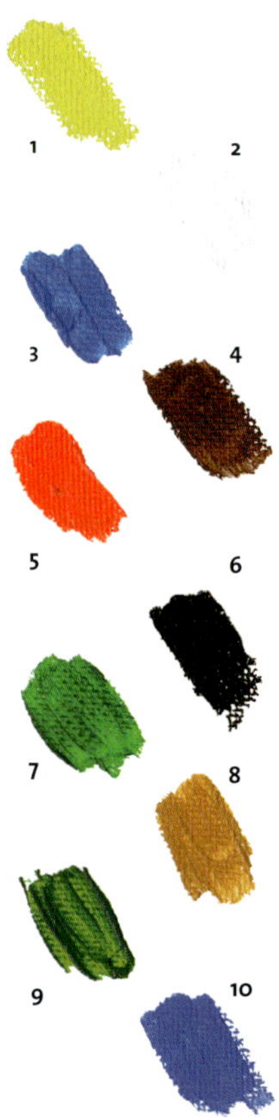

To create the directional, impasto brush strokes of Vincent van Gogh, you should be bold and daring with the way you apply the paint. If you look closely at his paintings, you can see the priming between the thickly impasted brush strokes. These brush strokes should be expressionistic, giving a feeling of restlessness. Keep the paint fluid and swirl it onto the canvas, checking that you are matching van Gogh's swirls.

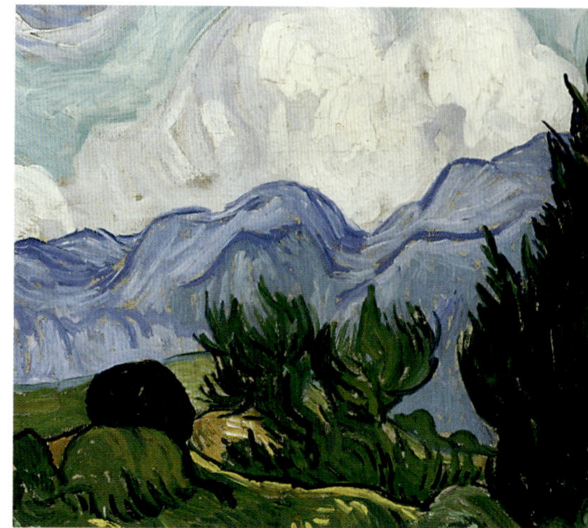

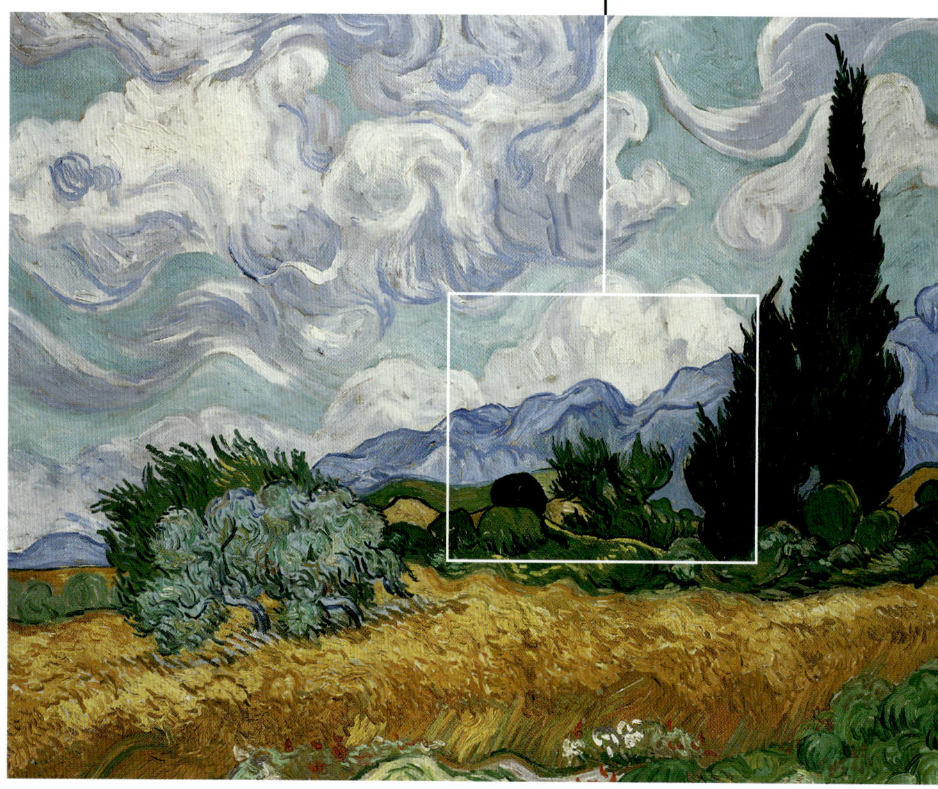

The main techniques

Use thin strokes for the background or wet paint on dry in unblended dabs. The brushes you use will make a big difference to the effects you build up. Flat brushes are good for broad marks, and the tips and sides can be used for long, narrow strokes. Round brushes are better for more defined marks. The stiffer the bristles, the better for this technique.

ABOVE
CORNFIELD AND CYPRESS TREES, 1889, oil on canvas, $28\frac{1}{4}$ x $35\frac{3}{4}$ inches (72 x 91 cm). *Traditionally planted in cemeteries, cypress trees had a symbolic association with death. Van Gogh applied paint vigorously and restlessly in this painting, as if he was reflecting the turbulent turn of events of his life. He has used heavy masses of organized color and short, curved strokes in bold and sweeping flourishes. The background is cool and calm, while the foreground is composed of wet-in-wet layers and short, choppy brush strokes.*

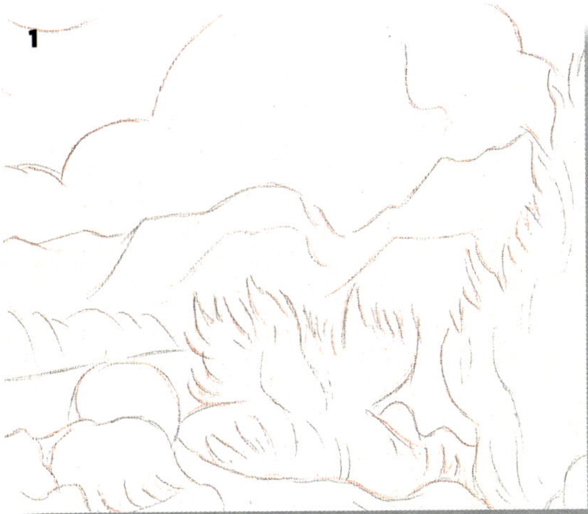

STEP 1 Choose a relatively smooth canvas or board and prime it with a couple of thin coats of white or, if you prefer, cream latex paint. Then, with a soft pencil or Conté stick, sketch in the outlines as you see them here.

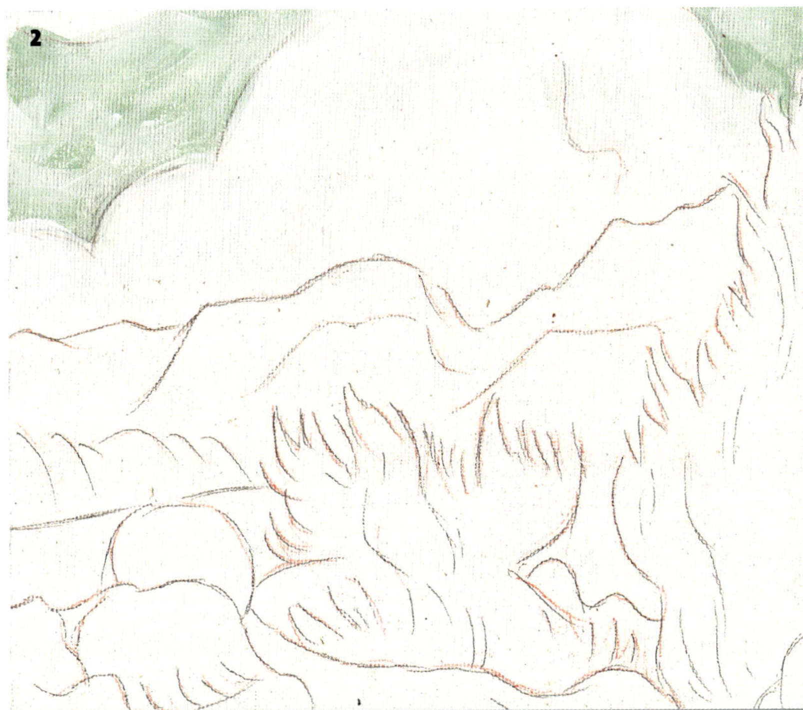

STEP 2 With Ceruleum Blue, Titanium White, and a touch of Chrome Yellow, begin to establish the outlines of the clouds in the background. Paint the whiter cloud formation in Titanium White straight from the tube.

STEP 3 Block in the distant mountains with a relatively thick mixture of Cobalt Blue and Titanium White, swirled onto the canvas, noting that the distant brush marks are thinner and less obvious than those in the foreground.

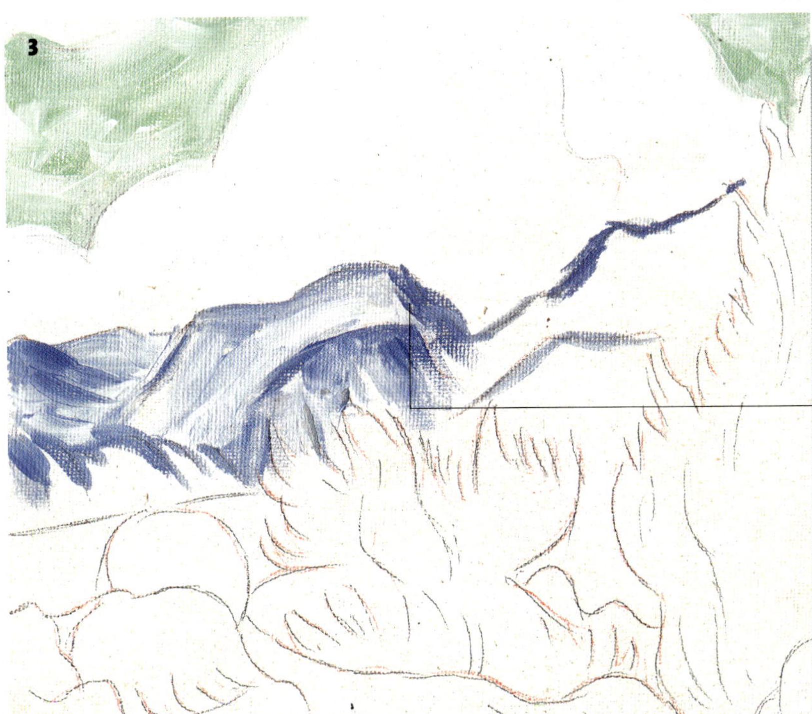

Use a No. 2 flat bristle brush, loaded with Cobalt Blue and Titanium White, to paint the mountains in the background.

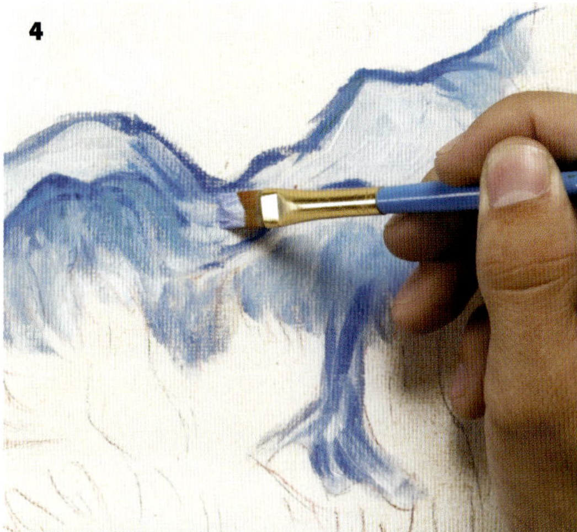

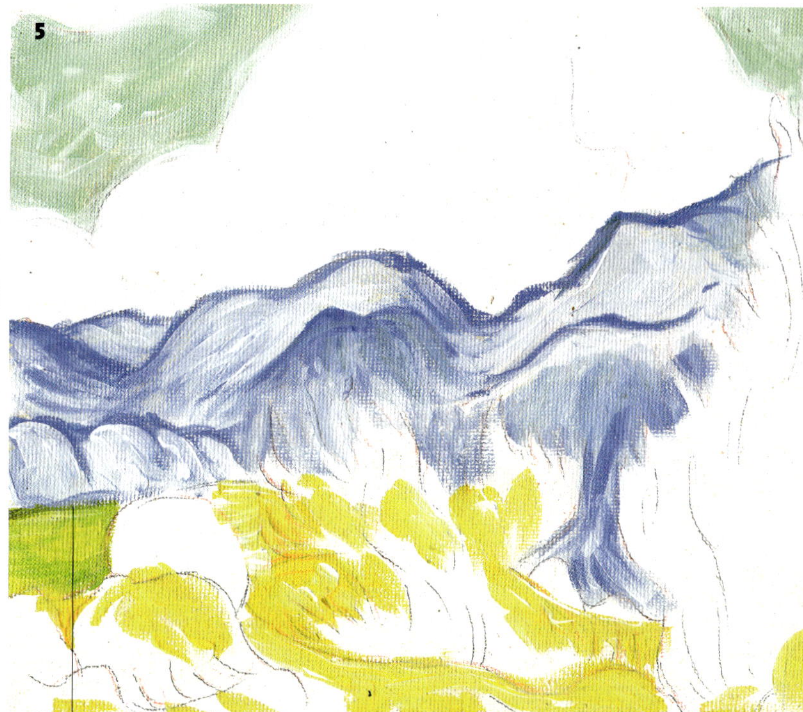

STEP 4 Deepen the mountains with additions of Cobalt Blue and Ivory Black. Brighten the sky with Viridian and Titanium White worked into the base color.

STEP 5 Now begin to build up the contrast of the front, relief painting and the distant, flatter marks. Use Chrome Yellow with a touch of Raw Umber and Yellow Ocher and add swirls of corn. For the green field in the distance, mix Sap Green, Cobalt Blue, Ceruleum Blue, and Chrome Yellow, and apply this mixture thickly to the small area beneath the blue mountains.

Build up the field gradually, working wet-in-wet to create van Gogh's smeared effect for this area.

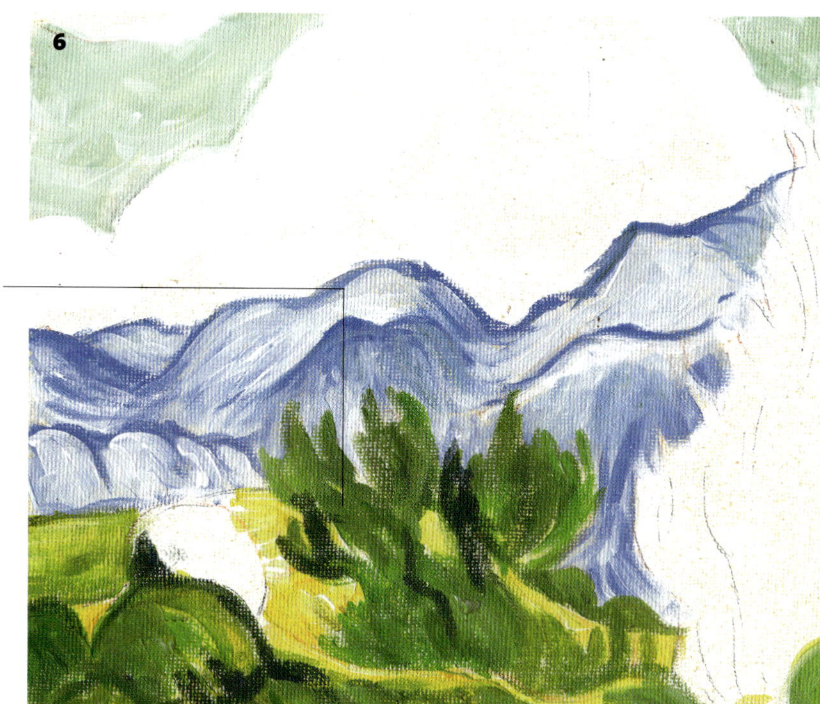

Vary the strength of the greens, applying them with a No. 2 flat bristle brush and following van Gogh's original brush strokes.

STEP 6 Use Viridian, Sap Green, Yellow Ocher, and Cobalt Blue for the curving cypress tree. Paint this with fluid paint in curling "tongues" as you see in van Gogh's work. Working wet-in-wet, apply thick swirls and twists in the same direction as van Gogh's, picking out green areas between the yellow corn.

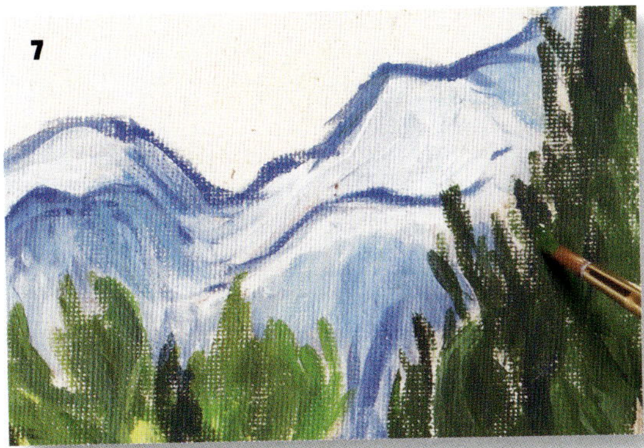

STEP 7 Mix some more of the green cypress tree mixture. Build up the bushes and foliage with a smeared effect ensuring that the different shades of green are relatively tacky as you apply them. The marks should not be too obvious or too blended.

STEP 8 Define the darkest contours of the tree with a round-tipped brush, using Sap Green, Cobalt Blue, Cadmium Red, and Ivory Black. Add more yellow to the foliage with Yellow Ocher and Titanium White. Use the paint in a thicker consistency now.

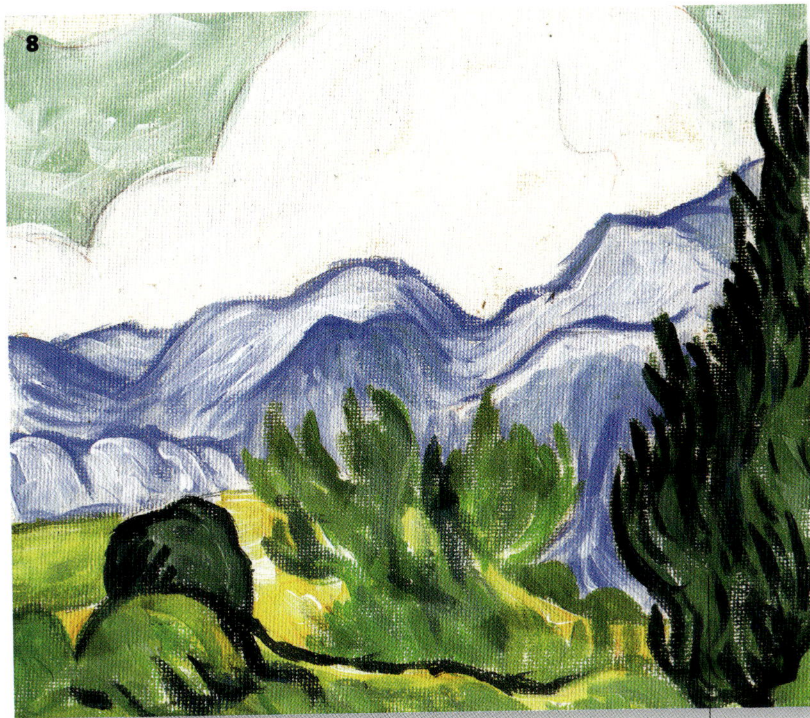

Use the paint in a thicker consistency. Add contrasting complementaries in shadows and highlighted areas.

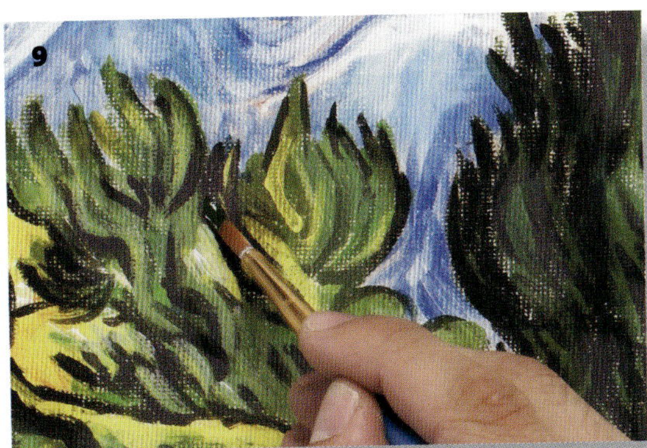

STEP 9 Take a look over the complete image. Go over any swirls or brush marks that don't correspond with van Gogh's and also compare tones to ensure that yours are defined enough. Bring out the density of the brush marks by adding pure colors in dabs straight from the tube here and there.

STEP 10 Using a little Cobalt Blue, add soft swirls to the distant cloud formations and smear on any further highlights needed. To finish, pick out the mountains with Cobalt Blue mixed with a tiny touch of Ivory Black, and enhance highlights with pure Titanium White.

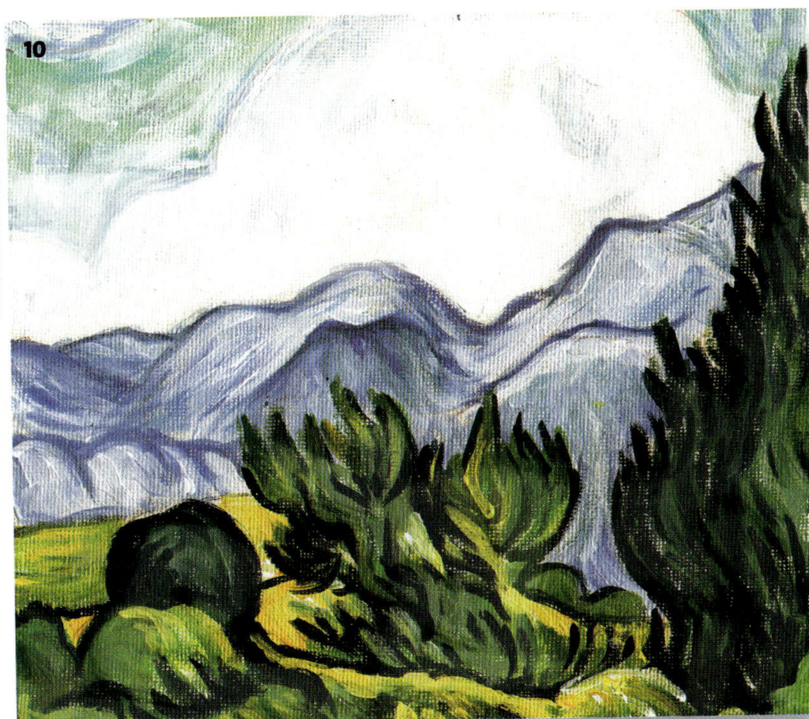

THE EFFECT OF JAPANESE PRINTS

VAN GOGH WAS highly intelligent, caring, and sensitive, but he lacked the training needed to become an academic painter. Although he had some lessons, he was mainly self-taught, building his early style on his admiration of past masters. When he moved to France, the Impressionists showed him other ideas, including lightening his palette and dabbing paint on the canvas in short, textured strokes. By the 1880s, when his

BELOW
SELF-PORTRAIT WITH BANDAGED EAR, detail.
It's easy to forget the influence of Japanese art when we look at van Gogh's fresh colors and compositional images. Relatively thick, textural brush marks describe the shape of his coat with a minimum of detail.

RIGHT
SELF-PORTRAIT WITH BANDAGED EAR, 1889, oil on canvas, 23½ x 19¼ inches (60 x 49 cm).
The descriptive quality of van Gogh's brushwork becomes more obvious on the clothes and face and less so in the background. This gives the impression that the background is receding. Most of the paint on the clothes and face was applied with a palette knife in dense, wet layers.

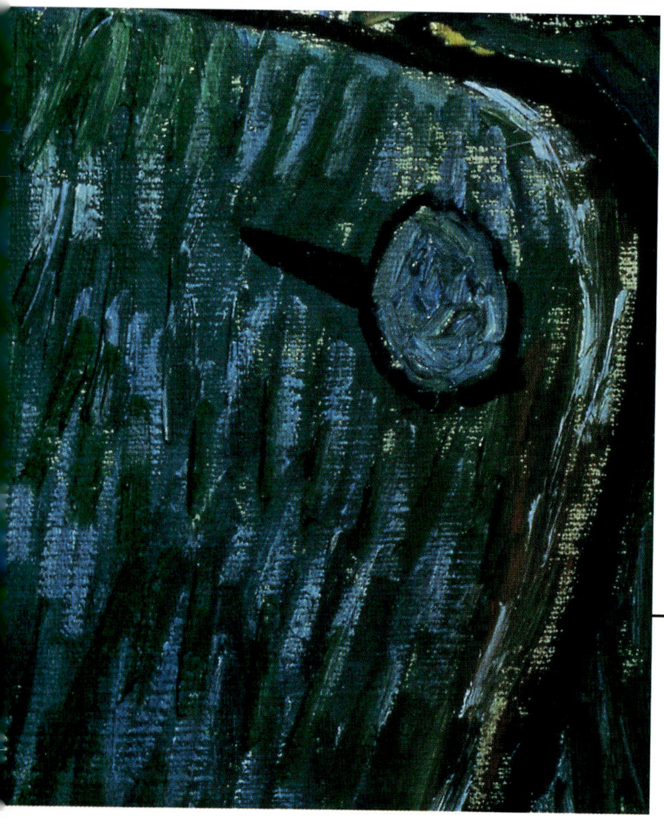

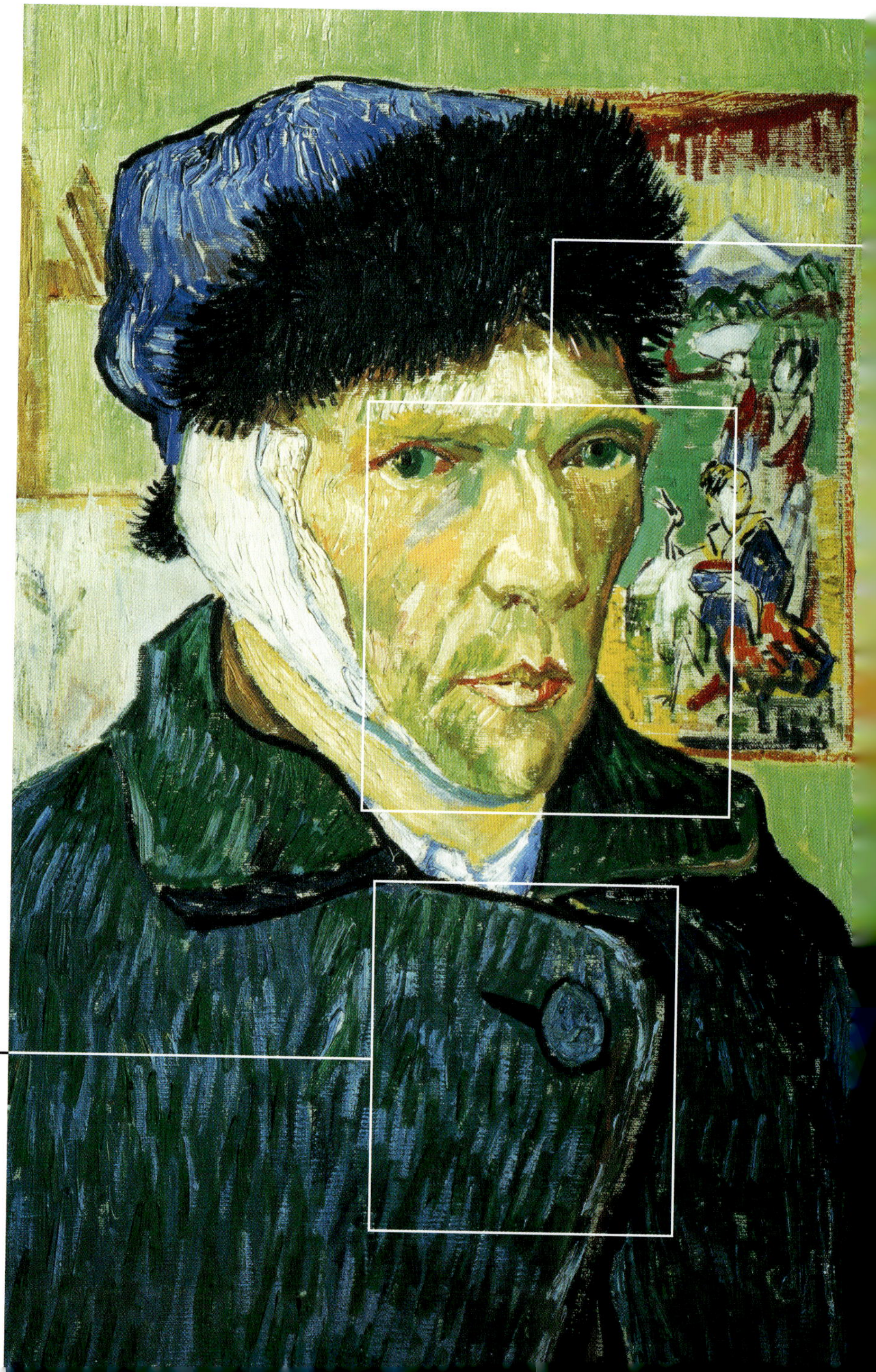

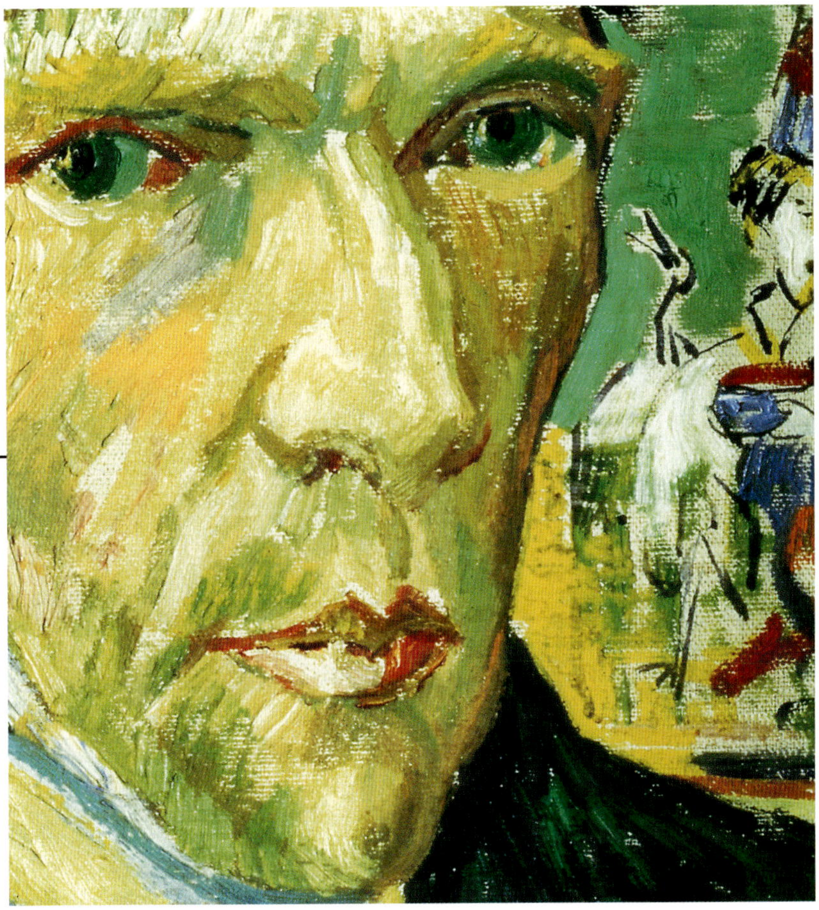

LEFT
SELF-PORTRAIT WITH BANDAGED EAR, detail.
Here, the facial features were painted in an almost abstract manner, showing the anger felt by van Gogh at the time, but retaining the calm composition of Japanese art.

painting career really began, the novelty of Impressionism was over. He picked up some of Gauguin's and Signac's ideas, and, when he moved to Arles, he believed that he could start a commune for artists. As we know, this never happened and he spent most of his life alone.

One of van Gogh's most acknowledged influences was Japanese art. The bold colors, decorative design, asymmetrical compositions, and flattened perspective all fascinated him, and, along with many of the Impressionists, van Gogh incorporated these ideas into his work. Even when he moved to Arles, he wrote to his brother Theo of the vibrant colors of the landscape, describing them: "... like a Japanese dream...."

Powerful depictions of nature

Van Gogh had collected Japanese prints avidly while living in Paris, mainly from Tanguy's store next to his apartment in Montmartre, and he eventually had around 400 prints in his collection. In Arles, he hung the prints on the walls of his yellow house. Some of these were by Japanese artists who were becoming well known in artistic circles, such as Toyokuni.

Although the craze for these prints was filtering across France, it assumed a special importance for van Gogh, as he believed that they depicted nature far more powerfully than Western paintings. He worked out ways of incorporating several of their unique elements in his own work and told Theo that he intended to "create his own Japan" in Arles and paint like a Japanese artist when he got there. First of all, he began including black lines to separate forms within pictures, which set him apart from the Impressionists right away. These are a direct link to the woodblock prints that he collected. Then he used domestic subjects, placing them in strong, bold compositions with areas of bright color placed side by side. Perhaps most famous of all was his use of asymmetrical compositions with unusual viewpoints, his rhythmical brush strokes, and harmonious curving lines.

HOW TO DO IT

YOUR PALETTE
This well-known image has a shimmering quality and is made up of:

1 Titanium White
2 Chrome Yellow
3 French Ultramarine
4 Vermilion
5 Cobalt Blue
6 Viridian
7 Raw Sienna
8 Yellow Ocher

For this detail, we are omitting the velvety blue sky and concentrating on the central area, which is painted predominantly in blues and yellows.

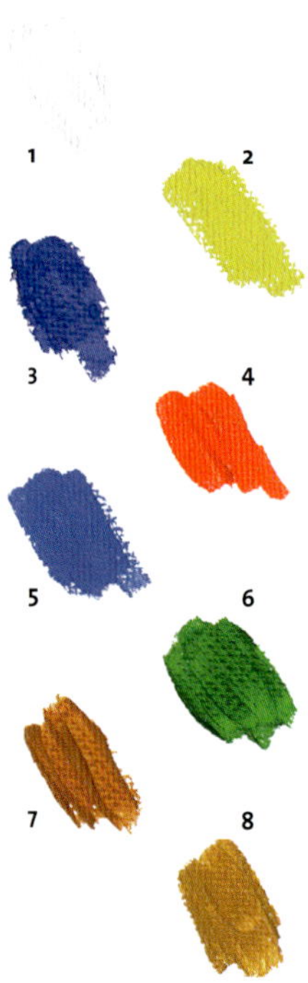

UNLIKE HIS CONTEMPORARIES, van Gogh was not so interested in the pictorial qualities of Japanese prints, but was fascinated by their bold color and representation of nature. It can be too easy to notice his textured brushwork, rich application of paint, and the bright yellows, blues, and aquamarines without really seeing his economy of composition and asymmetrical arrangements.

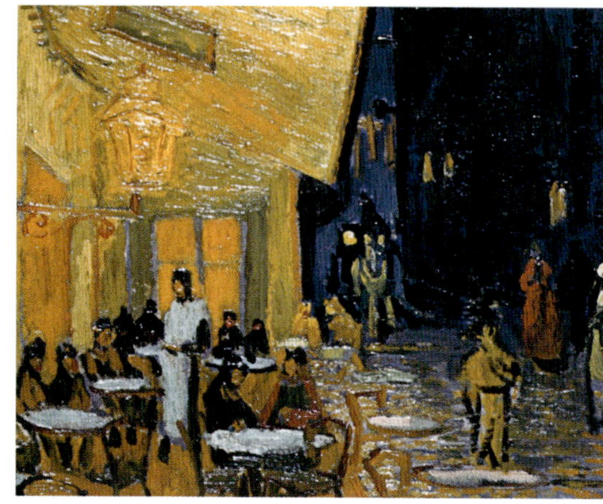

The main techniques

To pick up on the Japanese influence in the personal way it affected Vincent, once you've imagined the whole picture as a design and not worried about details, begin using a broken blue outline in specific areas. Once you have the design in place, then you can begin to pick out small, delicate details, such as contrasts of vertical figures and horizontal tables or areas where a lot is happening in contrast with parts where very little is going on.

RIGHT
CAFÉ TERRACE AT NIGHT, 1888, oil on canvas, 32 x 25¾ inches (81 x 65.5 cm)
This painting of a fashionable place in the Place du Forum demonstrates van Gogh's fascination with light, both natural and artificial, and his interest in painting night scenes in situ. This painting was executed in the fall, after he had spent the previous month drawing and painting the sunlit fields of wheat around Arles. The whole design and color scheme has come from his fascination with Japanese prints.

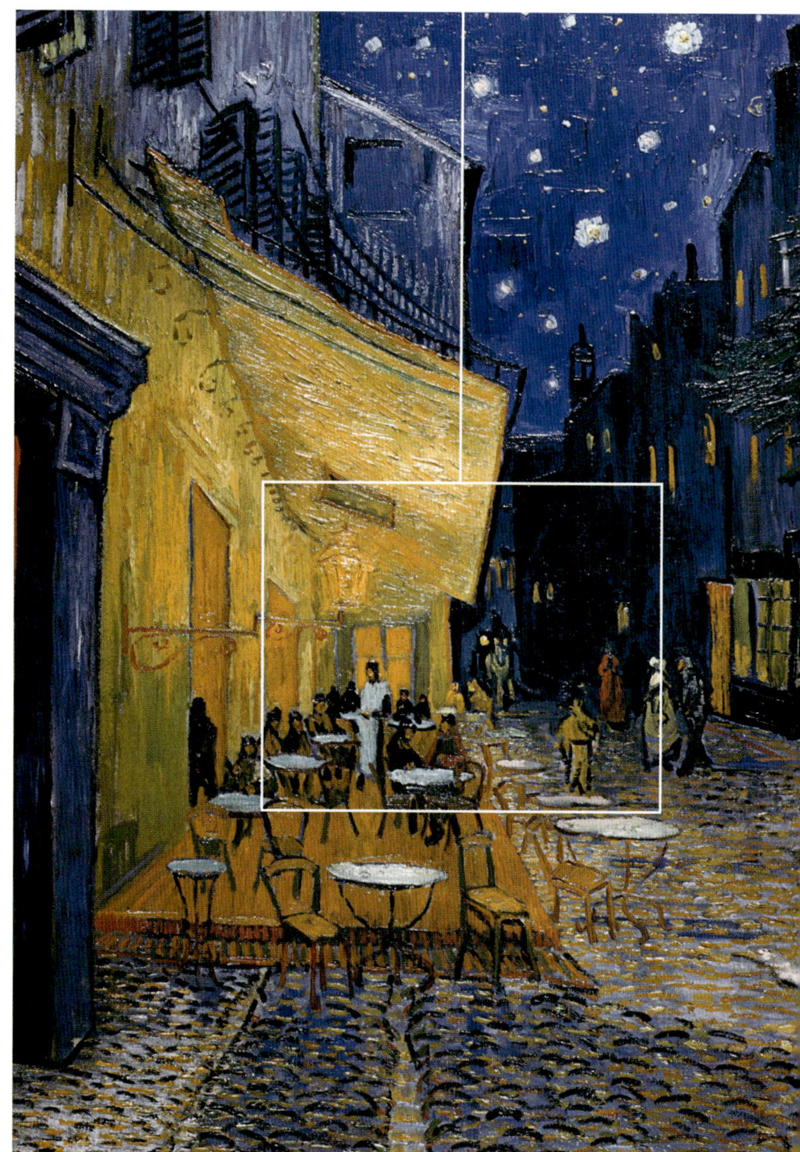

STEP 1 Use a white canvas or board, not too coarse, and prime it with a cream base coat using Yellow Ocher, Titanium White, and a touch of Cobalt Blue.

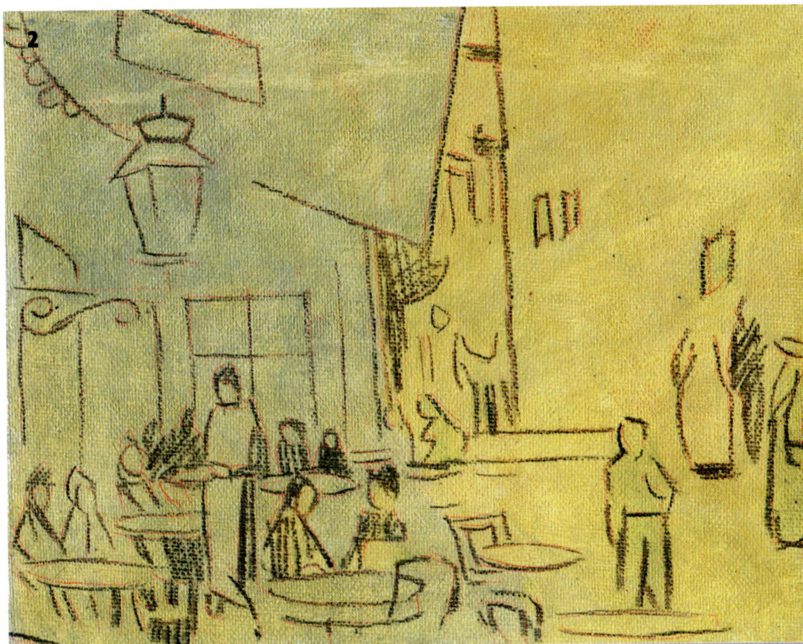

Using a No. 2 flat brush, apply French Ultramarine paint in relatively flat strokes over the yellow underpainting to the night sky and building opposite the café.

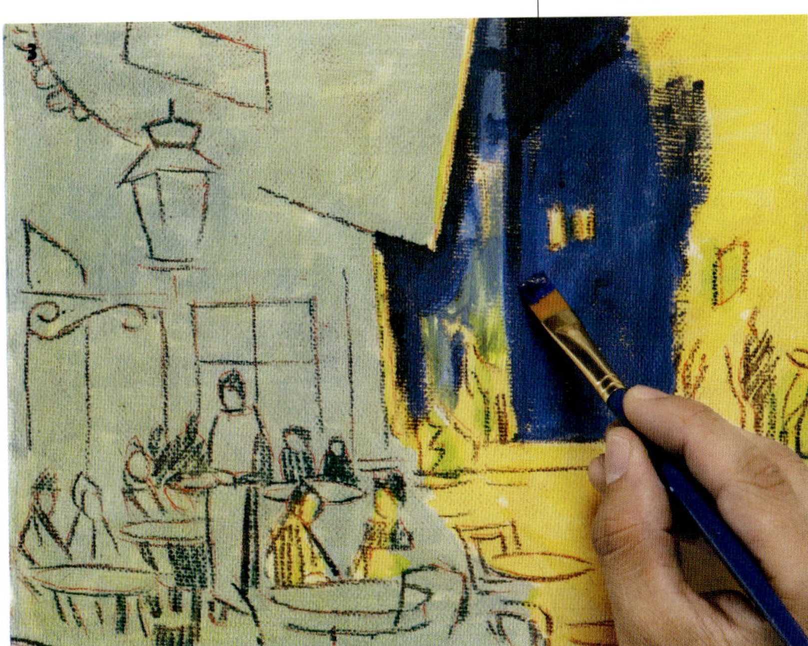

STEP 2 Lightly sketch this central section of the painting with red chalk, strengthened with charcoal, being aware of van Gogh's balanced composition and the "busy" and "quiet" areas of this image. Loosely work some French Ultramarine into the shadow areas on the left.

STEP 3 Using the paint in relatively transparent layers, work across your background surface, laying in light washes of the opposite colors you see. Where there is navy sky, paint a light yellow, and where there is a yellow-orange canopy and light from the bar, apply a light wash of French Ultramarine. When this underpainting is dry, paint wet-over-dry in a buttery consistency, using a small flat brush and small brush marks. For the blue here, use French Ultramarine plus a little Titanium White.

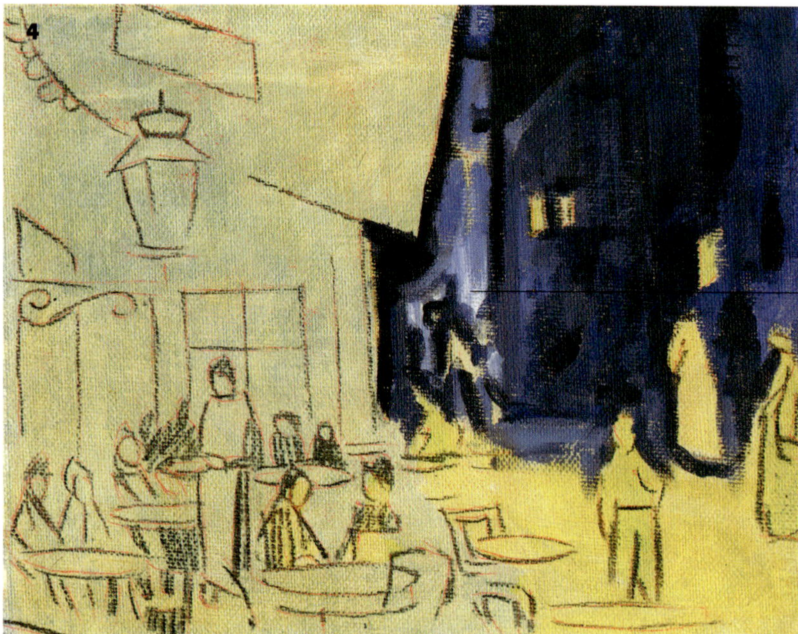

STEP 4 The Japanese rule of harmony means that contrasts are balanced across an image. This dark, velvety navy will be offset by bright orange-yellows. Using a flat brush, paint smooth strokes of French Ultramarine with a touch of Cobalt Blue and Raw Sienna mixed in.

Pull down the Cobalt Blue with the same flat brush, blending a touch of Vermilion in with it. Paint around the figures.

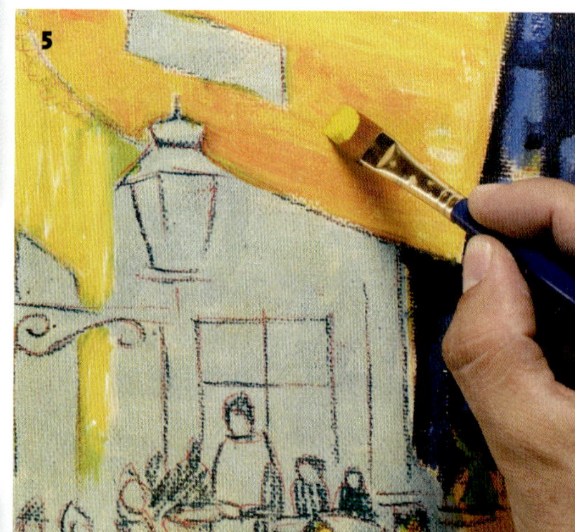

The large gas lamp is made out of Vermilion and Titanium White, applied in separate broken strokes straight from the tubes.

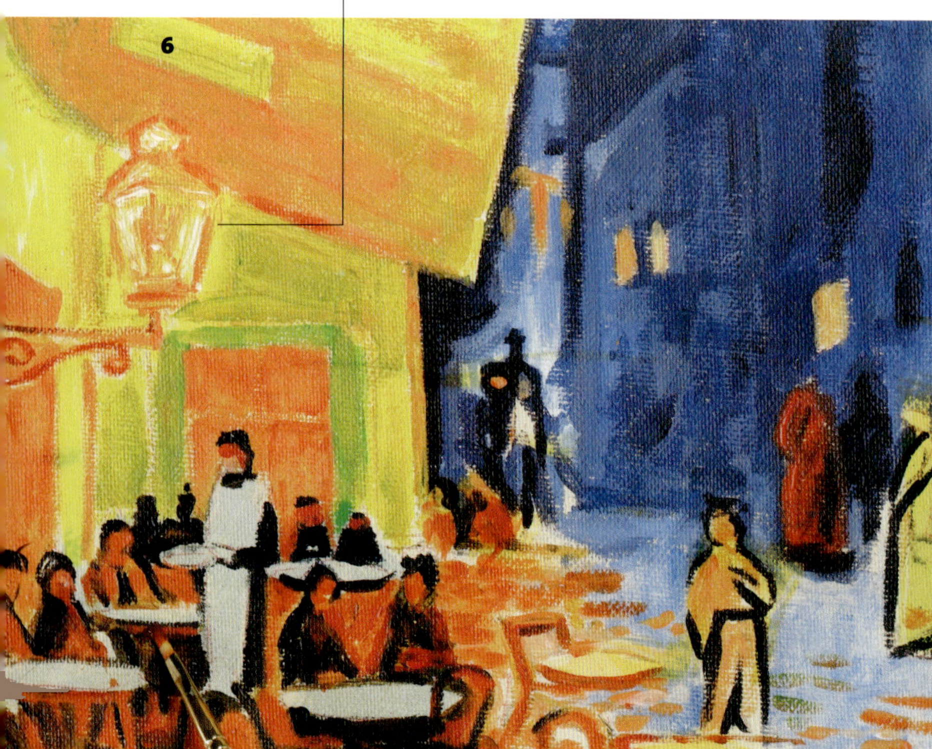

STEP 5 The light from the café illuminates the awning, so brush this lightly with Chrome Yellow, Vermilion, and Titanium White. Paint the yellow wall with Chrome Yellow and Titanium White.

STEP 6 Using a small round brush, begin working on the "busy" part of this composition. Paint in the door using Raw Sienna, Yellow Ocher, and Vermilion. Paint the back wall of the café with Viridian and Yellow Ocher, and begin to develop the silhouetted figures at the tables and on the sidewalk with Raw Sienna and French Ultramarine.

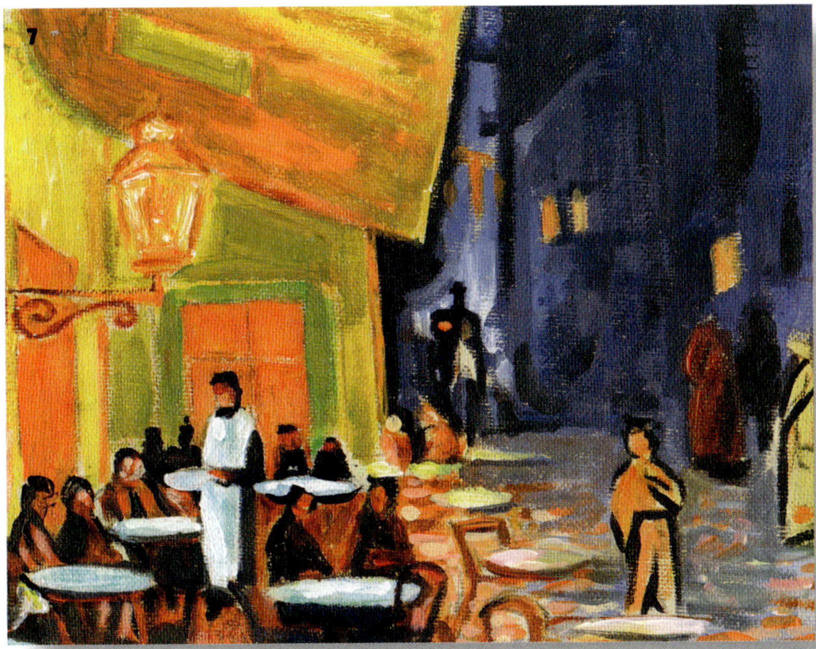

STEP 7 Keep the cobblestones quietly understated by painting the general image, but no specific details, in small slabs of French Ultramarine, Chrome Yellow and Viridian; Cobalt Blue and Titanium White; and Yellow Ocher and Viridian.

STEP 8 To finish, add the finer details to the picture, such as the horse and carriage and the figures in the middle distance. Adjust the density of the lighting, emphasizing the darkness on one side of the street and the brightness on the other side.

Emphasize the strong, diagonal composition by brightening the yellow of the café. Pick out the horse in the background with a small brush.

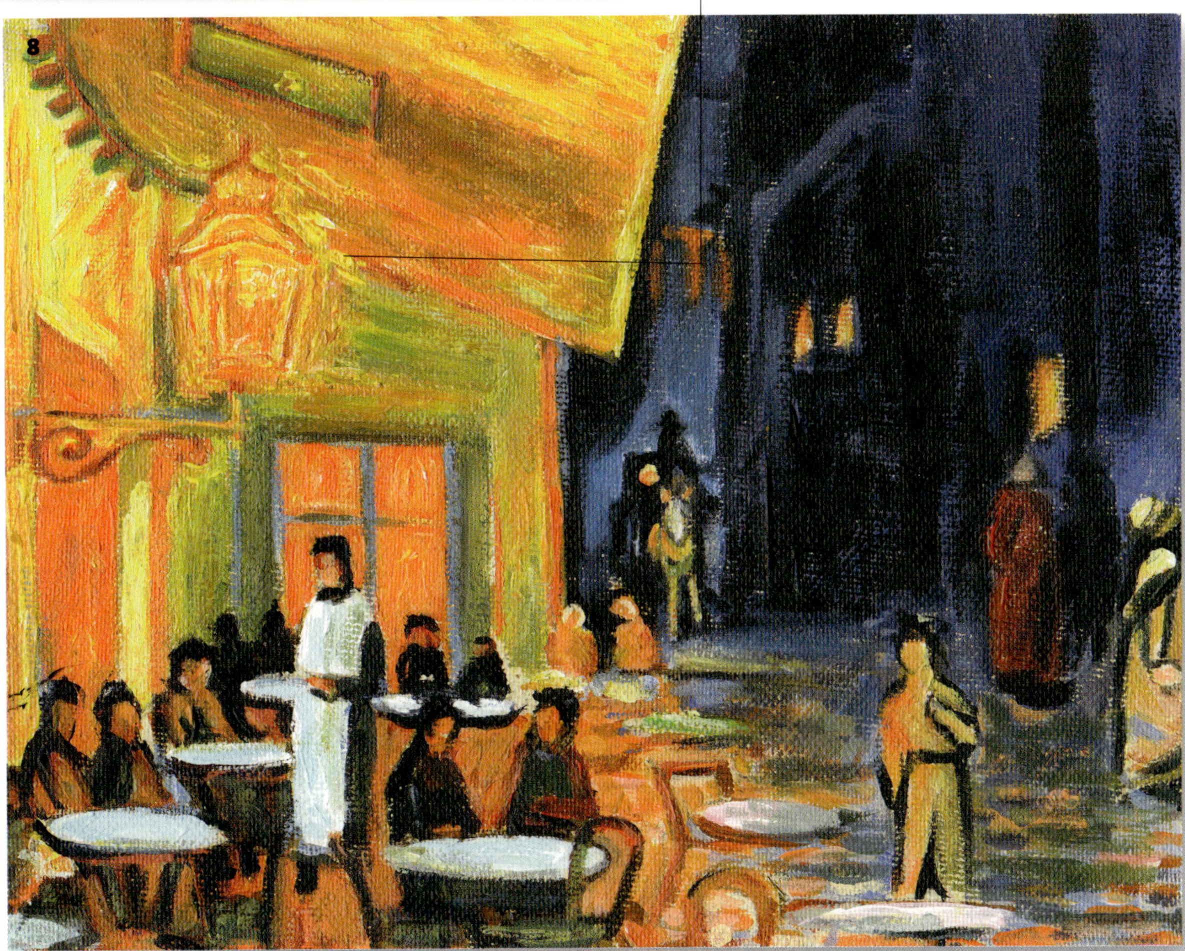

GLOSSARY

Alizarin A reddish purple pigment from the root of the madder plant. Combined with metal salts it creates the lake colors

Alla prima Original Italian term for an oil painting method whereby a complete painting is produced in one sitting

Atmospheric perspective Also called "aerial perspective." Distance and space are painted paler, bluer, and less distinct to the viewer, because they are seen through a haze of atmospheric particles

Au premier coup French term for alla prima

Background surface A surface specially prepared for painting

Blending Merging adjacent color areas, so the transition between colors is imperceptible, or mixing colors together completely

Broken color A method of painting in which colors are applied as areas of pure paint, instead of being blended or mixed. These colors combine in the eye of the viewer to create new colors

Cadmium Brilliant permanent pigments, including cadmium yellow, green, and red (the best substitute for vermilion)

Chiaroscuro The literal translation of this Italian term is "light-dark," and it describes the technique of painting form with smooth gradations of light and dark

Colored grays Hues that result from mixing complementary colors

Complementary colors Colors that are directly opposite each other on the color circle, such as red and green

Composition The layout or arrangement of a painting

Conté Trade name for synthetic chalks available most popularly in black, red, and brown

Cross-hatching A technique of laying tone by building up a series of criss-crossed lines

Dragging Brushwork technique used in oil painting, in which stiff brushes loaded with color are dragged across a textured dry or wet paint surface

Earth colors Pigments, such as brown or yellow, that occur naturally in earth or clay

En plein air In the open air

Foreshortening A distorted appearance caused by the effects of perspective—for example, when a hand is held out, it seems much larger than the body behind

Form Three-dimensional shapes

BELOW
From left to right: ***the shimmering light and shade of Monet's mature works; Pissarro's textured brush strokes; Renoir's smudging with thinned paint layers; Cassatt's carefully planned loose approach.***

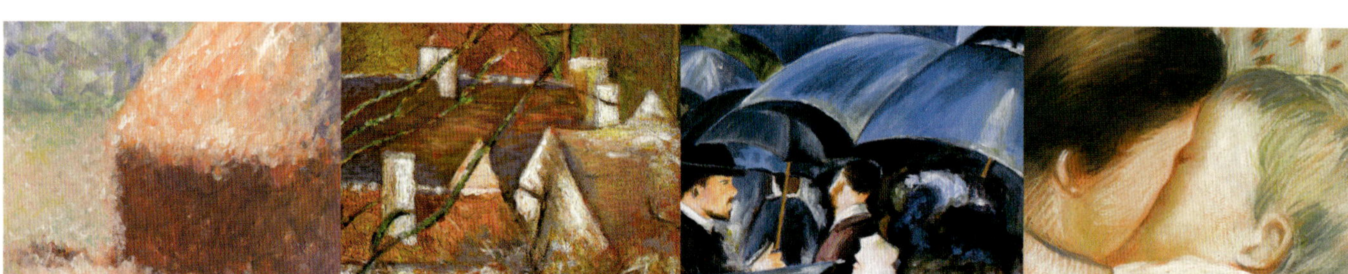

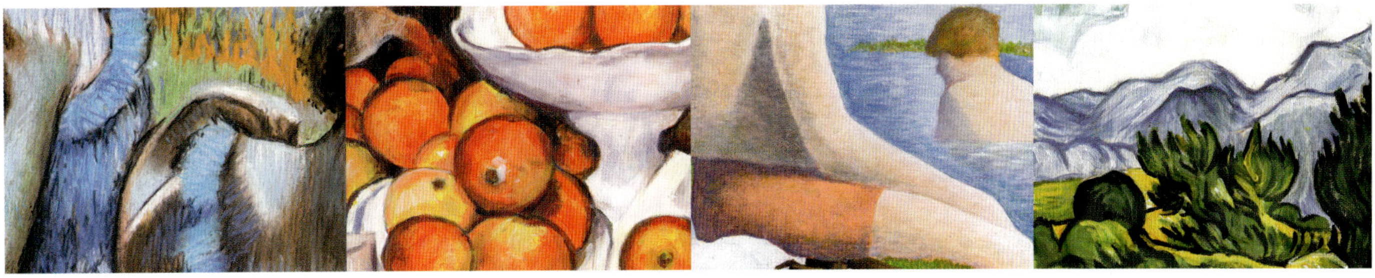

ABOVE
From left to right: ***Degas' scumbled, softly hatched pastel work; Cézanne's tonally balanced approach to still life; Seurat's tonal painting adhering to the laws of simultaneous contrast; van Gogh's directional impasto brush strokes.***

Glaze A transparent layer of paint applied over another layer

Gouache Opaque, water-soluble paint, similar to poster paint, also known as body color

Impasto Thick paint applied with a knife or brush

Linear perspective A method of creating an illusion of depth and three dimensions on a flat surface through the use of converging lines and vanishing points

Local color The actual color of the surface of an object, unmodified by light, shade, or distance

Modeling The representation of three-dimensional forms on two-dimensional surfaces so that they appear solid

Negative space The spaces between and around the main elements of the subject—for example, the skyline of a cityscape

Opacity The ability of a pigment to cover the surface or color to which it is applied

Optical mixtures Pure primary colors used in close juxtaposition, so that they appear to merge, producing secondary colors

Pointillism Dots of pure color placed beside each other. These were said to appear brighter than if the colors had been premixed. For example, the resulting green from juxtaposed blue and yellow dots was said to be more intense than if the blue and yellow was mixed beforehand

Priming Layer or layers of usually white or off-white paint applied to the support to seal it and prepare the surface for painting

Saturated color Pure color, free of black and white and, therefore, intense

Scumbling Rough application of a thin opaque layer of paint over another of a different color, so that the under layer shows through

Simultaneous contrast When two colors are placed side by side, they appear brighter. This particularly refers to the effect when complementaries are juxtaposed—the result is that each color makes the other appear more vivid

Support Rigid painting surface, such as canvas, wood, or board

Tonal value The lightness or darkness of a color on a scale from white to black

Underpainting Applying thinned paint of one color to create the basic tones of a painting before beginning the main work

Venetian method Painting a cool color over a dry, warm color, or vice versa

Wash An application of thinly diluted paint

Wet-in-wet Working wet paint into wet paint, so that the colors blend gently

Wet-over-dry Working wet paint over dry paint

INDEX